MW00399755

The Azrieli Papers:
Dimensions of Orthodox
Day School Education

The Azrieli Papers:
Dimensions of Orthodox Day School Education

Edited by
David J. Schnall
and
Moshe Sokolow

MICHAEL SCHARF PUBLICATION TRUST
OF YESHIVA UNIVERSITY PRESS
NEW YORK

The Azrieli Graduate School program of publication and scholarship is supported by the generosity of Henry and Golda Reena Rothman, to whom we are indebted for their ongoing kindness and beneficence. This is but the visible, public surface of their profound commitment to Jewish education, in general, and Azrieli, in particular, from which our entire community benefits.

Library of Congress Cataloging-in-Publication Data

Schnall, David J.
The Azrieli papers : dimensions of orthodox day school education / edited by David J. Schnall and Moshe Sokolow.
p. cm.
ISBN 978-1-60280-182-0
1. Jewish religious education. 2. Jewish religious schools. 3. Jewish day schools. I. Sokolow, Moshe. II. Title.
BM103.A97 2011
296.6'8083--dc22
2011014391

Distributed by
KTAV Publishing House, Inc.
888 Newark Avenue, Suite 119
Jersey City, NJ 07306
orders@ktav.com
(201) 963-9524

Contents

INSTRUCTION

SUBJECT MATTER

Foreword

David J. Schnall and Moshe Sokolow

Modern Orthodox Jewish day schools are like other schools, only more so; unlike other schools and, again, only more so. Day school educators, like their opposite numbers in the general sector, make assumptions about children and the way in which they acquire and process information; about adults and those interactions they have with children that constitute instruction; about schools as the loci in which these interactions occur and are, hopefully, nurtured; and, finally, about the nature of knowledge and which general and specific varieties of knowledge best serve the purposes and interests of the particular children for whose education they have taken responsibility.

In all those respects, day schools are like other schools and day school educators share the professional preparation, experiences, concerns, prerogatives and responsibilities of educators in the general sector, plus the additional role and responsibility peculiar to the transmission of the Jewish religious and national heritage. In this procedural respect, the differences between the two appear quantitative; in respect of the content of day school education, however, the distinction turns decidedly qualitative.

Modern Orthodox day school education is not simply the total of separate morning and afternoon educational programs; the whole, here, is greatly in excess of the sum of its parts. A look at nomenclature alone will illustrate the point. While *limmudei kodesh*, generally the AM component, is usually rendered as "Jewish studies," *limmudei hol*, its PM counterpart, has several renditions including: secular studies, general studies and English studies. [In the more extremely isolationist day schools, the term "gentile" (*goyische*) studies has been used.] These translations differ appreciably from one another and bespeak alternative philosophical or ideological perspectives on the relationship between knowledge in the realms of religion and reason.

The children who are enrolled in modern Orthodox day schools share the interests and predilections of their non-Orthodox and non-Jewish peers. They, too, IM, "twitter," blog, and have Facebook ac-

counts; they, too, have their favorite musical and cinematic perform-
ers, favorite sports and sports stars; they, too, organize their lives'
priorities around summer vacations, mid-winter semester breaks and
extended legal-holiday weekends. Day school students, in addition—
or, perhaps, in contradistinction—regulate their lives by the weekly
sidrah (Torah reading) and the annual cycle of festivals and high holy
days, which because they occur in September or October frequently
result in making the rest of the year seem comparatively anticlimac-
tic—a perennial challenge to spiritual education.

The parents of day school students share the aspirations and anxieties of the parents of students who attend public and private schools.
They are all concerned lest their children fall prey to on-line or virtual predators, they worry about the company they keep and whether
peer-pressure will entice or induce them to take up drugs or alcohol,
and, above all, they fret over their grade point averages and whether
they will be accepted to elite colleges and universities and remain on-
track for lucrative and prestigious professional careers, while acquit-
ting themselves honorably of their social and political obligations as
American citizens. Day school parents, in addition—or, perhaps, in
contradistinction—are concerned over their children's acquisition of
the particular skill set that denotes their ability to take their appropriate place in the ongoing life of the local and national Jewish community, and they aggravate over their choices of a year (or, increasingly,
two-year) commitment to study in Israel and their concomitant attachment to the State of Israel.

It is customary in educational discourse to speak about four "commonplaces," the common denominators of all formal educational experiences. They are: the milieu, the learners, the instruction, and the
subject matter.[1] This anthology is designed to focus attention on each
of these critical areas of educational concern and its contents are distributed along those same lines of inquiry.

MILIEU:
* Daniel Pollack and David J. Schnall: *The Right to Education in
  the American and Jewish Legal Traditions*
* Howard Deitcher and Alex Pomson: *Jewish Day Schools Worldwide; Achievements, Challenges, and Aspirations*

---

1. Joseph Schwab: *Science, Curriculum and Liberal Education* (Chicago
1978), 365.

Pollack-Schnall

American legal and political theory typically place heavy emphasis upon individual rights, both enumerated and reserved. By contrast, classic Jewish thought posits a complex of detailed and interlocking obligations, broadly dichotomized between the ritual, i.e. those that define relationships with the Deity, and the social, i.e. those that define individual and communal responsibilities toward one's fellow. As a result, educational issues are addressed in the former system in the courts and constitutions, whereas the locus of discussion in the latter system is the family unit.

Although education is not a fundamental right under the Constitution, the Supreme Court has stated that "the appropriate means of school discipline is committed generally to the discretion of school authorities subject to state law." This allowed several state constitutions to explicitly provide for education as a fundamental right and to invoke a strict standard of review when such rights are compromised. Other states do not offer education such a heightened level of protection.

Whether or not a state affords education the status of a fundamental right will have broad ramifications on matters relating to suspension and expulsion, the infrastructure of private institutions, enforcement of zero tolerance policies, and accommodations for students who have been removed from the regular educational setting.

The scope of Jewish educational thinking was largely grounded in *talmud torah*: its purpose was to shape and mold young students to follow the paths of righteousness, leading moral and ethical lives, and fulfilling detailed personal obligations to God, to their neighbors, and to their community. In Jewish law, education is defined as a lifelong obligation simultaneously extended to one's children. Still, in their original formulation, such obligations and any consequent benefits were by no means universal. For an obvious example, they did not include instruction for women, save for religious and ritual requirements specific to their gender. The traditional Jewish school bears some similarity to the contemporary private institution, in that both, to a large extent, have the freedom to select their own admissions criteria and to establish internal policy. Schools that are part of the public school system are significantly more restricted by court mandates and standards.

Deitcher-Pomson

The day school is one of the most remarkable creations of Jewish communal life. Its organizational characteristics are derived from a cultural template that originates beyond the Jewish community in the purposes and practices of public education: the preparation of large numbers of children for productive adult life by nominated specialists in an all-day setting. And yet the mission of the Jewish day school is profoundly counter-cultural, for it seeks to socialize children—and increasingly their families—into a way of life and set of values that often depart from the public norm.

Deitcher and Pomson discuss day school demographics, speculating on the effects of the economic downturn on enrollments. They note that increased disposable wealth among Jews has been only one factor among others that contributed to increased day school enrollment. It is therefore reasonable to assume that a decline in families' capacity to pay fees will lead only to a moderate decline in enrollment, just as lowering the cost of schooling will probably increase enrollment only at the margins. In sum, they attribute the growth in the number of day schools to a combination of the decay of public education, Jewish embourgoisement, the confluence of multiculturalism and the "school choice" movement, and concern over Jewish continuity.

As increasing numbers of Jewish children are educated in Jewish day schools, the social roles of these schools have expanded beyond the classroom to include family education, the celebration of religious and life-cycle events, and the provision of a wide range of Jewish experiences. Hence, they observe: the growth of family-education programs, co- and extra-curricular activities such as *shabbatonim*, and Israel education, which the authors—based in the Melton Center of the Hebrew University—analyze in painstaking detail, as well as the role of the Hebrew language in Jewish day schools. Indeed, there is a powerful sense that, as schools take on many practices once seen in camps, they are seeking not only to stretch students' intellects but to cultivate their commitments to community and people.

They then address the challenge of recruiting, training, and retaining qualified, able personnel who will teach subject matter in a rigorous way while engaging students meaningfully beyond the cognitive realm. Concurrently, as the number of day schools has mushroomed, so has demand for qualified principals. Also, the dramatic changes in the role and function of day schools have placed a heavy burden on incoming principals, demanding skills and knowledge that many do not possess or were not trained to assume.

Their examination of the integration of Judaic and secular studies in the day school curriculum reveals an enormous gulf between aspiration and accomplishment, with schools facing obstacles in all the "commonplaces."

Finally, a prospective looks at the most critical challenges that Jewish day schools face today, including the cost and quality of schooling, concern about the nature and extent of the impact of schools on students, and two significant lacunae in research about day schools: To what extent their positive effects are a consequence of what children learn and experience in school, or are a banal outcome of the fact that Jewish children spend so much time together in these settings, and developing a cross-cultural mode of inquiry.

LEARNERS:
- David Pelcovitz: *The At-Risk Adolescent in the Orthodox Jewish Community;* Implications and Interventions for Educators
- Rona Novick: *Bullying, Harassment, and Social Exclusion in Jewish Schools*; Unique Opportunities and Challenges to Promote Positive Peer Culture
- Jay Goldmintz: *Religious Development in Adolescence; A Work in Progress*

Pelcovitz
In attempting to uncover the etiology of the at-risk phenomenon, Pelcovitz notes that it is impossible to attribute this behavior to a single cause. At the same time, he does observe one theme that seems to be consistent among adolescents who tread this course, namely feelings of alienation and exclusion.

Though behavior problems were once three times more frequent among males than females, research suggests that the gap is narrowing in both the general and Orthodox populations. Pelcovitz notes some of the difficulties unique to Orthodox females who are among this cohort. Their problem is complicated by the absence of alternative schools for disorderly girls, so their expulsion from the regular school system means their further marginalization from the Orthodox community. Another complication stems from the Orthodox community's differing attitudes towards sexual behavior in girls as compared to boys. A reputation for promiscuous behavior on the part of girls is likely to lead to more enduring consequences than is the case with boys.

Familial factors commonly associated with at-risk children include: parental disciplinary styles that are overly heavy-handed or excessively permissive; physical or emotional abuse directed at spouse and/or child; preferential treatment towards siblings; parental mental illness; financial stress; and being a child of immigrants. Children of immigrants are often called upon to be their translators and advocates to the wider community, a role that is often at odds with their need to separate from their parents.

Since academic failure has been correlated with at-risk behavior, Pelcovitz urges educators to engage in early identification and prompt intervention, actively advocating for appropriate referral, assessment, and intervention. Mentoring programs, for one, can serve as a very powerful preventative force against the at-risk phenomenon. He cautions, however, that positive outcomes were found specifically when mentors were involved with their protégés for a minimum of a year. Adverse effects were noted when this relationship was terminated after three months or less.

Novick
There is a wide range of benefits to be accrued from implementing school-wide bully prevention programs, including: increased academic achievement; a more positive school climate; a decrease in behavioral disturbances; heightened religious identity; enhanced moral development; and a lower incidence of substance abuse in later years. Though many schools are concerned that curricular pressures preclude allotting time to bully prevention, Novick emphasizes that, in the long run, bully prevention programs yield academic profits as well as many other forms of dividends. The cost of not addressing it, however, is disproportionally high.

Many mistakenly assume that "bullying" is limited to physical aggression. Novick clarifies that "bullying" most frequently refers to a deliberate capitalization on an imbalance of power in order to cause physical, social, or emotional harm to another. Emotional bullying involves teasing, name-calling, and other behaviors that damage a student's self-esteem. Social bullying comprises those actions which damage a student's social standing, including social exclusion.

While the bully and the victim are certainly central figures on the bullying stage, bystanders play an incredibly critical role in determining the outcome of a given bullying incident. If bystanders can play a critical role in bully prevention, why do they often stand by idly? Novick explains that they tend to refrain from intervening because they are afraid that they will become the bully's next victim, because they don't possess the strength of character to fight the current of peer pressure, or because they come to dehumanize those that they consistently witness being degraded.

Creating awareness and sensitivity to issues surrounding bullying is very important; but it is only a first step. An effective bullying prevention program not only increases theoretical knowledge and heightens awareness, but also empowers students with the requisite skills to effectively and safely assume the role of peer leader. Suggested strategies include: using distraction or humor; being socially inclusive; telling adults; standing up to bullies; supporting victims; leaving no one out; and refusing to be involved in spreading rumors.

Novick examines various bully prevention approaches, and identifies three key components that are essential to an effective program: it should engage all levels of the school community; address the critical role of bystanders; and include clearly defined and consistently implemented protocols.

Goldmintz

In an era when accommodating diverse academic needs is at the fore of the collective educational consciousness, the process of understanding and addressing individual religious needs, particularly in developmental terms, is lagging behind.

Goldmintz suggests possible explanations for this religious decline: an expression of a desire for autonomy; a natural outgrowth of increased cognitive sophistication, whereby juvenile notions of faith are no longer satisfying; and a general need to engage in personal identity formation.

It is important for educators and parents to recognize that religious turbulence, and a concomitant reduction in commitment to observance, is a normal part of the adolescent trajectory, and to react accordingly. There is no reason to get into a tug of war with adolescents about all aspects of their observance; teachers and parents need to consider when to insist on conformity and when to look the other way.

Goldmintz presents educators with a number of strategies to address religious doubts in the context of the classroom and beyond: instituting a class in *mahshevet yisrael* [Jewish thought]; capitalizing on "teachable moments" in pre-existing *limmudei kodesh* and *limmudei hol* curricula; convening departmental meetings to discuss the most pressing religious questions and planning how and when to deal with them; surveying students about which questions they feel have not been sufficiently addressed; involving parents in the process; and hiring a non-teacher to serve as religious advisor.

Gender differences play a role in students' religious experiences and perspectives, and educators should avail themselves of research on this topic in order to design religious programming that is suitable for the target audience. While girls, for example, tend to emphasize qualities of loving relationship (God becomes the ideal confidant, who understands everything), boys, on the other hand, tend to look at God as the perfect being, and think of him in terms of His power and authority. Might this distinction not better help us understand why girls seem to be better *daveners* than boys? Is it not easier and more natural to enter into an intimate dialogue with God as confidant than with God as authority figure?

Goldmintz emphasizes that religious commitment is not only a function of an individual's cognitive development, but is largely affective as well. Spirituality is composed not only of knowing about God, but also of cultivating an intimate relationship *with* Him. He contends that it emerges "naturally" only if students see the text as having that potential from the start and, even then, they may need assistance. Both boys and girls are in need of role models who can not only model religious behavior but religious feelings as well.

INSTRUCTION:
*   Michael Rosenak: *Pictures and Models*; An Exploration in Jewish Educational Thought
*   Jeffrey Glanz: *The Ethics of Exclusion*; Pedagogical, Curricular, Leadership and Moral Imperatives for Inclusive Practice in Jewish Schools

Rosenak
Models enable us to represent and organize the world or some significant part of it by way of somewhat simplified pictures of reality. In

an especially metacognitive piece, Rosenak discusses the varieties of models available for educational use, while highlighting the potential limitations of being guided by models. Though models can inform and direct, they can also constrain when one is unwilling or unable to evaluate and then re-evaluate, thereby ensuring their continued validity.

Rosenak highlights several models of learning and teaching that bear ideological, theological and pedagogical worlds of meaning and obligation. Three such conceptions of learning are: the child as an empty mind that is waiting to be filled; a learner who is capable of absorbing only that which he or she on some level already knows; and one who is meant to be taught binding principles. In studying the ways in which the models help us to understand the educational enterprise, we are also examining and evaluating these ideologies and attempting to understand more clearly how they affect our thinking on educational issues and where they are leading us.

Rosenak calls upon the teachings of John Locke, Plato, Immanuel Kant, Zvi Lamm, Siegmund Freud, Martin Buber, Rabbi Joseph B. Soloveitchik, Kieran Egan, Nehama Leibowitz and others to illustrate different models of teaching. He proceeds to give a detailed description of three models pertaining specifically to Jewish education, each one framing the role of teacher, learner, and tradition, and the interaction between them, in a unique way. In the "traditional-existential model," in particular, the educator daringly empowers the learner with the responsibility and freedom to independently make moral assessments and to engage in Torah learning in search of self.

Glanz

Learning is a social experience enhanced by interaction with diverse abilities, cultures, values, and interests. Learning environments should also allow for the appreciation of and interaction with diverse learning styles.

Glanz cites theories and research from the areas of social justice, the ethics of caring, differentiated instruction, constructivism, and cultural diversity, as well as traditional Jewish sources, to support the notion that Jewish schools should intensify their commitment to inclusionary practices. He references the "paradigm effect," wherein individuals continue in their practices because of unquestioned notions and assumptions, remaining closed to the possibility that superior alternatives may exist. According to Glanz, inclusion hasn't been embraced because it is far afield from the methods with which educators are comfortable and familiar, whether or not those methods are most efficacious.

He further emphasizes that exclusion in the classroom doesn't only refer to differential treatment of students of diverse academic abilities; it applies equally to children of minority cultural backgrounds who may feel marginalized or ashamed when their traditions are less celebrated than those of the majority culture. In particular, he refers to Sephardic students who attend predominantly Ashkenazi schools. When administrators are focused on promoting the best interest of each student, teachers follow suit by tending to the academic, social, and emotional needs of their pupils, and students internalize the critical values of justice and respect.

SUBJECT MATTER:
- Lawrence Schiffman: *Making the Bible Come to Life;* Biblical Archaeology and the Teaching of *Tanakh* in Jewish Day Schools
- Moshe Sokolow: *Tefillat Rav, Educating for Prayer Utilizing the Writings of Rabbi Joseph B. Soloveitchik*; Curricular and Instructional Guidelines

Schiffman
Limmudei kodesh, in general, and Tanakh, in particular, is one of the main arenas in which Torah U'Madda, the synthesis of traditional learning and scientific analysis, must occur, and archaeology is one of the disciplines that can be brought to bear on their integration. Schiffman notes, however, that the wealth of biblical archeological findings have very little, if any, effect on contemporary American Orthodox Jewish education.

The discussion of the Bible in the contemporary American Orthodox community, he observes, is dominated by commentaries and homiletical discussions that do not seek to interpret the Tanakh as did the medieval commentators. Rather, they seek to use the Bible to convey messages generated centuries after the close of the Bible. Possible explanations for the reluctance of educators to incorporate biblical archeology into the Jewish studies curriculum include: "fears of wandering into possible heterodoxy," the possible implication that scientific support is required in order to maintain the veracity of Torah, and the increasing number of academics who assume the agenda of disproving the Torah's historicity and accuracy.

Schiffman highlights the many benefits to be accrued by including archeological findings into day school curricula: appreciating the innovation of the Jewish code of ethics in contrast to those of ancient cultures, providing important background information on biblical characters and stories; attributing historical veracity to biblical events, informing our understanding of contemporary political issues, and bringing to life the legacy and heritage of our forefathers. The combination of archeology and geography can greatly help to instill a historic connection to the Land of Israel while it helps to bring about greater understanding of the biblical narrative.

At the same time, he cautions that we need to teach students what can reasonably be expected of historical and archeological evidence. We need to carefully explain to students that the role of archeology remains merely to be an aid to understanding the Bible and an ancillary support for our beliefs. On a practical level, in order for teachers to incorporate archeological findings into their curriculum, ample training and informative workshops must be provided, as well as access to archeological materials and user-friendly resources.

Sokolow

Addressing educators' perennial distress over the inadequacy of student prayer, Sokolow diagnoses a "devotional deficit disorder" that he attributes to a de-emphasis on spirituality in traditional Jewish education where curricular measures tend overwhelmingly to the "cognitive"—academic or intellectual—dimension of education, with comparatively less consideration for the "affective"—emotional or value appreciation—dimension.

Sokolow adopts the pedagogical language and form of preeminent theories in curriculum development to guide educators in incorporating Rav Soloveitchik's powerful ideas into standard Tanakh classroom lessons that incorporate insights into *tefillah*. This curriculum both addresses pressing questions related to *tefillah* and brings to life the experiential man-God encounter intrinsic to the prayer experience. Among the issues raised in this piece are: the purpose of prayer; personalization of *tefillah* despite a canonized text and regimented time intervals; the role of the presence of a *minyan*; and unanswered prayers.

Sokolow eloquently expresses the Rav's view of prayer as a basic expression of one's humanity. Prayer is both an ennobling majestic enterprise of conversing with God, and also a stark, harsh encounter with one's frailties, needs, and fears. Just as the presence of other worshippers alleviates the loneliness of man's existence, the use of liturgical formulas relieves him of the burden of identifying and classifying his needs before making proper petition to have them met. Instead of leaving man to blunder in the maze of real or presumed needs, the Halakhah canonizes them and requires him only to recite them.

The second part of the essay comprises model Tanakh lessons: Adam and the first prayer; Abraham prays for Sedom; the Patriarchs as personifications of prayer; slavery and redemption as a prerequisite for prayer; and prayer as dialogue. Each lesson incorporates traditional objectives and instructional means appropriate for Biblical texts, simultaneously introducing Soloveitchikian ideas and concepts of prayer.

Acknowledgments

This book is an outgrowth of the *Azrieli Papers*, an ongoing forum dedicated to highlighting excellence in teaching, administration, and research in Jewish education. Monographs in this series have appeared as stand-alone publications and in special editions of academic journals. This program of publication and scholarship, a project of the Azrieli Graduate School and bearing its imprimatur, is supported by the generosity of Henry and Golda Reena Rothman, to whom we are indebted for their ongoing kindness and beneficence. This is but the visible, public surface of their profound commitment to Jewish education, in general, and Azrieli, in particular, from which our entire community benefits.

Dr. Herbert Dobrinsky, Vice President for University Affairs (and a graduate of Azrieli!), has been at the forefront of the revitalization of the Azrieli board and, along with board Chairman, Moshael Straus, is a trusted counselor and colleague in our school's renewed focus and efforts. Chancellor Norman Lamm and President Richard Joel have spared none of their considerable skills of persuasion in directing university resources towards Jewish education. President Joel, we believe, takes particular pride in the accomplishments of Azrieli, among whose students and graduates are several of his children.

On a more prosaic note, yet of no less significance, we are indebted to our colleagues for their generosity of time and spirit. Azrieli faculty members Shani Bechhofer, Chaim Feuerman, Scott Goldberg, Moshe Krakowski, Laya Salomon and Karen Shawn have contributed their individual talents and collective wisdom to the deliberations that often preceded these publications and have been unstinting in their constructive criticisms in the discussions that have followed. We look forward in the next volume of this incipient series to publishing their notable efforts as well. No less deserving of recognition are Louisa Wolf, Karen Oliver and Ilana Turetsky all of whom had a hand (or an eye) in the preparation of the original manuscripts.

As should be evident from the Table of Contents, our definition of Jewish education is expansive. We see the classroom instructor of a day school as a partner with the school's administration, the local pulpit rabbi, the summer camp director, the community and family educator, the youth leader, and all related others. With appropriate adaptation, these contents can be applied to the numerous environments within which Jewish children are raised and educated, and to the training provided for the professional educators involved in that education, foremost among whom are our own Azrieli students whose interests and aptitudes have given inspiration, shape and substance to much of these contents.

Finally, we are intimately grateful to the day school graduates who have enriched our lives as our spouses and children. As Rabbi Akiva quipped to his students in reference to his own wife: "What is mine and what is yours is truly theirs."

Milieu

Ve-Shinnantam le-Banekha:
Exploring the Right to Education in the
American and Jewish Legal Traditions*

Daniel Pollack and David J. Schnall

Introduction

The right to a basic education in the United States is taken for granted. Young children understand that from the time they begin school by about the age of five years, while their older brothers and sisters expect to remain there at least until they reach sixteen. It would seem to follow, therefore that in this country children between these ages have a right to an education. Given its broad emphasis upon study as both an instrumental value and a religious obligation, a cursory glance at classic Jewish legal tradition might yield a similar conclusion. Yet, in both instances, the discovery and the identification of such a right is no simple matter, especially as it impacts upon the public obligation towards children who do not conform to social and educational standards.

The intent of this paper is to examine this question within the context of both legal traditions. First, it will survey recent American legal opinion, considering fundamental versus non-fundamental rights relative to how individual states determine their own educational policies. Constitutional "due process" safeguards regarding suspension or expulsion of students will be covered, including non-public schools and public schools with newly initiated policies of zero tolerance toward drugs and weapons.

---

* An earlier version of this paper appeared as "Expelling and Suspending Students: American and Jewish Legal Perspectives," *New England Journal of International Comparative Law* (Summer, 2003).

This will be followed by a parallel survey of Biblical, Talmudic and rabbinic attitudes toward education as a fundamental right, considering the legal venue of that right and the obligations that it places upon public authority and private initiative. A following section will attempt to apply these considerations to cases of children who cannot be educated in the mainstream because of their own disabilities or because of problems of behavior and motivation. A concluding section will attempt to compare and summarize the elements that highlight both the Jewish and American legal traditions.

The American Legal Perspective

The United States Supreme Court classifies certain rights as particularly valuable to individuals labeling them as "fundamental rights." Rights that have been deemed fundamental include the right to procreate,[1] the right to marry,[2] the right to vote,[3] and the right of interstate travel.[4] Non-fundamental rights are those whose roots, while in the Constitution, are less clear.[5] This distinction is vitally important because it determines how courts will scrutinize state actions that infringe upon those rights.

Fundamental rights are afforded the highest level of protection under the Constitution and receive strict scrutiny. In order to intrude upon a fundamental right, the state must show that there is a compelling interest that necessitates infringing upon that right. In order to survive a strict scrutiny level of review, the means chosen by the state must be the least restrictive and narrowly tailored to achieve the desired end.[6]

1. *See* Skinner v. Oklahoma, 316 U.S. 535, 541 (1942) (holding that the right to procreate is implicitly fundamental "to the very existence and survival of the race").
2. *See* Loving v. Virginia, 388 U.S. 1, 12 (1967) (holding that marriage is one of the basic civil rights and this is a fundamental right).
3. *See* Harper v. Virginia Bd. Of Elections, 383 U.S. 663, 670 (1966) (the right to vote is implicitly fundamental because it is preservative of other Constitutional rights).
4. *See* Shapiro v. Thompson, 394 U.S. 618, 630 (1969) (the right to travel is implicitly fundamental because of its connection to the Privileges and Immunities Clause and the Commerce Clause).
5. *See* Bowers v. Hardwick, 478 U.S. 186, 196 (1986) (upholding a Georgia law forbidding sodomy because there is no fundamental right to engage in sodomy under the Constitutional right to privacy).
6. San Antonio Independent School District v. Rodriguez, 411 U.S. 1, 16–17 (1973).

When a non-fundamental right is infringed upon, courts will use a rational relations test, which merely requires that the state have a legitimate purpose for restricting or denying a non-fundamental right. The means chosen by the state need only be rationally related to achieving the desired end.[7] Courts will generally defer to a state when applying the rational relations test, and will assume both a legitimate purpose and rationality without requiring the state to demonstrate that the means chosen are the best possible.[8]

A third level of review has evolved because not all rights can be classified as either fundamental or non-fundamental. The level of review for these rights falls between the rational basis and strict scrutiny tests. This intermediate level of review requires the state to have an important purpose for its infringement, and the means chosen by the state to be substantially related to achieving that important purpose.[9] This intermediate level of review is similar to strict scrutiny in that it requires a legitimate state objective, but unlike strict scrutiny, the means used to achieve this end do not need to be the least restrictive.[10]

Education as a Fundamental Right

By and large, the Court has held that education is not a fundamental right per se, and thus strict scrutiny protection does not automatically apply. Rather, through several landmark decisions, the Court has permitted each state to make its own determination whether to classify education as a fundamental right. As a result each state is permitted to place its own level of protection on educational laws. In *San Antonio Independent School District v. Rodriguez* residents of San Antonio brought an action against a local school district claiming that the Texas school system's reliance on local property taxes to finance public schools favored the wealthy.[11] The plaintiffs maintained that there was a violation of Equal Protection under the Fourteenth Amendment because of the large disparities in per-pupil expenditures resulting

---

7. *Id.* at 40.

8. *See* Williamson v. Lee Optical, Inc, 348 U.S. 483, 487 (1955).

9. *See* Craig v. Boren, 429 U.S. 190, 197 (1976) (holding that a classification based on gender must serve important governmental objectives and must be substantially related to achievement of those objectives).

10. *See* Califano v. Webster, 430 U.S. 313, 317–320 (1977) (holding permissible different treatment of men and women in attempting to equalize traditional inequalities).

11. San Antonio Independent School District v. Rodriguez, 411 U.S. 1 (1973).

from the differences in the values of assessable property among the districts.[12] The Supreme Court held that no suspect class was involved and that *education is not a fundamental right guaranteed by the Constitution* (emphasis added).[13]

In determining that equal protection was not violated, nor was a fundamental right denied, the Court went on to apply a mere rational relation standard of review.[14] In using such a standard, the Court found that the school funding system was rationally related to a legitimate state purpose of permitting participation in and control of educational programs at the local level. Therefore, the Court concluded that there had been no violation of Equal Protection under the Fourteenth Amendment.[15]

Almost ten years later, the Supreme Court in *Plyler v. Doe* expanded its view on education to acknowledge that "education is more than some governmental benefit indistinguishable from other forms of social welfare legislation." The Court went on to impose what may be interpreted as a stricter level of scrutiny on state regulations of education by requiring the states to show a "substantial state interest" when abridging or eliminating educational rights.[16] Although the Court did not explicitly recognize this to be a heightened level of review, the concurring opinions acknowledged that the Court applied or could have applied a somewhat higher standard of review in this case.[17]

Although education is not a fundamental right under the Constitution, the Supreme Court has stated that "the appropriate means of school discipline is committed generally to the discretion of school authorities subject to state law."[18] This allowed several state constitutions to explicitly provide for education as a fundamental right and to invoke a strict scrutiny standard of review when such rights are com-

---

12. *Id.*
13. *Id.* A "suspect class" is a presumptively unconstitutional distinction made between individuals on the basis of race, national origin, alienage or religious affiliation, in a statute, ordinance, regulation, or policy. The concept of suspect classifications was first discussed by the Supreme Court in the case of Korematsu v. United States, 323 U.S. 214 (1944).
14. *Id.*
15. *Id.*
16. 457 U.S. 202 (1982).
17. *Id.* at 238–39. (Powell, J. concurring); *Id.* at 235 n.3 (Blackmun J., concurring).
18. Ingraham v. Wright, 430 U.S. 651, 682 (1977).

promised. For example, in *Horton v. Meskill*, the Connecticut Supreme Court held that "the right to education is so basic and fundamental that any infringement of that right must be strictly scrutinized."[19] Similarly, in *Rose v. Council for Better Education, Inc.*, the Kentucky Supreme Court held that "a child's right to an adequate education is a fundamental one under our Constitution,"[20] and in *Wilkinsburg v. Wilkinsburg Education Association,* the Pennsylvania Supreme Court stated that "public education in Pennsylvania is a fundamental right."[21]

By contrast, other states do not offer education such heightened level of protection. In *Claremont School District v. Governor*,[22] for example, the New Hampshire Supreme Court did not explicitly find education to be a fundamental right, but rather found that it was "at the very least an important, substantive right."[23] This opened the possibility that education would only receive an intermediate level of scrutiny. Indeed, some state courts have explicitly found that there is no fundamental right to an education, such as the Massachusetts Supreme Judicial Court, which in *Doe v. Superintendent of Schools*, held that the state's constitutional education clause did not incorporate a fundamental right to education.[24]

Suspension and Expulsion

Expulsion and suspension are two of the means by which school personnel can enforce rules and regulations. School authorities have the power to expel or suspend a student who disobeys a reasonable rule or regulation.[25] Suspension is the short-term removal of a student from school or the "denial of participation in regular courses and activities."[26] Suspension may be classified as a removal that lasts longer than "ten days but less than the time between the start of the sus-

---

19. Horton v. Meskill, 376 A.2d 359 (Conn. 1977).
20. Rose v. Council for Better Education, Inc., 790 S.W.2d at 212.
21. 667 A.2d 186, 212 (1989).
22. 635 A.2d 1375 (N.H. 1993).
23. *Id.* at 1381.
24. 653 N.E.2d 1088, 1095 (Mass. 1995).
25. Goss v. Lopez, 419 U.S.565 (1975) and Tinker v. Des Moines Independent Community School District, 393 U.S. 503(1969).
26. Philip T. K. Daniel & Karen Bond Coriell, *Suspension and Expulsion in America's Public School: Has Unfairness Resulted from a Narrowing of Due Process?,* 13 Hamline J. Pub. L. & Pol'y 1, 10–11 (1992).

pension and the end of the [school] term."[27] Expulsion, on the other hand, is the compete removal of a student from school for an extended period of time,[28] usually for the remainder of the school term.[29]

Although education appears not to be deemed a federal right under the Constitution, the Supreme Court has held that school districts must comply with important procedural safeguards before suspending or expelling a student. In *Goss v. Lopez*, the plaintiffs, nine high school students who had been suspended from public school without a hearing, challenged an Ohio law that empowered public school principals to suspend students for misconduct for up to ten days or to expel them.[30] The law provided for parental notification and an appeal of the decision to the Board of Education for those students who were expelled, but did not extend such right to students who were merely suspended.[31] The Supreme Court upheld the lower court's finding that the plaintiffs were denied due process by not being afforded a hearing before their suspension or within a reasonable time thereafter.[32]

The Court, in reaching its holding, ruled that when a state decides to provide public education, it must recognize that students have a property interest in education protected by the Due Process Clause.[33] Additionally, the Court held that students have a liberty interest in their standing with fellow students and teachers and in their opportunity for higher education and employment.[34] Thus, because the Due Process Clause protects these interests, the court concluded that states are not permitted to suspend students, even on a short-term basis, without notice and a hearing.[35]

27. Lawrence F. Rossow, The Law of Student Expulsions and Suspensions 3 (1989).
28. Daniel & Coriell, *supra* note 26, at 7.
29. Rossow, *supra* note 27 at 3. *See* Matthews v. Eldridge, 424 U.S. 319 (1976).
30. 419 U.S. 565 (1975).
31. *Id.* at 567–68. And *see* Draper v. Columbus Public Schools, 760 F.Supp. 131 (S.D. Ohio 1991).
32. *Id.* at 572.
33. *Id.* at 574. The state cannot deprive a person of life, liberty or property without due process of law. The protections of this procedural due process right attach when there has been a deprivation of significant property interest. Cf. Boddie v. Connecticut, ,401 U.S. 371 (1971).
34. *Id.* at 574–75. "Liberty interest" refers to an interest in freedom from governmental deprivation of liberty, especially when accomplished without due process.
35. *Id.* at 576.

For long-term suspension and expulsion, Due Process requirements are more stringent. The notice requirement must warn students
that certain types of behavior can result in long-term suspension or
expulsion, and the student and his or her parent must be informed of
the specific charges and grounds for expulsion.[36] The hearing requirement mandates that the hearing must take place before the student is
expelled and the charges against the student must be supported by
substantial evidence.[37] However, as long as the hearing is performed in
good faith without a gross deprivation of rights, courts will generally
uphold the decision of school authorities.[38]

Private Institutions

Although some procedural safeguards must be followed in private school settings, private institutions are permitted to structure their
school policies and discipline students who violate such policies with
little interference from the state. The Constitution bars public—but
not private!—schools from using invidious entrance criteria. Public
schools may not deny entry on the basis of race or gender.[39] In contrast, private schools may bar admission on such grounds, although
there may be some limitations, by state action, on the tax benefits or
other forms of general public assistance given to such schools.[40]

Just as private institutions do not have to follow race-neutral and
gender-neutral laws regarding admission, they do not have to follow
state policies regarding the suspension or expulsion of students from
their schools. In order to raise a Constitutional claim, even one that
would receive merely a rational review, the infringed upon right must
be caused by state involvement, and such involvement must be sub-

---

36. Rossow, note 27 (citing Grayned v. City of Rockford, 408 U.S. 104
(1972); Epperson v. Arkansas, 393 U.S. 97 (1968); Dixon v. Alabama State
Bd. Of Educ., 294 F.2d 150 (5th Cir.), *cert. denied*, 368 U.S. 930 (1961).
37. *Id.* at 21 (citing Birdsey v. Grand Blanc Community School, 344 N.W.2d
342 (Mich. Ct. App. 1983) .
38. *Id.* at 8 (citing Greene v. Moore, 373 F. Supp. 1194 (N.D. Tex. 1974).
39. *See* Brown v. Bd. of Educ., 347 U.S. 483 (holding that admission to a
public school cannot be denied because of race). *See also* Mississippi Univ.
for Women v. Hogan, 458 U.S. 718 (1982) (holding that the denial of admission based on gender to a public university is unconstitutional).
40. Allen v. Wright, 468 U.S. 737 (1984) (the Court denied standing to plaintiffs seeking to challenge what they claimed was an inadequate system of
detecting the existence of racial discrimination in private schools).

stantial.[41] This holds true even in situations where conduct is initially private and later becomes "entwined with governmental policies or so impregnated with a governmental character as to become subject to the constitutional limitations placed upon state action."[42]

The Court has assumed a three-pronged approach to determine whether the extent of the public involvement is so great that it may be protected under the Fourteenth Amendment. It looks to the constitutional interests on both sides: to the public function served by the private institution, as well as to state regulation of the very activity that allegedly deprives the plaintiff of a constitutional right.[43] For a private institution to be in violation of the Fourteenth Amendment, the state must have significant control over its policy-making process, or be so involved in the financing and running of the institution that it effectively facilitates the constitutional violation complained by the plaintiffs.[44] Mere financial assistance by the government, absent evidence of substantially greater state involvement, cannot alone be a basis for finding state action.[45]

Private schools, regardless of whether they include religious teachings, are governed by a contract between the parent and the school. It is difficult for a child to raise a valid Constitutional claim when suspended or expelled because these schools cannot usually show substantial government involvement. Although there are no uniform guidelines governing suspension and expulsion from private schools, most state courts are extremely reluctant to interfere because of their private nature.

For example, in *Hutchenson v. Grace Lutheran School*, a first grade student in New York was expelled because of behavioral problems and the parents brought suit to compel the reinstatement of their child. [46] The court determined that its power was limited to a determination as to whether there was a rational basis in the exercise of the school's discretion, or whether the action to expel was arbitrary and capricious.[47] The court noted that private schools are afforded broad discretion in conducting their programs, including decisions in-

41. Reitman v. Mulkey, 387 U.S. 369 (1967).
42. Evans. v. Newton, 382 U.S. 296 (1966).
43. *See* Pendrell v. Chatham College, 370 F.Supp 494 (W.D.Pa 1974).
44. Wisch v. Sanford School, Inc., 420 F.Supp. 1310 (D. Del. 1976).
45. *Id.*
46. 132 A.D.2d 599, 517 N.Y.S.2d 760 (2nd Dep't, 1987).
47. *Id.*

volving the discipline, suspension, and expulsion of their students.[48] Thus, when a private school expels a student "based on facts within its knowledge that justify the exercise of discretion, then a court may not review this decision and substitute its own judgment."[49]

In *Flint v. St. Augustine High School*, a student was expelled for violating the private school's no smoking policy.[50] The student challenged the expulsion by filing a lawsuit. The Louisiana Court of Appeals held that private institutions have a near absolute right and power to control their own internal disciplinary procedure which, by its very nature, includes the right and power to dismiss students.[51] Therefore, the court ruled that so long as there is due process, that is enough.[52] Additionally, in private and religious schools the contentious policy of retention, i.e. not promoting a student to the next grade level also involves only the contract signed between parents and the school, and does not involve constitutional laws.[53]

Zero Tolerance Laws

Although states are required to provide many procedural safeguards before lawfully suspending or expelling a student, there are no protections to ensure that those students receive an education once removed from the school. Children who are expelled from private institutions can enroll in public schools. But what happens when a child is expelled from a public institution? In states that recognize education as fundamental right, suspended and expelled students possess rights that may be protected to a greater extent than under the Federal Constitution. But problems ensue for those students who are expelled in states where education is classified as non-fundamental.

The rampant use of drugs and the violence that invade the public school system are a growing concern. Some years ago, President Clinton issued a memorandum on the "Implementation of Safe School

---

48. *Id.* at 599, 517 N.Y.S.2d at 761 (citing Matter of Carr v. St. John's Univ., N.Y., 17 A.D.2d 632, 634, 231 N.Y.S.2d 410, *aff'd* 187 N.E.2d 18, 12 N.Y.2d 802, 235 N.Y.S.2d 834).
49. *Id.*
50. 323 So.2d 229 (1975).
51. *Id.*
52. Id.
53. *See* Debra P. v. Turlington (1981); G I Forum et al. v. Texas Education Agency et al., 87 F. Supp. 2d 667 (2000); Eric V. et al. v. Dr. James F. Causby et al., 977 F. Supp. 2nd 384 (1997).

Legislation," which requires public school districts to expel students found with weapons on school grounds for at least one academic year, or risk losing federal educational funds under the Elementary and Secondary Education Act.[54] Additionally, public outrage over the violence in public schools has led lawmakers in various states to adopt a "zero tolerance" policy, which requires the automatic suspension or expulsion of students who possess weapons on school grounds.[55]

In 1994, Michigan lawmakers passed legislation mandating that any student found with a weapon on school grounds, or found guilty of arson or rape, would be permanently expelled from all public school districts in the state.[56] Although several other states have adopted a similar policy, Michigan is especially strict because there is no provision for alternative educational programs to accommodate such offenders. Thus, the discussion for new law now focuses attention on whether alternative programs should be provided to keep these youth off the streets.[57] The biggest criticism of a "zero tolerance" policy is that students found carrying weapons are given no second chance, no appeal, and no guarantee of alternative school programs or education.[58]

A majority of states require school districts to provide alternative education or instruction to those students of compulsory-attendance age who are expelled pursuant to the "zero tolerance" weapon policy. New Jersey, for example, provides that if a pupil is removed from the regular education program, the student must be placed in an alternative education program. If such placement is unavailable, home program or instruction or other programs shall be provided.[59] Virginia also requires that a board of education establish a program that consists of

54. Kennet J. Cooper, *President Directs Schools to Bar Students with Guns: Law Threatens Elimination of Federal Funds,* WASH. POST, October 23, 1994 at A8.
55. *See,* e.g. Ala. Code § 16–1–24.1 (1997); Ariz. Rev. Stat. Ann. §15–841 (1997); Ga. Code Ann. § 20–2–751.1 (1997); Kan. Stat. Ann § 72–8900 (1997).
56. Mich. Comp. Laws. Ann. §380.1311 (West 1994).
57. Paul M. Bogos, Note, *"Expelled. No Excuses. No Exceptions."— Michigan's Policy in Response to School Violence: M.C.L.A Section 380.1311,* 74 U. DET. L. REV. 357, 359 (1997).
58. Gary Borg, *Schools Expel 247 with Weapons,* CHI TRIB., October 10, 1995, at 7.
59. N.J. Stat. Ann. § 18A:37–8 (West 1997).

alternative education options.[60] Such programs for students not only provide an education, but place an emphasis on building self-esteem and the promotion of personal and social responsibility.[61]

However, the states that have enacted a zero-tolerance policy, absent legislative mandate, have no duty to furnish alternative schooling programs during the period of expulsion.[62] The North Carolina Court of Appeals, in *The Matter of Jackson*, held that a student's right to an education may be constitutionally denied when outweighed by the school's interest in protecting other students, teachers, and school property, and in preventing the disruption of the educational system.[63]

The Jewish Legal Perspective: An Overview

Jewish tradition and culture have always placed a high value upon education, both as an end in itself and as a mechanism for improving the individual and the society in which he resides. The Talmud poetically records that our world exists only for the breath of schoolchildren. Moreover, a town with no facilities for educating its young deserves to be razed.[64] It should be understood, however, that the primary locus of this concern was not the pursuit of vocational or professional skills and credentials, though provision was made for such training. Rather the scope of Jewish educational thinking was largely grounded in *talmud torah*: the study of Torah, including the Hebrew Bible and Talmud, alongside related rabbinic writings and commentary. Its purpose was to shape and mold young students to follow the paths of righteousness, leading moral and ethical lives, and fulfilling detailed personal obligations to God, to their neighbors and to their community.

Chief among these obligations and, according to some, equal to all others combined, was a lifelong commitment to continued learning and reflection through programs of formal, informal and individual study.[65] Adults were adjured to attend classes and lectures, to study with friends and family, and to fill spare moments with personal reflections on the traditions and practices of their culture. Equally, they

---

60. Va. Code Ann. §221–257 (Michie 1995).
61. *Id.*
62. Bogos, *supra* note 57, at 377.
63. 352 S.E.2d 449 (N.C. Ct. App 1987) .
64. Talmud Bavli: Shabbat 119a. An alternative version reads: "Should be placed under a ban."
65. Talmud Bavli: Peah 1:1; Talmud Shabbat 127a.

carried a primary obligation to educate their young and to socialize them in the ways of God and society.

As with many other aspects of Jewish thought, therefore, primary responsibility falls upon the individual before the collective, following a religious and moral rather than utilitarian trajectory. Any comparison of American and Jewish law related to education and its place in an ordered society must be understood within these parameters. Indeed, before detailing these trends, it may be well to consider components of Jewish public law.

Jewish law exhibits several characteristics that distinguish it from much of contemporary Western thought. One relates to the role of obligation in both personal relationships and public policy. American legal and political theory typically place heavy emphasis upon individual rights, both enumerated and reserved. By contrast, classic Jewish thought posits a complex of detailed and interlocking obligations, broadly dichotomized between the ritual, i.e. those that define relationships with the Deity, and the social, i.e. those that define individual and communal responsibilities toward one's fellow.

This generates an organic, even corporate, social framework that establishes differentials of power and status as standards for custodial responsibility, more than privilege. It venerates neither a struggle for freedom from executive and administrative power, nor a "sovereign people," from whom a political or administrative elite derives the right to govern—both of which often contribute an adversarial flavor to much of American legal culture. Instead, executive authority and the rights of the governed each derive from and are limited by the "word of the Lord" and those who interpret it.

Familiarity with Jewish history will confirm, however, that for centuries conditions were far less than ideal. Juridical development and public practice were pressed to accommodate capricious overlords and hostile host cultures, without undermining the tradition and its essential integrity. This followed at least three related paths, rooted in early sources and carefully elaborated over time.

The first was a substantial allowance for local custom to assume precedence when strict adherence to tradition would cause undue hardship and make daily life untenable, or merely to help fill the breach when tradition was silent. While this occurred primarily in the secular arena, e.g. in civil, financial and social relations, it was more than occasionally applied to ecclesiastical concerns as well. Such tolerance for local diversity allowed flexibility in confronting the unstable and insecure nature of medieval and modern Jewish history.

Second, and related to the first, though attempts at regional hierarchy met with occasional success, the locus of power in medieval Jewish life was generally municipal or local, especially in Europe, lending an early "federalism" to communal administration. This fit neatly with the feudal societies within which Jewish communities found themselves and was, in part, shaped by that reality. Therefore, it is appropriate to speak of a tolerance for diversity between Jewish communities in Poland, Germany or Morocco. However, within those communities, adherence to local practice was more rigidly enforced. Those who would reside or do business there were expected to conform to local practice, occasionally in the face of Scriptural or Talmudic precedent to the contrary.

Finally, Jewish legal and political culture is characterized by a well-developed sense of the dialectic. For each position, there is an opposition, for each proof-text, a counter-text—grounded in deductive argumentation, precedent and homily. Dissenting and minority opinions are preserved for their intrinsic worth and for their use as future precedent, should circumstances require normative re-examination. In this sense, classic Jewish study tends toward scholastic "ahistoricity," favoring the argument upon its merits and almost, though not quite, regardless of its context. The result provides a framework for change while promoting fluency with the past, a formula that has stood well in hostile and hospitable environs alike.[66]

---

66. See Stuart Cohen, *The Three Crowns: Structures Of Communal Discourse In Early Rabbinic Society*. Oxford: Cambridge University Press,1990; Robert Cover (1987), "Obligation: A Jewish Jurisprudence of the Social Order" *Journal Of Law And Religion* 5:65–90; Daniel Elazar, *Kinship And Consent: The Jewish Political Tradition And Its Contemporary Uses*. Lanham: University Press of America, 1983; Daniel Elazar, *The Jewish Polity: Jewish Political Organization From Biblical Times To The Present*. Bloomington: Indiana University Press, 1985. Steven Friedell, (1992) "The Different Voice in Jewish Law: Some Parallels to a Feminist Jurisprudence," *Indiana Law Journal*, 67:915–949; Suzanne Stone, "In Pursuit of the Counter Text: The Turn to the Jewish Legal Model in Contemporary American Legal Theory," *Harvard Law Review*, 106:813–894.

Talmud Torah is Equivalent to All Else

Early Talmudic sources establish a set of mutual obligations, social and ritual, that inhere in the relationship between parent and child.
Among these, the parent is expected to teach the child Torah, to see
that he marries, to teach him a trade and also to swim.[67]

In the course of discussion, later Talmudic sources link these specific responsibilities to biblical proof texts, thereby establishing the
centrality of both character education (*talmud torah*) and career training in the pursuit of successful living. Medieval commentaries added
that in this context, teaching one's child to swim is basic to survival,
and perhaps emblematic of other physical competencies integral to
good parenting.

Additionally, through careful manipulation of several Biblical
sources, Talmudic authorities placed the primary obligation of education upon fathers toward their sons, with daughters largely excluded
from the basic duties, and benefits, of *talmud torah*. This confirmed
a more general predisposition expressed elsewhere in the Talmud.[68]

Such sources provide several insights key to our analysis. First,
apparently education was understood as a private responsibility whose
parameters, whether religious, social or utilitarian, fell upon the family. Indeed, authors of later codes of Jewish law were most aggressive
in stipulating that fathers who neglected to pay appropriate support
for the care and education of their children could have their properties
attached and their public social and religious privileges withheld.[69]

However, whether by malevolence or inadvertence, if a child
reached his majority without proper education, the obligation for *talmud torah* now transferred to him. Indeed, the sources fall silent in
regard to available redress for damages against neglectful parents or
their estate to cover the future costs of educating a now adult child.
Nor do they provide compensation for consequent loss or suffering related to their failure to provide an education. This confirms still further
the apparently personal nature of these requirements.

Additionally, it is clear that the wide-ranging private obligations
to educate the young grounded in Jewish sources were not universal
but differentiated, most especially by gender. Indeed, related sources
questioned the wisdom of allowing females any access to Jewish edu-

---

67. Talmud Bavli: Kiddushin 29a.
68. Talmud Bavli: Kiddushin 29b, 82a and Sotah 20a.
69. Shulchan Arukh: Even Haezer 94:1.

cation, save for the practical details of their specific religious obligations along with a facility in reading Scripture.[70]

Moreover, absent a clear mandate for women to be formally educated, it was inferred that mothers, regardless of their capacities, were
free of any direct obligation to educate their children, male or female.
Early sources suggest, however, that mothers did have some contact
with teachers, and were typically involved in seeing to the welfare of
their children at school. Nevertheless, this bias toward male responsibility for education even interceded upon judicial decisions regarding
child custody. In the case of marital dissolution, for an example, Jewish courts were predisposed to leave young children and older daughters with their mothers. Sons beyond the age of six or seven, however,
were generally assigned to their fathers whose exclusive responsibility
it was to see that they were properly schooled. [71]

Talmud Torah in the Public Square

This system of largely private initiative eventually proved inadequate
to the task, especially in the face of important social inequities and
dislocations. Consequently, the Talmud tells us of a major change in
public policy regarding education, associated with the efforts of one
Joshua ben-Gamla, a high priest whose administration spanned the
early part of the first century of the Common Era. In the words of the
Talmud:

> Had it not been for him, Torah would be forgotten in Israel. At
> first one who had a father, taught him Torah. One who had no
> father learned no Torah. So they ruled that teachers be retained
> in Jerusalem. Then, one who had a father brought him to Jeru-
> salem, while one with no father did not reach Jerusalem. And
> so they ruled that teachers be appointed in each district, and
> children entered at the age of 16 or 17. But one whose teacher
> was cross with him [the child] would leave, until Joshua ben-
> Gamla established teachers in each town, and children were
> brought at the age of 6 or 7.[72]

70. Talmud Bavli: Sotah 21b, Kiddushin 29b; Yad Hahazakah: Hikhot Talmud
Torah 1:13; Shulchan Arukh: Yoreh Deah 246:6.
71.Talmud Bavli: Kiddushin 29a, 83a Ketubot 65b; Yad Hahazakah: Hilkhot
Ishut 21:17; Shulchan Arukh: Even Haezer 82:7; Sylvan Schaeffer, "Child
Custody: Halacha and the Secular Approach," *The Journal of Halacha and
Contemporary Society*, 6:3 (Fall, 1983) pp. 33–45.
72. Talmud Bavli: Bava Batra 20b–21a.

The reference is informative both for its historical value and for what it reveals about Jewish attitudes toward education as a fundamental right and public obligation. Apparently, the extant system of home schooling and family responsibility left an important social gap in regard to those who "had no father," i.e. those orphaned, abandoned or neglected. Such circumstances may have reached crisis proportion in the midst of the political turmoil and social instability of the Roman persecutions contemporaneous with ben-Gamla's administration. As we will see, later authorities expanded these provisions to include families financially unable to care for the education of their children.

Historians have employed this source to draw inferences regarding the evolution of public education in ancient Israel and the values implicit therein. Educational reform, they argue, began originally in Jerusalem, the Jewish national, religious and social center. Children who had been educated at home until the age of 16 or 17 would be brought to academies established there to pursue advanced study. However, this still excluded the large portion of adolescents whose parents were unable to sustain them there, and so parallel schools were established in each district to meet that need. [73]

Apparently, this too proved untenable for the broad majority of students, perhaps less able or less motivated than those with resources to study at the academies in Jerusalem. With little experience in a formal classroom, they ran afoul of their teachers and took umbrage with attempts at discipline. Having reached their majority, they simply left school.

It was the innovation of ben-Gamla to ordain that teachers for elementary level students be retained in each locality. Children would be schooled in the basics of Scripture at home until the age of six or seven years. Then they were brought to the local classroom, generally designated in a synagogue building or as part of quarters provided for the teacher. These arrangements were publicly supported from the general treasury and provided free for those orphaned or abandoned. Moreover, to reinforce its support for this reform, the Talmud provides, and later codes endorse, that in a locality with 25 children, citi-

73. *See* e.g. Nathan Drazin, *History of Jewish Education: From 515 BCE to 220 CE.* Baltimore: The Johns Hopkins Press, 1941. Also Ephraim Kanarfogel, *Jewish Education and Society in the High Middle Ages.* Wayne State University Press, 1992.

zens may petition for a mandatory fund to create such a program, even if an adequate facility exists in the next district.

Those with parents able to arrange for their education privately, retained a number of important options. The small minority who had both the time and the skill to instruct their own children beyond the rudiments of Scripture could execute their individual responsibilities directly, through something akin to home schooling. They would personally provide for *talmud torah* until their young took charge of their own obligations of education into adulthood. They were not required to send them to the local school, though they continued their support through contributions to the community fund. Similarly, parents with sufficient resources could engage private tutors rather than enroll their children in the local schools, so long as they continued to pay their assessment to the fund. Alternatively, those with adequate resources could enroll their children in the town school, though they were required to pay private tuition costs, over and above any taxes assessed for the local fund.

The Problem Child

Evaluating the position of Jewish law in regard to suspending or expelling students for cause is also no simple matter. With some exception, classic sources are largely silent on the matter, suggesting broad discretion in practice for private teachers, school administrators and lay leaders. Moreover, those early sources that do confront the issue appear to run in contrary directions. There are, for an example, those that suggest patience and forbearance with even the least able of students. "Educate the child according to his path," we read in Proverbs (22:6), implying, on its face, that teachers tolerate various learning styles, extending freedom and flexibility to their students. If one among them proved stubbornly unable or unwilling to learn, the Talmudic sages add, the wise educator ought to neither reprove him heavily nor remove him from class. Rather, allow him to remain with his friends for the social benefits that may accrue. Eventually he will absorb his studies.

This generally conforms to individual Talmudic rulings and anecdotes celebrating large increases in students due to a relaxation of entrance requirements under the academic leadership of Rabbi Eliezer ben Azariah. Similarly, Bet Hillel favored education for all, in apparent disregard for their moral or academic qualifications, so that they may be brought closer to Torah.[74]

Others are more rigorous. They understand the same Scriptural verse very differently. Indeed, "educate the child according to **His** path," i.e. according to the strict pathways of the Lord. Reprove him handily during his early years, filling him with stern words of moral instruction and rebuke lest he veer from the pathways of righteousness. Late adolescence appears to have been a period of particular concern and the parent was well advised to "rest your hand on your son's neck," during this time.[75] In keeping with this severity, the Talmud warns "let no man teach a student who is not appropriate," and one who accepts such a student, "will descend to purgatory." Such actions are like unto "tossing [precious] stones before an idolater." Later authorities ruled that a teacher or the school should "return him to the straight path," after which he may be re-admitted to the study hall.[76]

For the most part, the contexts of these discussions suggest that the student in question was deemed inappropriate on moral or religious grounds. To continue his Torah study without correcting these dissonant proclivities, would only contribute to further delinquency. Contemporary authorities generally have applied these rulings to theological differences between various Jewish denominations. The sources are generally silent regarding disorderly students, or those who threaten the security and wellbeing of others. [77]

As a result, recent rulings are found on both sides of the issue. One author for example, gives testimony to a verbal statement issued by Rabbi Abraham Karelitz, author of the *Hazon Ish*. Proscriptions against teaching unfit students, he argued, presumed that suspension or expulsion would serve as a deterrent for children and their families. Indeed, in an earlier age, the embarrassment and social sanction that followed would assure that they would work to correct their offenses so that they might be readmitted to study with their peers. In a contemporary world, absent such a cohesive and supporting environment, expulsion merely dooms such students to spiritual oblivion. It

74. Talmud Bavli: Bava Batra 21a, Berachot 28a and Avot D'Rabbi Natan 9:9.
75. Talmud Bavli: Kiddushin 30a.
76. Talmud Bavli: Makkot 10a, Hullin 133a; Yad HaChazakah: Hilkhot Talmud Torah 4:1.
77. Rabbi Ovadiah Yosef, Yabiah Omer: Yoreh Deah (2:17) and Rabbi Eliezer Waldenberg, Tzitz Eliezer (8:15).

is worthwhile to note that this thinking was presaged by Rabbi Shneur Zalman of Lyady.[78]

The bulk of opinion appears to emerge on the other side of the issue, however, particularly regarding students whose behavior endangers others or makes it difficult for them to learn. However, such rulings have not generally been grounded in the early precedents discussed above, perhaps in tribute to their ambiguity. For an example, in closing his extensive assessment of issues related to synagogue membership and school admission criteria, Rabbi Herschel Schachter suggests:

> We may expel a child from school for being a nuisance even if by Jewish law he is not accountable or punishable. Our rationale in essence is that we are not punishing him. We are simply trying to prevent him from affecting his peers or other children in the school.[79]

It is notable that his decision is not rooted in deliberations over Jewish educational tradition or policy. Rather, it emerges from general discussions of preventive detention, especially as they relate to strictures imposed on Jewish holy days.

Finally, we have an epistle to educators written by Rabbi Moshe Feinstein. There, the sage and religious leader wrote, almost as an afterthought, that a student whose behavior threatens to "spoil others, certainly should be removed." This should be done, however, only with the most careful deliberation, for withholding his education may be "tantamount to a capital offense."[80]

Rabbi Eliezer Shach makes the point still more forcefully, though he offers no reasoning or text in support. He rules that no consideration should be given to a student whose presence constitutes a danger for others. Such danger includes disrupting and distracting them from their studies. He adds however,

---

78. Cited in Rabbi Chaim Naftalin, "Kiruv VeRichuk: Birur Hilchati," Niv Hamidrasha (Spring, 1970) p. 154. See also Rabbi Abraham Karelitz, Kovetz Iggerot, nos. 89 and 93 (Bnai Brak: Greinneman, N.D.), Shulhan Arukh Ha-Rav: Hilchot Talmud Torah, no. 13, and Rabbi J. David Bleich, Contemporary Halachic Problems II, (New York: Yeshiva University, 1983).

79. Rabbi Herschel Schachter, "Synagogue Membership and School Admission," The Journal of Halacha and Contemporary Society, 12:3 (Fall, 1986) pp. 50–68.

80. Rabbi Moshe Feinstein, Iggerot Moshe: Yoreh Deah, 3:71.

If there is no danger to others, only that he has no success in his studies, then we do not distance him, for perhaps over time he will be strengthened and succeed. Particularly in these times, if he will leave the Yeshiva it is impossible to know what types of friends he will accrue. He may, heaven forbid, cease to observe mitzvot.[81]

Summary Comparison

Comparing Jewish and American legal perspectives over the issue of education as a fundamental right yields important similarities and contrasts. Both traditions understand the great importance of education as a functional route toward independence and self-sufficiency, as a modality for improving the personal and social quality of citizenship, and a means to pursue the good life. They each posit an obligation to provide education to the young, which is understood in its public and private context.

Deciding whether it is a fundamental right, however, is no simple matter. It appears that the Supreme Court does not find clear justification for assuming a right to education that obligates public authorities throughout the country. Still, it agrees that the public has a substantial interest in the education of its citizens, representing more than merely another publicly sanctioned social service. For the most part, the Court has left its formulation as a right and public obligation to the constitutions and the courts of the individual states.

Moreover, there appears to be a consensus regarding the freedom of private and parochial schools to develop structures and policies that do not conform even to generally accepted fundamental rights. They retain the power to restrict their educational institutions by race, religious affiliation or gender and they may exclude students based on behavior that might otherwise be acceptable in publicly funded institutions. In addition, given increased concern over violence and drug abuse in the schools, programs of zero-tolerance—whereby students are suspended or expelled for specific infractions—may well leave these students without recourse to alternative venues to continue their education.

In Jewish law, education is defined as a lifelong obligation simultaneously extended to one's children. Still, in their original formula-

---

81. Rabbi Eliezer Menahem Shach, Mikhtavim U-Maamarim, V. I and II (Bnai Brak: 1988) no. 65.

tion, such obligations and any consequent benefits were by no means universal. For an obvious example, they did not include instruction for women, save for religious and ritual requirements specific to their gender. In the many centuries since these discussions were initiated, much has been done to advance the case for female education in Jewish law on par with what is provided for men. Nevertheless, it would be no simple task to designate it as a fundamental right for purposes of our discussion.

Further, even publicly funded educational agencies for males appear to have been established as a concession to social disruption and dislocation. Once established, their original mission appears to have been aimed primarily at the needs of the underprivileged. Absent such need, a child might not have claim to his education as a basic right, nor was there a clear mandate for his parents to avail themselves of services provided.

Two further considerations underscore the point. In the first instance, its great importance notwithstanding, education in Jewish thought appears less as a personal right or public responsibility, than a private obligation resting primarily upon the individual family. Beyond usual taxes and assessments, parents of means also are expected to pay tuition for each child attending the local schools, their communal assessments notwithstanding. This allows them a fair amount of discretion in choosing and structuring that education but they have little claim upon the public to free them of this financial burden.

Finally, our overall formulation may be inadequate to the analysis, given the subtle but important distinction between a personal "right" and an "obligation" incumbent upon a public other. In the American legal tradition, rights inhere in the sovereign individual and on their basis he may make demands upon the public. By contrast, an obligation is bestowed from without as a function of a relationship. It yields little power of claim.

Indeed the notion of a fundamental right, as typically connoted in American constitutional law, may be foreign to the original intent of Jewish tradition. Thus, while parents have an obligation to provide *talmud torah* to their children, and all Israel has a portion in the Torah itself, it may be incorrect to suggest that children have a "right" to *talmud torah*. Even if parents are negligent, the obligation simply transfers to children upon their majority, with no claim against either their parents or the public authority.

Jewish Day Schools Worldwide:
Achievements, Challenges, and Aspirations

Howard Deitcher and Alex Pomson

The Diaspora Jewish day school is one of the most remarkable creations of Jewish communal life. Its organizational characteristics are derived from a cultural template that originates beyond the Jewish community in the purposes and practices of public education: the preparation of large numbers of children for productive adult life by nominated specialists in an all-day setting. Yet the mission of the Jewish day school is profoundly counter-cultural, for it seeks to socialize children—and increasingly their families—into a way of life and set of values that often depart from the public norm. In many countries, this task calls parents, many of whom are professionally and socially well integrated into the public culture, to invest significant portions of their personal wealth into this endeavor. The sustainability and vitality of Diaspora Jewish day schools depend, therefore, on a delicate balance of forces: They require that parents see the value of nurturing particular Jewish literacies and lifestyles in a setting that prepares children for success in societies that promote and nurture a more universal and inclusive lifestyle.

The first modern Jewish day schools, in 19th-century Europe and 20th-century America, were intended to serve narrowly delineated constituencies. In Europe, day schools were constituted as "free schools" by wealthy benefactors, intended to help the children of poor, usually migrant, Jews become worthy and well-integrated members of society (Eliav, 1960). In the United States, on the other hand, such schools were conceived as fortresses against social integration. Their mission was to train the future leadership of the Jewish people—its priesthood, as one advocate put it—and to protect Judaism from being overwhelmed in America (Dushkin, 1948; Sarna, 1998).

The emergence today of the Jewish day school as a school of choice for so many Jews—rich or poor, religiously liberal or Orthodox, immigrant or native—would surely have surprised even the most ardent day school advocates of previous generations. Examining why this change has occurred and what it has produced may shed light on future prospects and challenges for these important institutions.

Day School Demographics

Today, more than 1.4 million Jewish children—an unprecedented number—are enrolled in Jewish day schools worldwide. Three quarters of these children are in Israel (State of Israel, 2007). At the time of writing, an additional 260,000 children attend day schools in North America, and another 125,000 are in day schools scattered across the globe.[1] These numbers represent an increase of just under 130,000 students (or just over 65%) since DellaPergola and Schmelz (1989) calculated Diaspora day school enrollment as 232,000 in 1982–1983.

A major proportion of the students enrolled in day schools are affiliated with the ultra-Orthodox community. In the United States today, ultra-Orthodox students make up 60% of total day school enrollment, an increase of more than 40% in ultra-Orthodox student numbers in 10 years (Schick, 2009). In the UK, data from 1999 indicate that 48% of students were affiliated with ultra-Orthodox streams (Valins, 2003); their numbers have most likely grown since. In the southern hemisphere, where day school enrollment has historically been more diverse, similar trends have been playing out. Although the numbers are sketchier, a combination of school closures and mergers, as well as general shifts in community demographics, has led to a significant increase in the proportion of ultra-Orthodox students in the day schools of Argentina, Brazil, and Mexico (Goldstein & Ganiel, in press).

Much of the growth of day schools over the last 50 years can be attributed, therefore, to the natural population growth among ultra-Orthodox Jews. However, it is the increase in the number of liberal day schools and in the number of students enrolled in such schools that has been truly remarkable. The first non-Orthodox day school in North America opened in 1951, some 50 years after the first Orthodox day school. Today, there are approximately 165 North American day

---

1. The enrollment numbers for Diaspora schools are extrapolated from Schick (2005), Pomson (2004), Miller (2001), Cohen (2007), Gitelman, (2009) and Goldstein and Ganiel (in press).

schools either affiliated with non-Orthodox denominations or organized as pluralistic or non-denominational institutions, with an enrollment estimated to be just under one fifth of the total day school population (Schick, 2005). In Australia, some of the largest day schools in
the world have been, and continue to be, constituted as cross-commu-
nal institutions. Even in the UK, where almost all day schools have
traditionally been affiliated with Orthodox organizations, the first ever
community high school will open in 2010.

Diversification in the profile of day school families has occurred
in most countries as well. Until as recently as the 1980s, parents whose
children attended day school in northern hemisphere countries were,
typically, residents of Jewish neighborhoods and synagogue members
who had themselves received a relatively intensive Jewish education
(Ackerman, 1989; Beinart, 1999; Murphy, 2001). With few exceptions, these parents were Jewish from birth, Orthodox in denominational orientation, and married to other Jews; they were people for
whom paying for all-day Jewish schooling constituted the unquestioned expression of an already intensely engaged Jewish identity. Today, in many countries, Jewish day schools have successfully recruited
increased numbers of families with diverse religious commitments.
Many of these newer families lack an intensive Jewish education of
their own and depend on the schools to teach them Jewish practices
and concepts, a phenomenon that challenges schools, as will be seen
below (Pomson & Schnoor, 2008).

Changes in the profile of day school families have meant that day
school enrollment in the northern hemisphere increasingly resembles
that in the southern hemisphere. Since the Second World War, more
than 70% of all Jewish children in Australia, South Africa, and Latin
America attended Jewish day schools. In the northern hemisphere, the
level was far lower, barring exceptional cases such as Montreal, where
all public education was organized along religious denominational
lines. In the United States, the United Kingdom, and France fewer
than a quarter of Jewish children attended all-day Jewish schools. Today, the situation is much altered. While enrollment in the southern
hemisphere has eroded by a few percentage points, particularly among
the non-Orthodox, in the northern hemisphere it has increased dramat-
ically. By 2007, a majority of all Jewish children in Britain, aged 4 to
18, attended Jewish day schools, up from 20% in 1975; in the United
States, more than a quarter of Jewish children attended day schools

compared with 10% in 1975; and in France, close to 40% attended day schools compared with 16% in 1986 (JPPPI, 2007).

Since the onset of the acute financial downturn of 2008, there has been much debate as to whether growth in day school enrollment has peaked (Kramer, 2009; Rosenblatt, 2009; Sarna, 2009). Because Jewish day schools are privately funded in most jurisdictions (with the exception of the UK and some of Canada's provinces), there has been acute speculation as to whether there will be a slide in total enrollments over the coming years as families struggle to pay annual fees that can often exceed $20,000 per child. It is commonly assumed that while highly affiliated and highly Orthodox Jews are less sensitive to the high cost of day school education because of an *a-priori* commitment to parochial Jewish schools, moderately affiliated families will be much more likely to withdraw from schools if school fees continue to rise or if family incomes significantly fall (Continental Council for Jewish Education, 2003).

Although, as financial advisers like to caution, past performance does not necessarily indicate future results, a better sense of what might happen to day school enrollment in coming years will come from a precise analysis of what in the last three decades has caused day school growth, especially in the northern hemisphere.

Causes of School Growth

Day school growth, apart from that associated with the ultra-Orthodox community, has generally been attributed to four main causes:

Decay of Public Education

Jewish families, it is commonly said, have turned their backs on public schools as part of a larger withdrawal of the middle classes from public institutions left to decay by the public policies of governments in many Western countries (Himmelfarb, 1989; Shapiro, 1996). In an era when publicly funded institutions have become increasingly affiliated with the poor, and when the public perceives standards in public schools as increasingly inferior to those of private schools, Jewish parents, who often are themselves graduates of public schools, have been reluctant to sacrifice their children to an ideal of public education no matter how strongly felt (Zeldin, 1988). Parents, from this perspective, have turned to day schools not so much out of an interest in Jewish education per se, but rather because Jewish schools seem to

offer a quality of general education superior to that offered by most
public schools (Kelman, 1984). Day school advocates, therefore, have
argued that if schools are to continue to appeal to ever wider constituencies, their marketing and advocacy should focus on their capacity
to "provide top-notch preparation for a broad range of colleges and
universities, including those that are the most selective" (Lieberman
Research Worldwide, 2004).

Jewish Embourgoisement

In a related vein, it has been said that the decay of the public school
system has coincided with the steady rise in the sociocultural status of
the Jewish community and the concomitant ability of many families
to pay for private education. Increasingly, Jewish parents have chosen not between public schools and day schools but between different
forms of private education, with the Jewish parochial school as one
option (Beinart, 1999). The effect of increased affluence on school
choice has been seen most vividly in the creation of "boutique" day
schools with small enrollments, catering at great expense to families
with particular educational tastes. (According to Schick, 2000, 40% of
U.S. day schools enroll 100 or fewer students, and in most instances,
the geographical location and/or religious orientation of these institutions means they are unlikely to grow much larger.) Diamond has
argued that a kind of religious consumerism has produced this phenomenon, made possible by an expanding spending power that has
also spawned a substantial kosher lifestyle industry (Diamond, 2000).
From this perspective, increased disposable income among Jewish
families has resulted in day school growth.

Some commentators have framed this particular account of day
school growth in broader sociological terms by suggesting that the
shift to day schools is not only the product of greater spending power,
but is also a reflection of the socioeconomic evolution of the Jewish
community that, with few exceptions, no longer consists of first-gen-
eration immigrants (Ackerman, 1989). The two great waves of Jewish immigration to North America/the United States occurred at the
start of the 20th century and in the immediate aftermath of the Second
World War. For new arrivals at those times, the public school system
served as an important vehicle for socialization into the majority society. Today, after two or more generations of deepening assimilation
into the majority culture, Jewish parents willingly send their children

to separate parochial schools, either because they no longer fear being viewed as outsiders or because they have indeed become insiders (Shrager, 2002).

The Confluence of Multiculturalism and the "School Choice" Movement

Some have argued that the turn to day schools has less to do with changes within Jewish society and culture than with a transformation in the larger sociopolitical milieu of Western societies that has seen an unexpected confluence in aspects of progressive and conservative educational visions (Shapiro, 1996). Over the last 20 years, the increased receptiveness to the incorporation of multiculturalism in the public domain has allowed, with different degrees of integrity and effectiveness, a greater diversity of voices in public schools (Banks & Banks, 1995). It has also legitimized efforts by minority communities to counteract the dissolution of their cultures and identities in the public school system, even if that choice involves withdrawal from the system itself (Miller, 2001). The increased acceptance of the multicultural project has coincided with the proliferation of calls in right-wing circles for government aid for private schools, or at least for the use of public funds to support separate or distinctive schools. This move, generally couched in the rhetoric of school choice, has seen the advance of voucher programs and charter schools in a number of American states.

The convergence of these trends has reduced concerns among minority ethnic and faith communities about withdrawing from common public schools to create their own separate schools. Within the American Jewish community, some liberal organizations that once advocated for Jewish participation in public education have developed their own networks of day schools. Those who once led opposition to public aid for private religious schools have been reassessing their stance on the separation of church and state in educational matters (Wertheimer, 1999).

Concerns About Jewish Continuity

Within the organized Jewish community, day schools are invariably depicted as the most effective available vehicle for promoting the development of a distinct Jewish identity at a time when rates of Jewish-Gentile intermarriage have risen to unprecedented levels (JESNA, 1999). Until recently, it was difficult to determine to what extent this issue was important to families when choosing schools; nonetheless there is little doubt that for parents interested in providing their children with a substantial Jewish identity, a polarization of educational options has occurred. Alternatives to day school have withered. Jewish supplementary schools have cut back instructional time from more than 10 hours a week to 5 hours a week or less, enabling few such schools to claim that they can provide children with a significant foundation in Jewish literacy. If parents want their children to participate actively in Jewish cultural life, or if they seek a better-than-even chance that their child will marry another Jewish person, day school may be their only option (Cohen & Kotler-Berkowitz, 2004).

Some measure of confirmation for this argument has surfaced in recent years with emergent qualitative research data depicting how a great many of the non-Orthodox families enrolled in schools actively wrestle with commitments both to public education and to Jewish engagement, and of how "students and parents navigate among [multiple] worlds" when choosing day school (Shapiro, 1996; Goldberg, 1999). While few liberal parents seem ready to say (to researchers) that they chose to enroll their child in a day school because they wanted to increase the likelihood that their offspring will marry another Jew, there is accumulating evidence that in making this choice these parents find that day school satisfies deep values they discover they want for their children and even for themselves (Pomson & Schnoor, 2008; Prell, 2007).

Arguments such as these that emphasize the potential of day schools not only to combat Jewish cultural decline but also to inspire some kind of Jewish cultural renaissance have strongly influenced the creation of new schools, that is, the supply rather than the demand side of day school growth. Indeed, in the United States, a significant proportion of the day schools created during the last 15 years has resulted from the intervention of activist philanthropic foundations that have identified Jewish day schools as a highly effective means to intensify Jewish awareness and solidarity (PEJE, 2006).

Beyond Sociology to Policy

As we have argued elsewhere, broad accounts of the causes of a social phenomenon such as this operate at a high level of generality and therefore cannot predict or explain the choices made by particular individuals in particular communities at particular moments (Pomson, 2008). This account, for example, seeks to explicate trends in communities and countries far removed from one another, and therefore possesses the force of blunt generalization rather than the sharp nuance of the particular in attempting to make sense of the growing appeal of Jewish day schools. Thus, as we showed in a critique of this sociological account, day school growth in Toronto—a community where day school enrollment is more than 50% higher than the norm across the United States—was probably caused by improved rates of student retention within the system rather than by improved recruitment brought about by a combination of the factors surveyed above (Pomson, 2004). In fact, day school retention in Toronto has improved so much over the last 2 decades that the improvement may have masked an overall decline in the proportion of Jewish children in the city who at some point in their lives receive a day school education, a trend that runs contrary to the account just presented.

Despite its limitations, this account's general applicability does make it possible to anticipate with some confidence the likely consequences for day school enrollment of the economic challenges that many families currently face. For instance, we have seen that increased disposable wealth among Jews has been only one factor among others that contributed to increased day school enrollment. It is therefore reasonable to assume that a decline in families' capacity to pay fees will lead only to a moderate decline in enrollment, just as lowering the cost of schooling will probably increase enrollment only at the margins (Cohen 1999; Abba, 2002). An exception to this generalization was noted in Seattle where a tuition reduction program doubled the enrollment of the incoming high school class at Northwest Yeshiva High School. However, this program proved to be too expensive to maintain and within 5 years, it was totally revised and the original guidelines were significantly altered (Toren, 2005) Overall, the shift to day school in recent decades seems to reflect a change in the social status of Jews and in their values and priorities no less (and perhaps more) than any change in the capacity of Jewish parents to pay for private education. For these reasons, one might speculate that only financial distress on a scale previously unimagined by American Jews would result in a significant decline in enrollment.

Changed Responsibilities That Accompany School Growth

As increasing numbers of Jewish children are educated in Jewish day schools, the social roles of these schools have expanded beyond the classroom to include family education, the celebration of religious and life-cycle events, and the provision of a wide range of Jewish experiences. Some of those accumulating responsibilities can be directly attributed to the stimulus and pressures produced by growth. Accordingly, the funders who have financed an expanding system have started to expect, and even demand, that schools make the greatest possible contribution to the development of Jewish life not only for those who attend schools but also for those who do not. Furthermore, schools have responded to the diversification in the profile of day school families that accounts for some of the growth in enrollment by taking responsibility for providing these families with the Jewish social and cultural capital (that is, relationships with other Jews and knowledge of Jewish culture) that parents might previously have been expected to possess and employ in support of their children's Jewish education (See, for example, the autumn 2009 special issue of *Hayidion*, a Jewish teacher journal that is devoted to this development.)

Schools report that this is delicate work. First, in terms of determining their goals, they wonder whether or to what extent they should be involved in the nurture of families' private Jewish lives. They know they have an immediate responsibility to children, but they're less comfortable intervening in adult lives. Second, they are challenged by how to do this work in ways that are both respectful and productive. Unlike older adult Jewish learners who sign up for lecture programs in synagogues and JCCs, even parents who indicate that they want to learn are rarely attracted by adult education programs (Pomson & Schnoor, 2008). Instead, parents learn while doing or in order to do. For example, they learn while sitting on a committee or in order to help in the classroom; also they learn more from their peers than from an instructor. Indeed, it turns out that many parents learn a great deal about Jewish life and practice from what their children bring home from school (Pomson & Schnoor, 2009).

The expanding responsibilities of schools towards their students and their students' families may reflect changes in the roles of schools in society in general. For most of the last 150 years, and at least since the introduction of free compulsory education by modern nation-states in the 19th century, the primary function of schools was to prepare children for life as productive workers in a post-agricultural industrialized society. Today, schools are asked to do much more. No longer the exclusive preserve of religious and economic elites, schools are called on by governments to take up roles once performed by families, religious institutions, and workplaces. In recent times, schools have been asked to instruct their pupils on how to drink sensibly, eat healthily, vote conscientiously, and take a responsible attitude towards sex.

Jewish schools have not been free from this growing burden of social tasks. Jewish children were once expected to acquire knowledge of Judaism, develop attitudes about the Jewish world, and learn Jewish behaviors from people and places in their immediate surroundings—in the family, at the synagogue, even on the street (Soloveitchik, 1994; Blidstein, 2003). Today, responsibility for the emotional, moral, and interpersonal development of Jewish children has been increasingly devolving to schools, and day school educators find themselves no less challenged by these changes than their peers are in other school systems.

We sense that the consequences of this extending weight of responsibilities have not yet fully materialized. In one unexpected development, for example, Jewish day schools have become some of the major providers of informal Jewish education, a field once considered the preserve of youth movements and summer camps. Faculty trained to teach academic subjects in classroom settings are now asked to provide Jewish experiences such as religious holy day celebrations, residential Shabbat retreats, and trips to Israel that were once the responsibility of synagogues, families, or youth groups.

In a study of Israel education in day schools (about which we will say more below), we have observed changes in how schools conduct a major component of Jewish education—Israel education—that reflects this shift. In the course of our research, we asked heads of school to reflect on where they have the greatest impact on students' connection to and understanding of Israel. The great majority pointed to programs and interventions that occur outside the classrooms in which students spend the bulk of their time For the non-Orthodox, it tended to be the Israel trip that a majority of schools now organize, and for the Orthodox it was the special programs and experiences provided during the course of the year or the relationships children developed with Israeli personnel in the school. When we looked closely at the curriculum materials that schools use in the classroom to teach about Israel—whether designed by teachers themselves or by external providers—we found that they tended to be heavily skewed towards what can be called an "experiential" rather than a "cognitive" perspective; that is, they emphasized the relevance of the material to students' lives and experiences rather than focusing on abstract concepts or academic content.

It is too soon to say with any certainty whether what we observed in the field of Israel education is also occurring in other sub-disciplines of Jewish studies. Anecdotally, we suspect it may be. We have observed Orthodox high schools scheduling Friday afternoon *kumsitzes*, Monday morning *cholent kiddushes*, and Carlebach sing-alongs at almost any time of the week. There is a powerful sense that as they take on many practices once seen in camps, schools are seeking not only to stretch students' intellects but to cultivate their commitments. These practices and programs indicate that educators are not fully convinced of their students' loyalties or commitment. This concern may not be unreasonable, given the inclusion in modern Orthodox and especially in liberal day schools, of increasing numbers of students who don't come from religiously engaged families. To that extent, the roles now played by day schools may be starting to resemble those played over the last 50 years by congregational schools, as they attempt to socialize the moderately affiliated into a life of Jewish engagement and practice.

New/Old Challenges and Opportunities

Day schools serve as centers of Jewish life and, by definition, must cater to the diverse needs of a wide range of stakeholders. In attempting to realize this mandate, schools confront a series of perennial challenges whose outcomes oftentimes determine their particular character within their communal context. Schools wrestle with these issues on an ongoing basis and are ultimately judged on their ability to respond effectively to them. The following challenges have confronted schools over time, but have recently taken on a new sense of urgency that requires creative and strategic thinking and additional resources.

1.   Personnel Recruitment, Retention, and Professional Development

One challenge that has accompanied the rapid growth of day schools is that of recruiting, training, and retaining qualified, able personnel who will teach subject matter in a rigorous way while at the same time engaging students meaningfully beyond the cognitive realm. Whether this challenge is conceived as a crisis probably depends on one's tolerance for disequilibrium, but there is no doubt that teacher recruitment has been a chronic problem for schools and communities over many years, and that day school growth has only made it worse.[2] An even more acute challenge is the need to provide qualified, competent, even dynamic, day school leaders who can effectively address the formidable realities that schools face. The dearth of such personnel has led some to fear for the future of the day school system. As a key executive from one national Jewish organization put it: "Without good people, we have nothing" (Sales, 2007, p.18).

For much of the 20th century, most Jewish day schools met their staffing needs from three major sources, all of which became less and less adequate by the late 1970s, just when day school growth started to accelerate. The most important of these sources was immigrant, Hebrew-speaking educators from Europe. As members of this group grew older, they could not be replaced, their home communities having been destroyed by the Holocaust (Sarna, 1998). In fact, the disappearance of this source of teachers predates the Holocaust. Through legislation and executive order, Canada and the United States made immigration increasingly difficult in the 1920s and 1930s. These teachers, alumni of either a traditional or an "enlightened" European Jewish education, had formed the backbone of a school system which from its origins was committed to the *Ivrit be-Ivrit* (Hebrew-immersion) educational method.

The second source of educators in the prewar era came from ultra-Orthodox North American seminaries and yeshivas, which graduated some students who were prepared to enter the teaching profession. These young men and women, however, were not trained to teach in a Hebrew-immersion setting or to relate to the children from Conservative, Reform, secular, and modern-Orthodox homes who had become a day school demographic (Goldberg, 1999). Another potential source of personnel was the Hebrew teachers colleges. Their alumni were few, however, and in any case, these colleges tended to focus not on the preparation of classroom teachers but of supervisory and administrative personnel mainly for supplementary schools whose low salaries were a deterrent to developing full-time careers (Davidson, 1989).

---

2. Evidence of this challenge's pervasiveness is seen in the following studies and reports. Although concerned with the challenges facing day school education in different parts of the world, they all end up underscoring the critical need to prepare greater numbers of qualified and competent teachers and leaders. See Goldring, Gamoran, and Robinson. (1999), Sales (2007), Gefen (2007), Valins (2005), Gitelman (2009), and Lippman-Kanfer Institute (2009).

From the late 1960s, modern-Orthodox schools started to rely heavily for staff on *shlichim*, Israelis who came on short-term contracts. Israeli teachers brought with them knowledge of Hebrew and a special spirit unique to their background in the young state. For these reasons, they were well suited to communities with a Hebraic and Zionist orientation, such as Toronto and Cleveland. The adaptation to North America of *shlichim* was sometimes slow, however, and it was often difficult for them to serve as accessible role models. By the late 1980s, this staffing strategy was becoming complicated. The frequent and large-scale turnover of staff contributed to some instability in the schools, and changing immigration regulations were making it difficult to hire teachers from abroad.

Today, the situation regarding staff in Jewish day schools is probably more complex than ever. In *The Educators in Jewish Schools Study* (EJSS), Ben-Avie and Kress (2007) examined 195 congregation schools and 110 day schools and found that 48% of day school Jewish studies teachers hold a secondary degree and 9% have completed a tertiary degree. These figures compare favorably with public school educators; on the other hand, 44% of day school educators who responded to the EJSS did not have valid teaching certification that is both recognized by the state or province in which they teach and is not an emergency credential. The study also revealed that nearly a quarter (24%) of both Judaic studies and general studies day school educators across North America were newly hired for the 2005–2006 school year, with most hired to replace exiting teachers. This has created a sense of personnel instability in the field that carries significant policy implications.

In spite of the high level of turnover among school personnel, the EJSS study reported that educators express an overall sense of job satisfaction with their career choices, with the majority of respondents affirming items such as, "If I knew at the outset what I now know about my current job, I would still choose it." Only a small minority felt that if they could start again, they would select a different career path. This may suggest that those who do not enjoy the work of teaching leave quickly, while those who remain are relatively satisfied with their choices. All the same, a worrying number of day school educators (34%) still see themselves leaving the field of Jewish education in the next few years. The EJSS reports that for Jewish day schools the most pronounced predictors of retention include: (a) personal and professional support, whereby the teacher feels that she is being supported by administrators, colleagues, and parents; (b) satisfactory salary and benefits; and (c) allocation of non-contact time for lesson preparation.

A coalescence of factors has created both an acute shortage of day school principals and a perception that the demand for qualified and talented heads of school far exceeds the number of individuals who can successfully fill the available positions. As the number of day schools has mushroomed, so has demand for qualified principals. Also, the dramatic changes in the role and function of day schools have placed a heavy burden on incoming principals, demanding skills and knowledge that many do not possess or were not trained to assume (Schick, 2007). Furthermore, there is a perception that the tenure of current principals is shorter than in the past, as volunteer leaders have found the qualifications of principals to be lacking, or as successful principals have opted for more lucrative positions in other places (Raab, 2006). Finally, the significant increase in principals' salaries may have created unrealistic expectations about the range of roles that heads of school must fill, thereby generating feelings of frustration and disillusionment among both lay and professional leaders.

The perceived high turnover rate of principals is validated in Schick's (2007) study, which reports that nearly two thirds of the principals surveyed had been at their current schools for less than 10 years, with one quarter having been there less than 4 years. Equally significant is the finding that only one third of the principals were recruited by the same schools where they were previously employed. Several explanations shed light on this unusual phenomenon: First, career advancement is often predicated on job mobility. Second, an assistant principal aspiring to become a head of school may find herself in a situation whereby the incumbent principal triggers a search process for alternatives outside the community. Finally, Schick argues that lay leaders tend to prefer selecting candidates from outside their institutions.

When discussing principals' retention, Schick was surprised to discover a very high degree of job satisfaction, with more than 80% of the principals characterizing their experience as rewarding, and another 14% describing it as satisfactory. This concurs with his finding that more than 75% of the respondents characterized their decision to make Jewish education their career a wise one.

As for principals' training, a third of the respondents to Schick's study reported that they were not adequately prepared for their first principalship. This is significant considering that 80% reported that they had previously taught at a day school and knew the inner workings of their schools as well as the day school system more generally. Furthermore, more than half had never participated in a formal training program, but felt that they had been thrust into leadership positions without sufficient knowledge, skills, or a support system to help them meet emerging challenges. This corroborates an earlier report (Goldring, Gamoran, & Robinson, 1999) that claimed that educational leaders in Jewish day schools have inadequate formal preparation in the areas of education administration and supervision. According to this report, only 36% of day school leaders have certification in administration, and a mere 19% have completed a degree in educational administration. In addition, attendance of day school leaders at professional development programs is poor. At the time of this earlier research, day school leaders attended 4.4 workshops over a 2-year period, a mere fraction of what was required in many public educational systems. If we assume that a workshop lasts 3 hours on average, 4.4 workshops over 2 years is approximately 33 hours over 5 years. For the reports' authors, this compared most unfavorably with the requirements of many American states, where school administrators had to attend 100 hours of workshops over the same 5-year period. In comparing the level of professionalism between day school heads and their public school counterparts, Gamoran comments: "Principals of Jewish schools are more professionalized than those in other private schools, but less trained than public school principals" (Gamoran, Goldring, & Robinson, 1999, p.457).

Taken together, these data point to several conclusions that warrant further deliberation. On the whole, heads of Jewish day schools are committed, professionally satisfied, well-compensated, mobile educators. At the same time, they are not generally formally certified nor sufficiently prepared in educational leadership and administration, and they do not they take adequate advantage of professional development opportunities. Day school teachers, in contrast, are not well compensated financially. Though the majority of teachers hold a degree beyond a B.A., few have a valid teaching certification, and they too participate in only a minimal number of professional-development programs over the course of their careers.

The emerging picture raises several questions that deserve the attention of policy makers and educational leaders: (a) What strategies can address the issues of retention for both teachers and administrators? (b) What are the available pools of qualified individuals who can fill these positions? (c) What types of training programs are available for incoming teachers and administrators, and how are these educators supported on an ongoing basis? (d) What practical implications do these studies carry for schools that are attempting to recruit and train young educators?

To start answering these questions, we provide an overview of current training programs for teachers and administrators, and then explore how these programs can be developed in order to meet growing demands from the field. The number of initiatives has increased significantly over the past few years as new strategies and accompanying resources have been created to address these challenges. Pre-service programs train educators in an array of different areas including curriculum and instruction, classroom management, educational philosophy, developmental psychology, and foundations in Jewish education. Most programs include a practicum of fieldwork that allows participants to gain practical experience and integrates theoretical courses with the realities in the field. In the United States, the majority of programs grant a master's degree in Jewish education, qualifying the participant to enter the teaching field.[3]

In addition to master's programs, several non-degree programs have recently begun that provide new opportunities for individuals who don't need a formal graduate degree. In recent years, these new programs have attempted to accommodate the hectic lifestyles of educators by offering a series of intensive programs that do not require full-time, yearlong residence or that can be accessed by distance learning. Some of these programs have added a new training component of induction, helping to socialize new educators into the culture of the school and nurture them during their initial period of work. Oftentimes these programs provide novice educators with professional mentors who have successfully weathered such challenges themselves and are now prepared to share their wisdom and experience with younger colleagues. This process also creates new roles for veteran educators, who

---

3. For a listing and description of these various programs, see Sales (2007). For a list of the various pre-service programs for Orthodox educators, see Feuerman, (2002).

generally view these opportunities most positively, allowing them to employ a new set of leadership skills that are highly regarded and appreciated. Moreover, mentoring serves a critical role in the retention of successful veteran educators who keenly seek these kinds of roles in the school context (Ben-Avie & Press, 2007).

A second area of professional development focuses on in-service training of day school educators. A host of different research reports (McLaughlin & Talbert, 2001; Darling & Hammond, 1999; Knapp, 2003) underscore the importance of well-qualified teachers who work in a thriving professional ambiance that encourages and supports multiple opportunities for professional development. As long as teachers feel that they are growing professionally and continuing to wrestle with relevant challenges, they will succeed in connecting with children, and their ability to impact the lives of their students will increase over time. Comer notes: "In well-functioning schools, educators thrive and stay, and in turn, the students learn and develop well" (Comer, 1997, p. 143). Thus, if teachers are encouraged to pursue opportunities for professional growth, the payback is rich and worthwhile. Unfortunately, these findings have had limited impact on the field of Jewish teacher education. As noted above, Jewish educators engage in relatively few in-service training opportunities, a critical factor in their professional growth and development (Stodolsky & Dorph, 2007). Furthermore, in analyzing the content of various in-service programs for Judaica teachers, Holtz and Gamoran (2000) reported: "Unfortunately, far too many examples of professional development in Jewish education have not caught up with the latest thinking in general education" (p.180). In addition to the few formal professional development programs, little time is allocated for teachers to work together, discuss professional issues, and observe each other teaching. Several new programs are addressing this problem, but these have mostly targeted lead teachers, and their impact has been limited (Stodolsky & Dorph, 2007)As a response to the shortage of qualified leadership for Jewish day schools, there has been a recent upsurge in the number of leadership development programs for school principals. These programs generally combine formal classroom learning with practical ongoing instruction and mentoring, a critical mix that is widely accepted as the most efficient and engaging form of professional development for educational leaders (Garet, Porter, Desimone, Birman, & Yoon, 2001). The efficacy of these programs should be monitored over time in order to determine their impact on the field.[4]

2. Israel Education

Israel education continues to play a pivotal role in Jewish day schools worldwide. Myriad curriculum packages, a wide array of professional development programs for educators, and an abundance of short- and long-term experiences in Israel for students, teachers, and family groups are organized by schools. In large part, the proliferation of activity in this area can be understood as a reaction to the growing indifference of young Diaspora Jews to Israel, as well as the perception that a significant attachment to Israel bolsters Jewish identity among day school students (Cohen & Kelman, 2007).

There are currently about 300 day schools in North America whose values are informed by Zionist (or Israel-centric) commitments. This small and loose network is characterized by a common interest in providing students with opportunities to forge a meaningful relationship with Zionist ideals and the State of Israel. However, the range of goals as well as the lack of clarity about how to achieve them is some times hard to believe. Most striking is the sharp difference between how Israel education is approached in modern-Orthodox and liberal schools.[5]

Liberal schools are 50% more likely to sponsor some kind of Israel trip for their students and their families than are Orthodox schools. At the same time, the proportion of liberal high school graduates attending a gap-year experience in Israel is significantly lower than among the Orthodox graduates (Berger, Jacobson, & Waxman, 2007). A second difference is noted with respect to curricular materials on teaching Israel: Liberal schools are more than twice as likely as Orthodox schools to employ commercially produced curricula rather than school-produced programs. Liberal schools are only half as likely as Orthodox schools to employ Israelis on short-term contracts as either teachers or informal educators, opting instead to hire local educators

4. Note Schick's disturbing remark: "For all of the recent emphasis on training programs, not as many as one in five (of principals who responded to the AVI CHAI survey) credit this (professional development) as helping to prepare them" (Schick, 2007, p. 19).
5. When referring to liberal schools, we mean community, Conservative, and Reform schools, because there do not appear to be statistical differences among their approaches to Israel education.

to teach about Israel. Finally, liberal schools are almost twice as likely to provide professional development for their faculty about Israel education as are their Orthodox counterparts.[6]

In attempting to explicate the multiple challenges that day schools face in providing engaging and meaningful Israel education, we focus on the following: (i) the absence of clear and realistic purposes for Israel education; (ii) the dominant role of experiential education; (iii) the range of available curricular materials on Israel education, and (iv) the decreasing stature of Hebrew language in schools.

(i) Confused purposes

Educational research underscores the need for schools to articulate intelligible and achievable educational objectives, a need that is particularly relevant for Jewish schools that wrestle with a host of challenging goals (Fox, Scheffler, & Marom, 2003). Although a significant number of day schools have in recent years invested significant time and energy in articulating their overall Jewish mission, scant attention has been paid to the area of Israel education (Margolis, 2008; Kopelowitz, 2007; Schnall, 1991). Rather than confronting the challenge of drafting a coherent and binding vision regarding the place of Israel in their schools, many day schools have co-opted the AVI CHAI Foundation formulation: "The creation of the State of Israel is one of the seminal events in Jewish history. Recognizing the significance of the State and its national institutions, we seek to instill in our students an attachment to the State of Israel and its people as well as a sense of responsibility for their welfare." Typically, such schools talk in general terms about a love for or commitment to Israel, goals that are as likely to be declared by elementary schools as by high schools. The schools promise sweeping affective outcomes, but do not identify a more nuanced set of goals to guide the development of educational programs (especially for teaching Hebrew) and the allocation of resources or teaching time.

(ii) An over-reliance on experiential education

As noted earlier, when school heads reflect on which aspects of

6. Significant portions of this section are based on studies we conducted for the AVI CHAI, Schusterman, and Jim Joseph Family Foundations. See Pomson, Deitcher, and Muszkat-Barkan (2009) and Pomson, Deitcher, and Rose (2009).

Israel education have the greatest impact on students, the great majority point to programs and interventions that occur outside the classroom spaces where their students spend most of their time. They point to special calendar events and ceremonies, relationships with Israelis working in their schools or in partner communities, and, of course, their programs in Israel. As seen in Table 1 (summarizing responses to one item on a system-wide survey we conducted), other than at the lowest grade levels where schools do not provide trips to Israel, and where Israel education is centered in the Hebrew language classroom, Israel education is perceived to have its greatest power when conveyed by the vehicles of informal or experiential education.

Table 1. "Of all the programs in your school, which in your view has the greatest impact on students' connection to Israel?

All combined	Partnerships	Informal events	Curriculum	Personnel	Trip	
5%	15%	25%	30%	20%	5%	K–6 (15 schools)
2%	10%	23%	17 %	16 %	31%	K–8 (78 schools)
3%	8%	30%	15%	13%	31%	K–12/9–12 (56 schools)

The materials that schools use in the classroom also tend to be heavily skewed towards what we call an "experiential" rather than a "cognitive" perspective. Having analyzed more than 70 curricula for teaching about Israel published over the last 10 years by both commercial and not-for-profit publishers, we found that these programs predominantly emphasize their relevance to the students' lives and experiences rather than focus on abstract concepts or academic content. They eschew teaching-for-understanding and instead try to cultivate an emotional or personal response.

Of course, a preference for informal/experiential education is not necessarily problematic. Our concern is with the tendency towards informal education in a setting whose raison d'être was, historically at least, the provision of formal education. It leads us to wonder whether in the field of Israel education we are witnessing what Isa Aron once called a paradigm of "enculturation" rather than one of "instruction."

Aron drew upon the work of Christian educator John Westerhoff, who points to the critical role of John Dewey and other early 20th-century philosophers in underlining the importance of these concepts in educational practice. Enculturation, Aron explained, constitutes the broadly conceived task of introducing children into a set of values and norms, and initiating them into a culture and its commitments. Instruction is a more narrowly conceived task that assumes the child's preexisting commitment to a culture, and is therefore focused on helping children acquire knowledge of the ideas and skills which that culture values. Whereas enculturation is advanced by providing young people with well-conceived and positive Jewish experiences, instruction occurs typically within the walls of the classroom in an interaction between the teacher and learner (Aron, 1987).

We sense that when it comes to Israel education, schools are engaged in enculturative, not instructive, work. Schools, whether Orthodox or non-Orthodox, are seeking to cultivate commitments and inculcate values by providing students with formative experiences. Schools don't seem ready to assume that students' commitments are firm enough for educators to focus only on instruction. Rather, the educators must engage in Israel advocacy work with their own students.

This is no small matter. First, the great majority of those who work in schools were trained as classroom-based instructors and not as enculturative (or experiential) educators. One can only wonder how students respond to the fact that this one area of Jewish studies is relegated to a different type of educator, or in some cases to educators who have not been trained in experiential education. In Eisner's terms, what explicit, implicit, and null messages about Israel education are internalized by the students (Eisner, 1979). Are schools aware of the consequences of this approach and if so, have they deliberated about its impact?

A second problem with the emphasis on informal education afflicts all informal education programs: How does one conduct proper assessment of student progress? When the goals of an educational process are attitudinal or emotional, it is hard to determine when and what to assess as indicators of learning.

Finally, the tendency toward experiential learning results in a "dumbing down" of Israel education in contrast to the academic rigor that is generally associated with other areas of the Jewish studies program. In 2004, Mansdorf published a study in which he evaluated the levels of knowledge about modern Israel among graduates of modern-Orthodox Jewish day schools participating in post-high school programs in Israel. He found an apparent gap between the students' limited knowledge about modern Israel and their sophisticated knowledge in other areas of Jewish studies (Mansdorf, 2004; see also, Eldar, 2004). These findings confirm the existence of what appears to be a double standard with respect to the competing educational goals of the disciplines of Jewish studies. Consistently, schools pursue a less rigorous approach towards Israel education. Thus, during field-based study of Israel education in North American day schools we were told by a head of school that she advises new cohorts of Sherut Leumi women (Israeli national service program): "What you teach is not as important as who you smile at." Evidently, schools try hard to make children *feel* good about Israel, but attach less importance to what they *know* about it.

(iii) Israel in the curriculum

Though many well-conceived educational programs about Israel do exist (in spite of occasional complaints to the contrary), we believe that certain underlying issues contained in these curricula need to be addressed. For example: What are the goals of the curricular encounter? In what disciplines and subject areas are these goals anchored? What forms of pedagogy are employed, and why? How are these curricula adapted for use in accordance with the various ideologies of the schools, the attitudes and beliefs of the teachers, and the needs and backgrounds of the students and their families?

As mentioned above, in attempting to address these questions we reviewed more than 70 publicly available curricula produced by commercial publishers or by not-for-profit agencies such as the Jewish Agency for Israel, boards of Jewish education, and a number of independent bodies. We gleaned several critical lessons about the goals of these programs, the curricular messages they impart, and the challenges that teachers face in teaching these materials. When teachers contemplate the implementation of a particular Israel education program, they face the dilemma of its place in the overall curriculum. How do they determine in which discipline or subject area Israel education should find a home? Most teachers find this question particularly troubling because similar problems do not arise in other areas of their teaching, and oftentimes little guidance is provided by the school leadership or by the curriculum programs. Furthermore, if a program has no obvious subject-area setting in the timetable, it may well be rejected as an indulgence, regardless of how engaging it might be. A teacher might conclude, upon further investigation, that the most common focus for Israel education is in "contemporary society," a category that does not fit into any of the conventional subject area categories; or she might categorize it as "history," the next most frequent subject focus for Israel education. However, this raises a host of other problems when the study of Israel ends at a particular historic date and does not include contemporary Israel or a study of its current challenges.

Another concern that teachers have when they review Israel curriculum involves the pedagogic orientation of the materials and the types of messages that are conveyed in the educational process. We identified four broad and distinct pedagogic orientations: traditional (concerned with the transmission of subject content); experiential (focused on making meaning, relevant to the present moment and the student's life); behavioral (concerned with developing skills irrespective of the particular content employed); and cognitive (focused on the comprehension of abstract concepts). Although there were instances of overlapping orientations, the majority of materials highlighted one dominant orientation. Overall, we found that 67% of curricula employed a traditional orientation; 43%, an experiential orientation; 23%, a cognitive orientation; and 7%, a behavioral orientation (usually as Hebrew language curriculum). This breakdown is consistent with what we observed earlier concerning the experiential orientation of Israel education in day school more generally: that there is a tendency towards making sure that students have positive Israel (related) experiences, but not that they generate questions of their own or develop a deep knowledge and understanding about Israel.

(iv) The role of the Hebrew language in Jewish day schools

Over a period of years, and interwoven with the role Israel plays in day schools and their communities, a consensus has emerged that the place of Hebrew in day schools worldwide is steadily declining (Deitcher, 2007). We offer several reasons for this phenomenon and attempt to envision possible responses to this process. In attempting to comprehend the rapidity and widespread prevalence of this decline, our initial discussion focuses on the overarching role that Hebrew plays in Diaspora Jewish life today. In other words, how does the Hebrew language shape and inform modes of Jewish identity in Diaspora communities around the world?

First and foremost, Hebrew no longer serves as an ethnic language of communication for Jews around the world (Rodman, 2003). When Jews assemble in order to discuss issues of common concern, the *lingua franca* is not Hebrew. Furthermore, Hebrew language use is not a cultural or social norm, and as a result the incentive for the engaged leadership of the world Jewish community to study Hebrew is greatly depreciated. As Deborah Lipstadt notes: "To say that virtually none of the major leaders of the American Jewish community are fluent in Hebrew is to state the obvious. With the exception of rabbis and a portion of those who come from the Orthodox community, the number of Jewish communal leaders of national stature who could conduct a fluent conversation in Hebrew or read a Hebrew text and be able to glean the meaning could probably be counted on the fingers of one hand" (Lipstadt, 1993, p. 309). In short, Hebrew no longer carries its previous ethnic import, and as a result, Jewish leaders around the globe do not regard Hebrew literacy as a *sine qua non* for filling these formative positions (Bouganim, 2007; Myhill, 2004; Cohen 1993).

As noted earlier, all day schools face a time crunch. Typically, school leadership must determine how best to build a robust Jewish studies program within the limited available hours. Perennial questions about the proper balance between "meaning making" and Hebrew skills acquisition confront schools on a regular basis, with the overwhelming majority of school leaders opting for the former, assuming that in the larger scheme of things, this experience will better serve the long-term needs of students (Gross, 1990).

Interestingly, the reduction of hours for Hebrew instruction is prevalent in many non-English speaking communities as well. The perceived need to acquire English proficiency has, in some of these communities, impinged on the place of Hebrew in the school curriculum, and consequently, the number of hours devoted to Hebrew instruction has been reduced. Worryingly, such trends have been observed even in communities such as Argentina and Mexico, which were previously more committed than most other Diaspora communities to maintaining the highest standards of Hebrew instruction (Rodman, 2003).

3. Integration of Jewish and general studies

The challenges with which Jewish day schools struggle today cannot all be attributed to their recent growth. Some challenges, such as the goal to integrate Jewish and general studies, seem inherent in the day school enterprise. For the pioneers of Orthodox day school education, a key element in their mission was to introduce students to two heritages or two bodies of knowledge. As argued by Samson Raphael Hirsch, founder of what for many became the template institution for Orthodox day school education, if "in real life a Jew, to perform his duty, as a man and a citizen, should combine Jewish with general culture, so in the nursery of life, in the school, provision should be made for fostering both sides in unison and harmony" (1956, p.188). This message was adopted by the founding head of one of America's pioneer Orthodox day schools, who espoused commitment to ensuring that "general knowledge should find a home in the academies of Jewish learning . . . where it should be viewed as an essential ingredient in the development . . . of a proud and religious American Jew and Jewess" (Lookstein, 1978, p.38).

Similar intentions were articulated by theorists of liberal day school education too. Walter Ackerman, a day school head teacher at an early stage of his career, writing three years before the Conservative Solomon Schechter Day School Association was founded, made an argument that has been repeated down the years: "The public school is concerned with the child as an American; the afternoon religious school is concerned with him as a Jew; the Conservative day school is concerned with the child who is heir to two traditions, and addresses itself to the synthesis of this dual heritage within the embracive framework of Torah" (Ackerman 1961, p. 47).

Over time, a number of theoretical models and examples have been developed to bring together—harmonize, as Hirsch put it—the two parts of the school curriculum. Lukinsky, a pioneer in this respect, proposed a set of concepts for the integration of curriculum across Jewish and general studies (Brown & Lukinsky, 1979), as well as within the disciplines of Jewish studies (Lukinsky, 1978). Holtz (1980) mined his experience teaching both Talmud and English literature in a liberal day school to propose the "thematic integration" of subject matter that "draws on the best thinking of both Jewish and non-Jewish minds." Solomon, as the principal of a Solomon Schechter school committed to "creating integrative experiences" for his students, provided a case study drawn from his own experience (1989), and also a more theoretically grounded map of what integration promised (1984).

Despite the best intentions of curriculum designers, however, various factors have militated against such outcomes. As Ingall and

Malkus (2001) show, the terrain that connects Jewish learning with the rest of the curriculum is a "border-land" that requires careful negotiation between powerful interest groups who tend to pull in different directions. As a result, there is often a disconnect between practices in the Jewish and general studies classroom, or what Bekerman and Kopelowitz (2008), in a study of the teaching of Jewish texts in modern-Orthodox and non-Orthodox schools, call a secular/religious dichotomy. In her research on moral education in a range of school settings, Simon was surprised to find that in a school with a school mission statement that highlights "the idea of the integration of 'secular knowledge' and 'Jewish ideals'," "serious discussion of moral and spiritual matters are primarily relegated to religion classes" (Simon, 1998, p. 42). Tanchel (2008) and Hyman (2008) show that even in liberal day schools, Judaic studies teachers often seem reluctant to engage students in the kind of critical thinking that is the hallmark of the general studies curriculum, although Tanchel shows how this might done by taking up her own experiences teaching biblical criticism in a community day school. As Zeldin (1998) indicated in an influential programmatic piece, it seems that successful "integration and interaction in Jewish day schools" calls (challengingly) for schools to pay attention to all four of what Bolman and Deal (2003), in their study of organizational change, identify as the frames of school (and actually, all organizational) life: human resources (concerned with the needs of individuals in an organization); structure (concerned with organizational efficiency); politics (where members of an organization compete for power); and symbol (where members find meaning and inspiration).

An examination of curriculum integration in the Jewish day school reveals an enormous gulf between aspiration and accomplishment. Schools face obstacles in every one of Schwab's four "commonplace" components of curriculum:

1. *Subject matter:*

As Beiler (1986) has acknowledged, it is immensely difficult to translate complex philosophical constructions of integration into curriculum guidelines, no matter how inspiring the words and personal example of those who have expressed them. For example, while there is no disputing the existential appeal of Soloveitchik's (1986) halachic man, who "orients himself to the entire cosmos and tries to understand it by utilizing an ideal world which he bears in his Halachic consciousness" (Soloveitchik, 1986, p.19), it is difficult to translate such a finely crafted ideal into a conception of the texts and experiences most crucial in inculcating this desired persona, whatever the character of teachers, students, or milieu.

More recently, Lehmann (2009) has argued that the different assumptions, norms, and objectives of Jewish and general studies classrooms are impossible to reconcile because of the different status (one might say sanctity) of the texts studied in different subject areas.

2. *Teachers:*

The integrated curriculum ideal is necessarily dependent on the participation of teachers who themselves embody or "typify the concept of integration" (Lookstein, 1978, p.38), for if teachers of Jewish or general studies can themselves only provide partial examples of the integrated and integrative personality, students will find it difficult to make their own ways towards this ideal (Berman, 1972). An integrated curriculum cannot be delivered without integrative teachers, for no matter how subjects are organized or texts are chosen, it requires, as Buber noted, only "the raising of a finger, perhaps, or a questioning glance from the teacher" (Buber, 1979, p.115) for the student really to learn of a teacher's commitments and ideals. Unfortunately, integrated Jewish educators continue to be rare because there are few programs that prepare teachers who are not exclusively Jewish studies specialists or specialists in other subject areas.

3. *Students:*

Jewish philosophies of integration invariably assume the commitment of the individual to his or her own religious tradition (Lamm, 1990). They presuppose the individual's commitment to God and His laws, and explore how that individual can be committed both to humankind in general and to the particular society in whose midst he or she lives. Research has shown, however, that many students in Orthodox day schools do not exhibit the foundational Jewish commitments on which a philosophy of integration is predicated (Eisenberg & Pelkovitz, 2009). In the non-Orthodox day school sector, we have seen that many students have enrolled primarily because of excellence in general studies and not for "Jewish reasons" (e.g. Kelman, 1979). In these circumstances, Jewish day school educators have been reluctant to develop curriculum models that encourage an encounter between

Torah and worldly wisdom because they are unsure about the extent of the students' commitment to, or interest in, Torah.

4. *Milieu:*

Our earlier discussion points to another significant reason for the paucity of successful examples of curriculum integration. When families do not share their school's vision of the goals of Jewish education, a school finds it difficult to sustain a truly integrative curriculum. Thus, some modern Orthodox schools have been pressed into downgrading integrative aspects of their curriculum by a "contra-acculturative" shift in their own parent or governing bodies (Heilman & Cohen, 1989, p.188–199). There is evidence, also, that many community and Conservative day schools have been pulled away from pursuing an integrated model both by an influx of families who have fled a decaying public sector (Zeldin 1990) as well as by others, who in rejecting supplementary Jewish education, have displayed "a significant turn towards particularism" (Wertheimer, 1989, p.104).

With so many of their goals at cross-purposes, Jewish educators may well despair of ever achieving the kind of balance they seek in their schools. Integration may be an important but ultimately unachievable ideal: something desirable but not deliverable.

Looking Forward

The most critical challenges that Jewish day schools face today are those that test the delicate balance between the cost and quality of schooling. The costs of day school education threaten to take it out of reach for increasing numbers of families, while at the same time there has been intensifying debate about whether day schools have been and are capable of satisfying the educational and ideological outcomes they promise. We will examine each of these challenges more closely, as well as one further problem that complicates discussion about these matters: the thinness of research knowledge about day school education.

1. Financial challenges

Cost is a major concern day for all day schools. In a recent study of the challenges facing North American day schools, administrators reported that parents who do not enroll their children in day schools usually cite high tuition and the lack of adequate scholarship assistance as the reasons for their decision (Lippner-Kaunfer, 2009). If the product was cheaper, or they had access to great discretionary funds, parents say that they would keep their children in schools. As mentioned above, under these circumstances, it is not surprising that some have started to question whether the day school system can be viable for much longer for many of those it currently serves (Kramer, 2009; Sarna, 2009; Prager, 2005; Rosenblatt, 2009).[7]

A number of explanations have been offered as to the sources of this financial crisis (Wertheimer, 2001; Schick, 2003; Prager, 2005; Baker, 2006; Lippmann-Kanfer Institute, 2009; Friedman, 2009; Zucker, 2009). Some point directly to the economic turmoil that has challenged all of the world's economies. From this perspective, "the economy" has had an impact on schools' income in two immediate ways: It has led to an overall increase of 10%–20% in scholarship requests and, at the same time, it has triggered a 10%–25% reduction in major gifts and mid-level donations to the schools; this is apart from a reported 7% decline in enrollment in some sectors (Solomont, 2009). These factors have dealt a heavy blow to the economic viability of schools, with a small number being forced to close before the start of the 2009/2010 academic year (Zucker, 2009).

A second explanation for the current financial crisis looks past present economic circumstances to a systemic problem that predates any of the present turmoil. To put it bluntly: too many day schools are too small. Forty percent of day schools enroll fewer than 100 children. With a small base of demographic support, they are incapable of benefitting from any kind of economies of scale. There is evidence that larger schools (those with more than 300 students) collect greater proportions of their funding from tuition (Prager, 2005). Unfortunately, nearly 80% of day schools in the United States enroll fewer than 350 children (Schick, 2005).

A third thesis argues that the current crisis is linked to the recent growth of day schools across North America. Ironically, in this view, schools have been victims of their own success. As day schools started to appeal to a greater diversity of Jewish families, it is said, they began to appeal to less Jewishly engaged families who have been more likely

---

7. At the time of writing, Wertheimer (2010) published an incisive prognosis of the threat posed by escalating tuition to the inclusiveness and sustainability of the day school system. His advocacy of government assistance for day schools drew sharp criticism.

to withdraw their children and reduce the number of tuition-paying students when funds become tight (Cohen, 1999; Prager, 2005). In fact, the most recent data from Schick's "Census of Jewish Day Schools" reports that while Orthodox day school enrollments have continued to grow significantly since 2003–2004, enrollment in non-Orthodox schools is down 2.5% in this same period (Schick, 2009).

The enormity of the economic challenge facing Jewish schools has inspired several responses, each of which holds promise but at the same time poses challenges to educational leaders. The most widely discussed response focuses on the need for increased philanthropy, either from private donors or foundations, or from communal-based sources, to lower the per capita level of tuition. Studies show that reduced tuition can be of special help to schools serving non-observant families (Cohen, 1999; Abba, 2002; Lippmann-Kanfer Institute, 2009; Gold and Aronson, 2003). In the past 15 years, several bold and creative efforts have succeeded in increasing tuition support for day schools. Several examples include AVI CHAI's Jewish Education voucher incentive program, and similar initiatives by the Paula and Jerry Gottesman Foundation, the Harold Grinspoon Foundation, Charles and Lynn Schusterman Foundation, and the SAMIS Foundation. In a similar manner, the Day School Endowment Fund is a project of the Bureau of Jewish Education and the Jewish Federation in Los Angeles that helps families enroll and keep their children in day schools. Another noteworthy example is the UJA-Federation of New York's trust that garners grandparents' support for day school tuition (Tobin, 2000). Finally, George Hanus created the Jewish Day School Scholarship Committee, which attempted to stimulate the creation of endowment funds for day schools by asking every Jew to allocate 5% of his estate to a Jewish education endowment of his or her choice (Hanus, 2005)

Yet, in order to have a significant impact on the system, enormous sums would need to be raised (Wertheimer, 2001). Zucker (2009) offers the following example as a means of grasping the challenge at hand: In order to reduce the average tuition in Bergen County, NJ from $13,000 to $10,000, an infusion of approximately $13.6 million of "new money" would be needed, which would then have to be raised on an annual basis. In the current financial climate, this challenge seems more elusive than ever.

A second strategy centers on cutting school costs. Though Zucker (2009) offers a range of possible ways to achieve this goal, others maintain that it is unrealistic to believe that such measures will provide the kind of relief that is needed. As both Friedman (2009) and Prager (2005) have argued, day school education is not expensive compared to the public school system. In the northern New Jersey towns of Bergen County, for instance, the cost of public school per student is more than $16,000, compared to $13,000 per student for day schools (Zucker, 2009). If we factor in that day schools provide a dual curriculum and generally don't achieve economies of scale, the viability of this cost-cutting option seems limited.

A third strategy that has generated much controversy in recent years is to look to the possibility of creating Hebrew charter schools. Charter schools are publicly funded but privately run schools. They are exempt from many public school rules and regulations and operate independently, but are held accountable for student performance to the same degree as public schools (National Alliance for Public Charter Schools, 2009). In 2007, approximately 1.1 million students were enrolled in 4,000 charter schools; their rate of growth is 10% per year. The first Hebrew charter school opened in 2007 in Hollywood, FL and serves as an elementary school for that area. Approximately 80% of the students had transferred from other public schools and the remaining 20% came from private Jewish day schools (Goodnough, 2007).

The Steinhardt Foundation supported the opening of a Hebrew-language charter school with kindergarten and first grades in Brooklyn, NY, and plans to add one grade each year until reaching grade 5 (Weiss, 2009). Advocates of Hebrew charter schools argue that this is an affordable option for families that otherwise would not be able to provide their children with a quality Jewish education. Opponents, however, contend that "religious" charter schools threaten the viability of other private schools and could pose a serious threat to Jewish day schools. They cite evidence from Florida where shortly after Ben Gamla Hebrew charter school opened, a Jewish day school located in the same area closed its doors because of insufficient enrollment (Lippmann-Kanfer Institute, 2009).

A fourth approach seeks to increase government assistance, whether through direct subsidies to schools or vouchers to parents, through tax credits, by recognizing the cost of religious studies as tax deductible, or by other financial incentives. This strategy appears to be widely endorsed among day school leaders, but to date, little progress has been made, and most agree that these efforts will take much time and are unlikely to show results in the near future (Prager, 2005; Friedman, 2009).

One final strategy focuses on the need to galvanize wider communal support for the ongoing development of day schools. It is commonly accepted that day school education is the most effective vehicle for instilling lasting Jewish commitment, including Jewish marriage, communal involvement, and support of Jewish causes (Cohen, 2004). It therefore behooves Jewish communities to rank day school enrollment as a top priority and allocate significant resources to ensure their ongoing growth. This could be accomplished by a group of school volunteer leaders assuming a more active role in approaching Jewish federations and enlisting their support in increasing allocations to their schools. There is a perception among day school principals that their board members have not been actively engaged in identifying potential donors and helping to cultivate them (Bloom, 2009). Encouraging board members to leverage the Jewish federations could be an effective means to increase communal support for the schools (Tobin, 2000). Alternatively, community leaders could be prodded to launch campaigns that tap into synagogues, preschools, camps, and other community organizations in order to make certain that they serve as pipelines for entry into day schools. This approach reflects the spirit of Wertheimer's (2005) *Linking the Silos* report and maximizes limited communal resources to advance this goal. An alternate form of communal support envisages local Jewish federations convening a meeting of school leaders and other communal organizations and encouraging them to explore ways to pool resources (Woocher, 2009). In light of Schick's finding that 40% of day schools enroll fewer than 100 students, the need for communities to examine models of sharing resources and cutting operating costs is both relevant and urgent.

2. Performance anxiety

While concerns about the rising costs of day schools have grown, there has been—in some sectors at least—increased concern about the nature and extent of the impact of schools on students. Jewish day schools engage in counter-cultural work. Fundamental to their raison d'être—wherever they are in the world—is the aspiration to ensure the survival and development of Jewry and Judaism in an open society. Although, as noted above, a developing research consensus has found that day schools have a special capacity to produce such outcomes, especially when compared to the available educational alternatives, it has seemed, in recent years, that modern Orthodox day school educators have become increasingly anxious about how well their schools are fulfilling this mission.

Because of the lack of research into the attitudes and beliefs of Jewish educators, evidence of this anxiety is piecemeal rather than systematic, anecdotal rather than comprehensive.[8] However, in the few published and public sites where Orthodox educators reflect on their work, this anxiety has seen vivid expression. More than 35 years ago, in one of the first-ever-published symposia on the state of day school education, the mood was quite different, even triumphalist. Introducing a collection of reflections in the journal *Tradition* about the modern Jewish day school, Walter Wurzberger (1972) found it appropriate to paraphrase Winston Churchill, and proclaim: "Never before in the history of American Jewry have so many owed so much to so few Day Schools." He was restating a consensus, he said, when he argued that there was no doubt that day schools "offer the best hope for producing the kind of Jew who is genuinely dedicated to Torah and the Jewish people." His upbeat judgment echoed an opinion expressed often during the same period in the journal *Jewish Education*, at that time under the editorial leadership of Alvin Schiff, a vocal advocate for day school education.[9]

Since the mid-1980s, by contrast, there started to appear with nagging frequency in the same publications and in others a tendency to question the effectiveness of the Orthodox or yeshivah day school. Writing in *Tradition*, Goldberg (1981) questioned the quality of day school graduates in a piece entitled "A critique of the American Jewish day school." In *Jewish Education*, the tone was also much changed. In a special issue devoted to the day school, articles called attention to the lack of "quality curriculum," a "personnel crisis," problematic finances, and, more ominously, to what one contributor called "some sobering concerns," all of which questioned the day school's capacity to provide what it had once promised (Siegal, 1983). Schiff him-

---

8. A few small-scale studies have explored teacher's beliefs about particular aspects of their pedagogy (for example, Dorph (1993) and Shkedi (1993)), but there have been no such studies, whether on a limited or large scale, into teachers' views of their schools' larger purposes and products.

9. Typical of Schiff's stance was a piece from 1967 entitled, "An appreciation of the Jewish day school in America," *Jewish Education*, *37*(1–2), 69.

self, reflecting on the journal's contents during the period 1975–1986, mused that schools needed to respond effectively to the challenges that derived from rapid and continuous growth, and especially to those posed by a changing student population (Schiff, 1986).

In recent years, these proliferating concerns have come to concentrate on doubts about what and how much students learn from the many years they spend in schools. Troubling phenomena, such as students "flipping out," "dropping out," "acting out," or simply being generally drawn to the norms and behaviors of non-Jewish culture, have drawn great attention from lay and professional commentators. These concerns have been expressed most vividly in two recent symposia on modern Orthodox education, one in 2008, sponsored by ATID, the Academy for Torah Initiatives and Directions, and one in 2009 in the online journal, *Meorot*, published by Yeshivat Chovevei Torah.

Serving as a respondent to the ATID symposium, Levisohn summarized the mood he found in a preponderance of contributions:

> ... the responses collected here indicate that we are not doing as well as we would like. The essayists talk about the prominence of materialism, entitlement, and egocentrism. Shalom Berger describes the "challenge of no challenges." . . . Some also point to educational environments that are not conducive to the healthy development of character, environments that emphasize control and authoritarianism, that prioritize image, that promote demeaning behaviorism and mindless competition . . . [As] I read the contributions of my colleagues in these pages, I find repeated expressions of concern for a Modern Orthodox education towards spiritual integrity, an education oriented towards the inculcation of virtue.

There were no respondents to the *Meorot* symposium; however, Finkelman (2009), one of its contributors, pointed out that the way in which the editors framed the questions for contributors indicated a sense of a system that was falling short of its goals, even though, as Finkelman himself powerfully argued both in the symposium and elsewhere, this general sense seems to have been inspired more by supposition than hard information. At this time, he argued, there is little reliable research available about what impact day schools have on which sectors of their clientele.

Substantiated or not, these same anxieties are evident in another setting that has only come in to existence with the dawn of popularly accessible Internet. With more than 2,000 subscribers, LookJed is the largest online forum for computer- mediated discussion among individuals interested in Jewish education. Its most active contributors are concentrated within the educational leadership of a narrow segment of modern or centrist Orthodoxy. Their conversations during a single calendar year in the forum's most active discussion threads reveal a concern with issues prevalent in the symposia: Orthodox day school educators feel embattled both within and without, are concerned about their limited or miseducative impact on students, and are struggling to navigate an appropriate relationship with the non-Jewish world and with popular culture (Pomson, 2009).

As suggested above, the impulse behind these concerns may not be new; educators and school leaders may simply be giving expression to a myth that "everything depends on the school," the expectation that the continued vitality of a community depends first and foremost on its schools. Paradoxically, one might say that this is the ambiguous burden of the day school's special mission. The intensification of these concerns in recent years, therefore, may not indicate a decline from a golden age of day school education, as much as it reflects a diversification in the profile of those who attend these schools (Waxman, 2009). Day school growth may have challenged schools in ways that have not yet been fully absorbed.

3. Too much supposition: a lack of research.

Empirical research into all-day Jewish schooling has tended to be concerned with inputs and outputs, focusing primarily on those who teach in or lead schools, and on those who graduate from them.[10] This research has produced a growing appreciation of the motivations, dispositions, beliefs, experiences, and satisfactions of those who teach and work in schools. A number of doctoral studies have focused, for example, on the identities and characteristics of teachers and princi-

---

10. Of course, there has also been no lack of theoretical work on day schools. This has concentrated around the questions of, first, what the distinctive goals and outcomes of day school education are and how these might be extended or transformed; and second, what the place of the different disciplines of Jewish studies in the day school curriculum is, and what the relationships of these disciplines are to one another and to the general studies curriculum.

pals in schools (Dorph 1993; Markose, 1998; Kramer, 2000; Reiss Medwed, 2005). While Ingall's (2006) study of the short-lived careers of three idealistic and well-qualified day school teachers remains the only book-length study in this field, there is an accumulating body of peer-reviewed work that broadens our understanding of those who choose to become day school teachers (Feuerman, 2003; Backenroth, 2004; Pomson, 2005; Shkedi, 1993). Finally, in recent years there have been a number of important commissioned reports concerning day school educators that compare them with other personnel working in other sectors of Jewish education (Gamoran et al. 1998; Schaap & Goodman, 2006; Ben-Avie & Kress, 2007).

Research on the outputs of day school education has been no less abundant, constituting a kind of obsession with the lasting effects of day school education on the Jewish identity and behavior of graduates. While we might have expected that studies of this kind, to have validity, would need to be of a scale that goes beyond the efforts of individual doctoral candidates, a number of doctoral dissertations have nonetheless examined different outcomes of day school education (see, for example, Charytan, 1996, and Shapiro, 1988). More typically these topics have been explored as part of larger projects that seek to compare the impact of day schools with other vehicles for Jewish education (for example, Barack Fischman & Goldstein, 1993; Schiff & Schneider, 1994; Cohen & Kotler-Berkowitz, 2004; Chertok et al 2007). There have also been a few case studies that focused on the impact of individual schools on their alumni (Jacobs, 2003; Dickson, 2004). The combined "message" of these studies is that day schools do have a superior impact on measures of Jewish identification when compared with other forms of Jewish education. Nonetheless, as Chertok (2007) and her colleagues caution, the relatively recent development of liberal day school education means that there is currently a lack of systematically gathered data on the long-term impact of this educational option.

Research on day schools continues to proliferate. Within the research, however, are two significant lacunae whose redress would serve its further development and without which it is hard to resolve concerns about the quality of schools. First, while it is generally agreed as we discussed above, that day schooling has a positive effect on measures of Jewish education that no other educational vehicle can match, little is known about *why* these schools produce the effects they do. We don't know, for example, to what extent these positive effects are a consequence of what children learn and experience in school, or are a banal outcome of the fact that Jewish children spend so much time together in these settings. The Jewish day school remains a black box; what happens inside is hidden from view. Thus, a first task in the development of day school research is analogous to the cognitive revolution in the study of teaching that moved from the investigation of inputs and outputs of teaching to an examination of what goes on inside the classroom. We need to know what goes on inside Jewish day schools.

Of course, literature of this kind exists in abundance in the field of general education, where it is likely to be produced by sociologists, ethnographers, and historians, or by practitioners writing in an autobiographical or confessional vein. There is no shortage of evocative accounts of life in schools and classrooms that shape and are shaped by theories of learning. Such literature is rare, however, when it comes to Jewish day schools. The careful study of classroom life in day schools by Lehmann (2007), Krakowski (2008), and Hyman (2008) are, however, recent promising exceptions that demonstrate how nuanced doctoral work can contribute to the field.

A second task for research is that of developing a cross-cultural mode of inquiry. The Jewish day school has emerged as a popular and frequently normative option for the education of Jewish children in almost every community where there are at least 1,000 Jewish households. The day school is an international phenomenon, and has been studied in a wide variety of international settings such as the Czech Republic (Foltynova, 2007); Denmark (Anderson, 2008); and Argentina (Goldstein, 2009). There are sharp differences between the ways schools are funded, governed, and educationally organized in different countries, yet there has never been an attempt to compare the commonalities and differences between schools in a systematic and well-grounded fashion. In the same way that studying the insides of schools would open up a black box, so studying the outsides of schools—their contexts—in relation to their particular cultural settings would clear a good deal of the mystery that surrounds them.

Conclusion

As stated at the outset, the Jewish day school is a signal achievement of Jewish communities worldwide. The dramatic rise in day school enrollment and its accompanying pivotal role in shaping Jewish identity testify to the significant changes that Jews have undergone both as a community and in their relationship to the majority culture. In the course of this monograph, we have attempted to describe the multiple reasons for the growth of these schools and their impact on Jewish life in their host communities. In addition, we explored ways in which different communities have been shaped by the growth and proliferation of these schools, beyond what the children learn in their classrooms. Finally, we discussed a variety of new social, religious, financial, and educational challenges that day schools are facing, as well as some of the strategies that are being adopted in order to address those challenges. In conclusion, we believe that based on the respect they have earned in communities throughout the world and on their significant accomplishments in a host of different areas, Jewish day schools will continue to grow and flourish in the coming decades and continue to shape Jewish life in future generations.

References

Abba, S. (2002). *Forecasting the demand for enrolment in Toronto Jewish day schools*. Toronto: UJA Federation of Greater Toronto, Board of Jewish Education.

Ackerman, W. (1961). The day school in the Conservative movement. *Conservative Judaism, 15*(2), 46–57.

Ackerman, W. (1989). Strangers to tradition: Idea and constraint in American Jewish education. In H. Himmelfarb & S. DellaPergola (Eds.), *Jewish education worldwide: Cross-cultural perspectives* (pp. 71–116). Lanham, MD: University Press of America.

Anderson, S. (2008). *The competition, the rabbi, and the prize: Anger, guilt, and inclusion in a pluralistic Jewish day school*. Paper presented at the American Anthropological Association, November 11, 2008.

Aron, I. (1987). *Instruction and enculturation in Jewish education*. Paper presented at the conference on research in Jewish education, Los Angeles, June 1987.

Backenroth, O. A. (2004). Art and Rashi: A portrait of a Bible teacher. *Religious Education, 99*(2): 151–166.

Barack Fischman, S., & Goldstein, A. (1993). *When they are grown up they will not depart*. Waltham, MA: Cohen Center for Modern Jewish Studies, Brandeis University.

Banks, J. A., & Banks, C. M. (Eds.). (1995). *Multicultural education: Theory and education*. New York: Macmillan.

Beinart, P. (1999). The rise of the Jewish school. *Atlantic Monthly, 284*, 21–23.

Bekerman Z., & Kopelowitz, E. (2008). The unintended consequences of liberal schooling: A comparative study of the teaching of Jewish texts for the purpose of cultural sustainability. In Z. Bekerman & E. Kopelowitz (Eds.), *Cultural education-cultural sustainability* (pp. 323–342). New York: Routledge.

Beiler, J. (1986). Integration of Judaic and general studies in the modern orthodox day school. *Jewish Education, 54*(4), 15–26.

Ben-Avie, M., & Kress, J. (2007). *A North American study of educators in Jewish day and congregation schools* (EJSS).

Berger, S. Z., Jacobson, D., & Waxman, C. I. (2007*). Flipping out? Myth or fact: The impact of the year in Israel.* New York: Yashar Books.

Berman, S. J. (1972). The Jewish day school: A symposium. *Tradition, 13*(1), 95–130.

Blidstein, Y. (2003). Halacha: The Jewish normative world. In A. Berholtz (Ed.), *A journey into the world of halacha* (Hebrew). Tel Aviv: Yediot Aharaonth.

Bloom, H. (2009). *Survey of the governance and advocacy practices of Jewish day schools.* [Report]. New York: Yeshiva University, Institute for University-School Partnership.

Bolman, L. G., & Deal, T. E. (2003). *Reframing organizations: Artistry, choice and leadership.* San Francisco: Jossey-Bass.

Bouganim, A. Hebrew in the era of globalization (Hebrew). In *The Hebrew language in the era of globalization.* Jerusalem: Magnes Press.

Brosh, H. (1996). Hebrew language diffusion through schools and universities in America. *Journal of Jewish Education, 62*(3), Fall.

Brown, S. I., & Lukinsky, J. S. (1979). Integration of religious studies and mathematics in the day school, *Jewish Education, 47*(3), 28–35.

Buber, M. (1979). *Education: Between man and man.* (R. G. Smith, Trans.). Glasgow: Fontana-Collins, 109–131.

Charytan, M. (1996). *The impact of religious day school education: A study of changes in seven modern Orthodox day schools and the impact on religious transmission to students and their families.* Unpublished doctoral dissertation. Graduate Faculty of Sociology. City University of New York.

Chertok, F., L. et al. (2007). *What difference does day school make?* Boston, MA: Maurice and Marilyn Cohen Center for Modern Jewish Studies, Brandeis University.

Cohen, E. H. (2007). *Heureux comme Juifs en France?* Étude sociologique. Jerusalem-Paris: Akadem.

Cohen, S. M. (1993). The eclipse of Hebrew as the national language of the Jewish people. In A. Mintz (Ed.). *Hebrew in America: Perspectives and prospects.* Detroit: Wayne State University.

Cohen, S. M. (1999). Money matters: Incentives and obstacles to Jewish day school enrollment in the United States. In Y. Rich & M. Rosenak (Eds.), *Abiding challenges: Research perspectives on Jewish education* (pp. 251–274). London: Freund Publishing House.

Cohen, S. M. (2004) Jewish education and its differential impact on adult Jewish identity. Retrieved from http://www.peje.org/advocacy/MakingCase.asp

Cohen, S. M., & Kelman, A. Y. (2007). *Beyond distancing: Young adult American Jews and their alienation from Israel.* Jerusalem: Andrea and Charles Bronfman Philanthropies.

Cohen, S. M., & Kotler-Berkowitz, L. (2004). The impact of childhood Jewish education on adults' Jewish identity: Schooling, Israel travel, camping and youth groups. *United Jewish communities report series on the national Jewish population survey 2000–01.* New York: United Jewish Communities.

Comer, J. P. (1997). *Waiting for a miracle: Why schools can't solve our problems-and how we can.* New York: Dutton.

Conference on the Future of the Jewish People. (2007). Background Policy Documents. Jerusalem: Jewish People's Policy Planning Institute. 14–15.

Continental Council for Jewish Education. (2003). Day school tuition subvention, reduction and scholarship programs. New York: JESNA.

Darling Hammond, L., & Sykes, G. (1989). *Teaching as the learning profession: Handbook of policy and practice.* San Francisco: Jossey Bass.

Davidson, A. (1989). *The preparation of Jewish educators in North America: A status report.* Report submitted to the Commission of Jewish Education in North America.

Deitcher, H. (2007). We were as dreamers: The impact of the communal milieu on the place of Hebrew in Diaspora Jewish education.

In N. Nevo & O. Olstain (Eds.), *The Hebrew language in the era of globalization.* Jerusalem: Magnes Press.

DellaPergola, S., & Schmelz, U. O. (1989). Demography and Jewish education in the Diaspora: Trends in Jewish school-age population and school enrolment. In H. Himmelfarb & S. DellaPergola (Eds.), *Jewish education worldwide: Cross-cultural perspectives* (pp.43–68). Lanham, MD: University Press of America..

Diamond, E. (2000*). And I will dwell in their midst: Orthodox Jews in suburbia.* Chapel Hill: University of North Carolina Press.

Dickson, S. (2004). Kadimah: The pursuit of scholastic excellence and religious commitment. *Journal of Jewish Education, 69*(3), 15–47.

Dorph, G. Z. (1993*). Conceptions and preconceptions: A study of prospective Jewish educators' knowledge and beliefs about Torah.* New York: Jewish Theological Seminary of America.

Dushkin, A. (1948). Jewish Education in New York City. *Jewish Education, 20*(1), 15.

Eisenberg, S., & Pelcovitz, D. (2009). *Religious change after the year of study in Israel: Psychological and social correlates.* Paper presented at the Network for Research in Jewish Education, 23rd Annual Meeting. New York.

Eisner, E. (1979). *The educational imagination.* New York: Macmillan.

Eldar, A. (2004). Orthodox students gap year experience in Israel. Jerusalem: JAFI.

Eliav, M. (1960). *Jewish education in Germany during the Enlightenment and Emancipation period*s (Hebrew). Jerusalem: Jewish Agency for Israel.

Feuerman, C. (2002). Professional development initiatives for aspiring *menahalim. Ten Da'at, XV.* 18-20.

Feuerman, C. (2003). In quest of the ideal teacher: divergent perspectives and emergent goals for pre- and inservice training, *Ten Da'at, XVI.* 33-49.

Finkelman, Y. (2009) [No title] *Meorot, 7*(2), 16–20.

Foltynova, T. (2007). *Jewish education in the Czech Republic: A case study of the Lauder schools in Prague.* Rappaport Center for Assimilation Research and Strengthening Jewish Vitality: Bar Ilan University.

Fox, S., Scheffler, I., & Marom, D. (2003). *Visions of Jewish education.* Cambridge: Cambridge University Press.

Friedman, A. (2009). The tuition hole: How we dug it and how to begin digging out of it. *Meorot, 7*(2), 2–6.

Gamoran, A., & Goldring, E. B. (1998). *The teachers report: A portrait of teachers in Jewish schools.* New York: CIJE.

Gamoran, A., Goldring, E. B., & Robinson, B. (1999). Towards building a profession: Characteristics of contemporary educators in American Jewish schools. In Y. Rich & M. Rosenak (Eds.), *Abiding challenges: Research perspectives on Jewish education,* Tel Aviv: Freund Publishing.

Garet, M. S., Porter, A. C. Desimone, L., Birman, B. F., & Yoon, K. S. (2001). What makes professional development effective? Results from a national sample of teachers. *American Educational Research Journal, 38*(4), 914–945.

Gefen, P. (2007). Creating an educational philosophy: Lessons from Abraham J Heschel. In *Ten years of believing in day school education.* Boston, MA: PEJE.

Gitelman, Z. (2009). Do Jewish schools make a difference in the former Soviet Union? In A. Pomson & H. Deitcher (Eds.), *Jewish day schools, Jewish communities: A reconsideration* (pp. 109–138). Oxford: Littman Library of Jewish Civilization.

Gold, B., & Aronson, R. (2003). Day school tuition subvention, reduction, and scholarship programs, *Continental council for Jewish day schools.* New York: JESNA.

Goldberg, H. (1981). A critique of the American Jewish day school, *Tradition, 19*(4), 29–296.

Goldberg, H. E. (1999). A tradition of invention: Family and educational institutions among contemporary traditionalizing Jews. In S. M. Cohen & G. Horencyzk (Eds.), *National variations in Jewish identity: Implications for Jewish identity* (pp. 85–106). Albany: State University of New York Press.

Goldmintz, J. (2008). Back to Basics. In *Teaching towards tomorrow: Setting an agenda for modern Orthodox education.* Jerusalem: ATID, 31.

Goldring, E. B., Gamoran, A., & Robinson, B. (1999). *The leaders report: A portrait of educational leaders in Jewish schools.* New York: Mandel Foundation.

Goldstein, Y. (2009). Community school versus school as community: The case of the Bet El community in Buenos Aires. In A. Pomson & H. Deitcher (Eds.), *Jewish schools, Jewish community: A re-*

consideration (pp. 172–192). Oxford: Littman Library of Jewish Civilization.

Goldstein, Y., & Ganiel, D. (In press). Jewish education in Latin America: Challenges, trends and processes. In H. Miller, L. Grant, & A. Pomson (Eds.), *International handbook of Jewish education.* New York: Springer.

Goodnough, A. (2007). Hebrew charter school spurs dispute in Florida. *New York Times,* August 24, 2007.

Gross, M. (1990). Why Hebrew? Jewish identity and the need for new directions in Jewish education, *The Reconstructionist,* January–February. 17–38.

Hanus, G. (2005). The greatest threat to Jewish survival, *World Jewish Digest,* November.

Heilman, S., & Cohen, S. M. (1989). *Cosmopolitans and parochials: Modern orthodox Jews in America.* Chicago: University of Chicago Press.

Himelfarb, H. S. (1989). A cross-cultural view of Jewish education. In H. S. Himelfarb & S. DellaPergola (Eds.), *Jewish education worldwide: Cross-cultural perspectives* (pp. 3–41). Lanham, MD: University Press of America.

Hirsch, S. R. (1956). On Hebrew instruction as part of general education. In *Judaism eternal* (pp. 188–202). London: Soncino Press.

Holtz, B. (1980). Towards an integrated curriculum for the Jewish school. *Religious Education, 75*(5), 546–557.

Holtz, B., & Gamoran, A. (2000). Changing the core: Communal policies and present realities in the professional development of teachers for Jewish schools. *Journal of Jewish Communal Service. 76*(3).

Hyman, T. (2008). *The liberal Jewish day school as laboratory for dissonance in American-Jewish identity formation.* Unpublished doctoral dissertation. Steinhardt School of Culture, Education, and Human Development. New York, New York University.

Ingall C. K., & Malkus, M. (2001). Negotiating the borderlands: Implementing and integrated curricular unit in a Jewish day high school. *Journal of Jewish Education, 67*(1/2), 36–47.

Ingall, C. K. (2006*). Down the up staircase: Tales of teaching in Jewish day schools.* New York: Jewish Theological Seminary of America.

Jacobs, M. R. (2003). The Jewish Academy of Metropolitan Detroit: The experience of the pioneering graduating class. PEJE. Retrieved from http://www.peje.org/docs/DetroitHSgraduates.pdf

Jewish Educational Services for North America & United Jewish Communities. (1999). *Task force on Jewish day school viability and vitality*. New York: Jewish Educational Services for North America.

Kopelowitz, E. (2005). Towards what ideal do we strive? Survey commissioned by RAVSAK and the Jewish Agency for Israel, Jerusalem.

Kelman, S. (1984). Why parents send their children to non-orthodox Jewish day schools: A study of motivations and goals. *Studies in Jewish Education, 2*, 289–298.

Knapp, M. S. (2003). Professional development as a policy pathway. *Review of Research in Education, 27*, 109–158.

Krakowski, M. (2008). *Isolation and integration: Education and worldview formation in ultra-Orthodox Jewish schools*. Unpublished doctoral dissertation. Evanston, IL: Northwestern University.

Kramer, M. N. (2000). *The pathways for preparation: A study of heads of Jewish community day schools affiliated with the Jewish community day school network, 1998–1999*. Unpublished doctoral dissertation. New York: Teachers College. Columbia University.

Kramer, M. N. (2009). The perfect storm, *Forward,* August 12.

Lamm, N. (1990). *Torah Umadda: The encounter of religious learning and worldly knowledge in the Jewish tradition*. Northvale, NJ: Jason Aronson.

Levisohn, J. (2008). Jewish education in pursuit of virtue. In Y. Finkelman (Ed.), *Teaching toward tomorrow: Setting an agenda for modern Orthodox education* (pp, 84–90). Jerusalem: Academy for Torah Initiatives and Directions.

Lieberman Research Worldwide. (2004). Understanding the needs of Jewish parents in the Greater Boston area to more effectively market day schools. Retrieved December 12, 2008, from http://www.peje.org/docs/DAFStudy.pdf

Lippman-Kanfer Institute. (2009). *Day school education in challenging times: Examining the strategic options*. New York: Jewish Educational Services for North America.

Lipstadt, D. E. (1993). Hebrew among Jewish communal leaders. In A. Mintz (Ed.), *Hebrew in America: Perspectives and prospects*. Detroit, MI: Wayne State University Press.

Lehmann, D. (2009). Calling integration into question: A discourse analysis of English and *Humash* classes at a modern Orthodox yeshivah high school. *Journal of Jewish Education, 74*(3), 295–316.

Lipstadt, D. E. (1993). Hebrew among Jewish communal leaders. In A. Mintz (Ed.), *Hebrew in America: Perspectives and prospects,* Detroit, MI: Wayne State University Press.

Lookstein, J. (1978). True integration. *Jewish Education, 46*(4), 37–38.

Lukinsky, J. S. (1978). Integration within Jewish studies. *Jewish Education, 46*(4), 39–41.

Mansdorf, I. (2004*). Knowledge and attitudes of post high school Jewish-American orthodox students in Israel.* Retrieved from www.lookstein.org/resources/israel_students.pdf_

Margolis, D. J. (2008). Towards a vision of education reengagement with Israel in day schools. *Jewish Educational Leadership, 7*(1).

Markose, J. O. (1998). *Individualism and community: A study of teachers in a Canadian Jewish day school.* Unpublished doctoral dissertation. Ontario Institute for Studies in Education. Toronto: University of Toronto.

McLaughlin, M. W., & Talbert, J. (2001). *Professional communities and the work of high school teaching,* Chicago: University of Chicago Press._

Miller, H. (2001). Meeting the challenge: The Jewish schooling phenomenon in the UK, *Oxford Review of Education, 27*(4), 501–513.

Murphy, C. (2001). Longing to deepen identity, More families turn to Jewish day school, *Washington Post,* April 7, 2001, B1.

Myhill, J. (2004*). Language in Jewish society,* Tonawanda, NY: Multilingual Matters National Alliance for Public Charter Schools (2009). Retrieved, from http://www.uscharterschools.org/pub/uscs_docs/blk/about.htm

PEJE. (2006). *Making the case for Jewish day schools.* Retrieved from http://www.peje.org/docs

Pomson, A. (2004). Jewish day school growth in Toronto: Freeing policy and research from the constraints of conventional sociological wisdom. *Canadian Journal of Education, 27*(3), 321–340.

Pomson, A. (2005). Parochial school satisfactions: What research in private Jewish day schools reveals about satisfactions and dissatisfactions in teachers' work. *Educational Research, 47*(2), 163–174.

Pomson, A. (2008). Dorks in yarmulkes: An ethnographic inquiry into the surprised embrace of parochial day schools by liberal American Jews. In Z. Beckerman & E. Kopelewitz (Eds.), *Cultural edu-*

cation-cultural sustainability: Minority, diaspora, indigenous and
ethno-religious groups in multicultural societies (pp. 305–321).
Mahwah, NJ: Erlbaum.

Pomson, A. (2009). What are they talking about? Listserv discussion
as a window on the concerns of Orthodox Jewish educators. Contemporary Jewry, 29,49–66.

Pomson, A., Deitcher, H., & Muszkat-Barkan, M. (2009). Israel education in North American day schools: A systems analysis and
some strategies for change. Unpublished report submitted to the
AVI CHAI Foundation.

Pomson, A. Deitcher, H., & Rose, D. (2009). Israel curriculum in
North American Jewish day schools: A study of untapped transformative potential. Unpublished report submitted to the Schusterman and Jim Joseph Family Foundations as a project of the
iCenter.

Pomson, A., & Schnoor, R. F. (2008). Back to school: Jewish day
school in the lives of adult Jews. Detroit, MI: Wayne State University Press

Pomson, A., & Schnoor, R. F. (2009). Home-made Jewish culture at
the intersection of family life and school. In A. D. M. Pomson &
H. Deitcher (Eds.), Jewish day school, Jewish community: A reconsideration (pp. 307–323). London: Littman Library of Jewish
Civilization.

Prager, Y. (2005). The tuition squeeze: Paying the price of Jewish education. Jewish Action, 66, 13–18.

Prell, R. E. (2007). Family formation, educational choices, and Amer-
ican Jewish identity. In J. Wertheimer (Ed.). Family matters:
Jewish education in an age of choice (pp. 3–33). Waltham, MA:
Brandeis University Press.

Raab, Y. R. (2006). Why they leave: A study of Jewish day school administrators who left Jewish education. Unpublished doctoral dissertation, Florida State University.

Reiss Medwed, K. G. (2005). Three women teachers of Talmud and
rabbinics in Jewish non-orthodox day high schools: Their stories
and experiences. Unpublished doctoral dissertation. New York,
New York University. Humanities and Social Sciences in the Professions.

Rodman, P. (2003). Israel and the place of modern Hebrew in Jewish
education worldwide: A consultation about the possibilities for
Hebrew language institution. Jerusalem: JAFI.

Rosenblatt, G. (2009). Jewish day school model may now be thing of past. *The Jewish Week,* June 5. Retrieved July 22, 2009, from http://www.thejewishweek.com/viewArticle/c52_a15707/Editorial__Opinion/Gary_Rosenblatt.html

Sales, A. L. (2007). *Mapping Jewish education: The national picture.* Report for the Jim Joseph Foundation.

Sarna, J. (1998). American Jewish education in historical perspective. *Journal of Jewish Education 64*(1–2), 8–21.

Sarna, J. (2009). Lesson from the past, EJewishPhilanthropy.Com, February 22. Retrieved July 22, 2009, from http://ejewishphilanthropy.com/lessons-from-the-past/

Schaap, E., & Goodman, R. L. (2006). *Recruitment of college students into the field of Jewish education: A study of the CAJE Schusterman college program alumni* (1990–2003). New York, CAJE.

Schick, M. (2000). Jewish day schools. In D. Ravitch & J. P. Viteritti (Eds*.), Lessons from New York: City schools* (pp. 269–290). Baltimore, MD: John Hopkins University Press.

Schick, M. (2003). *The impact of the economic downturn on Jewish day schools.* New York: AVI CHAI Foundation.

Schick, M. (2005). *A census of Jewish day schools in the United States, 2003–2004.* New York: AVI CHAI Foundation.

Schick, M. (2007). *A survey of day school principals in the United States.* New York: AVI CHAI Foundation.

Schick, M. (2009). Summary of key findings: A census of Jewish day schools in the United States, 2008–2009. Retrieved, from http://www.avi-chai.org/Static/Binaries/Publications/Key_Findings_of_2008_09_Day_School_Census_Final.pdf

Schiff, A. (1967). An appreciation of the Jewish day school in America. *Jewish Education, 37*(1–2).

Schiff, A. (1986). What this index is all about. Some thoughts on the content of *Jewish Education* 1975–1986. *Jewish Education, 54*(1), 3–7.

Schiff, A. (1995) The Jewishness quotient of Jewish day school graduates: A study of the effects of Jewish education on adult Jewish behavior. *Ten Da'at, VIII*(1). 15-22.

Schiff, A. & Schneider, M. (1994). *Far reaching effects of extensive Jewish day school attendance: The impact of Jewish education on Jewish behavior and attitudes.* New York: David J.Azrieli Graduate Institute of Jewish Education and Administration, Yeshiva University, Research Report 2.

Schnall, D. (1991). Religious Zionism and yeshiva education. *Ten Da'at, V*(2). 29-31.

Shapiro, S. (1988). *From generation to generation: Does Jewish schooling affect Jewish identification?* Unpublished doctoral dissertation. New York: New York University.

Shapiro, S. (1996). A parent's dilemma: Public vs. Jewish education. *Tikkun, 17,* 13–16.

Shkedi, A. (1993). Teachers' workshops encounters with Jewish moral texts. *Journal of Moral Education, 22*(1), 19–30).

Shrager, H. (2002). More Jewish day schools open as parents reconsider values. *Wall Street Journal.* May 21. Retrieved December 7, 2003, from http://groups.yahoo.com/group/SepSchool/message/5277?source=1

Siegel, M. (1983). Some sobering concerns. *Jewish Education, 51*(1), 30.

Simon, K. G. (1998). Bring it up with the rabbi: The specialization of moral and spiritual education in a Jewish high school. *Journal of Jewish Education, 64*(1 & 2): 33–43.

Solomont, E. B. (2009). U.S. Jewish schools mostly 'hanging on.' *Jerusalem Post,* September 13. Retrieved from http://www.jpost.com/servlet/ Satellite?cid=1251804553875&pagename=JPArticle%2FShowFull

Soloveitchik, H. (1994). Rupture and reconstruction: The transformation of contemporary orthodoxy. *Tradition,* 28(4). 64-131.

Soloveitchik, J. B. (1983). *Halachic man.* (L. Kaplan, Trans.). Philadelphia: J.P.S.

State of Israel, Ministry of Education, *Internet Vemeda Chinuchi,* 2007. Retrieved from http://cms.education.gov.il/EducationCMS/Units/Owl/Hebrew/ UvdotNetunim/netunim/Stat.htm

Stodolsky, S., & Dorph, G. (2007). *Community report: Are our schools places where teachers thrive as professionals? A survey of teachers in Bay area Jewish schools,* San Francisco: Goldman Fund and Mandel Foundation.

Tanchel, S. (2008). A Judaism that does not hide: Teaching the documentary hypothesis in a pluralistic Jewish high school, *Journal of Jewish Education, 74*(1), 29–52.

Tobin, H. (2000). Promising Strategies for increasing day school philanthropy: An overview. *PEJE Day School Assembly.*

Toren, R. (2005). Thoughts on giving. *Jewish Action,* Fall.

Valins, O. (2005). The future of Jewish schooling in the United Kingdom, *Ten Da'at, XVII.* 41-48.

Valins, O. (2003). Defending identities or segregating communities? Faith-based schooling and the UK Jewish community, *Geoforum, 34*(2), 235–247.

Waxman, C.I. (2009). The "good old days" weren't so good: What about today? In Y. Finkelman (Ed.), *Teaching toward tomorrow: Setting an agenda for modern Orthodox education* (pp. 66–70). Jerusalem: Academy for Torah Initiatives and Directions.

Weiss, A. (2009). New York approves plan for fits public school with Hebrew focus. *The Forward*, January 18.

Wertheimer, J. (1989). Recent trends in American Judaism. *American Jewish Yearbook, 89*, 63–162.

Wertheimer, J. (1999). Who's afraid of Jewish schools? *Commentary, 108,* 49–54.

Wertheimer, J. (2001). *Talking dollars and sense about Jewish education.* New York: AVI CHAI Foundation.

Wertheimer, J. (2005*). Linking the silos: How to accelerate the momentum in Jewish education today.* New York: AVI CHAI Foundation.

Werthimer, J. (2010). The high cost of Jewish living. *Commentary,* March, 17–25.

Woocher, J. (2009). Doing more with less? *JESNA Blog,* March 17.

Wurzberger, W. (1972). Symposium: The Jewish day school, *Tradition, 13*(1), 95.

Zeldin, M. (1988*). Cultural dissonance in Jewish education: The case of reform day schools.* Los Angeles: Hebrew Union College, Jewish Institute of Religion.

Zeldin, M. (1998) Integration and interaction in the Jewish day school. In R. E. Tornberg (Ed.), *The Jewish educational leader's handbook* (pp. 579–590). Denver, CO: A.R.E.

Zeldin, M. (1990). *In yesterday's shadow: Case study of the development of a Jewish day school.* Paper presented at the Fourth Annual Conference of the Network for Research in Jewish Education. New York.

Zucker, S. (2009). The economic crisis and Jewish education. *Meorot, 7*(2), 7–11.

The At-Risk Adolescent in the Orthodox Jewish Community: Implications and Interventions for Educators

David Pelcovitz

Preface

In recent years, there has been an unfortunate increase in the number of adolescents from observant Jewish families who have been seriously disruptive, rebellious and defiant. This essay will summarize the current literature on the nature and scope of the problem, some hypothesized causes for such difficulties, as well as provide a summary of recommended interventions for educators.

Definition

Since the term "at-risk" adolescent has been widely used, we will continue its use. However, it should be noted that there are a number of difficulties with this terminology; it is overly vague and has different meanings based on the setting, observer, and context. Keeping that caveat in mind, the term, "at-risk," as it will be used in this paper, refers to a set of difficulties with parents and/or school that an adolescent may experience in complying with the rules of home, school, and community. Using the common yardstick typically employed in the field of child mental health, these difficulties will be defined as meeting the criteria for "at-risk" only when the adolescent crosses the threshold into behavior that causes significant distress in the adolescent or his/her family, and is also accompanied by significant levels of impairment in the adolescent's functioning. Specific examples may include:

- A reduction or absence of religious observance relative to the accepted norm of observance expected by home and school

- Drug or alcohol use or abuse
- Defiance of parental rules that leads to significant parent-adolescent conflict
- School truancy

In light of the almost complete absence of empirically based information on the at-risk problem in the Orthodox Jewish population, this review will rely heavily on the general research literature regarding the etiology, prevention and treatment of serious behavioral difficulties in adolescents. This literature generally falls into two categories: research on juvenile delinquents and studies of conduct disordered adolescents. The literature on juvenile delinquency typically defines delinquency either in legal terms based on records of arrests or adjudication or on adolescent self-report of illegal behavior (Mulvey, Arthur & Reppuci, 1993). Conduct disorder, which overlaps to a considerable degree with delinquency, is a psychiatric disorder which the mental health diagnostic system (DSM-IV, American Psychiatric Association, 1994) defines as including a wide array of aggressive and antisocial behaviors including "a repetitive and persistent pattern of behavior in which the basic rights of others or major age-appropriate societal norms or rules are violated." The assumption of this review is that although cultural differences between adolescents living in the secular world and those living as Orthodox Jews will lead to subtle differences in etiology, prevention, and intervention, the basic knowledge garnered from decades of research in the general population will help inform conclusions about Orthodox youth as well.

Scope of the Problem

The insular nature of the Orthodox community, as well as the sense of shame that typically accompanies this problem, makes it very difficult to get a handle on the true scope of the at-risk problem. In the most comprehensive survey of the incidence of at-risk behavior in the Orthodox community, the Metropolitan New York Coordinating Council on Jewish Poverty conducted a study of the scope of the problem in the Brooklyn Orthodox Jewish community. Their methodology was a survey of 25 Brooklyn based organizations that work with Orthodox youth, including schools, hot lines, and mental health professionals who work with adolescents in the community. Based on this approach, the researchers concluded that Brooklyn's 23,000-student yeshiva system includes approximately 1,500 at-risk 14–17 year-old youths. These adolescents were found to be engaging in "serious" at-risk behavior including theft, substance abuse, truancy, and running away from home. The study's authors acknowledge that limitations of their methodology would bias their results in a manner that significantly underestimated the scope of the problem. They estimate that an additional 2,500 adolescents are engaged in similar behavior but have not been identified. It is important to note that while the conclusions of the study reflect a higher than expected incidence of at-risk adolescents in the Brooklyn Orthodox community, the estimates are noted by the survey's authors to be less than the incidence of similar difficulties reported in the general population of Brooklyn.

Clinical Presentation

Dr. James Garbarino, a noted expert on adolescent psychology, describes a study that he conducted a number of years ago (J. Garbarino, Personal communication, September 26, 2002). In an attempt to understand the different faces that adolescent rebellion might take in diverse cultures, he interviewed adolescents in different parts of the world. In an Amish community, a group of adolescents described a rebel in their community as a boy who wore a pink handkerchief in his suit jacket. The most "extreme" case of rebellion they could think of was a teen from a neighboring Amish town who hitched a ride on a tractor. In contrast, a group of Lebanese adolescents he interviewed at the height of the civil war in Lebanon, said that the only way to rebel in their society was to open fire on members of their own clan. Garbarino concluded that while the content of adolescent rebelliousness differed drastically in different cultures and different parts of the world the process was essentially similar, i.e. a need of certain adolescents to push against whatever limits are set by their family and community.

Where in the Orthodox Jewish world is this "line" crossed into at-risk behavior? Nefesh, an international organization of Orthodox mental health professionals, held three two-day conferences to arrive at a consensus on how to define and approach the problem of at-risk adolescents (Blumenthal & Russell, 1999, Russel & Blumenthal, 2000 and Russel & Blumenthal, 2003). Each of these conferences was attended by approximately 70 invited "experts"—rabbis, educators, outreach workers, and psychotherapists who worked with this population in the United States, Canada, England and Israel. Consensus definition emerged regarding the clinical presentation of the at-risk adolescent. The conferences resulted in three editions of a manual that outlined the consensus of the attendees regarding identification, prevention and intervention for the troubled adolescents and their families.

SOFT SIGNS: **Generally in a Thirteen to Fourteen Year Old**
Changes from typical behavior within his/her community group:
- The music listened to is changed
- Not learning well; showing great impatience with academics
- Language is changing with greater usage of slang

MEDIUM SIGNS: **Generally in a Fifteen to Sixteen Year Old**
- She/he will be in their second *yeshiva* by their sophomore year
- Smoking cigarettes
- Beginning to have family conflict
- Symptoms of sexuality are out of the norm for his/her community
- Change in clothing and hairstyles
- May not have used marijuana but knows the language of the drug culture
- Consistently downs a few shots of whisky or beer at *kiddush*

HARD SIGNS: **Generally in a Sixteen to Nineteen Year Old**
- Is a chronic truant or a dropout
- He/She is no longer following any rules of the house; conflict with parents is routine; conflict spills over into relationships with siblings, and parents will worry about the effect on their other children
- Attending parties without parental knowledge or permission, going to clubs or partying at friends' houses whose parents are on vacation and the house is empty for a few days
- Spending an excessive amount of time out of the home
- Use of marijuana and/or other drugs
- Stealing may be commonplace
- Shabbat observance, *kashrut*, and *tefillin* are, for the most part, dropped

Etiology: Risk Factors

Perhaps the only agreement among those who work with this population about the cause of at-risk behavior in Orthodox adolescents is that such difficulties can rarely be attributed to a single source. Among the most prominent hypothesized causes is any persisting condition that makes an adolescent feel marginalized and not accepted by family, peers or society. It is logical that in such situations, the adolescent seeks a sense of solace and belonging by finding similar-minded peers who pull the adolescent into deviant behavior. In recent years, organizations such as Priority One, a Long Island based organization that specializes in reaching out to at-risk Orthodox youth, has conducted weekend retreats for families and professionals struggling with this issue. A major component of the weekend is a panel made up of a group of adolescents and young adults who are either currently engaging in at-risk behavior or have overcome their difficulties to return to the mainstream. The focus of these sessions is a discussion of how they view the reasons for their rebelliousness. What is striking is that although there are a wide variety of reasons perceived by the adolescents for their rebellion, the common thread that consistently runs through their narratives are feelings of alienation and exclusion. Whether their inability to feel connected stems from a history of academic failure, abuse, intense conflict with parents or spiritual alienation, these youngsters were not able to find a connection with role-models who helped them feel a part of their family, school or peers. They consistently described finding such feelings of belonging only when among similarly alienated friends.

Biological and Genetic Factors

A growing body of evidence has documented that, particularly in situations where serious behavior problems have an early onset, biologically driven and/or genetic influences can play an important role in placing a child at-risk for significant behavioral difficulties in adolescence. For example, adoption studies have found that serious conduct problems in children, particularly those that include aggressive behavior, have a strong genetic component that interact with environmental influences (Cadoret, Yates, Troughton, Woodworth & Stewart 1995).

Recent research has found that children who present with early onset behavioral difficulties often have subtle deficits in the frontal part of the brain (Davidson, Putnam, & Larson, 2000). The frontal lobes, the foremost region of the brain, have been found to be involved in key personality traits ranging from affect regulation to capacity for empathy and ability to self-monitor. In what is often termed "executive function deficits," such children suffer from an often subtle dysregulation in this part of the nervous system and typically present with the following behavioral difficulties, all of which involve functions served by the frontal regions of the brain:

- Difficulty shifting from one mind-set to another, inability to flexibly shift from one strategy to another in problem solving.
- Organizational deficits which may lead to difficulty: anticipating problems, formulating goals in response to problems, selection and evaluation of appropriate responses.
- Deficits in working memory (e.g., a child will blurt out an answer in order not to forget it).
- Problems with goal-oriented planning, i.e. choosing the best goal from a range of possible choices.
- Difficulty self-monitoring; this refers to experiencing problems tuning in to the impact of one's behavior on others or failure to check in with one's self to insure that tasks and behavior are appropriately planned and thought out.

Of course, biology is not necessarily destiny. With proper support from family and school, such children can learn to overcome these executive functioning deficits, in spite of their dysregulated temperament. However, when parents and teachers are not able to effectively teach the child how to override this predisposition, he or she is at increased risk for becoming a member of the next generation of at-risk adolescents.

PSYCHIATRIC CO-MORBID DISORDERS

Attention Deficit Hyperactivity Disorder (ADHD)

Educators will recognize that the above described difficulties are often part of the constellation of symptoms seen in children with ADHD or other students presenting with seriously disruptive behavior. In fact, recent research using neuroimaging techniques, has found subtle frontal abnormalities in children diagnosed with ADHD (Castellanos et al., 1994; Tannock, 1998). The inattentiveness, low frustration tolerance and high activity level that are core ingredients of

ADHD have been found to be highly correlated with increased risk for significant behavioral difficulties in adolescence (Vermeiren, 2003). It is estimated, based on epidemiological research, that a child with ADHD is 10 times more likely to be diagnosed with a conduct disorder (Angold, Costello & Erkanli, 1999). This connection is further documented in research finding that between 20% and 72% of incarcerated adolescents meet criteria for ADHD (Vermeiren, 2003). Richards (1996) hypothesizes that the higher estimates in this range are more accurate than the studies that find lower comorbidity. The low estimates are thought to be spurious because there were few sources of accurate data regarding the early histories of the inmates. In addition, differential diagnosis is often difficult because of significant overlap between antisocial and ADHD symptoms.

When children present with a combination of ADHD and significant conduct problems, they need to be followed very carefully since the "double trouble" of ADHD plus behavioral disorders places them in a pool of children at particular risk for more pervasive and serious behavioral difficulties in adolescence (Loeber, Burke & Lahey, 2000). This high-risk group of children is also more likely to develop significant difficulties with anxiety, impaired self-concept and aggression (Kuhne, Schachar & Tannock, 1997).

In the only study of ADHD in at-risk Orthodox Jewish adolescents, Feldman (2004) compared 24 at-risk Orthodox adolescents to a comparison group of 25 Orthodox Jewish adolescents studying in yeshiva high schools in the same neighborhoods as the at-risk adolescents. The comparison adolescents were screened to insure that their behavior was consistent with the expectations of the Orthodox community. The at-risk adolescents scored significantly higher than the comparison group on a standardized measure of ADHD. Feldman found that between 14 and 29% of the at-risk adolescents received scores that placed them above the 95th percentile on measures of ADHD.

Oppositional Defiant Disorder (ODD)
Oppositional defiant disorder is a psychiatric diagnosis, which as outlined in DSM-IV (American Psychiatric Association, 1994), is characterized by a pattern of frequent negativistic, hostile, and defiant difficulties that lasts for at least six months and causes significant impairment in the child's ability to function well at home, in school or with peers. This pattern of behaviors is characterized by some or all of

the following: frequent loss of temper, argumentativeness with adults, an active defiance or refusal to comply with adults' requests or rules, repeated attempts to deliberately annoy people, a tendency to blame others for his or her mistakes or misbehavior. Such children are also often described as touchy, resentful and easily annoyed by others. If angered, they may respond by becoming spiteful or vindictive.

ODD is more likely to be predictive of risk for later severe conduct problems when characterized by high levels of severity and persistence (Cohen et al., 1993). In one study, for example, when children met criteria for ODD in their preschool years, almost 70% were presenting with more serious behavioral difficulties by age 9 (Campbell, 1991) . In addition to early onset and symptom severity, specific symptoms have been found to be of particular concern. For example, Loeber, Burke & Lahey (2000) report that when preadolescents present with frequent fighting, cruelty to peers, or running away, they are particularly likely to develop more severe conduct problems as adolescents. These researchers conclude that proactive as compared to reactive aggression is a particularly ominous predictor.

A model that has particular relevance for educators in identifying elementary school children who are at greatest risk for serious behavioral difficulties as adolescents has been described by Loeber et al. (2000). These researchers marshal considerable evidence from the literature supporting the finding that those children with ODD who also have ADHD are more likely to develop more serious behavioral difficulties as they grow older. When ODD presents without the accompanying inattentiveness, impulsivity or high activity levels of attention-deficit, there is lower risk for later serious behavioral problems.

Depression and Withdrawn Behavior
A number of studies have found a strong connection between delinquency and depression. Vermeiren's (2003) review of the co-morbidity of delinquency and depression reports that between 11% and 33% of delinquents have been diagnosed with a full blown depressive disorder. The wide range in estimates is likely a combination of differing methods of measuring depression (self-report questionnaires or structured interviews) as well as variation between studies regarding whether adolescent or parental reports are used. It is well known, for example, that parents tend to underestimate the level of depression in their child.

Up to an additional 50% have been found to have milder forms of depression. In a review of 16 epidemiological studies investigating the connection between severe behavioral difficulties and depression, Angold, et al., (1999) conclude that children with conduct disorders are 6 times more likely to be diagnosed with depression. The depression-disruptive behavior connection is particularly strong in girls as compared to boys (Ulzen & Hamilton, 1998).

The depression-conduct disorder link is a particularly important one for educators to be aware of. Because of the often silent nature of child and adolescent depression, it is typically more difficult to identify depression in the classroom than disruptive behavior. The earlier depression is diagnosed and treated, the better the long-term prognosis. When a teacher refers such children for diagnosis and treatment the teacher can play an important role in preventing the depression from putting a child on a trajectory that can later lead to substance abuse and/or other kinds of serious behavioral difficulties. Another important practical implication for educators is that when depression is identified in an at-risk adolescent the risk for suicidal behavior is increased. Researchers have found that both depression and disruptive behavior independently increase risk for suicidal ideation and attempts. When such a child self-medicates their depression by abusing drugs, there is a particularly lethal combination that can greatly increase the risk for self-destructive behavior (Brent, Perper & Moritz, 1993).

Shyness and behavioral inhibition tend to protect children from risk for later delinquent behavior (Kerr, et al., 1997). A temperament characterized by fear of others and anxiety about new situations understandably makes it less likely that an adolescent will be pulled into the novelty seeking behavior that typifies many adolescent delinquents. In contrast, Kerr and colleagues found in their longitudinal study, that children who are socially withdrawn and present in a manner that combines low levels of anxiety, a low need for approval from adults and a preference for being alone, are at increased risk for developing significant behavioral problems as adolescents.

FAMILY FACTORS

There are a number of factors that have been found to be associated with families that have an at-risk adolescent. Although not exhaustive, the following variables have been found to be strongly associated with increased likelihood of disruptive behavior in adolescence:

• *Disciplinary Style*

Researchers have consistently found that a parental discipline style characterized by high levels of emotionalism, criticism, lecturing or physical punishment, is associated with an increased chance that a child will be non-compliant and rebellious (Loeber & Hay, 1997).

Additional risk factors include parental inconsistency, particularly if accompanied by failure to adequately monitor one's child's activities outside of the home (Kilgore, Snyder, & Lentz, 2000).

• *Attachment Problems between Parent and Child*

When parental emotional difficulties get in the way of their ability to establish a secure attachment with their child, the risk for later behavioral difficulties increases. For example, when a parent is depressed during a child's early years, the child has increased risk for presenting later with aggression and disruptive behavior (Sharp, Hay & Pawlby, 1995). There are likely multiple determinants underlying the parental depression-child conduct problem connection. Since irritability is often a component of depression, depressed parents are more likely to respond to child misbehavior in an unproductive, emotional manner. Furthermore, the pessimism inherent in depression makes it more likely that there will be a focus on the negative in the child's behavior. Such children may come to think that they can't win since any efforts at improvement are squelched when their depressed parent fails to recognize these attempts.

• *Parental Powerlessness*

When financial problems or high levels of marital conflict deplete parents' emotional resources, they are often not able to place appropriate limits on their child's behavior. Research has consistently shown a robust connection between such difficulties in parents and subsequent behavioral difficulties in their children (Pelcovitz & Kaplan, 1994).

• *Parental Interest in Child's Performance in School*

Parents who take an active interest in a child's performance in school and are able to create a partnership with educators in maximizing the ability of their child to reach their academic potential are more likely to raise children who do not develop serious behavioral difficulties (Reid & Eddy, 1997).

• *Favoritism towards siblings*

Children who feel that they are not loved and appreciated by their parents, particularly when they feel that a sibling is consistently favored, are more likely to develop behavioral difficulties. For example, Dunn found that older siblings who felt that their behavior was unfairly controlled as compared to younger siblings, whom they perceived as being treated more leniently, were more likely to engage in externalizing behavior (Dunn, Stocker & Plomin, 1990).

In his study of 24 at-risk Orthodox Jewish adolescents, Feldman (2004) found that the adolescents in the comparison group were more likely to describe their parents as using an "authoritative" disciplinary style characterized by striking an ideal balance between appropriate limits and sufficient warmth and love. This finding suggests that the literature regarding the parenting difficulties in the parents of at-risk adolescents is applicable to the Orthodox Jewish family as well.

History of Abuse or Trauma

Research on abused children and adolescents consistently documents significantly increased risk for disruptive behavior disorders and substance abuse (Kaplan, Pelcovitz & Salzinger, 1998). Abuse victims have been found to develop behavioral difficulties at an earlier age and of a more severe nature than their non-abused delinquent counterparts (Henry & Moffitt, 1997). When history of trauma and abuse is investigated in groups of delinquent adolescents, alarmingly high prevalence rates of interpersonal trauma are evident. Approximately 60% of delinquent girls report having been victims of attempted or completed sexual assault and 27% of delinquent boys report witnessing violence in their families (Vermeiren, 2003). These traumatic events translate into approximately one third of delinquent adolescent boys and 65% of adolescent girls having a lifetime diagnosis of PTSD (Cauffman, Feldman, Waterman & Steiner, 1998). There are numerous causes hypothesized to be behind the trauma-behavioral disturbance connection. In addition to the impact of aggressive role-models, neurobiological changes that accompany exposure to chronic trauma such as abuse can lead to serious disruption in a victim's affect regulation (van der Kolk, Pelcovitz & Roth, 1996).

Although there is only anecdotal research documenting the abuse-at-risk connection in the Orthodox Jewish community, there is ample anecdotal evidence to support such a connection. The insular nature of the Jewish community, coupled with an accompanying reluctance to report abuse to secular authorities, may have led to an exacerbation of the abuse problem in a community that otherwise has numerous protective factors (e.g. community support, religious restrictions) against the possibility of child abuse (Pelcovitz, 1988). A presentation at an Orthodox Jewish conference on the at-risk problem (Nefesh-Ohel conference on Children in Crisis, 2000) included a symposium with a number of presentations that anecdotally documented the high rate of undisclosed sexual abuse in at-risk Orthodox adolescents.

Children of Immigrants

It has long been noted that particular challenges face adolescents whose parents emigrated from other countries. The cultural chasm that often exists between parent and child heightens whatever feelings of parent-adolescent conflict might accompany adolescents whose parents are born in the same country. In Israel, the phenomenon of "kippot zerukot"—cast away yarmulkes, has been noted to be particularly prevalent in adolescent children of Orthodox parents who moved to Israel from other countries (Fisherman, 1998). Although not systematically studied, anecdotal evidence suggests that a driving force behind these adolescents' feelings of alienation is a pervasive sense that they don't belong in either world. They don't feel accepted by their Israeli classmates who view them as "foreigners" and they don't feel fully connected to the idealism that brought their parents to Israel.

In a study of Russian children of parents who left Russia to move to Israel, Slonim-Nevo and Sharaga (2000) found that the children of immigrants reported higher levels of emotional distress relative to their Israeli counterparts. It is of note that the researchers found that the longer these adolescents lived in Israel, the more their alcohol consumption increased relative to their peers who were children of Israeli parents. These studies clearly suggest that educators should pay attention to this population, who are at particular risk for feeling isolated and marginalized, in a manner that makes them uniquely vulnerable.

Similarly, children of immigrants in the United States also face a number of issues that increase their risk for rebellion. Increased risk for educational problems and behavioral difficulties in school are particularly prevalent in children of various American Jewish immigrant groups. This phenomenon is related to a variety of influences that differ with the particular immigrant group. For example, in the Bukharan community, cultural values that emphasize financial success over educational success play a pivotal factor in the educational adjustment of Bukharan adolescents attending day schools in the United States (Halberstadt & Nikolsky, 1996). An equally important contributor to increased risk for educational failure is language based difficulties that are often present to a greater degree in bilingual populations (Green & Bychkov, 1996).

The developmental demands of adolescence often clash with the reality of the lives of children of immigrants. Increased likelihood of adolescent-parent conflict has been noted in the literature on children of Jews immigrating to the United States from the former Soviet Union (Zicht, 1993, Halberstadt & Nikolsky, 1996) and children of Syrian Jewish immigrants (Zicht, 1996). Adolescence calls for disengagement from parents, increased attachment to peers and formation of a stable identity. These demands are typically accompanied by heightened levels of self-consciousness. Each of these components of adolescent development can be compromised by the pressures inherent in the immigrant experience. Fearing the negative influences of American society parents often respond with overprotective and/or authoritarian parenting styles. Both of these styles have been associated with increased risk for rebelliousness on the part of adolescents (Pelcovitz, Kaplan & Ellenberg, 2000).

Because of their greater proficiency in English, children of immigrants are often called on to be their parents' translators and advocates with the wider community. This role is often at odds with their need to separate from their parents and high levels of discomfort are often reported by adolescents who view their parents' "foreign" behavior as a source of embarrassment.

In summary, it is not surprising that children of immigrants are at heightened risk for significant educational and conduct problems as adolescents. A dangerous combination of too little time spent with the adolescent because of financial pressures necessitating long work hours and parenting styles shaped by high levels of stress and differing cultural values can be a potent recipe for producing alienated and rebellious adolescents.

Academic Achievement

In the last several decades, there have been a number of studies that have shown that poor school achievement increases risk for later serious behavioral difficulties (Farrington, 1987). In a study using a longitudinal design, Tremblay, Masse & Perron (1992) found that poor school achievement in first grade increased risk for disruptive behavior in elementary school and predicted a "delinquent personality" by age 14. Similarly, a number of researchers have documented reduced risk for delinquency in children from low-income families who attend preschool programs that improve their academic readiness (Schweinhart, 1987). Language difficulties have been singled out as having particular import in predicting later behavioral difficulties. A number of studies have documented the importance of early identification and remediation of verbal deficits as a core ingredient in the primary prevention of adolescent at-risk behavior (Henggeler, Schoenwald & Borduin, 1998).

Academic difficulties play a particularly crucial role in the genesis of behavioral difficulties in yeshiva students. The central importance the Orthodox community places on education, coupled with the greater demands of the curriculum and the lower tolerance towards children who don't fit the mold, are among the forces that can fuel rebelliousness in the child who encounters failure in a yeshiva. In the only systematic evaluation of the association between academic difficulties and behavior problems in the Orthodox Jewish community, Goldberg (2004) investigated the association between reading problems and behavior problems in 77 fifth grade boys attending modern Orthodox elementary schools. Consistent with previous literature, Goldberg found a significant relationship between reading and externalizing behavior problems. Of particular interest was his finding that feelings of social exclusion played a mediating role in the relationship between Hebrew decoding and externalizing behavior problems. Given the central role that reading Hebrew plays in the academic success of yeshiva students, Goldberg's finding suggests that core academic deficits may contribute to a child feeling set apart from peers in a manner that can fuel disruptive behavior. Further research is needed to expand on this finding, and to explore alternative hypotheses. For example, a high co-morbidity between reading difficulties and ADHD suggests the possibility that the impulsivity, social difficulties and inattentiveness that accompany ADHD may be a pivotal factor that, together with the reading difficulties, increase risk for externalizing behaviors.

Peer Influences

Association with deviant peers is clearly associated with increased risk for problem behavior in adolescence (Patterson (1993). Researchers have found that when exposed to peers who also engage in rebellious behavior, children are more likely to engage in substance abuse, delinquency and aggression (Dishion, McCord & Pouling, 1999). In one of the most comprehensive and long-standing studies of the roots of delinquency ever undertaken, the Cambridge-Somerville Youth Study followed adolescents at-risk for delinquency who attended a summer camp that exposed them to other troubled adolescents. These youngsters were found to have suffered numerous negative effects over the next 30 years of their lives, including increased risk for incarceration, early termination from school, and, ultimately, earlier death, than a comparison group that received no such exposure (Dishion et al., 1999).

In light of the central role played by deviant peers in promoting the development of delinquent behavior, it is not surprising that therapeutic intervention aimed at disengaging adolescents from associating with delinquent peers while simultaneously increasing their association with conventional well-behaved peers through such activities as organized athletic events or youth groups has been found to significantly decrease problematic behavior (Huey et al., 2000). For example, in the most carefully documented treatment for delinquent adolescents, Multisystemic Therapy, therapists teach parents how to better monitor their child's activities and encourage parents to better familiarize themselves with their child's peers. Simultaneously, unpleasant consequences are established for continued association with deviant peers. When parents are successful in disentangling their child from these negative influences, enduring improvement often follows.

Community Support

There is a clear connection between the quality of a neighborhood and a child's risk for serious behavioral difficulties. Children residing in neighborhoods having high levels of poverty or crime engage in delinquent and violent behavior at younger ages than children living in more advantaged or safer environments (Loeber & Hay, 1997). Research has found that neighborhoods that have a strong sense of community are less likely to experience significant behavioral difficulties in their youth (Sampson, Raudenbush & Earls, 1997). The process by which tightly knit communities exert this type of positive influence includes such activities as adults monitoring the spontaneous public social gatherings of adolescents coupled with a willingness to intervene when they see truancy or adolescents engaging in wild behavior. In a survey of 343 neighborhoods in Chicago, Sampson found significantly lower levels of violence in communities populated by adults who felt a sense of collective responsibility for the young residents of their neighborhoods.

In light of the above, it is not surprising that experts who work with the at-risk problem of Orthodox youth have informally noted increased risk in neighborhoods that aren't cohesive. For example, relatively higher rates of serious adolescent behavioral difficulties have been noted in large communities where a child's absence from regular attendance at synagogue services is not noticed. In contrast, communities that are cohesive enough to take note of a child's absence from services, or where a child's acting out behavior is addressed by caring adults, may prevent small behavioral difficulties from degenerating into more serious rebellious behavior.

Female vs. Male At-Risk Behavior

Epidemiologic research has documented that, in the general population, there is a threefold higher prevalence of serious conduct problems in males as compared to females (Cloninger & Svrakic, 2000). In recent years, however, researchers have documented that this gap may be narrowing as the number of girls who exhibit significant levels of antisocial behavior has been noted to be on the rise (Molidor, 1996). In most areas of mental health, more severe impairment in functioning relative to boys is seen when girls override the inherent protection of their gender and cross the threshold into presenting with what is usually considered a male dominated disorder. Conduct disorder is no exception to this general rule. In a review of 20 carefully constructed studies of female delinquency and antisocial behavior, Pajer (1998) found that antisocial girls were at-risk for a variety of serious difficulties as adults, which portends a more serious outcome than their male counterparts. As adults, this research documents, antisocial girls emerge with a host of serious difficulties including poor marriages, job difficulties, significant problems functioning adequately as parents and generally high levels of psychiatric disturbance and attempts at suicide.

Anecdotal evidence suggests that the increased prevalence of conduct disorder seen in girls in the general population is mirrored in the Orthodox community as well. For example, in recognition of the growing problem seen among Orthodox girls the second Nefesh conference on the at risk problem in the Orthodox community made a better understanding of the assessment, intervention and prevention needs of at-risk girls their main focus (Russel & Blumenthal, 2000). More recently, the Caring Commission of the New York UJA Federation formed a special task force charged with addressing the problem of behaviorally at-risk girls in the Orthodox population.

There are a number of unique difficulties facing Orthodox girls who are at-risk. Anecdotal evidence presented by mental health specialists who work with this population suggests that girls are more likely than boys to begin their trajectory into serious behavioral difficulties by presenting with a variety of subtle behaviors that often elude early detection. Such early indicators of impending behavioral difficulties as eating disorders, depression and suicidal ideation, all more likely in females, are less likely to come to the attention of adults in their early stages than the more obvious acting out behavior which are the typical early indicators of risk for boys (Russel and Blumenthal, 2000).

Girls encounter even more serious difficulties when their problems have been identified and intervention is sought. For example, there are fewer alternative schools for behaviorally disordered girls, making it more likely that if their behavior leads to their expulsion from a yeshiva high school, they will be further marginalized from the community by being forced to attend public schools. Another complication stems from the Orthodox community's differing attitudes towards sexual behavior in girls as compared to boys. A reputation for promiscuous behavior on the part of girls in the Orthodox community is likely to lead to more enduring consequences than is the case with boys. Once sexually active, girls can't regain their virginity. In contrast, boys who are sexually active are more easily rehabilitated, particularly if they return from a year of study in Israel with newly acquired zeal for a religious life style. All of these forces combine to make at-risk girls even more likely to be marginalized than their male counterparts. As noted earlier, such feelings of isolation and marginalization are at the core of the dynamic that can feed an escalating spiral of difficulty.

SCHOOL BASED INTERVENTIONS

Early Identification

Primary prevention of at-risk behavior in Orthodox adolescents has as its cornerstone the identification of children at greatest risk for later difficulties before such vulnerabilities blossom into more serious and intractable behaviors. The most effective prevention efforts would involve early identification and intervention by educators of difficulties that present in the following areas.

Individual Factors

As noted earlier, children with frontal deficits are at increased risk for later at-risk behaviors. Educators can play a key role in prevention by facilitating early identification and intervention for children diagnosed with the "double trouble" of ADHD and oppositional defiant disorder. As a practical matter, elementary school teachers who are struggling with what many consider their most challenging students—those who present with a combination of inattentiveness, impulsivity, and oppositional and defiant behavior—should keep in mind that actively advocating for appropriate referral, assessment and intervention has more than the short-term benefits of improved classroom behavior. It is easier to teach skills such as improved compliance and self-regulation to a child than an adolescent, who is more likely to resist adult intervention.

The pivotal role that academic success plays in a child's long-term sense of self-worth and connection to the community makes early identification of areas of academic vulnerability another cornerstone of early intervention. Since children with reading problems and/or language difficulties are at particular risk for later behavioral problems, educators should be aware of the potential far-reaching consequences of a child living with a continuing sense of academic failure. Such difficulties can be subtle, and may not emerge until the increased demands of later grades. Educators should regularly reevaluate the match between their students' academic abilities and the demands placed on them by the curriculum.

Transitional periods can place vulnerable children at heightened risk for behavioral difficulties. Educators should be particularly tuned in to the possibility of emerging difficulties during critical periods such as when a child begins departmental studies, when they move to a new building (for example if the Junior high school is in a different building than the elementary school) during the bar/bat-mitzvah year and in the year that the student applies for admission to high school. Particular attention should be given to the vulnerable child during these transition periods to insure that they don't elude early detection of emerging behavioral difficulties.

Untreated depression is another common pathway to serious later behavioral difficulties in adolescence. While the glaring and overt nature of disruptive behaviors is easy for educators to identify, the often silent nature of depression is far easier to miss. Educators should keep in mind that depression may primarily present in the classroom as chronic irritability, negativity and sensitivity. Difficulty with attention is another symptom of depression that might present in the classroom as a lack of motivation rather than an indication that a child is experiencing a mood disturbance. In addition, a child who has difficulty enjoying himself or herself or is prone to focus on the negative may also be manifesting subtle signs of a pervasive mood disorder. It is also important to keep in mind that underlying depression often co-occurs with disruptive behaviors.

Educators should also be aware of how depression might present during different developmental phases. A preschooler might present with a somber appearance, lack the bounce of non-depressed peers, make frequent negative self-statements, and show tearful and spontaneously irritable behavior far more frequently than their non-depressed peers. In school-aged children, depression might present with frequent irritability and a tendency to hate themselves and everything around them.

History of Past or Current Abuse

As noted earlier, many adolescents who present with at-risk behaviors in high school later disclose that their feelings of alienation, anger, and isolation have their roots in undisclosed abuse. Although far from comprehensive, the following behaviors have been noted by experts to trigger suspicions on the part of educators as to the possibility of abuse.

Sexual Abuse
- Sexual behavior or knowledge which is unusual in a *yeshiva* setting.
- Child forces sexual acts on other children.
- Fear or avoidance of a specific place or person, such as sudden change in child's willingness to go to gym or swimming pool.
- Extreme fear of being touched; e.g. unwilling to submit to physical examination.
- Excessive guilt, self blame, sense of being damaged.

- Refusing to talk about "secret" he/she has with an older child or adult.

Physical Abuse
- Improbably explained bruises and welts
- Behavioral Indicators:
  - Wary of adult contact
  - Apprehensive when other children cry
  - Extreme fear of others
  - Afraid to go home, early to school or stays late (as if afraid to go home)
  - Wears clothing that covers body when not appropriate

Physical Neglect
- Consistent hunger
- Inappropriate hygiene, dirty or unkempt, offensive body odor
- Inappropriately dressed for weather
- Consistent lack of supervision (especially in dangerous activities)
- Unattended physical problems; e.g untreated lice
- Behavioral Indicators:
  - Constant fatigue, exhausted
  - Begging or stealing food
  - Frequent school absence or tardiness

Family Factors
When the above described child vulnerabilities are coupled by a family environment that fails to help the child override their predispositions to disruptive behavior, educators should heighten their level of concern. Early intervention is at its most effective when educators successfully enlist parents of their disruptive students into an effective school-parent partnership. Changes made in families of difficult young children can have a more pervasive and far-reaching impact than when change is attempted with parents of an adolescent who have already experienced many years of perceived frustration and failure with their child.

Parental disciplinary style
Risk is increased whenever parenting relies on a rule structure that is dominated by extremes that are either overly permissive or overly strict. Either extreme on the emotional connection continuum is also

of concern. Thus, families that are both so enmeshed and overprotective that the child feels smothered or, at the other extreme, parents who seem emotionally cold and disconnected from their children. Additional concerns should be raised when educators note a parenting style marked by inconsistency, vacillating between neglect and high levels of emotionalism, marked by yelling or excessive criticism.

High-conflict divorce or severe marital conflict

Risk is particularly high in the early stages of a divorce, when parents often become so preoccupied with the emotional devastation that typically accompanies the first few years of a divorce that they have little energy left for their child. Exposure of a child to interparental physical violence or emotional abuse that accompanies marital fighting has been found to have a particularly strong association to child and adolescent behavioral difficulties.

Parental depression or other serious mental illness

As noted earlier such difficulties can seriously compromise a parent's ability to provide their child with the stability that provides the foundation for adequate behavioral control.

Ongoing family stress

Economic stress, particularly when other children in a class come from economically advantaged homes, can be a correlate of child behavioral difficulties. Similarly, other ongoing stressors in the family that can increase risk include frequent relocation, children who are first generation Americans, or families where members suffer from life-threatening medical conditions.

Environmental Factors: School and Community Climate

As noted earlier, a sense of living in a caring community where the child is valued and respected as a contributing member of their family, school and community is a crucial buffer against serious at-risk difficulties. Researchers have documented a number of variables that are associated with establishing a school climate that is conducive to reducing antisocial behavior (Hawkins & Lam, 1987). These include:

- A predictable, fair, calmly administered and consistent set of rules
- A curriculum that is perceived by students as relevant
- Teachers who make time for their students
- A strong and effective principal

- A perception on the part of the students that they have some input into the educational process

Of course, the above "wish list," once implemented, does not guarantee an absence of serious rebellious behavior on the part of students. However, schools that provide a safe, warm and nurturing environment are more likely to temper a student's rebelliousness in a manner that can ultimately lead to a turn around in their feelings of alienation.

MENTORING

Perhaps the most common intervention promoted by the Orthodox community, targeting the at-risk problem, is the implementation of various types of mentoring programs. Mentors are often recruited naturally in the course of a typical adolescent's life. In a study of 770 adolescents, Zimmerman, Bingenheimer & Notaro (2002) found that most of the teens in their study had naturally occurring mentors and that those who did were less likely to engage in delinquent behavior, used marijuana less frequently, and had more positive attitudes towards school. What are the ingredients identified by adolescents as being particularly helpful in such naturally occurring relationships? Beam, Chen & Greenberger (2002) interviewed 55 adolescents who were in a relationship with naturally occurring mentors in their communities. When asked what they found most helpful about such relationships, the teens reported that the opportunity to spend time with somebody who respected them and made them feel heard and supported was at the core of what they valued most about the relationship.

While naturally occurring mentors are a reality in the lives of many adolescents, those who need such support the most are often not able to find role-models in their day to day lives. In the last several decades, major shifts in society have changed the nature of adolescent exposure to adult role models. There are increasingly high percentages of families which are either single parent households or in which both parents work outside of the home. In addition, there are increasing expectations that adolescents take part in after school extracurricular activities that are typically age segregated and have changed the availability of role-models for adolescents (Rhodes, 2002). The research suggests that at-risk adolescents can benefit from structured mentoring experiences, provided that such relationships are provided by committed and well trained mentors. In a systematic review of 55 studies of the efficacy of mentoring programs, Dubois, Holloway, & Valentine (2002) found that the benefits which such programs brought to at-risk youth were most likely to be beneficial when mentors had sufficient training and supervision and when protégés had developed enduring, and genuine relationships with their mentors.

The research on the core ingredients of successful mentoring suggests that the following characteristics are present in the most effective adolescent-mentor relationship:

1. Commitment to a long-term relationship

In a landmark study of the crucial role played by length of time spent by mentors with their protégés, Grossman & Rhodes (2002) analyzed the outcome data from over 1,000 youngsters served by the Big Brothers/Big Sisters program. They found that when mentors remained committed to their protégés for 12 months or more, there were clearly beneficial effects including improved relationships with parents, lower levels of drug and alcohol use, improved self concepts, an enhanced sense of social acceptance and increased feelings of academic competence. In contrast, when mentors abandoned their protégés after a short period of time (3 months or less), the children suffered significant drops in their self-concepts and feelings of academic competence. Children in the premature termination group were found to actually have been harmed by the experience of mentoring and would have been better off had they not been assigned a mentor.

2. Training and supervision of mentors

Sipes and Roeder (1999) surveyed the training practices of 700 mentoring programs. They found that more than half offered less than two hours of training. The strongest mentor-protégé relationships were reported in those who received at least six hours of training from their program. Ongoing supervision of mentors is also reported to be a key ingredient predicting success (Rhodes, 2002).

While there is a great deal of variability in the content of what is offered by various mentoring training programs, the most successful programs show a commitment to training as a process rather than an event; i.e. mentors are provided ongoing training and supervision. For example, Big Brothers/Big Sisters of New York City has a training center that offers a wide range of training opportunities for mentors as well as a mentoring supervisor certificate program and ongoing workshops (www.bbbsny.org/training/). Typical topics of training include sessions that teach basic communication skills with adolescents, activity planning with protégés, strategies for developing a positive alliance with parents, and approaches for helping children deal with instability in their lives (Rhodes, 2002).

3. Involvement in enjoyable activities

A number of experts on mentoring have found that it is important that the mentor provide enjoyable social activities like going out to lunch, bowling or other enjoyable events with their protégé. Relationships and communication are most likely to thrive through indirect forces like shared fun than through direct efforts at establishing relationships (Rhodes, 2002, Sipe & Roeder, 1999).

In recent years, in recognition of the need to service at-risk adolescents in the Orthodox community, a number of mentoring programs have been established. Examples of site-based mentoring are the "Clubhouse" in London, a drop-in center where protégés are provided with opportunities for recreation as well as mentoring relationships that have a vocational education component, typically in jobs related to working with computers, a medium that many at-risk adolescents find inherently interesting. Another promising on-site program is Bridges, in Queens, New York. This program, which is unique, in that its focus is on elementary school age children, is an after-school homework center that provides students who fall in the risk categories described above with homework support from high school students who are trained to be mentors as well as tutors. School based mentoring programs such as TOVA, on the south shore of Long Island, provide well trained and supervised mentors who come to schools several times a week and meet with the child providing either tutoring or a break. These mentors often meet with the child off-site approximately once a week as well. The advantages of school based programs are both the convenience and the added benefit of the mentor being able to serve as an advocate for the child to the school. While there are no systematic efforts, as yet, to measure the efficacy of these programs, word of mouth has provided strong anecdotal evidence of their efficacy. The research literature reviewed above, however, should serve to highlight the importance of investing in proper screening, training, and supervision of these mentors.

GUIDELINES FOR TEACHERS AND CONCLUSIONS

Once a child is already presenting as overtly rebellious it is important for educators to keep in mind that, since the key dynamic underlying such behavior is feeling alienated and set apart from the mainstream, teachers can play a pivotal role in helping a child or adolescent feel connected. Perhaps the most potent antidote to feeling angry and alienated is feeling appreciated and understood. When teachers make harsh or belittling remarks or treat a child in a manner that the child perceives as unfair, the downward spiral that the child is already caught up in can be accelerated. Conversely, a combination of time, support, and understanding can go a long way towards bringing a rebellious adolescent on the path towards reconnecting to more productive and meaningful behavior. The following recommendations can be considered:

1. A rebellious child does best with a balance between love and limits. Research (Barkley, 1998) indicates that consequences that work best with disruptive children and adolescents are:

- Brief, unemotional, clear, consistent, and not overly harsh.
- Stem logically from the misbehavior and make sense to the child.
- Viewed as being delivered in the context of a child feeling liked and appreciated, in spite of the punishment. When a teacher shows that he or she doesn't take the child's misbehavior personally and disapproves of the behavior and not the child, consequences tend to be far more effective.

A parent once pointed out to me that he always wondered why his child bristled at the slightest criticism from either parent but was able to take even the toughest and most demanding direction from the coach of his basketball team. It was explained to the parent that when a child knows that everybody is "on the same team" they will accept even the most demanding set of rules willingly. They are most likely to rebel when they feel that their parent or teacher isn't on the same team.

2. A set of strategies that can be used to guide teachers in dealing with disruptive children in the classroom have been developed by Greene (2000) at the Harvard Medical School. These include:

- Develop a perspective that sees the child's behavior as coming more from the child's wiring rather than from willful misconduct. Most of these children have their behavioral difficulties either fueled by neurological factors (i.e. frontal deficits) or stressors at home that make it difficult for them to regulate their affect. While this does not mean that limits and consequences are not necessary, it does mean that the teacher can respond calmly as he or she would to any misbehavior that is coming more from a child who "can't" rather than "won't" behave properly.

- Respond to child before he or she is at their worst
- Anticipate and modify situations which will likely trigger defiance by cueing in to specific factors which fuel explosiveness
- Use of distraction, logic, empathy may work if employed before meltdown
- Choose only worthy battlegrounds
- Address recurring patterns by identifying specific situations that routinely cause significant frustration

3. Whenever possible, address the spiritual. Rebellious adolescents often describe feeling alienated from spirituality, yet, at the same time, being thirsty for greater spiritual understanding and connection. An at-risk child who returned from a summer program that emphasized spirituality with growth through *musar* explained the reason for the dramatic improvement in his behavior after the summer. "Until now," he explained, "I never knew who God was. God was always about what I couldn't do. Don't' watch TV on *shabbos*, don't go to inappropriate movies. Nobody ever told me who God was until this summer. Now that I understand what God is about, Judaism makes more sense to me, and for the first time, I'm interested in what Judaism has to offer."

4. Schools need to build in a system for systematically tracking the progress of students who fall into the risk categories described above. The formation of Child Study Teams that include administrators, school mental health support staff and a teacher, who serves as a grade representative, can help facilitate an atmosphere that creates a safety net that makes it less likely that a child will fall through the cracks.

5. Promoting effective parent-school partnerships is an essential part of any program for addressing the needs of the at-risk child. Research has consistently shown that at-risk children do better when they perceive their parents as being actively involved in their education (Henggelar et al., 1998). Helping parents gain an appreciation of the importance of overtly supporting teachers, monitoring homework as-

signments and grades and supporting extracurricular school activities have all been found to develop the kind of prosocial behavior that can serve as an antidote to the influence of acting out peers. Educators can help promote this type of partnership by providing parents with regular feedback regarding their child's academic and behavioral progress and scheduling parent-teacher conferences in a manner that is flexible enough to accommodate parents' work schedules.

6. A commitment on the part of school administrators to ongoing training of teachers and parents regarding strategies for dealing with at-risk children can be valuable both for dealing with this population once problems emerge and for prevention of problems in students who have not yet developed such difficulties. Some yeshivot have implemented mandatory teacher and parent training focusing on how to deal constructively with defiant and disruptive behavior and on how to maximize the chances of creating a strong parent-school partnership. Such programs tend to be most effective when schools create in-service days for teachers that do not require the teachers to attend sessions on their own time. Content of teacher training should include classroom management strategies for defiant students as well as training on how to identify high risk situations, when to refer and how to talk to parents. A strategy that has proven effective for maximizing parent attendance at parent-training sessions, is scheduling programs as part of parent-teacher conference nights.

7. Expelling a child from a school should be considered only as an extreme step when all alternatives have been exhausted. Yeshivot that have a low threshold for expelling rebellious adolescents have unwittingly exacerbated the problem for the entire community by creating a growing group of such children on the streets, thereby fostering the kind of "deviancy training" that can contaminate more mainstream adolescents in the community (Dishion et al., 1999). Some alternatives to expulsion that have been successfully implemented in various communities include alternative schedules such as providing adolescents with a modified program that allows them to work for part of the day and attend school for part of the day. This allows these adolescents to remain part of their peer group and find success in non-academic areas of strength where they are more likely to achieve. Some schools have experimented with "exchange" programs where they "trade" a disruptive child in one school for a disruptive child in another school. When a child is given a totally fresh start in a new school, they often experi-

ence success that isn't possible in an environment where they are perceived by teachers and peers as troubled. Finally, although many high schools frown on early graduation, when rebellious adolescents are allowed to graduate after their junior year, they often thrive. Success can come as a result of a number of factors including being given a fresh start in an environment where they aren't viewed in a preconceived way, being given the opportunity to make more appropriate friends, and the benefits that are part of the greater academic flexibility present in post high school environments.

IN SUMMARY

A review of the literature on identifying and intervening with at-risk adolescents suggests that the Orthodox community has a number of significant strengths that can be harnessed to help this troubled population. The strong value placed by the community on family and community cohesiveness, coupled with a tradition that promotes concern for the welfare of children are powerful forces that likely account for the relatively lower prevalence of this problem in many Orthodox communities. On the other hand, unique stressors in the community such as the financial and emotional stresses that can accompany raising large families and the strong stigma that the community places on academic weakness are two forces that can serve to amplify risk. Educators can play a pivotal role in combating this problem. Research has repeatedly confirmed that the core ingredient in predicting which at-risk children are resilient in the face of multiple risks is the ability to form a relationship with at least one person who cares. Teachers often play that crucial role in the lives of alienated adolescents. Repeatedly, experience has shown that a teacher reaching out to a troubled adolescent can begin a process that gradually helps that child recover from feelings of alienation, pain, and anger. Such relationships, coupled with a commitment to early identification and intervention, and efforts at forging a strong parent-school partnership should ultimately reduce the growing problem of the at-risk adolescent.

References

American Psychiatric Association. (2000). *Diagnostic and statistical manual*—Text Revision (DSM-IV-TR). Washington, DC: American Psychiatric Association.

Angold, A., Costello, E., & Erkanli, A. (1999). Comorbidity. *Journal of Child Psychology and Psychiatry and Allied Disciplines, 40*, 57–87.

Barkley, R. (1998). *Attention-deficit hyperactivity disorder: A handbook for diagnosis and treatment* (2nd ed.). New York, Guilford Press.

Beam, M., Chen, C., & Greenberger, E. (2002). The nature of adolescents' relationships with their "very important" nonparental adults. *American Journal of Community Psychology, 30* (2), 305–325.

Blumenthal N., & Russell, S. (Eds.). (1991). *Children in crisis: Detection and intervention: A practical guide for educators, parents and mental health professionals.* New York: Nefesh, the International Network of Orthodox Mental Health Professionals.

Brent, D., Perper, J., & Moritz, C. (1993). The validity of diagnoses obtained through the psychological autopsy procedure in adolescent suicide victims: Use of family history. *Acta Psychiatrica Scandinavica, 87*, 118–122.

Cadoret, R. J., Yates, W. R., Troughton, E., Woodworth, G., & Stewart, M. A. (1995). Genetic-environmental interaction in the genesis of aggressivity and conduct disorders. *Archives of General Psychiatry, 52*, 916–924.

Campbell, S. B. (1991), Longitudinal studies of active and aggressive preschoolers: Individual differences in early behavior and outcome. In D. Cicchetti & S. L. Toth (Eds.), *Rochester Symposium on Developmental Psychopathology* (pp. 57–90). Hillsdale, NJ: Erlbaum.

Cauffman, E., Feldman, S., Waterman, J., & Steiner, H. (1998). Posttraumatic stress disorder among female juvenile offenders. *Journal of the American Academy of Child and Adolescent Psychiatry, 37*, 1209–1216.

Cloninger, C., & Svrakic, D. (2000). Personality disorders. In H. Kaplan, B. Sadock, & V. Sadock (Eds.), *Comprehensive textbook of psychiatry* (7th ed.). Baltimore, MD: Lippincott, Williams & Wilkins.

Cohen P., Cohen J., & Brook, J. (1993). An epidemiological study of disorder in late childhood and adolescence, II: Persistence of disorders. *Journal of Child Psychology and Psychiatry, 34*, 869–877.

Davidson, R. J., Putnam, K. M., & Larson, C. L. (2000). Dysfunction in the neural circuitry of emotion regulation: A possible prelude to violence. *Science, 289,* 591–594.

Dishion, T., McCord, J., & Pouling, F. (1999). When interventions harm: Peer groups and problem behavior. *American Psychologist, 54,* 755–764.

Dubois, D., Holloway, B., Valentine, J., & Cooper, H. Effectiveness of mentoring programs for youth: A meta-analytic review. *American Journal of Community Psychology, 30*(2), 157–197.

Dunn J., Stocker, C., & Plomin, R. (1990). Nonshared experiences within the family: Correlates of behavioral problems in middle childhood. *Developmental Psychopathology, 2,* 113–126.

Farrington, D. P. (1987). Early precursors of frequent offending. In J. Q. Wilson & G. C. Loury (Eds.), *From children to citizens* (Vol. 3). Families, schools, and delinquency prevention (pp. 27–50). New York: Springer-Verlag.

Feldman, A. (2004). *Parenting style and behaviors associated with ADHD in at risk adolescents in the Orthodox Jewish community.* Unpublished doctoral dissertation. Georgia State University, College of Education, Department of Counseling and Psychological Services.

Fisherman, S. (1998). *No'ar ha-kipot ha-zerukot.* Elkanah: Orot Yisra'el, Mikhlalah Akademit le-Hinukh.

Goldberg, S. J. (2004). *The relationship between English (L1) and Hebrew (L2) reading and externalizing behavior amongst orthodox Jewish boys.* Unpublished doctoral dissertation. New York University, Steinhardt School of Education.

Grossman, J., & Rhodes, J. (2002). The test of time: Predictors and effects of duration in youth mentoring relationships. *American Journal of Community Psychology, 30*(2), 199–219.

Green, S., & Bychkov, I. (1996). Bilingualism in immigrant children: A preliminary essay. *Journal of Jewish Communal Services, 72,* 339–343.

Greene, R. (2000). *The explosive child: A new approach for understanding and parenting easily frustrated, chronically inflexible children.* New York: HarperCollins.

Halberstadt, A., & Nikolsky, A. (1996). Bukharan Jews and their adaptation to the United States. *Journal of Jewish Communal Service, 72,* 244–255.

Hawkins, J., & Lam, T. (1987). Teacher practices, social development, and delinquency. In J. D. Burchard & S. N. Burchard (Eds.), *Prevention of delinquent behavior* (pp. 241–274). Newbury Park, CA: Sage.

Henggeler, S., Schoenwald, S., & Borduin, C. (1998). *Multisystemic treatment of antisocial behavior in children and adolescents.* New York: Guilford Press.

Henry, B., & Moffitt, T. (1997). Neuropsychological and neuroimaging studies of juvenile delinquency and adult criminal behavior. In D. M. Stoff, J. Breiling, & J. D. Maser, (Eds.). *Handbook of antisocial behavior* (pp. 280–288). NY: Wiley.

Huey, S., Henggeler, S., & Scott, W. (2000). Mechanisms of change in multisystemic therapy: Reducing delinquent behavior through therapist adherence and improved family and peer functioning. *Journal of Consulting and Clinical Psychology, 68*, 451–467.

Kaplan S., Pelcovitz, D., Salzinger, S., Weiner, M., Mandel, F. S., Lesser, M. L. et al. (1998). Adolescent physical abuse: Risk for adolescent psychiatric disorders. *American Journal of Psychiatry, 155*(7), 954–959.

Kerr, M., Tremblay, R., Pagani, L., & Vitaro, F. (1997). Boy's behavioral inhibition and the risk of later delinquency. *Archive of General Psychiatry, 54*, 809–816.

Kilgore, K., Snyder, J., & Lentz, C. (2000). The contribution of parental discipline, parental monitoring, and school risk to early-onset conduct problems in African American boys and girls. *Developmental Psychology, 36*, 835–845.

Kuhne, M., Schachar, R., & Tannock, R. (1997). Impact of comorbid oppositional or conduct problems on attention-deficit hyperactivity disorder. *Journal of the American Academy of Child and Adolescent Psychiatry, 36*, 1715–1725.

Loeber, R., & Hay, D. (1997). Key issues in the development of aggression and violence from childhood to early adulthood. *Annual Review of Psychology, 48*, 371–410.

Loeber, R., Burke, J., Lahey, B., Winters, A., & Zera, M. (2000). Oppositional defiant and conduct disorder: A review of the past 10 years, Part I. *Journal of the American Academy of Child and Adolescent Psychiatry, 39*, 1468–1484.

Danziger, Y. (1999). *Metropolitan NY coordinating council on Jewish poverty survey: The incidence of at-risk youth in the Orthodox*

Jewish community of Brooklyn, NY. Report to the New York City Department of Youth and Community Development, Metropolitan Council on Jewish Poverty.

Molidor, C. E. (1996). Female gang members: A profile of aggression and victimization. *Social Work, 41,* 251–257.

Mulvey, E., Arthur, M., & Reppuci, N. (1993). The prevention and treatment of juvenile delinquency: A review of the research. *Clinical Psychology Review, 13,* 133–167.

Pajer, K. (1998). What happens to "bad" girls? A review of the adult outcomes of antisocial adolescent girls. *American Journal of Psychiatry, 155,* 862–870,

Patterson, G. R. (1993). Orderly change in a stable world: The antisocial trait as a chimera. *Journal of Consulting and Clinical Psychology, 61,* 911–919.

Pelcovitz, D. (1988). Identifying the abused child: The role of day school educators. *Ten Da'at, 2,* 9–11.

Pelcovitz, D., & Kaplan, S. (1994). Child witnesses of violence between parents: Psychosocial correlates and implications for treatment. *Child Psychiatric Clinics of North America, 3*(4), 745–758.

Pelcovitz, D., Kaplan, S., Ellenberg, A., Labruna, V., Salzinger, S., Mandel, F. et al. (2000). Adolescent physical abuse: Age at time of abuse and adolescent perception of family functioning. *Journal of Family Violence, 15*(4), 375–389.

Reid, J., & Eddy, J. (1997). The prevention of antisocial behavior: Some considerations in the search for effective interventions. In D. M. Stoff, J. Breiling, & J. D. Moser (Eds.), *Handbook of antisocial behavior* (pp. 343–356). New York: Wiley.

Rhodes, J. (2002). *Stand by me: The risks and rewards of mentoring today's youth.* Cambridge, MA: Harvard University Press.

Richards, I. (1996). Psychiatric disorder among adolescents in custody. *Australian and New Zealand Journal of Psychiatry, 30,* 788–793.

Russell, S., & Blumenthal, N. (Eds.). (2000). *Children in crisis: Detection and intervention: A practical guide for educators, parents and mental health professionals* (2nd ed.). New York: Nefesh, the International Network of Orthodox Mental Health Professionals.

Russell, S., & Blumenthal, N. (Eds.). (2003). *Children in crisis: Detection and intervention: A practical guide for educators, parents and mental health professionals* (3rd ed.). New York: Nefesh, the International Network of Orthodox Mental Health Professionals.

Sampson, R. J., Raudenbush, S. W., & Earls, F. (1997). Neighborhoods and violent crime: A multilevel study of collective efficacy. *Science, 277,* 918–924.

Sharp D., Hay, D., Pawlby, S., Schmucker, G., Allen, H., & Kumar, R. (1995). The impact of postnatal depression on boys' intellectual development. *Journal of Child Psychology and Psychiatry, 36,* 1315–1336.

Schweinhart, L. J. (1987). Can preschool programs help prevent delinquency? In J. Q. Wilson & G. C. Loury (Eds.), *From children to citizens* (Vol. 3). Families, schools, and delinquency prevention (pp. 135–153). New York: Springer-Verlag.

Sipe, C., & Roeder, A. (1999). Mentoring school-age children: A classification of programs. Philadelphia, PA: Public/Private Ventures.

Slonim, N. V., & Sharaga, Y. (2000). Psychological and social adjustment of Russian-born and Israeli-born Jewish adolescents. *Child and Adolescent Social Work Journal, 17,* 455–475.

Tannock, R. (1998). Attention deficit hyperactivity disorder: Advances in cognitive, neurobiological, and genetic research. *Journal of Child Psychology and Psychiatry, 39,* 65–99.

Tremblay, R., Masse, B., & Perron, D. (1992). Early disruptive behavior, poor school achievement, delinquent behavior, and delinquent personality: Longitudinal analyses. *Journal of Consulting and Clinical Psychology, 60,* 64–72.

Ulzen, T., & Hamilton, H. (1998).The nature and characteristics of psychiatric comorbidity in incarcerated adolescents. *Canadian Journal of Psychiatry, 43,* 57–63.

Van der Kolk, B., Pelcovitz, D., Roth, S. Mandel, F. McFarlane, A. C., Herman, J., (1996). Dissociation, affect dysregulation and somatization: The complexity of adaptation to trauma. *American Journal of Psychiatry, 153*(7), (Supplement) July, 83–93.

Vermeiren, R. (2003). Psychopathology and delinquency in adolescents: A descriptive and developmental perspective. *Clinical Psychology Review, 23,* 277–318.

Zicht, G. (1993). The effects of emigration on Soviet Children. *Journal of Jewish Communal Services, 69,* 57–63.

Zicht, G. (1996) The immigration of Syrian Jews to New York 1992–
    1994. *Journal of Jewish Communal Services, 72*, 256–262.
Zimmerman, M., Bingenheimer, A., & Notaro, P. Natural mentors
    and adolescent resiliency: A study with urban youth. *American
    Journal of Community Psychology, 30*(2), 221–243.

Bullying, Harassment, and Social Exclusion in Jewish Schools:
Unique Opportunities and Challenges to Promote Positive Peer Culture

Rona Novick

Introduction

"Much have I learned from my teachers, more from my colleagues, but most from my students" (*Talmud, Ta'anit 7b*)

Educators who speak with students about their school experiences quickly learn that school is as much a social setting as it is an academic one. As such, it can contribute to children's sense of self and belonging, or it can fuel self-doubt and reinforce loneliness. Schools' increasing focus on addressing their social climate and promoting students' social development has been motivated, in part, by the growing body of research demonstrating the clear connection between academic and social-behavioral issues (Benninga, Berkowitz, Kuehn, & Smith, 2006; Goldberg, 2005). Among the most pressing reasons for schools to address peer culture, however, is the cost of not addressing it. Depression, alienation, and even suicide and violence are possible outcomes for students who cannot find their social niche (Espelage & Swearer, 2003).

Jewish schools have unique, compelling reasons for addressing peer relationships and social issues. Character education is not an afterthought in religious, value-based education. It is central to Torah living, and to Torah-based education. Jewish educators therefore, have significant opportunities and avenues to support the development of positive peer culture. Secular educators may bemoan the extent of bullying, peer cruelty, or poor social skills in their schools, blaming inadequate time or the failure of their curriculum to address these critical issues. Jewish educators, however, must explore how and why in settings where the spirit and *halakhot* of *ve-ahavta le-rei`akha kamokha* is regularly and repeatedly taught, these negative peer phenomena persist.

This chapter will address the critical issue of developing a positive peer culture in schools. Jewish schools are already investing time and effort in this crucial task. This discussion will focus on the negative phenomenon of bullying as an example of a concrete issue that schools can successfully address. It is sobering to realize that our schools are not all they can be, but it is the author's hope that this chapter will uplift rather than depress. If we focus on bully prevention as both an end in itself, and a means to fulfill Jewish schools' larger mission to create socially responsible and responsive *mensches* and leaders, then addressing bullying becomes a necessity, and a privilege.

Bullying and related social difficulties are complex, and may manifest quite differently at different developmental levels. An exhaustive discussion of social development and bullying is beyond the scope of this chapter. The focus here will be on students of upper elementary and middle school grades, as the research on bully prevention centers on those years when the frequency of bullying is the highest.

This chapter follows the sequence required for effective bully prevention. First one must understand the **Rationale for Bully Prevention**. Next, it is critical to explore the **Scope of the Problem and Issues in Definition**. Before beginning bullying programs, schools need accurate information about the **Characteristics of Bullies, Victims and Bystanders,** and whether there are critical **Gender Issues.** The **Components of Effective Bully Prevention** must be included. Finally, **Practical Recommendations** are often needed to address particular issues.

Rationale for Bully Prevention

There has been considerable debate over whether students' autonomy and self-expression is compromised by moral or social-emotional education. An increasing number of researchers and theorists support the clear imperative for schools to transmit not only knowledge, but values. As reports of school violence and students' cruelty to each other continue to emerge, Sommers cautions:

> Leaving students to discover their own values is a little like putting them in a chemistry lab full of volatile substances and

saying, "Discover your own compounds, kids." We should not be surprised when some blow themselves up and destroy those around them (2006, p. 37).

In Jewish educational settings, character education and focusing on the social-emotional learning of students should be less controversial. Schools wishing to address it, however, feel the burden of completing other curricula and supporting students' academic success. Research on the positive academic benefits of addressing the behavioral, social and emotional world of the student should provide reassurance that it is a worthy investment.

The impact school and class social climate have on academic outcomes has been consistently documented (Fraser, 1998; Moos & Moos, 1978) including the positive impact character education and social emotional learning initiatives have on grades and test scores. Benninga et al. (2006) cite four character education/social emotional learning programs with documented impact on academics. Schools employing the Peaceful Schools Project or the Responsive Classroom approach reported greater gains on standardized test scores. Similarly, middle school students who attended elementary schools utilizing the Child Development Project fared better both in class grades obtained and on achievement tests, as did students in schools participating in the Seattle Social Development Project.

Concerned that the data represented the relatively limited number of schools utilizing pre-packaged character education programs, Benninga and colleagues undertook an examination of the impact of a wider variety of character education approaches on academic outcome. In a sample of 120 California elementary schools, they found a positive relationship between the extent to which character education was implemented and current and future academic achievement in both language and mathematics. They conclude that good quality character education is "positively associated with academic achievement, both across academic domains and over time" (Benninga et al., 2006 p. 2).

Another area of study of school climate supports the rationale for and relevance of character education. School-wide Positive Behavioral Interventions and Supports (PBIS) requires that schools create clear behavioral expectations for all students, provide necessary instruction to allow students to meet those expectations, and offer incentives for students who demonstrate both effort and success (OSEP Center on Positive Behavioral Interventions and Supports, 2004). Through this focus on clear behavioral and social expectations, PBIS attempts to impact overall school culture. An approach that is founded on data-driven decision making, data on PBIS schools is collected and analyzed regularly. Understanding the need to tie behavioral and social improvements to academic achievement, Putnam, Horner, and Algozzine (2006) summarized data on the academic benefits of effective PBIS implementation. Assuming that time in instruction is an important contributor to academic success, the authors reported gains of the equivalent of 169 days of instruction in a six month period in PBIS schools compared with similar schools in an urban setting. They document a 24% increase in on-task behavior in classrooms using positive behavior support. The authors report significant impact of PBIS on grades and standardized test performance, with reading and math percentile ranks increasing between 18 and 25 percentage points. A review of Illinois PBIS schools found that 62 percent of their students met third grade state reading standards, compared with 47 percent of students in non-PBIS schools, further supporting the connection between behavioral and social environment and academic outcome.

Are there academic benefits to addressing bullying in particular, beyond those demonstrated for character education in general? A large scale study of bullying in the United States documented a significant association between involvement in bullying and student perception of academic achievement (Nansel, et al., 2001). Whether students were bullies, victims, or both, they had significantly lower achievement scores than bystanders. The cross-sectional design of the research did not allow determination of causality: Did bullying place students at academic risk or vice versa? Prior research has documented the negative impact being bullied has on concentration, a clear requirement for academic success. The authors caution that since studies of bullying and school outcome focus on achievement scores, a narrow indicator of school success, "a number of important things learned in school such as social skills, ability to collaborate, ability to accept criticism and learn from it, helping others, persistence when facing problems, ability to pay attention, and a host of other skills" are being ignored (p. 1030). A longitudinal study of over 1,500 students in their first year of middle school confirmed that victimization in the fall predicts poor academic functioning in the spring (Nishina, Juvonen, &

Witkow, 2005). The bullying-academic connection is both strong and pervasive. Nansel and colleagues (Nansel, Craig, Overpeck, Saluja, & Ruan, 2004) expanded their study of bullying and school adjustment to 25 countries, including the United States and Israel. Significantly worse school adjustment in students involved in bullying, whether as bullies or victims, persisted in all but one country.

Dual curriculum schools, challenged with meeting academic standards in reduced time, may fear that focus on social or emotional issues will interfere with meeting curricular goals. Cohen, Kress and Elias (2002) argue that as is true in secular settings, focus on social and affective tone in the learning environment is not only helpful, but "crucial for complete academic, social, emotional and Jewish growth" (p. 22). Jewish schools strive to create graduates with a strong affiliation to Jewish values and practices. Critical goals in their own right, these goals are that much more pressing given the research that failure to create affiliation contributes to a score of other difficulties for Jewish youth. Students who become disenfranchised or alienated are more likely to engage in anti-religious and high-risk behavior such as substance abuse (Pelcovitz, 2005; cf. previous chapter).

Bullying is a phenomenon that touches every level of school functioning, from the individual student to the classroom to school-wide culture. When a school successfully addresses bullying, it cannot help but create a positive social culture with benefits far and above simply decreasing bullying behavior. Such schools not only see improved grades; their students exhibit greatly improved behavior and decreased substance abuse in later years (US Department of Health and Human Services, 2006).

Scope of the Problem and Issues in Definition
Research suggests that bullying is a part of the school experience for virtually all students. The National Resource Center for Safe Schools (NRCSS) released estimates in 2001 that suggest 30% of American students are *regularly* involved in bullying, as bullies, victims or both. Advances in technology have increased the spread, frequency and variety of bullying, creating more and different bullies and victims (Smith, et al., 2008). As the US Department of Education argues, others are significantly affected as well: "Children and teens who regularly witness bullying at school suffer from a less secure learning environment, the fear that the bully may target them next,

and the knowledge that teachers and other adults are either unable or unwilling to control bullies' behavior" (1998).

To date, no studies of bullying in American Jewish schools have been published. International research confirms that Israeli rates of bullying are similar to those in United States public schools (Nansel et al., 2004). Research on the BRAVE bully prevention curriculum has included student surveys of over 2,000 middle school students in US co-educational Jewish day schools. Preliminary review of the first year data (approximately 800 students) reveals rates and patterns of bullying similar to those found in public schools in the United States (Novick, Winkler, Czarka, & Isaacs, 2009).

Bullying has been studied from Norway to New Zealand to Japan, and not surprisingly is both experienced and defined in various ways depending on the cultural context. There is, however, significant consensus on three critical elements of definition: bullying is intentional, involves an imbalance of power, and causes harm. There is less agreement on the fine points of whether bullying requires a chronic, repeated process, and if it involves many against one, or can have a solo perpetrator (Olweus, 1993). For the purposes of this paper, we will define bullying as the deliberate use or abuse of power by one or more students to cause harm to another student. As such, this definition encapsulates the three agreed upon essential elements of bullying as follows:

Bullying is the **deliberate** (intentionality) **use or abuse of power** (power imbalance) **to cause harm** (causes harm) to another student.

There is a variety of ways in which students may attain power. Physical size is the most obvious, but social standing, academic or athletic skill, financial resources, attractiveness, position (i.e. class president), *protectzia* (who you are related to and/or who you know), and even membership in a particular cultural or ethnic group can empower students. In Jewish schools, many of which draw students from multiple segments of a community, power may derive from address (which side of town you inhabit), membership at a particular synagogue, country of origin, and parents' or other family members' positions in community and school organizations. The author has encountered power imbalances in *yeshivot* and day schools based on skin tone, and in immigrant schools, on status in the students' country of origin generations before emigration.

Intentionality, the purposeful nature of bullying is often obscured by perpetrators who excuse their behavior with the statement "I didn't mean to hurt him/her." No one enjoys being ridiculed, harassed or excluded. Typically, bullies explain their continued cruelty by stating that the victim did not look or act upset. A seasoned eighth grade teacher provided the following example to the bullies in his class: In nature movies, you often see predators, such as lions, stalking a herd of antelope. An antelope that is wounded is compelled to "act" unhurt, to avoid becoming the predator's next meal. "Is it possible," this wise teacher asked, "that when classmates are hurt by your words or actions, they act unhurt to avoid additional attack?"

Although the clearest evidence of harm from bullying comes from physical bullying, social and emotional harm are actually more frequent. Emotional bullying involves teasing, name-calling, and other behaviors that damage a student's self-esteem or mood. Social bullying are those actions which damage a student's social standing, including social exclusion. This latter form of harm has contributed to the creation of the term relational aggression (Underwood, 2002). Despite researchers' awareness of these varying forms of bullying, students may need to be educated to broaden their notion of bullying. A study of 14 year old students in England found that while over 90 percent identified verbal teasing and physical aggression as bullying, only 62 percent agreed that social exclusion qualified (Smith, Cowie, Olafsson, & Liefooghe, 2002).

Characteristics of Bullies, Victims, and Bystanders

Children's literature and popular culture provide stereotyped portrayals of victims and bullies. From classic Disney movies such as *1001 Dalmatians*, to modern films such as *Toy Story*, bullies are recognizable through their dress and obvious cruel behavior, lacking the subtlety seen in real-life situations. Movies and children's stories may explain a bully's cruelty as a response to mistreatment the bully experienced, and suggest that such meanness can be reversed with extra kindness. In *The Berenstain Bears and the Bully* (Berenstain & Berenstain, 1993), a young bully develops when she is mistreated at home. The canine bully in *Martha Walks the Dog* (Maddaugh, 1998), after being mistreated by his owner, is reformed when he is called a "good dog." Other bullies in literature are given a taste of their own cruelty, as in Caple's picturebook *The Wimp* (1994). In this story, Arnold and his sister strand bullies who are spray painting the school on the roof, resulting in the bullies receiving punishment for their crimes. The story ends there, whereas one would wonder what retribution real world bullies might deliver to Arnold and family. The recent film *The Ant Bully* illustrated retribution and forced empathy as a boy who bullies ants is made to live among them and experience their struggles.

Bully plots in films (*Mean Girls, Radio*), television shows and children's books often suggest that entrenched and on-going cruelty or social exclusion can be reversed with one dramatic intervention or within a 30 minute episode. The title character in Spinelli's popular book *Loser* (2002), socially excluded from first through sixth grade, assists in the search for a missing child and is invited to join the popular students' team. Howe's *Pinky and Rex and the Bully* (1996) has a bully crumbling in the face of character's new confidence. In the popular Mercer Mayer series, *Just a Bully* (1999), teachers are portrayed as unhelpful, exacerbating the bullying and recommending physical retaliation that would result in disciplinary action in virtually any school. Unfortunately, these fictional bullies and victims contribute to widely held but largely incorrect notions about bullying and the means necessary to address it.

Research documents the following characteristics of students who are frequently victimized (Hawker & Boulton, 2000; Card, 2003):
- Shy
- Reactive, show extreme emotion when victimized
- Anxious
- Depressed
- Low self-esteem
- Poor social skills

The commonly held opinion that children are bullied because they are different in some physical or academic way has been largely proven wrong. Only two specific child characteristics result in victimization, being overweight or being perceived as having an atypical sexual orientation. Children with other physical differences become victims only when they are sufficiently reactive when teased or excluded. This reaction fuels the bullying. It is tempting, therefore, to "blame the victim," arguing that they bring harassment upon themselves, either by provoking the bully, or by appearing weak and defenseless (Banks, 2000).

Secular settings may attempt to protect students by developing bully free zones, or zero tolerance policies. Torah based educational settings need only invoke the dictum *lifnei ivver lo titen mikhshol* (Vayikra, 19:14). Bullying is a major roadblock for victims, and Torah educators and students cannot expect such victims to overcome it alone. The Torah reminds us, *v'ger lo tilhatz ve-atem yeda'tem et nefesh ha-ger ki gerim heyitem be-eretz mitzrayim"* (Shemot, 23:9), that all Jews were once victims, and we should therefore have clear empathy for the victimized. Jewish educators can understand and teach that *no circumstances make bullying acceptable.*

With victimization comes serious physical, social and emotional sequalae.

Depression is common, as is anxiety in students who are frequently bullies (Espelage & Swearer, 2003). Victims report frequent somatic complaints, including head and stomach aches. In many cases, victims may experience impaired sleep and even bedwetting, and suicidal ideation is not uncommon (Nansel, Overpeck, Pilla, Ruan, & Simons-Morton, 2001).

A great deal of myth and misinformation surrounds bullies. A common misconception is that bullies lash out at others as a result of poor self-esteem. In fact, research provides a very different picture. Persistent bullies are generally aggressive, and have a view of relationships that condones aggression as a means of achieving power and influence (Smith, Schneider, Smith, & Ananiadou, 2004). Bullies have little empathy and desire power and control (National Resource Center for Safe Schools, 1999). A study of over 1,900 students in the Los Angeles area found that bullies were the most psychologically "healthy" students studied, with no evidence of anxiety, depression or poor self-esteem (Juvonen, Graham, & Schuster, 2003).

Developing a clear picture of bullies and victims is complicated by the fact that some children seem to be at times victim and, at times, perpetrator. These bully-victims, or provocative victims are equally likely to respond with aggression as with anxious distress when bullied. They are consistently found to be at highest risk for emotional distress and psychosocial difficulties (Smith et al., 2004). Students with nonverbal learning disorders, social skills deficits, and attention deficit disorder are over-represented in this group. This group presents a particular challenge for educators, as they may require fairly extensive support and skills training, as well as consequences for their negative behavior.

Victims, bullies and provocative victims actually comprise a relatively small part of a school's culture. The vast majority of students in any school will be bystanders, observers of the bullying that occurs. In fact, 85% of all bullying is witnessed by peers. Almost 30 years ago, Olweus' seminal work on decreasing bullying in schools demonstrated the importance of this large group of students (1978). As bullying is about power, bullies gain little in social status or power unless they have an "audience." Rarely evident to adults (Olweus, 1993), the typical audience for bullying consists of peers. How those peers respond provides bullies with critical information; is my cruelty celebrated, does it earn me social status, or does it cost me reputation and standing with my peers?

Understanding Bystander Behavior

Why don't students tell bullies that their behavior is unacceptable, and put an end to school bullying? Student bystanders do not send bullies this clear message because they are afraid they will become the next victim, or suffer other social consequences (Mellor, 1993).

Several well studied social psychology phenomena may help explain why student bystanders do not exert their power. Solomon Asch, interested in understanding how citizens could not only tolerate but support the Nazi rise to power, began studying conformity in the 1950s. In one of his classic studies, eight subjects were seated in a semi-circle and asked to identify which line matches a target line on a card. Seated in chairs 1–7 are confederates of the experimenter, and each gave the same blatantly wrong answer. In chair 8, the unknowing subject valiantly disagreed, at least initially. When the procedure was repeated subjects became hesitant and appeared depressed, and 35 percent of the time, caved in to peer pressure, conforming despite clear knowledge that what they were doing was wrong (Asch, 1956). Varying the study finds that when one confederate gives the correct answer, the likelihood of blind conformity is markedly reduced.

Repeated with many variations and populations, Asch's work reminds us what a challenging task we present to student bystanders. Since bullying often involves repeated attacks, bystanders may hear that a peer is deficient or defective many times. Even when a bystander knows this is incorrect, what strength of character is required to say differently?

Another social psychology phenomenon to consider is the tendency to dehumanize those we see frequently victimized or degraded. In the classic study conducted at Stanford University by Zimbardo and colleagues (Haney, Banks & Zimbardo, 1973), students appointed as "prison guards" monitoring other student "convicts" were so cruel that the planned two week study was ended in half the time. The process of dehumanization has been cited as an explanation for instances in history and in the recent past in which labeling an individual or a group as "victims" led to grossly malevolent and inhuman treatment by those in power. Today's students have seen headlines about the abuse of prisoners at Abu Ghraib. In Jewish schools, where the Holocaust is almost uniformly taught, the impact of dehumanization of victims should be readily appreciated.

The failure of bystanders to act in helpful ways raises the question of why individuals who know an ethical or moral imperative do not follow it. The relationship between moral knowledge and moral behavior has been of interest for centuries. Haidt (2001), arguing for the role of social intuition in moral judgment, summarized two views useful to consider, those of Metcalf and Mischel (1999) and Batson and Thompson (2001). Metcalf and Mischel explain human behavior in the face of moral temptation; two systems, the "hot" (temptation) and "cool" (ability to resist temptation) systems, interact to determine the outcome. Metcalf and Mischel further suggested that the cool system relies on hippocampal memory and frontal planning and inhibition centers of the brain. They argued that a child's ability to demonstrate moral behavior is determined by the strength of the cool system, which increases over development.

Batson and Thompson (2001) offer a different view, with motivational considerations central. Their empathy-altruism hypothesis states that empathy aroused by another's suffering evokes an altruistic motivation to reduce the victim's distress. How can we explain the common failure of bystanders to act to ameliorate the suffering of the victims of bullies? Batson and Thompson explain that both *moral hypocrisy*, aiming to appear moral, while, if possible avoiding the cost of being moral, and *overpowered integrity*, being moral only until the costs of moral actions become extreme, are motivational conditions that lead people to act immorally. In the social culture of the elementary or middle school, Mellor (1993) reminds us of the cost of moral behavior bystanders anticipate: social rejection, intimidation and/or personal harm.

The above discussion suggests that shifting bystanders from a passive stance to an active, pro-social one will be challenging and requires specific focus as part of a comprehensive bully prevention strategy. Jewish educators have a plethora of sources to support the active role bystanders can and should take. We read in *Vayikra* (19:16), *"lo ta `amod al dam re `ekha"* exhorting us to act, to help, when one among us is hurt. Torah provides examples in the behavior of Torah figures of the responsibility to act when another suffers. Moses can not tolerate the abuse of a slave; Esther risks her own safety on behalf of the Jewish people. Similarly, Torah teaches us the consequences of failing to come forward and act on another's behalf. The depravity of Sodom which resulted in its destruction, was evidenced in part by the failure of even one of its citizens to stop the attack on Lot and his guests (Bereishit 19:4–5).

Gender Issues

Researchers are increasingly recognizing that the complex phenomenon of bullying may be quite different for boys and girls. This is of particular interest in Jewish schools where classes and buildings may be single or mixed gender for part or all of the day. Early research focused almost exclusively on boys, and suggested an overwhelming percentage of bullying involving boys as compared to girls (Olweus, 1993). This may have represented sampling biases in that experimenters were more likely to notice boys' physically aggressive bullying than girls' more subtle social and emotional aggression (Leckie, 1997).

Cillessen and Mayeux (2004) reviewed existing studies on children's aggression and completed a longitudinal examination of relational aggression (social bullying) and popularity, following children from grades 5 through 9. Despite the hypothesis that physical *and* relational aggression would result in increased popularity for boys and girls, their data suggested very different routes to popularity for the genders. High status-boys were able to both achieve and maintain their popularity via friendliness. Popular girls, however, resorted to more negative behaviors, including social aggression and bullying. Their longitudinal design allowed consideration of the chicken/egg question, in that it appeared that "status led to behavior more often than the reverse" (2004, p.160). This was true especially for girls who were first perceived as popular, then exhibited relational aggression. This is consistent with other research which documents girls' use of meanness and manipulation to control peers and establish dominance.

The debate over gender differences in aggression and social aggression is far from resolved (Underwood, Galen, & Paquette, 2001). In their thorough review, Merrell, Buchanan, & Tran (2006) report that girls exhibit relational aggression more frequently than boys, view it as hurtful as physical aggression, and direct their socially aggressive behavior mostly towards other girls. To confuse the issue, there are some studies that find greater relational aggression in boys. These studies, however, focus on younger children, suggesting an interaction of gender and age. The authors conclude that although additional research is necessary, relational aggression occurs in both genders and creates serious psycho-social sequelae for those who experience it.

Unfortunately, research is only beginning to evaluate how gender issues play out in single or mixed gender schools. The majority of research on single versus mixed gender educational settings has been conducted in non-Jewish settings and aims to evaluate academic and vocational impact. The National Association for Single Sex Public Education (2005), summarizing the evidence supporting single-sex education, cites the almost exclusive focus on grades and test scores, and urges consideration of breadth of educational opportunity. They catalog numerous studies which support the notion that boys in single gender schools are more than twice as likely to study foreign languages, art, music and drama. They quote interviews from boys at such schools who report feelings of comfort, and freedom from both bullying and intimidation in their all boy classes. Girls reportedly benefit from increased exposure to math and sciences, and demonstrate academic gains in these areas.

What is the impact of single-gender or coeducational format on the social culture of schools? Anecdotal reports from schools shifting to single gender include marked decreases in discipline referrals. A study of secondary students in both types of schools in Flanders found girls only had a greater sense of belonging in single gender schools (Brutsaert & Van Houtte, 2002). Students in single gender classrooms have reported more order, teacher control, discipline, and organization (American Association of University Women Educational Foundation, 1998). Students in single gender schools perceived less friction, and students in all female schools, the least friction of all (Richardson, 1990). Mael's review of socio-emotional and academic development in single-sex and coed schools revealed increased self-esteem in single-sex settings (1998). In addition, there was a suggestion at the middle school level that the presence of boys affects popularity issues among girls, resulting in an overemphasis on physical appearance that negatively impacts girls' friendships. In contrast, there was a trend for girls to have more positive perceptions of class culture when boys are in their class.

Shute, Owens, and Slee (2007) explored the victimization of girls in co-educational settings. In their interviews of students and teachers at a co-ed high school in Australia, they discovered that verbal harassment of girls by boys was a daily occurrence, with the vast majority of such victimization having sexual overtones. The authors state that cross-gender victimization of girls by boys is a well-documented phenomenon, but that its sexual nature has received limited study. Single-gender settings are not without difficulty, in that boys may be subject to significant teasing and harassment if they do not emulate masculine, macho norms of behavior (Frank, Kehler, Lovell, & Davison, 2003).

Does the above research, focusing primarily on academics and non-gender stereotyped learning and course choices or on sexually tinged harassment in co-educational public high schools, have any relevance to Jewish schools? Cohen et al., (2002) reviewed classroom climate in an Orthodox day school. In an earlier study of gender differences in coed, Conservative day schools, girls perceived more equality and fairness, achievement, motivation and parental involvement. In the Orthodox school studied, classes were coed until fourth grade, then separate for all subjects through graduation in eighth grade. Girls in the older grades (in single gender classrooms) reported the lowest levels of friction, compared with girls in the lower grades (mixed gender classrooms).

In Jewish settings, the gender mix of a class or school is correlated with other factors, such as *hashkafah,* curriculum content, and geographic location. Careful and significant research will be required to fully explore and understand how gender and school composition contribute to the school's social culture and bullying in particular. Only after such research can the question of what intervention adaptations are required to maximize success in all settings be addressed.

Components of Effective Bully Prevention
The first successful bully prevention programs grew out of tragedy in suburban Norway. Three students in Bergen committed

suicide leaving notes explaining that they could no longer tolerate the teasing and bullying they were experiencing (Olweus, 1993). Supported by the Norwegian government, Olweus began the study of school bullying and the development of methods to address it. Olweus' approach includes education of all members of the school community, including review of a student survey of bullying, empowerment of bystanders and school staff to share responsibility for creating bully-free environments, and policies and procedures for the discipline of bullies. Implementation of his approach yielded highly promising results in Norway, with a 50% reduction of bullying in the first year, and increases to 75% reduction by the second year of the program. In addition, all members of the school community were reportedly happier in the school environment, academic achievement improved and anti-social behavior decreased. Replication in 14 intervention schools in Bergen resulted in reductions of bully/victim problems ranging from 21–38%. An additional study in Oslo found reductions of bullying of 33% for girls and 48% for boys (Olweus Bullying Prevention Program, 2006).

Following Olweus' seminal work, the Department for Education in England supported evaluation of bully prevention programming (Smith & Sharp, 1994). Programs included similar components to those used by Olweus: gathering student information, establishing school-wide rules, training all adults in the school, improving adult supervision and building parental awareness, and were effective in significantly decreasing bullying and increasing students' willingness to report it. The English studies, not surprisingly, found the schools that accomplished the largest reductions in bullying were those that demonstrated the most thorough and consistent application of bully prevention programming.

In their 2004 review of bully prevention, Smith et al. cite 12 large-scale intervention studies completed internationally, in Germany, Belgium, Spain, Finland, Ireland, Austria, Switzerland, Australia and the United States. While none of the intervention studies has matched the impact of Olweus' original work, reductions of 5–20% in victimization rates are consistently accomplished. Smith argues that no "magic ingredient" has been determined, and the best predictors of outcomes include the extent to which schools take ownership of bully prevention, the length of the interventions, and an earlier (pre-secondary school) start.

The core components of the Olweus approach have been woven into programs world-wide, with attempts to replicate his findings. The American version of the Olweus program, recognized by the Department of Justice as a Blueprint Violence Prevention program (Olweus, Limber, & Mihalic, 1999) and operated out of Clemson University in South Carolina (Limber, 2004), has achieved more modest (30–40%) reductions of bullying. Imported in the early 1990's, eighteen participating South Carolina middle schools demonstrated significant decreases in students' reports of bullying others and significant decreases in boys' reports of being bullied and socially isolated (Limber, 2004). Further evaluation of the program in 12 Philadelphia area schools revealed significant reductions in self-reported bullying, and significant decreases in adults' observations of bullying when the program was implemented with moderate or better fidelity (Black, 2003). Reasons for the discrepancy between American and Norwegian outcomes include differences in educational systems, culture, and the student populations served.

Other programs and approaches have been utilized to ameliorate school bullying. In its 2001 review, the Northwest Regional Education Laboratory highlighted the Steps to Respect program (Committee for Children, 2001), the Maine Project Against Bullying (1997), and the Effective Behavioral Support program (Walker et al., 1996). Vignettes of schools employing these approaches are provided, but formal outcome measures are not offered. Frey et al. (2005) published a controlled study of the Steps to Respect program with over 1,000 students in grades 3–6. Steps to Respect aims to decrease bullying by building friendship skills, social problem-solving and assertiveness, as well as empowering bystanders to act pro-socially in the face of bullying, and by increasing staff-awareness and responsiveness. Students in the intervention group showed decreases in bullying and argumentative behavior on the playground, had more agreeable interactions, and demonstrated reduced negative bystander behavior. The intervention group also reported increased bystander responsibility, perceived greater adult responsiveness, and decreased acceptance of bullying.

Bully prevention initiatives have broadened to include training in social skills, anger-management and friendship building. Mikami, Boucher & Humphreys (2005) utilized a classroom-level intervention based on cooperative games and cooperative learning opportunities to decrease peer-rejection, with some success. Salmivalli (2001) trained peer counselors to develop and lead a week-long intervention campaign against bullying. There were strong gender differences, with girls showing decreases in bullying and increased willingness to influence bully problems in their classes. Boys also decreased their engagement in bullying, but less so than girls, and exhibited an unfortunate increase in bullying attitudes. DeRosier & Marcus (2005) reported on the one-year impact of a social-skills program addressing friendship and bullying. The participating third grade students achieved higher self-esteem and social acceptance, and decreased aggression. Some of these changes were not evident until one year after the training, leading the authors to suggest that children may not be immediately rewarded by their peers with acceptance after improving their social skills. Leff (2006) successfully decreased inner city girls' relational aggression with an intervention combining 20 group and 8 classroom sessions. The sessions included information on anger management, role playing opportunities, and skills training in social-problem solving.

BRAVE

Interested in creating a school-wide, user-friendly, evidence based approach, the Alliance for School Mental Health incorporated many Olweus elements into its BRAVE (Bully Prevention/Anti-Violence Education) program (Novick, 2000). BRAVE involves parents, teachers and students in education about bullying, and provides additional components to promote school-wide systems change. In place of a survey to build awareness of bullying, BRAVE employs a mock trial of cartoon bullies. To bolster the relatively weak skills training and rehearsal offered in the Olweus program, BRAVE developed specific instruction in and practice of critical bystander skills. Similar to many evidence-based bully prevention programs, BRAVE includes quality circles, a regular and ongoing mechanism for safe discussion of class social issues. Based on the concept introduced by Olweus, class quality circles are modeled after those used in manufacturing settings. Assembly line workers participate in quality circles to discuss how well they function as a team to create the best possible product; students in quality circles are given the opportunity to explore how well they work as a team to create a safe, caring classroom and school.

Initial evaluation of the BRAVE program included review of student self-report outcome data from two large suburban middle schools. In one school, participating students were less likely to dislike school (from 12% pre to 9% post). There were marked gender differences, with boys disliking school dropping from 19% at pre- to 13% post-intervention. Collapsing bullying across severity there was no change, but significant differences were found in students subjected to milder bullying. Rates of teasing yielded decreases for both boys and girls (31% pre and 26% post for girls and 33% pre and 28% post for boys). Similar gender differences were apparent in the percentage of students frequently excluded, with girls showing a decrease following the program (from 11% pre to 8% post, and actually increasing for boys, 5.9% pre to 10% post). This may be a result of increased awareness that social exclusion qualifies as bullying. Following participation, higher percentages of students reported that their teachers are active and effective in addressing bullying, and that they would come forward and tell someone if they were bullied. In one of the schools, the percentage of students who felt their teachers do a lot to stop bullying increased from 30% to 59% for girls, and from 31% to 58% for boys over a two year period.

A more elaborate and controlled multi-year study of the BRAVE program is currently underway. In the initial year of the study, three co-educational United States Jewish middle schools were compared with 2 similar wait-list control schools. Students in those classes that participated in BRAVE demonstrated reductions in aggressive problem solving in the first six months of the program, as compared with non-participating classes in the active schools and control schools. This is a particularly encouraging finding, as students received less than six months of programming. Data from the second year of the research is currently being collected and analyzed and includes four additional active schools (totaling seven) and two additional wait-list controls, as well as continued data collection to track further changes in first year schools.

Are there general principles or components shared by effective bully prevention approaches? Several key ingredients appear in the majority of programs. First, all relevant members of the school community are educated about bullying. Second, the central role of bystanders and the concept of shared responsibility are addressed and opportunities for ongoing social processing are included. Finally, rules and consequences are determined and delivered. These critical components, including a review of the challenges and opportunities for Jewish settings, are discussed below.

Knowledge about Bullying

System-wide education about bullying is accomplished in the Olweus approach by having students complete a bullying questionnaire. The original program involves results of this anonymous survey being reported to the entire student body and faculty during a full-day of programming around the topic of bullying. This has some advantages in that the completion of a survey also provides administrators and faculty with useful information for planning interventions. Not all schools recognize the value of a data-driven approach. A review by the British Department for Education of those schools utilizing their anti-bullying resource materials revealed that only 1% used the Olweus measure, with 42 percent using their own survey, and other schools using interviews, spot checks or other methods. Overall, only 66% of the schools used any form of survey or data collection (Oliver & Candappa, 2003).

Tabulating, interpreting, reporting, and utilizing data may present challenges for all schools and for Jewish schools in particular. Public schools may have mandated record keeping for discipline referrals, and technical support for testing and survey administration, which private Jewish schools lack. Even the presence of professionally trained counseling staff does not ensure comfort and skill in utilizing data. Wilkerson & Eshbach (2009) documented the need for specific training in data use, and the relative weakness of counselors' knowledge base in this area. With the availability of *Survey Monkey* and similar tools, Jewish schools may be able, with some guidance and support, to collect and analyze data to increase school wide awareness of bullying.

Knowledge about bullying can be presented in numerous ways, and the laws of pedagogy apply in the case of social-emotional issues exactly as they do for mathematics or reading. That is to say that one-day or large impact events, such as assemblies, serve a purpose in generating excitement and imparting basic knowledge. It would be as foolish to assume that a reading assembly creates readers as it would be to think that a bully prevention assembly creates responsible social citizens.

Exactly what knowledge do students and adults need to successfully address bullying? Most programs include a significant focus on awareness—developing an understanding of what bullying is. Students' definition of bullying is often limited to the physical. Helping students understand that verbal taunting and social character assassination is equally harmful is critical. Jewish schools have many

Torah and Rabbinic sources to support this notion. "Life and death are in the hands of the tongue," our scholars remind us (Mishlei 18:21). Rambam's *Hilkhot Teshuvah* cites the three behaviors that, when engaged in regularly, prevent one from a share in the world to come: inventing or using cruel nicknames, publicly shaming others, and disgracing one's teachers (3:14). Additional Jewish sources that support an expanded conceptualization of bullying are provided at the end of this chapter.

Many bully prevention programs teach students to recognize bullying and to share responsibility for addressing it. In limiting the education to this knowledge, however, such programs may place students in an unfair position. Such programs empower students with the responsibility to do something about the bullying in their environment, but often fail to provide instruction and practice in the specific tools or skills that would allow students to do so successfully and safely.

Shared Responsibility

Bully prevention programs generally include direct instruction in areas such as assertiveness, emotion regulation, social problem-solving, and other skills that allow bystanders to act both responsibly and effectively (Committee for Children, 2001; DeRosier & Marcus, 2005, Novick, 2000). Commercial programs to teach social skills, assertiveness, and other pro-social behaviors abound, and a review is beyond the scope of this paper. While the breadth and depth of these programs is, on some level, a strength, they often involve dozens of lessons and significant classroom instructional time, making them challenging to implement in secular schools, and quite impractical given time constraints in Jewish settings. The discussion that follows will therefore be limited to the promotion of concrete bystander strategies that support shared responsibility.

The Positive Behavior Supports technical assistance center launched a bully prevention component to its school-side behavior management approach, that includes three strategies for both victims and bystanders (Ross, Horner & Stiller, 2009). The three strategies are abbreviated as: *Stop, Walk and Talk.* Students are taught the language and means to tell bullies to stop, are encouraged to walk away from situations to avoid reinforcing the bully, and to talk to adults about what happens.

The BRAVE program (Novick, 2000) provides a broader array of bystander behaviors, identifying seven pro-social strategies that allow students to accept shared responsibility and intervene in an appropriate manner when bullying occurs. Using the acronym *LEADERS,* these strategies offer bystanders choices to lead rather than follow before, during and after bullying occurs. Suggested strategies include: using distraction or humor, being socially inclusive, telling adults, standing up to bullies, supporting victims, leaving no one out, and refusing to be involved in spreading rumors.

In dozens of classroom workshops, several patterns have emerged in students' responses to these strategies. Students often give lip service to the notion of **standing up** to bullies, and may even do so in role-plays. In reality, as research attests (Committee for Children, 2001), few students respond in this manner. Students clearly require practice in delivering assertive responses to bullies before they will confront them. **Distraction** is an indirect means of diverting the bully's or victim's attention, and requires minimal direct confrontation. Many students have not entertained this possibility and welcome it as a do-able and "safe" way to intervene. The strategy of **supporting victims** is inherently appealing to some students, and distressing to others. As a humanitarian act, students understand it is the right thing to do. As the Committee for Children suggests, empathy for bullied peers is more likely to result in a supportive response if "children have a repertoire of assertive response options" (2001, p.14). Students may need to learn to recognize the obvious and subtle ways support can be given, both in the moment and at a later time. Some students may have significant concern that supporting or including a victim, particularly one from an unpopular group, will cause negative social contagion— "*uncoolness*" will rub off. Significant opportunities for discussion should be provided to help students understand the difference between being inclusive and being everyone's best friend. **Humor** and other de-intensifying strategies also require considerable explanation and rehearsal.

Two of the strategies used in many programs present a challenge in that they relate to *leshon ha-ra`*. A critical component of a bully's power comes from the rumor mill that cements the reputation of both bully and victim. Even when they assume they are being helpful, students who spread rumors warning of a bully's impending attack further heighten the bully's status and highlight the victim's weakness. Most students accept that such rumors are not helpful and in Jewish schools where the prohibition against *leshon ha-ra`* has been inculcated from an early age, this notion is an easy sell. Since Jewish educators recognize that despite frequent lessons and ongoing *musar*, rumors continue in their settings (Amsel, 1987), this should be revisited and addressed directly in the context of bully prevention.

Central in virtually all bully prevention is the goal of having responsible bystanders **tell adults** when bullying happens. It is only with such open communication that all members of the school community can share responsibility for creating a caring environment. In secular settings, educators encounter the developmentally appropriate mistrust of adults, and the strong social prohibition against *ratting out* one's peers. Students have, by late elementary or middle school, been educated to "solve problems on your own" and to avoid "tattle-telling." In addition, it is not uncommon for students to have the experience of informing an adult and receiving no help, or the situation actually being worsened. In the 2003 study of students' views about bullying commissioned by the British Department for Education and Skills, students viewed telling teachers about bullying as accompanied by a "wide range of risks, particularly in relation to possible breaches of confidentiality, failure to act on reported incidents of bullying, and an inability to protect pupils from retaliatory action" (Oliver & Candappa, 2003, p.4). In Jewish schools, where education in avoiding *leshon ha-ra`* is in place, there is often an additional hurdle to overcome in expecting students to tell adults about bullying. Partnership with the Rabbinic leaders and with classroom Rebbeim may be crucial. It has been the author's experience that it is helpful to draw a parallel between how *piku`ah nefesh* supersedes the *issur* against *leshon ha-ra`* in the case of physical harm, and similar requirements to speak up when non-physical, but significant emotional or social harm is being done.

A word of caution is necessary at this point regarding the assertive strategy of **standing up to bullies**. Schools may discover a Machiavellian phenomenon. Students may feel that the only or best way to be responsible, active, bystanders is to stand up to bullies in powerful, aggressive means. This may include students considering the use of physical or verbal threats to the bully, or socially excluding him or her. Students need constant reminders that they can stand up to bullies, as well as use other bystander options, without themselves becoming bullies.

Ongoing Social Processing

Research documents that effective bully prevention is possible only when there are ongoing opportunities for student social processing. This usually takes the form of regularly scheduled discussion groups. Olweus' program (1993) adapted the concept of a quality circle and recommended that quality circles occur weekly in each class, and be conducted among staff as well. Many other programs include regular discussions, if not weekly, then on a regular basis.

No research is available on the specific content of ongoing discussion groups. Given the focus on shared responsibility, it should not be surprising that the Olweus program's quality circles center on discussions of how students did and could respond to actual instances of bullying in the school setting. The BRAVE program manualized quality circles, providing teachers with cue cards, and training and support on both process and content (Novick, 2000).

A compelling reason to include regular discussion groups in bully prevention programs is the clear message such discussions send students about adults' interest in and concern about the social climate of the school. Students are more likely to report bullying incidents to teachers who are better at listening to pupils, prepared to take them seriously, and known to take firm but fair action (Oliver & Candappa, 2003). What better way for educators to communicate these qualities than by sitting with students on a regular basis and helping them seriously review and address their social concerns.

Ongoing social processing groups also provide opportunities for additional practice of social problem solving and role-playing of bystander strategies. The BRAVE program uses quality circles to allow students to review and change the messages their behavior sends to bullies or victims, and to generate and practice alternate behaviors (Novick, 2000). Similar to learning the skills of math or Hebrew reading, learning the skills of bully prevention requires ongoing practice. The challenge for Jewish schools in providing such vehicles is the complexity of scheduling in the dual curriculum setting. No research yet exists to inform decisions as to whether such ongoing discussions should occur monthly with the same faculty, and therefore be limited to either religious or general studies, whether they should occur in class-sized groups or unite all sections of a grade as a social unit, or be single or mixed gender.

Rules and Consequences

A major component of effective bully prevention in Olweus and other programs is the establishment of rules and consequences both to prevent bullying and to address it when it occurs. In order to create the appropriate school culture, Olweus (1993) suggests the following three rules be established, posted and explained to students:

- We do not bully others.
- We do not stand by when others are being bullied.
- We tell an adult when bullying occurs.

A positive re-wording of these rules yields:

- We treat all students with respect and kindness.
- We do something to help when we see another treated disre-spectfully or unkindly.
- We tell adults when we see others treated disrespectfully or unkindly.

There is a strong movement in the public sector to mandate that schools establish formal policies and procedures regarding bullying. As of July 2003, fifteen states had enacted anti-bullying legislation and thirteen additional states had legislation that was related to, although not specifically named as anti-bullying (Furlong, Morrison, & Grief, 2003). As of December 2009, 41 states had some laws in effect, but eight of those were rated with a grade of C or poorer by the watchdog organization Bully Police, USA, and only fifteen states have achieved an A rating or better (Bully Police, 2009). State legislation may require that schools adopt anti-bullying programs, develop procedures for reporting and tracking bullying, provide disciplinary consequences, or offer training to faculty (Limber & Small, 2003). In the best case scenario, such policies are developed through a process that allows input from all members of the school community. The New Jersey Department of Education, recognizing the challenge of creating such policies, developed a website which includes model policy statement components for schools to adapt. The suggested language for the basic policy statement is:

> The board of education prohibits acts of harassment, intimidation or bullying. The board of education has determined that a safe and civil environment in school is necessary for students to learn and achieve high academic

standards; harassment, intimidation or bullying, like other disruptive or violent behaviors, is conduct that disrupts both a student's ability to learn and a school's ability to educate its students in a safe environment; and since students learn by example, school administrators, faculty, staff and volunteers should be commended for demonstrating appropriate behavior, treating others with civility and respect and refusing to tolerate harassment, intimidation or bullying (New Jersey Department of Education, 2002).

In addition, the New Jersey guidelines set the tone for school-wide, ongoing and cooperative efforts to address bullying.

The board of education believes that standards for student behavior must be set cooperatively through interaction among the students, parents and guardians, staff and community members of the school district, producing an atmosphere that encourages students to grow in self-discipline. The development of this atmosphere requires respect for self and others, as well as for district and community property on the part of students, staff and community members.

Policies and rules do not guarantee a bully-free school environment. The most effective bully prevention programs eliminate only 50–75% of bullying. It is critical, therefore, to establish clear procedures to handle bullying when it occurs. Schools typically utilize disciplinary measures that exist for other rule infractions, such as detention, suspension, loss of privileges, and letters or phone calls to parents. In secular settings, formal school discipline plans, written codes of conduct and specific anti-bullying policies are common place, and often mandated (Smith, Smith, Osborn, & Samara, 2008). Jewish schools may not be subject to such mandates, and may opt for more informal approaches to policy and discipline.

Establishing and implementing policies and consequences for bullying and other negative social behaviors can prove extremely challenging. Since many of these peer to peer social problems occur out of adult vision, school administrators are faced with difficult determinations of guilt. For this reason, it is highly recommended that schools keep a log of reported bullying difficulties (National Resource Center for Safe Schools, 1999). While a teacher may witness a single, seemingly unremarkable act, reviewing prior log entries may reveal that the same student has been seen to engage in similar behavior. Equally helpful is a regular forum for faculty to review the social climate of the class, grade and school, and to generate strategies for addressing those students with social difficulties. Such regular discussions are difficult in Yeshiva and Day School settings where *Limudei Kodesh* and general studies teachers often have limited time to co-plan, and may not be in the building at the same time. If face to face meetings are impossible to coordinate, alternate strategies for communicating about students and social climate may be necessary, such as using email and other technology, creating a log or journal system, or having each set of teachers discuss issues with a central staff member.

Jewish school settings face an additional challenge when developing policies and consequences to address bullying, harassment, and social exclusion. Unlike public schools, they are generally governed by or answer to a lay board. In some instances, this board may be comprised of powerful members of the community. Can teachers and administrators feel safe in establishing and enacting policies that may directly affect children of such powerful community members? This presents a significant dilemma for our community, since we are asking children to do the right thing, even when it is difficult and may have consequences, while adults may not feel comfortable doing so.

Practical Recommendations

Given adequate resources, financial and human, the clear choice in addressing bullying is the systematic, evidence-based, school-wide approaches addressed above. Fortunately, even when resources are limited, or schools are not prepared to mount a comprehensive initiative, there is much that can be done to build a caring culture and decrease bullying. The practical suggestions that follow begin with pitfalls to be avoided, and include actions teachers, administrators, and families in Jewish schools can take to make a difference.

Common Pitfalls

Indiscretion: Several years ago a girl in a coed day school complained that she was taunted by boys in surrounding classrooms when she walked towards the resource room. Standing at their classroom doors they would call "retard," or "there goes dummy." The third grader rallied her courage and shared her distress with a school administrator. Incensed at this non-appropriate behavior, the administrator promptly visited all the girl's classes, and delivered a powerful discussion of *mussar* centering on the proper respect due girls and women. The following day, on the bus, at recess and lunch, the girl was routinely berated for "getting us into trouble." The well-intentioned administrator had never revealed his source. How did the boys know who complained? The administrator did not realize that only one girl used the resource room in that hallway.

Invariably, adults want to fix painful situations, and our tendency is to do so through direct means. In the case of bullying, adults must always ask what the likely consequences of their actions will be. While a *Rebbe* can protect a child teased at recess by having him sit next to him, this may further identify him as different, or weak. When students do come forward to report bullying, it is critical that we protect both the victim and the informant from any further cruelty or retribution.

Conflict resolution and peer mediation: There are numerous resources and protocols available for engaging students in conflict resolution and peer mediation. Conflict resolution programs generally involve skills training for students on ways to independently solve interpersonal conflicts. Peer mediation programs train student mediators to conduct formal mediation sessions between fellow students who have experienced some conflict. To be done effectively, these approaches require significant ongoing adult supervision. In the case of bullying, traditional peer mediation is strongly contra-indicated. Peer mediation assumes a dispute has occurred between equal parties. When bullying occurs, by definition, one party (the bully) is a good deal more powerful than the other (the victim). The most likely outcome of peer mediation applied in bullying instances is that the victim will be re-victimized, but in a sanctioned, public way. This can be more damaging than the original bullying, as it leaves the victim feeling totally unprotected and without recourse.

Bullies as bosses: Schools may attempt to harness the power of bullies by placing them in charge. Bullies are not infrequently appointed bus counselor, hall monitor, etc. There is great danger in this approach, as Machiavelli suggested. Bullies have already experienced the corruption of power. Why would granting them additional power be helpful? Similarly, on occasion, schools have asked bullies to make retribution for their misdeeds in a way that provides them with inordinate power. Consider the Jewish high school that discovered seniors were creating hazing rituals for freshmen. These wise seniors convinced the administration that despite the humiliation and discomfort such rituals involved, they had the best interest of their schoolmates in mind; they wanted to insure the new students bonded with each other. The well-meaning administration, hoping to capitalize on the seniors' reported pro-social intentions, gave them the responsibility to plan all freshman social events. One can see how this might be a bit like asking a fox whose belly is full of chicken to guard the coop.

Expecting resolution and restitution: From their earliest days in school, students are taught to correct their errors. Students are asked to make restitution for their acts, and to offer apologies to those they have hurt. It is not recommended that bullies be made to face their victims and apologize. There is a significant risk that even in the context of an apology, the victim will be further humiliated, traumatized or frightened. It is appropriate, of course, to have the bully express remorse for their behavior. This can be done in writing, or to a school faculty member who can assess the genuineness of the sentiment and whether it can be communicated to the victim. There are similar risks in requiring bullies to make restitution to victims. The bully who torments a peer at lunch, and is made to carry that child's lunch, or clean the lunch table, may develop and express additional antagonism towards his victim.

Staff Attitudes and Behaviors

Since effective bully prevention centers on empowering students as bystanders, it is tempting to assume that staff attitudes and behaviors are of limited importance. In fact, one of the most effective ways to change student behavior is to change the behavior of the adults in the environment (OSEP Center on PBIS, 2004). School staff may need both knowledge and assistance to support bully prevention. Teachers often are inaccurate in identifying bullies (Leff, et al., 1999) and may feel less than confident in their abilities to deal with the issue (Boulton, 1997). Recent research on teachers in Jewish schools underscores the critical role feeling prepared to address bullying plays in supporting effective teacher efforts (Novick & Isaacs, in press). Often, however, it is not lack of educator knowledge or skill that hampers bully prevention, but the attitudes described below that are less than helpful.

I teach a subject—not friendship: Curricular demands can result in educators becoming overly focused on curriculum content and forget that first and foremost, schools teach *children*. To teach children effectively, educators must attend to all aspects of their development: academic, spiritual, moral, emotional, behavioral, and social. The creative teacher invariably finds a connection between these "non-academic" elements of development and the subject they teach. Recently a middle school science teacher commented that he planned on teaching a lesson on emulsifiers. "After the demonstration, I will tell the students that we all need to be social emulsifiers, to help the different groups in our school mix better," he remarked.

I do not have time to deal with these issues: Yeshiva and day school teachers are perennially provided with less on-task and teaching time than they would like or need. It is natural to assume that focusing on behavioral and social-emotional issues will further limit available teaching time. On the contrary, the research on PBIS has documented the gains in academic time with an initial investment in behavioral and school culture issues (Putnam, Horner & Algozzine, 2006). A third grade girl's teacher discovered this phenomenon when she initiated weekly post-recess discussions. On Friday afternoons, she led the students in a discussion of the concerns they had written in a recess "concerns" box. The teacher reported greatly improved concentration and increased teaching time as girls learned their issues would be addressed at the appropriate time.

Boys will be boys, girls can be mean: Many adults betray their sense of hopelessness and helplessness in statements that underscore the pervasiveness of bullying. Unfortunately, such statements become excuses for inaction. If bullying is seen as an integral part of growing up, something all children need to tolerate, why address it in schools? If students are certain to act with cruelty, why strive for niceness? Fortunately, forward thinking individuals throughout history have demonstrated that simply because a problem existed in the past, it does not need to remain problematic forever. It is with this attitude that polio has been all but eradicated and new technologies and strategies allow remediation of learning problems that previously were uncorrectable. When a commitment is made to creating safe, socially constructive schools, those schools can become a reality.

Staff attitudes are critical because they shape staff behavior. Educators have a major influence on bullying as role models. If students see teachers treat each other or treat students disrespectfully, they are likely to behave similarly. Effective bully prevention supports the notion that all people should be treated kindly, and that everyone is valued. Students cannot learn this lesson if their teachers or administrators model inequitable treatment, humiliation, or abuse of power. In a presentation at the 2004 Nefesh International Conference in Israel, Rabbi Abraham J. Twerski explained how even simple and subtle inequitable behaviors can send a powerful message. The person who, after grocery shopping, places their shopping cart behind the car next to them sends the message that "I am important, the people in that car don't matter . . . let them put my cart away." Educators need to be particularly aware of the messages about interpersonal equity their behavior sends to students.

Faculty's largest impact on bullying occurs when they themselves are bystanders. When students see an adult witness bullying, and that adult does nothing, multiple messages are communicated. Students read such inaction not as neutral, but as support for bullying. Bullies receive a clear signal that their actions will be tolerated, and are likely to continue and perhaps expand their aggression. Victims receive the devastating message that they cannot expect adults to protect them or end their torment.

Addressing the Needs of Victims

Even schools utilizing the most effective bully prevention programs will be confronted with victims who require support and guidance. Students identify counselors and other confidential sources of support as helpful in dealing with victimization (Oliver & Candappa, 2003). Since victims are often selected as targets because of their reactivity, counseling aimed at decreasing their emotionality may be helpful. Reactivity is, however, a temperamental factor, highly influenced by genetics and biology and helping students change it is particularly challenging. Cognitive behavioral strategies that teach both reinterpretation of events (cognitive restructuring) and alternative behaviors (assertiveness training, anger management) may be useful. The author has had some success helping students "act" in a non-reactive way, despite their subjective experiences. Often, such students have been told to "just ignore" bullying, and not to let it "bother you." For a reactive student, such advice is not only impossible; it indicates a failure of empathy on the part of the advice giver. In asking reactive students to "act" unaffected, students can feel validated and understood, while being encouraged to develop a temporary "performance" strategy.

Research consistently demonstrates the protective benefit of friendship for victims (Committee on Children, 2001). Parents and educators can greatly help victims by building their friendship skills and creating additional opportunities for developing friendships. Schools that feel friendship building is not their responsibility should recognize that through cooperative learning and other regularly occurring school activities there are numerous opportunities to provide students with this significant buffer against bullying.

Curricular Connections

The ideas and practices of effective bully prevention can be easily supported with standard content from the secular and *Limudei Kodesh* curricula. A few suggestions are offered below.

Limudei Kodesh:

Parashat HaShavua, *Humash*, and *Halacha* offer excellent materials for discussing the Torah view of interpersonal relationships. Many schools develop *middot* or *hesed* programs, which dovetail with the values necessary for bully prevention. Such programs are often focused outside the school setting; i.e. assisting the elderly, giving to the needy in other countries. It is critical to bring the lessons into the microcosm of the class and school. Students must be helped to understand *hesed* is as important, and at times more challenging to accomplish, when it is offered to the person next to you.

The Jewish calendar can provide tie-ins to bully prevention. *Rosh Hashana, Sefirat HaOmer*, and *Rosh Hodesh*, are times when taking-stock of behavior and committing to new goals is the norm. Hanukkah and Purim provide examples of social responsibility, where an individual or group assisted *K'lal Yisrael* through their brave actions. A *mishloah manot* lesson the author observed in a third grade boys class involved each student receiving blank cut-outs of candy and goodies. On each item, the boys wrote a compliment for one of their fellow students. Each boy proudly collected his *mishloah manot* compliments and placed them in a construction paper basket! The excitement and genuine sense of community in the room was palpable. *Sukkot, Pesach, Tu B'Shevat, Shavuot;* every festive holiday can be connected to the critical Torah teaching of *ve-ahavta le-rei-`akha kamokha*.

It is hard to imagine how one could teach the *Shoah* without addressing the issues bullying raises: intolerance, peer pressure, social responsibility, bystander apathy. I recently asked 7th grade day school students at a bully prevention workshop whether it is really so terrible to do nothing when bullying happens. A girl called out "I'll explain why in two words: Hitler and Czechoslovakia."

General Studies:

Both the content of general studies subjects, and the methods teachers use can support bully prevention. Literature and history offer natural connections to bullying issues. Videos allow teachers to stop the action and discuss social issues and solutions to interpersonal dilemmas. Students are often better able to demonstrate empathy when discussing characters in videos, novels or history than their own classmates. It is also "safer" for students to judge the social interactions of others than to admit their own shortcomings.

All teachers can contribute to bully prevention by developing a positive social climate in the classroom. Teachers influence this when they group students and teach them to work at cooperative learning tasks and when they help students learn how to respond when peers make errors. In a fourth grade classroom, a teacher underscored respect for peers in a concrete way. Whenever a student was called on to respond, she prompted, "Are we showing respect to our classmate, are we ready to listen?" At this, the students turned their bodies to face the called-on student and waited for his response. After class, when asked if this seemingly time-consuming strategy was worth while she replied: "The students are so much more respectful, and the class runs so smoothly, we're actually ahead of the other fourth grade classes!"

The Power of Positives

Focus on the positive behaviors that negate bullying can prove as productive as work to eliminate bullying behaviors. Educators do well to find and celebrate instances of kindness, leadership, social responsibility, and empathy in their students. In many cases, personal celebration may mean as much or more than a certificate, or posting on a bulletin board. A word from a teacher or *Rebbe* to a student who asked a socially excluded peer to sit with them can make a strong impression. Several years ago, a 6th grade teacher told of a student who had assisted another in the class for the entire year. She had done so without being asked, and despite the frequent taunts by classmates this slower student endured. Taken by the girl's kindheartedness, the teacher privately gave her a small gift at the end of the year. If this girl's acts of kindness were celebrated in a more public way, with genuine warmth and care, it could have served as a wonderful example for others.

Focusing on such moral exemplars, positive examples beyond the school building, can have a powerful impact (Walker, 2006). Current events and people who embody positive characteristics should be brought to students' attention. Classes may write letters of admiration or support to public figures who demonstrate the characteristics bully prevention strives to build.

Informal Settings—Camps, Community Organizations and Synagogues

Wherever there are children's social groups there can be bullying. In observant Jewish communities such social groups occur in schools, synagogues, youth groups and camps, with many children belonging to overlapping groups. No research has been completed on bullying in these settings, in either the Jewish or secular world, but consideration of their social dynamics may yield some suggestions.

Whether in the form of Shabbat groups or recreational trips and holiday events, synagogue programming for children is generally directed by a lay committee, staffed by one or a small number of paid young adults and teen and/or parent volunteers. Unlike school staff, there are neither requirements nor guarantees that any of those involved have professional training in child development or education. Similarly, in youth groups, primary contact with and responsibility for children is often in the hands of older teens and young adults who themselves were once members of the youth group. Many local youth groups are branches of national organizations, allowing children to socialize beyond their home community.

Camps, while less formal than schools, have significant structure and considerable paid staff, ranging in age and expertise. Moore, (2001) argues that camps have unstable and seasonal attendance creating temporary relationships and minimal rewards for popularity and social status. In the Jewish world, camps are often an extension of the school community, with fairly stable attendance and fostering significant and long-term, if long-distance relationships. Camp friendships and experiences may therefore play a significant role in the lives of Jewish children.

While research has yet to determine if bullying in the above settings is different in nature or intensity than that in schools, there is reason to be concerned. In these informal settings staff may not have had the benefit of education about bullying or social relationships. In some cases, staff may be only slightly older than their charges and barely recovered from their own experiences with cliques or bullying. Since many appropriate strategies for managing bullying issues are counterintuitive, it is both possible and likely that without training even well-meaning staff may inadvertently contribute to the problem. Even within the structured environment of school, bullying is most frequent in bathrooms, at recess, and other less structured or supervised venues. Camp and other informal settings offer additional times when children are unstructured and less supervised, perhaps allowing bullying of greater severity and frequency. Expanding the development of positive social environments beyond the school building is clearly necessary, and will require extensive outreach and engagement across the informal education spectrum.

Family Issues

It would seem logical that families contribute to the behavior of bullies, victims and bystanders. A great deal of research on aggression exists, but only a few studies have explored the relationship between families and bullying. Bullies' families are often described as lacking in nurturance, commonly using physical punishment and teaching that physical aggression is an acceptable way to address problems (Merrell et al., 2006; Oregon Resilience Project, 2003). High levels of marital conflict have also been associated with increased aggression in children. Rodkin & Hodges (2003) discuss parenting practices and victimization. Parenting practices that interfere with the development of children's autonomy may contribute to victimization. For boys, maternal over-protectiveness and intense mother-child closeness has been associated with victimization. Girls who are victims, however, are more likely to come from families that employ coercion and threats of rejection. The authors report an important contradiction. Whereas early research found a relationship between harsh home environment and victimization, this was only the case for children with few friends. Friendships, and other extra-familial factors can either ameliorate or exacerbate children's victimization.

Educators invested in creating positive social environments and addressing bullying will, undoubtedly confront a variety of parental attitudes. The educator's task, in bully prevention and all areas, would be made easier if families supported them fully. When addressing issues as sensitive as interpersonal relationships, families may have very different ideas than schools. Schools cannot require or expect that families change their parenting styles, or belief systems. A question frequently asked by school administrators and teachers is, therefore, "how can we expect students to follow rules and behave in a certain way, when their families have different expectations?" Children are capable, from quite an early age, to differentiate between divergent expectations in different settings. They know that Grandma gives cookies even if you do not finish your vegetables, but Mommy does not. Students quickly learn all the ways that the rules at school are different from those at home. Schools therefore have both the opportunity *and* the obligation to create expectations for student behavior that will support a positive social climate.

The fact that schools *can* create their social climate independent of family input does not mean that they *should* do so. Schools should make every attempt to engage families in bully prevention much as they engage them in supporting academic programs. For families to become involved, they must be kept informed. Newsletters and written information can be combined with workshops. Some schools have scheduled parent-child programs to boost attendance, or invited parents to bully-themed performances by their children. However it is accomplished, as is true with academic achievement, children benefit when parent-school partnerships are established and nourished.

Techno-bullying

As this article goes to print, it is likely that students are commandeering new technologies to build their social networks. The New York Times, reporting a Pew Internet and American Life study, reports that 87% of children aged 12 to 17 are regularly online, 11 million at least once each day! Eighty-four percent own cellphones and portable mp3 players, laptops and BlackBerrys. Unfortunately, in addition to the many social benefits technology offers, it also allows the anonymous, rapid, and widespread dissemination of social aggression. Many agencies and publications discuss cyberbullying, but current technology allows bullying to go beyond the computer. Smith, et al. (2008) identify 7 types of technological bullying including text message, picture/video clip via cell phone, email, chat-room, instant message and website bullying. Techno-bullying presents a number of challenges. Children are often more knowledgeable than adults about the latest technology, making supervision difficult. The vast majority of techno-bullying is accomplished outside the school building and after school hours, also complicating issues of supervision and jurisdiction.

There are a wide range of attitudes across Jewish educational settings regarding computer and technology usage. Restriction on technology is unlikely to eliminate techno-bullying. As students increasingly develop social relationships supported by technology, schools will be called upon to educate students about appropriate social behaviors for in-person and technological relationships.

Conclusion

Bullying is a complex social phenomenon that exists as part of the even more complex school social culture unique to each educational setting. Schools wishing to address this challenging issue require specific knowledge, since the most effective strategies are, at times, counterintuitive. Numerous areas of research including exploration of moral development, social development, group dynamics, peer relationships, and aggression contribute to our knowledge base in addressing bullying. Literature on bully prevention, in particular, offers educators a straightforward, if challenging formula for effecting social change in the school setting.

Increasingly, state and federal mandates are requiring schools to devote the time and energy necessary to create physically and emotionally safe environments for all students. Jewish schools do not require a government mandate to invest in the values that support bully prevention. Compelled to impart to students the Torah imperative: *Do not stand by while your brother bleeds*, day schools and Yeshivot cannot stand idle when bullying occurs in their midst. The significant body of literature and evidence based programs complement Torah teachings and should inform efforts in this area. But bully prevention in Jewish schools can and should be about more. It should be a means to a rather compelling end; an opportunity to fulfill the grandest mission of *Hinukh*. When Jewish schools teach students the concepts behind bullying, they teach them the central precepts of the Torah. When Jewish schools teach students the skills to be socially responsible peer leaders, as opposed to inactive followers, they contribute to the creation of a generation of *B'nei Torah* prepared to support *K'lal Yisrael* in the years to come.

Additional Torah/Rabbinic citations to support bully prevention:

Pirkei Avot, (2:10): "Your friend's dignity should be as precious to you as your own"

Pirkei Avot (4:12): "Let the honor of your student be as dear to you as your own."

Shulhan Arukh, Orah Hayyim (339:4): Avoidance of humiliating others can, in certain cases, take precedence over observance of halachot. The Ramah ruled that a wedding can be performed on Shabbat to avoid public shame or humiliation.

Bereishit (45:1): When Yosef is about to reveal his identity and confront his brothers, he asks all others to leave the room because he could not bear to let his brothers be embarrassed in front of bystanders (Rashi).

Megillat Esther (2:21–23): Mordechai overhears officers plotting to kill King Ahasverus. It is not considered Lashon Hara to act as he did and immediately have the information brought to the King.

Sanhedrin 11a: The story of Rabbi Judah who, while giving a lecture was annoyed by the smell of garlic. "Let the one who has eaten garlic go out" he announced. The great sage Rabbi Hiyya immediately stood and left. Rabbi Hiyya was not the one who ate garlic, but rather wanted to avoid the humiliation of a person who was not a renowned scholar and who would surely be embarrassed.

Moed Katan 27a: The practice was for rich people to bring food to the house of a mourner in silver *kelim*. Poor people brought their contributions in straw baskets. The Rabbis ruled that all should bring their contributions in straw baskets so as not to embarrass the poor.

Mishna Sanhedrin 4:5: "Let not a man say to his fellow, my father was greater than your father."

Rambam, Laws of Character Development (6:8): Do not humiliate your fellow in public, whether he is a minor or adult.

Sharei Teshuvah, Rabbi Jonah Gerondi (3:221): We are obligated to relate *Lashon Hara* if an innocent victim will suffer if you don't speak.

Taanit (20 a–b): This includes the story of Rabbi Elazar ben Shimon and the ugly man. The scholar asks an ugly person if everyone from his town is as ugly as him. The man replies "tell the craftsman

who made me, how ugly is the vessel that you made." The story ends with Rabbi Elazar begging for forgiveness.
Yiddish saying: What is a hero? One who suppresses a wisecrack.

References

American Association of University Women Educational Foundation. (1998). *Separated by sex: A critical look at single sex education for girls.* Washington DC: American Association of University Women.

Amsel, N. (1987). The *middot* and Jewish values crisis in our schools: What to do. *Ten Da'at, 2(2),* 8–10.

Asch, S. (1956). Studies of independence and conformity: A minority of one against a unanimous majority. *Psychological Monographs, 70*(9).

Banks, S. (2000). Addressing violence in middle schools. *The Clearing House, 73*(4), 209–211.

Batson, C. D. (1987). Prosocial motivation: Is it ever truly altruistic? *Advances in Experimental and Social Psychology, 20,* 65–122.

Batson, C. D., & Thompson, E. R. (2001). Why don't moral people act morally? Motivational considerations. *Current Directions in Psychological Science, 10*(2), 54.

Benninga, J. S., Berkowitz, M. W., Kuehn, P., & Smith, K. (2006). Character and academics: What good schools do. *Phi Delta Kappa International.* Retrieved October 27, 2006, from http://www.pdkintl.org/kappan/k0602ben.htm

Berenstain, S., & Berenstain, J. (1993). *The Berenstain bears and the bully.* New York: Random House Books.

Black, S. (2003). *An ongoing evaluation of the bullying prevention program in Philadelphia schools*: Student survey and student observation data. Paper presented at Center for Disease Control's Safety in Numbers Conference, Atlanta, GA.

Boulton, M. J. (1997). Teachers' views on bullying: Definitions, attitudes and ability to cope. *British Journal of Educational Psychology, 67,* 223–233.

Brutsaert, H., & Van Houtte, M. (2002). Girls' and boys' sense of belonging in single-sex versus co-educational schools. *Research in Education, 68,* 48–56.

Bully Police, USA. (2009). Retrieved December 13, 2009, from http://www.bullypolice.org/

Caple, K. (1994). *The wimp.* New York: Houghton Mifflin Company.

Card, N. A. (2003). *Victims of peer aggression*: A meta-analytic review. Presented at Society for Research in Child Development biennial meeting (April), Tampa, FL.

Cillessen, A. H. N., & Mayeux, L. (2004). From censure to reinforcement: Developmental changes in the association between aggression and social status. *Child Development, 75*(1), 147–163.

Cohen, I. J., Kress, J. S., & Elias, M. (2002). Classroom climate in an orthodox day school: The contribution of emotional intelligence, demographics and classroom context. *Journal of Jewish Education, 68*, 21–33.

DeRosier, M. E., & Marcus, S. R. (2005). Building friendships and combating bullying: Effectiveness of S. S.Grin at one-year follow-up. *Journal of Clinical Child and Adolescent Psychology, 34*(1), 140–150.

Espelage, D. L., & Swearer, S. M. (2003). Research on school bullying and victimization: What have we learned and where do we go from here? *School Psychology Review*, 32(3), 365–383.

Frank, B., Kehler, M., Lovell, T., & Davison, K. (2003). A tangle of trouble: Boys, masculinity and schooling—Future directions. *Educational Review, 55*, 119–133.

Frey, K. S., Hirschstein, M. K., Snell, J. L., Edstron, L. V. S., MacKenzie, E. P., &

Broderick, C. J. (2005). Reducing playground bullying and supporting beliefs: An experimental trial of the steps to respect program. *Developmental Psychology, 41*(3). 479–491.

Furlong, M. J., Morrison, R., & Greif, J. L. (2003). Reaching an American consensus: Reactions to the special issue on school bullying. *School Psychology Review, 32*(3), 456–470.

Goldberg, S. J. (2005). Hebrew reading difficulties and social exclusion: A path to aggressive behavior. *Jewish Leadership Journal*, Fall. Lookstein Center for Jewish Education in the Diaspora. Retrieved August 25, 2006. from http://www.lookstein.org/online_journal.php?id=74

Haney, C., Banks, W. C., & Zimbardo, P. G. (1973). Interpersonal dynamics in a simulated prison. *International Journal of Criminology and Penology, 1* (Fall), 69-97.

Haidt, J. (2001). The emotional dog and its rational tail: A social intuitionist approach to moral judgment. *Psychological Review, 108*(4), 814-834.

Hawker, D. S. J., & Boulton, M. J. (2000). Twenty years research on peer victimization and psychosocial maladjustment: A meta-analytic review of cross-sectional students. *Journal of Child Psychiatry and Psychiatry, 41*, 441–455.

Howe, J. (1996). *Pinky and Rex and the bully.* New York: Aladdin Publishing.

Israel, B. (2006). The overconnecteds. *New York Times,* Education Life Supplement, Sunday, November 5, 20–22.

Juvonen, J., Graham, S., & Schuster, M. A. (2003). Bullying among young adolescents: The strong, the weak and the troubled. *Pediatrics, 112*(6), 1231–1237.

Leckie, B. (1997). Girls, bullying behaviors and peer relationships: The double-edged sword of exclusion and rejection. Retrieved October 31, 2006, from http://eric.ed.gov/ERICDocs/data/ericdocs2/content_storage_01/0000000b/80/0d/ac/20.pdf

Leff, S. S. (2006). The friend-to-friend program: Initial evaluation of a school-based aggression-prevention program fro inner-city African American girls. *Developmental and Behavioral Pediatrics, 27*(5), 430.

Leff, S. S., Kupersmidt, J. B., Patterson, C. J., & Power, T. J. (1999). Factors influencing teacher identification of peer bullies and victims. *School Psychology Review, 28,* 505–517.

Limber, S. P. (2004). Implementation of the Olweus bullying-prevention program: Lessons learned from the field. In D. Espelage & S. Swearer (Eds.), *Bullying in American schools: A social-ecological perspective on prevention and intervention* (pp. 351–363). Mahwah, NJ: Erlbaum.

Limber, S. P., & Small, M. A. (2003). State laws and policies to address bullying in schools. *School Psychology Review, 32*(3), 445–455.

Mael, F. A. (1998). Single-sex and coeducational schooling: Relationships to socioemotional and academic development. *Review of Educational Research, 68*(2), 101–129.

Maine Project Against Bullying. (1997). Retrieved October 30, 2006, from http://lincoln.midcoast.com/~wps/against/bullying.html

Mayer, M. (1999). *Just a bully.* New York: Golden Books.

Meddaugh, S. (1998). *Martha walks the dog.* New York: Houghton Mifflin.

Mellor, A. (1993). Finding out about bullying. *SCRE Spotlights*, The Scottish Council for Research in Education.

Merrell, K. W., Buchanan, R., & Tran, O. K. (2006). Relational aggression in children and adolescents: A review with implications for school settings. *Psychology in the Schools, 43*, 345–360.

Metcalf, J., & Mischel, W. (1999) A hot/cool-system analysis of delay of gratification: Dynamics of willpower. *Psychological Review, 106,* 3–19.

Mikami, A. Y., Boucher, M. A., & Humphreys, K. (2005). Prevention of peer rejection through a classroom-level intervention in middle school. *The Journal of Primary Prevention, 26*(1), 5–23.

Moore, V. A. (2001). Doing racialized and gendered age to organize peer relationships: Observing kids in summer camp. *Gender & Society, 15*(6), 835–858.

Moos, R., & Moos, B. (1978). Classroom social climate and student absences and grades. *Journal of Educational Psychology, 70,* 263–269.

Nansel, T. R., Craig, W., Overpeck, M., Saluja, G., & Ruan, J. (2004). Cross-national consistency in the relationship between bullying behaviors and psychosocial adjustment. *Archives of Pediatrics and Adolescent Medicine, 158,* 730–736.

Nansel, T. T., Overpeck, K. G., Pilla, R. S., Ruan, W. J., & Simons-Morton, B. G. (2001). Bullying behaviors among U.S. youth: Prevalence and association with psychosocial adjustment. *Journal of the American Medical Association, 285,* 2094–2100.

National Association for Single Sex Public Education. (2005). Single-sex vs. coed: The evidence. Retrieved October 5, 2006, from http://www.singlesexschools.org/ research-singlesexvcoed.htm.

National Resource Center for Safe Schools. (1999). *Recognizing and preventing bullying.* (Fact Sheet No. 4). Portland, OR: Northwest Regional Educational Laboratory. Retrieved September 2, 2006, from http://www.safetyzone.org/publications/ fact4_index.html

New Jersey Department of Education. (2002). *Model policy prohibiting harassment, intimidation and bullying on school property, at school-sponsored functions, and on school busses.* Retrieved November 1, 2006, from www.nj.gov/njed/parents/bully.htm

Nishina, A., Juvonen, J., & Witkow, M. R. (2005). Sticks and stones may break my bones, but names will make me feel sick: The psychosocial, somatic and scholastic consequences of peer harassment. *Journal of Clinical Child and Adolescent Psychology, 34*(1), 37–48.

Novick, R. M., & Isaacs, J. (In press). Telling is compelling: Teacher impact of student bullying reports. *Educational Psychology.*

Novick, R. M. (2000). *BRAVE instructor manual.* New Hyde Park, NY: Alliance for School Mental Health.

Novick, R. M., Winkler, J., Czarka, A., & Isaacs, J. (2009). *Emerging trends in bullying in co-educational Jewish day schools.* Poster presented at Nefesh International Conference (December), Happauge, NY.

Oliver, C., & Candappa, M. (2003). Tackling bullying: Listening to the views of children and young people. *Research Report, 400,* Nottingham: DfES.

Olweus Bullying Prevention Program. (2006). Evidence of effectiveness. Retrieved October 1, 2006, from http://www. clemson.edu/olweus/content.html

Olweus, D. (1978). *Aggression in the schools. Bullies and whipping boys.* Washington, DC: Hemisphere Press (Wiley).

Olweus, D. (1993). *Bullying at school.* Malden, MA: Blackwell Publishing.

Olweus, D., Limber, S. P., & Mihalic, S. (1999*). The bullying prevention program: Blueprints for violence prevention* (Vol. 10). Boulder, CO: Center for the Study and Prevention of Violence.

Oregon Resilience Project. (2003). *Bullying in schools.* Retrieved November 3, 2006, from http://orp.uoregon.edu

OSEP Center on Positive Behavioral Interventions and Supports. (2004). School-wide positive behavior support implementers' blueprint and self-assessment. Center on Positive Behavioral Interventions and Supports, University of Oregon. Retrieved September 15, 2006, from http://www.pbis.org/researchLiterature. htm

Pelcovitz, D. (2005). The at-risk adolescent in the orthodox Jewish community: Implications and interventions for educators. *The Azrieli papers*: A project of the Azrieli Graduate School of Jewish Education and Administration. New York: Yeshiva University.

Putnam, R. F., Horner, R. H., & Algozzine, R. (2006). Academic achievement and the implementation of school-wide behavior support. *PBIS Newsletter, 3*(1). Retrieved October 10, 2006, from www.pbis.org/news/New/Default.aspx

Richardson, A. (1990). Classroom learning environments: Some differences among school types. *Perceptual and Motor Skills, 71,* 518.

Rodkin, P. C., & Hodges, E. V. E. (2003). Bullies and victims in the peer ecology: Four questions for psychologists and school professionals. *School Psychology Review, 32*(3), 384–400.

Ross, S., Horner, R., & Stiller, B. (2009). Bully prevention in positive behavior support for Middle Schools. Retrieved December 13, 2009, from http://www.pbis.org/common/pbisresources/publications/BullyPrevention_PBS_MS.pdf

Salmivalli, C. (2001). Peer-led intervention campaign against school bullying: Who considered it useful, who benefited? *Educational Research, 43*(3), 263–278.

Shute, R., Owens, L., & Slee, P. (2008). Everyday victimization of adolescent girls by boys: Sexual harassment, bullying or aggression? *Sex Roles, 58,* 477–490.

Smith, P. K., Mahdavi, J., Carvalho, M., Fisher, S., Russel, S., & Tippet, N. (2008). Cyberbullying: Its nature and impact in secondary school pupils. *The Journal of Child Psychology and Psychiatry, 49*(4), 376–385.

Smith, J. D., Schneider, B. H., Smith, P. K., & Ananiadou, K. (2004). The effectiveness of whole-school antibullying programs: A synthesis of evaluation research. *School Psychology Review, 33*(4), 547–561.

Smith, P. K., Cowie, H., Olafsson, R., & Liefooghe, A. P. D. (2002). Definitions of bullying: A comparison of terms used, and age and sex differences, in a 14- country international comparison. *Child Development, 73,* 1119–1133.

Smith, P., & Sharp, S. (1994). *School bullying: Insights and perspectives.* New York: Routledge.

Smith, P. K., Smith, C., Osborn, R., & Samara, M. (2008). A content analysis of school anti-bullying policies: Progress and limitations. *Educational Psychology in Practice, 24*(1), 1–12.

Sommers, C. H. (2006). How moral education is finding its way back into America's schools. In W. Damon (Ed.), *Bringing in a new era in character education.* Stanford: Hoover Press.

Spinelli, J. (2002). *The loser.* New York: Harper Collins Children's Books.

Underwood, M. K., Galen, B. R., & Paquette, J. A. (2001). Top ten challenges for understanding gender and aggression in children: Why can't we all just get al.ong? *Social Development, 10,* 268–271.

148 RONA NOVICK

Underwood, M. K. (2002). Sticks and stones and social exclusion: Aggression among girls and boys. In P. K. Smith & C. H. Hart (Eds.), *Blackwell handbook of childhood social development* (pp. 533–548). Oxford: Blackwell.
U.S. Department of Education. (1998). *Preventing bullying: A manual for schools and communities.* Washington, D.C. Retrieved September 20, 2006, from http://www.cde.ca.gov/ssp/bullymanual.htm
U.S. Department of Health and Human Services (2006). *SAMHSA model program: The Olweus bullying prevention program.* Retrieved October 25, 2006, from http://modelprograms.samhsa.gov
Walker, H. M., Horner, R. H., Sugai, G., Bullis, M., Sprague, J. R., Bricker, D. et al. (1996). Integrated approaches to preventing antisocial behavior patterns among school-age children and youth. *Journal of Emotional and Behavioral Disorders, 4,* 193–256.
Walker, L. J. (2006). Moral exemplarity. In W. Damon (Ed.), *Bringing in a new era in character education.* Stanford: Hoover Press.
Wilkerson, K., & Eschbach, L. (2009). Transformed school counseling: The impact of a graduate course on trainees' perceived readiness to develop comprehensive, data-driven programs. *Professional School Counseling, 13*(1), 30-38.

Religious Development in Adolescence:
A Work in Progress

Jay Goldmintz

Defining the Problem

Ironically, one of the primary principles that all Jewish educators hold dear is the demand: *hanokh la-na`ar al pi darko*, that we take into account the individual differences of our students.[1] It is ironic because for all of our sensitivity to this issue, our community has only relatively recently begun to make formal accommodations for the different learning needs of our diverse populations. We are finally beginning to tailor curriculum content and demands to better suit student learning styles. We can diagnose learning problems and present curriculum accordingly. We have learning centers and resource rooms to help individualize educational needs. And yet, when speaking of religious concerns, religious growth, religious development, one wonders what, if any, accommodations are made for individual differences.

The question itself goes to the heart of our mission as religious educators. And yet in all of the writing about modern Orthodox religious education, for all of the conferences and seminars, seldom does one read or hear much talk about what religious education means in terms of individual students. To be sure, there is often discussion about broad goals of commitment to *talmud torah* or *shmirat mitzvot* or *yirat shamayim* or *ahavat torah* and the like, but these do not speak to how we are to inculcate these values within the students who sit in our *Tanakh* or Talmud or *halakhah* classes every day. Put another way, there is much talk about teaching texts and ideas, but not enough about teaching students.

1. My sincere thanks to colleague and friend Dr. Jerry Zeitchik who acted as a sounding board for many of the ideas expressed here, to Dr. Joel Wolowelsky for his encouragement and support, and, as always, to Linda.

Part of the problem lies in trying to quantify such differences, to identify "where" an individual student "is religiously." It is facile to try to place them on a continuum of religious observance for we know that observance, its presence or absence, does not always tell us the full story about what a student is thinking or feeling about religious commitment. It is also difficult to assess in terms of what a student actually says about his or her religious life, since some students cannot always articulate what they feel or believe and, more important, the nature of religious discourse is such that words or concepts may mean different things to different students at different times in their lives.

Indeed, it is precisely these kinds of differences between ninth graders and twelfth graders or between a particular student when he was in the ninth grade and that same student three years later that made me begin to think of religious commitment not in static terms but in developmental terms. The notion of development implies that a human being goes through stages of maturation. No one has been more influential in our understanding of the intellectual component of this development than Jean Piaget. Suffice it to say for our purposes that Piaget characterized growth as a series of progressive and successive stages, each one being necessarily linked to the one before it. Each stage is marked by an equilibrium, a point at which the worldview is in balance and is understood in specific ways. New experiences are incorporated into this worldview and the mental structures (for example, the ability to understand numbers) are gradually changed in order to accommodate new experiences or information that doesn't quite fit. When there is so much change that old understandings do not suffice, then a disequilibrium is said to exist, thus marking a transition to the next and necessarily higher stage of understanding. The ultimate goal is formal operational thinking, a stage when one can think about mental images or about symbols, even in the absence of the objects about which one is thinking.

Most Jewish educators will be familiar with this system and there is certainly some evidence to suggest that if the jargon was unfamiliar to *Hazal*, the concept of cognitive development was not.[2] Many educators will also be aware of the subsequent work that was done in the field of moral development by Lawrence Kohlberg. Fewer Jewish educators, however, may be aware of the work of David Elkind or Ronald Goldman who applied Piagetian principles to religious educa-

---

2. See, for example, Avot, 5:21.

tion, particularly to the area of religious thought.[3] Similarly there is the work of James Fowler, who has explored the implications of this view of human development in terms of religious faith.[4] Fowler based himself not only on Piaget and Kohlberg but on Erikson's stages of emotional development.[5] Alternatively, there are those who see religious development not so much in terms of distinct limiting stages as much as they see that development in terms of a child's increasing experience.[6] And, most recently, and of special note for Jewish educators, Shraga Fisherman[7] has used Erikson's theory of psychological development to explore the spiritual identity of religious adolescents.

Needless to say, all of these efforts have come under intense scrutiny and criticism with scores of studies being written to replicate, expand, limit or disprove all or part of their findings.[8] My goal is not

3. David Elkind, *Children and Adolescents: Interpretive Essays on Jean Piaget* (NY: Oxford University Press, 1970). Also "The Child's Conception of His Religious Denomination: The Jewish Child," *Journal of Genetic Psychology* (99 1961), pp. 209–225. Ronald Goldman, *Religious Thinking from Childhood to Adolescence* (London: Routledge and Kegan Paul, 1964).
4. James Fowler, *Stages of Faith: the Psychology of Human Development and the Quest for Meaning* (New York: HarperCollins, 1981). Also "Faith and the Structuring of Meaning," in Craig Dykstra and Sharon Parks, *Faith Development and Fowler* (Birmingham: Religious Education Press, 1986). pp. 15–42.
5. Erik Erikson, *Childhood and Society* (New York: Norton, 1963) 2nd edition. *Identity Youth and Crisis* (New York: Norton, 1968).
6. See the works of Gareth B. Matthews: *Philosophy and the Young Child* (Cambridge: Harvard Univ. Press, 1980); *Dialogues with Children* (Cambridge: Harvard Univ. Press, 1984); and especially Gareth Matthews, *Philosophy of Childhood* (Cambridge: Harvard University Press, 1994). Also see, Robert Coles, *The Spiritual Life of Children* (Boston: Houghton Mifflin, 1990).
7. Shraga Fisherman, "Spiritual Identity in Israeli Religious Male Adolescents: Observations and Educational Implications," *Journal of Jewish Education.* 66:3 (Fall 2000/Winter 2001), pp. 6–18, which summarizes his findings. The original material as well as representative interviews which form the basis of that summary can be found in *No`ar ha-Kippot ha-Zerukot* (Elkanah: Mikhlelet Orot, 1998). Subsequently, Dr. Fisherman published another volume, focusing particularly on women: *`Almah Avdah: Zehutan ha-Emunatit shel Datlashiyot* (Elkanah: Michlelet Orot, 2000). My thanks to Rabbi Avi Weiss of Orot for facilitating my access to this volume.
8. See Kenneth Hyde, *Religion in Childhood and Adolescence: A Comprehensive Review of the Research* (Birmingham: Religious Education

to enter that fray, not only because I am unqualified to do so but rather because I believe that taking a more eclectic approach may even be more worthwhile. For there is much that the typical educator can learn and glean from these studies in our practice that can help us interact with our students in a more directed and meaningful way. As such, my goal here is not to provide a comprehensive theory of religious guidance. Nor is it my intent to deny or belittle the enormous success that we continue to have on a daily basis in helping to create or facilitate religious growth in our students. Rather, I seek to sensitize us all to think and talk to one another about that growth in a way that often finds too little articulated expression in our field and in our practice.

Adolescence

We all know that adolescence can be a turbulent and difficult time, the so-called "identity crisis" examined by Erikson.[9] At the very least, the expectations that others (parents, friends, teachers, society, popular culture, Judaism) have of the adolescent, to say nothing of the expectations that adolescents may have of themselves, make for a life of constant measuring of oneself and trying on different images. A student's value system can be called into question on a regular basis and it should therefore come as no surprise that his or her religious commitment, regardless of its level, will also be affected in some way.

Seen in this light, it should come as no surprise that a nearly universal key finding in the research on religious development is that there is a drop-off in religious commitment during the adolescent years. Many of us could intuit such a finding, but there is significant research, across cultural and denominational lines, to support the phenomenon.[10] On the one hand, such a finding should be liberating for those educators who unnecessarily chastise themselves for the fact that some students seemed "more religious" when they first entered the high school but now seem to be "less religious" or less observant. Instead, we need to realize that such a dip or decline may in fact be

---

Press, 1990). Also See Elie Gottlieb, "Religious Thinking in Childhood and Adolescence: Argumentative Reasoning and the Justification of Religious Belief." Unpublished doctoral dissertation, Hebrew University. I am indebted to him for his sharing his review of the research and bibliography early on in my own reading.

9. Erikson, *Identity Youth and Crisis, op. cit.*.

10. See Hyde, *op. cit.*.

very normal and is no indication that the state of affairs is a permanent or even long-term one.

It is a key fact to share, too, with parents who cannot understand why their child seemed so "religious" and motivated in the eighth grade but now that he is in the tenth grade seems like he has lost it all. (Surely, they maintain, the school is to blame!) But if a reduction in commitment to observance is common, then there is not necessarily a need for parents or teachers to panic. Neither is there a reason to get into a tug of war with adolescents about all aspects of their observance. Exactly where one draws the line, is of course a difficult question that is worth examining further.[11] Meantime, teachers and parents need to consider when to insist on conformity and when to look the other way. The father who once told me that "as long as this boy is in my house, he is going to wear *tzitzit*," may be backing his child into a corner that potentially has only a tragic exit. On the other hand, the parent who allows his child not to go to *shul* every *Shabbat*, may be headed for an equally tragic outcome. Such issues are important but educators, like parents, need to recognize them for what they often truly are: the normal adolescent struggle to try on different hats, testing or pushing limits, to find out what they truly believe.

In extreme cases, it will also do the teacher well to recall that a decline in religious behavior—if not outright rebelliousness—may have little to do with religious observance per se. I can think of a (thankfully small) number of students whose conduct in *davening* or their posture in Torah classes was so outrageous that they managed to try my patience regularly. These are students who came from "good religious homes" or "good *frum* communities," yet they seemed so oppositional. One would do well with such students to remember the words of one psychoanalyst who notes that:

> For some adolescents, the quest for independence can be pursued only through overthrowing and rejecting parental norms and standards. Religion in such cases may become the symbolic repository for parental authority and corresponding conflicts or continuing dependence. The adolescent who needs to

---

11. The complexity of the issue may be best illustrated by Hyde's summary of research related to attitudes to church attendance: "Most children regard worship as uninteresting and boring, nevertheless, it is the children who have been regularly involved in it who are more likely to retain the habit of church attendance when free to abandon it." Hyde, *op. cit.*, pp. 11–12.

reject authority may find this need penetrating his religious experience and his relation to God as well.[12]

When that student acts out, we need to remind one another that there may well be far more involved and religion is merely the venue where it is being played out before our eyes on a daily basis. We certainly need to be concerned about the self-destructive effects of such behavior, and we need to be concerned about the potential effects on other students, but it is critical that we recall that such behavior may have little to do with *davening* or *mitzvah* observance or Torah life per se. Such students may need general professional counseling, we may need to speak with parents, we may need to provide them with the alternative of *davening* in another place such as a local morning *minyan*. But the one thing such a child probably does not need is *musar* about the importance of *davening*. Nor should his behavior be seen as representing some failure of his teachers or his home. In any event, we need to think more creatively and in a more measured and directed way about such behaviors and we need to train teachers to respond appropriately.

Religious doubt or rebellion, then, may well be part of a norm. Such doubt can be explained in a number of ways. It "is often an expression of the adolescent's need for autonomy in the face of the regressively reactivated pull to dependency on parental objects."[13] Alternatively, one might see it simply in cognitive developmental terms: having achieved a level of formal operations thinking, the adolescent can now think in the abstract and juvenile notions of belief are discarded or called into question. Finally, it may be understood in the broader sense of identity formation: the adolescent "is unwilling to accept slogans blindly and prefers to consolidate his own spiritual identity, in a way that will let him feel that his parents' and teachers' influence on this identity is as small as possible."[14] The bottom line, however, is that doubt is often a very natural if not always healthy aspect of adolescence.[15]

---

12. W.W. Meissner, *Psychoanalysis and the Religious Experience* (New Haven and London: Yale University Press, 1984), p. 145.
13. *Ibid.*
14. Shraga Fisherman, "Spiritual Identity," p. 8.
15. All of this is separate from the specifically religious doubts that arise as a result of the pressures and influences of modern society. Israeli society is clearly no different in this regard. In addition to Fisherman, *loc. cit.*,

Doubting and Questioning

And yet, what is our response to these doubts? What opportunities do we provide for students to give voice to these doubts? Are they part of the very fabric of our classroom curricula and discussions, or are they reserved for only those rare moments at a *shabbaton* or during informal educational events? Or do they finally get our attention only when we perceive (too late) that a child is in crisis? Surely if doubt is an important part of adolescent growth, if it is a part of normal spiritual and cognitive maturation, then we should be finding ways to help students express their doubts. It would seem that we are not as sensitive to this issue as we can or should be. In Israel, there has been much concern of late about a whole generation of students who grew up in the *yeshivah tikhonit* whose questions were dismissed as heretical or irrelevant, with the result that large numbers have fallen into the category of *"yotz'im beshe'elah."* Rav Yehuda Amital has bemoaned the fact that

> We have before us a generation that "does not know how to ask." Not just that it does not *know* how to ask, but it does not even *think* to ask, due to educational indoctrination. Not knowing to ask, has evolved as an educational ideal throughout our educational system. . . Youngsters, who naturally know how to ask, have learned to restrict their questions to limited contexts, where the questions lack significance and are mainly technical and formal, not existential. Regarding any areas outside these realms, the youth have internalized the educational message that questions are, if not outright forbidden, then at least inappropriate. As a result, a process has emerged whereby a sizable portion of the youth refuses to ask, not because they are afraid to ask, but because they do not know how.[16]

see Shlomo Kaniel, "The Religious Zionist: Toward the New Era," *Religious Education* 9:4 (Fall, 2000), 453–473. [*"HaTzioni HaDati—Mabat l'Atid." BiSdeh Chemed, Gilayon* #4, 5758.] It is also separate from the theological implications of doubt which may be part and parcel of religious life or at least religious life in this age. See Norman Lamm, *Faith and Doubt* (New York: Ktav, 1971), pp. 1–40.

16. Rav Yehuda Amital. "The Search for Religious Enthusiasm Among Today's Youth." *Parshat Vayikra* 5760. www.vbm-torah.org/archive/sichot60/24vayik.ans. Recently republished as "The Generation 'That Does Not Know How to Ask,' " in *Between Religious Experience and Religious*

One might be tempted to say that this is not the case in Modern Orthodox high schools here in America. Perhaps; although one does hear from time to time that a student in our community who asks a sensitive question in class is simply told that the answer lies in To-rah—*tze u'lmad*.[17] More subtly, though, how often do students ask questions in class but the response they hear is something like "the question is not really relevant (!) to the topic at hand," or "it will take us too far afield," or "we don't have the time right now," or "if we finish this section in time then we will come back to your question"?

How often do we push off such questions because we think we don't have the time or because of our own discomfort? And when, in fact, there really is no time to talk about the issue at that moment, do we go out of our way to make the time during some later class? Our students quickly learn not to ask certain kinds of questions or not to ask questions at all! Instead, we need to take these questions and doubts very seriously and we need to find ways to address them, to give them a voice, to create environments where it will be comfort-able to ask. Students need to hear possibilities from us, ones that are not prescriptive or judgmental but which they can absorb and try on for size.

The question of what questions need addressing is a difficult one as are the questions of how and when they should be asked. But es-pecially if they are potentially an important and positive part of the educational process, as well as the process of religious maturation, then we should be thinking of ways to make the time and the place. Obviously, a *mahshavah* or philosophy class might be one possible venue, as long as it is students' questions that are raised there and not only the teacher's.[18] Yet another possibility is to examine the cur-

---

Commitment (Gush Etzion: Yeshivat Har Etzion, 5763), pp. 30–31.

17. See, for example, Sarah Shapiro, "Circles in the Sand: A Question of Questioning," in *Jewish Action* (Winter 5762/2001).

18. One senses that there are fewer and fewer schools teaching philosophy or *mahshavah*. For a more popular lament see Chaim Eisen, "Is Yeshiva Education Accomplishing What it Should? *Jewish Action* (Winter 5762/2001). On some reasons for this absence, see most recently David Shatz, "Remembering Marvin Fox: One Man's Legacy to Jewish Thought," *Tradition*, 36:1 (Spring 2002), pp. 59–88, especially pp. 61–69. Focusing more on student-centered issues of belief might make such courses more palatable and attractive. On students' ability to "do philosophy" alone or even within the context of other subject areas such as *Tanakh* or *halakhah*, see Gareth Matthews and Howard

ricula that are already in place. *Tanakh*, Talmud, *halakhah* are all subjects which provide what might be called "teachable moments" for hashkafic issues. One could not imagine, for example, teaching about Pharaoh and the *makkot*, without dedicating at least one lesson to the clash of free will and determinism. A class on *hilkhot oneg Shabbat* might include the question of doing something that is less than "*shabbosdig*" because an individual student needs to explore its outer limits. A *mahloket* in the Gemara may particularly lend itself to the question of *emunat hakhamim*. Rather than leave it up to the individual teacher, we should be planning together, as a department, as a school, to decide which issues we should be addressing at which points in the curricula and we should be sharing with one another as a faculty the different perspectives that might be possible.

General Studies as a Straw Man

Nor should such opportunities be restricted to the *limmudei kodesh* curricula. The issue of evolution and biology is the most obvious example, and the context for teaching history could be another. One thinks particularly of the English literature curriculum that could and should also be combed by religious faculty in search of loci for meaningful discussions about issues of belief, identity, religious inquiry and doubt.[19] To the extent that these issues cannot be addressed by the English literature faculty, then arrangements should be made for team teaching. As Fisherman points out:

> Adolescents are less hesitant to discuss doubts disguised as the feelings and musings of a literary protagonist. An open and penetrating discussion of the protagonist's questions, and presentation of diverse positions, should be encouraged. This route legitimizes doubts without worrying the participants about self-exposure. Further on, adolescents can be encouraged to move from third-person to first-person expression. Discussion (especially when projective) also facilitates hearing one's peers' solutions to similar questions and the ways in which they dealt with their doubts.[20]

Deitcher, "Doing Philosophical Theology in the Seventh Grade at Halevy School," *Religious Education* 88:2 (Spring 1993), pp. 294–304.

19. See Rav Aharon Lichtenstein, "Torah and General Culture: Confluence and Conflict," in Jacob J. Schacter, *Judaism's Encounter with Other Cultures: Rejection or Integration* (Northvale: Jason Aronson, 1997), pp. 217–292.

20. Shraga Fisherman, "Spiritual Identity," p. 12. It makes the most sense

The questions are not necessarily ones that can be provided by an outsider; rather, they are best when they emanate from the students themselves. One could easily imagine polling students for a list of religious or faith issues that never get talked about, collating such a list and then meeting together as a faculty to find places in the curriculum, both formal and informal, where it may be appropriate to address such questions either tangentially or head on. It might be appropriate to establish an email address where students can write to pose their questions and then have teachers respond. A collection of responses might be posted on a website as a kind of "FAQs (frequently asked questions) on Faith."[21]

Just being open to raising such questions, however, is only part of the story. Frequently, one has a sense that the questions that are raised by students in the ninth grade are qualitatively different than the questions raised in the twelfth grade. Here, again, looking at students' religious growth developmentally would be helpful. In the first place, it would make us rephrase the above statement to say that it is not the questions which are qualitatively different as much as are the ninth grade and the twelfth grade students who are asking the questions. I refer here not so much to cognitive or emotional differences alone. After all, younger and older students may understand, say, the problem of suffering, differently. Rather, I refer to religious differences between them, in terms of how they live or articulate their faith. To understand this better, some reference to James Fowler's work might be helpful.

Fowler's Stages

Fowler, as we have stated, is one of those theorists who maintains that humans go through a number of successive spiral stages where

---

in terms of adolescent development that discussions with peers should be particularly critical and beneficial. Evidence of this in a Jewish school setting can be found in a recent study of students in three different kinds of religious Israeli high schools, which found that a noticeable number of students spoke with no one about their struggles, but among the majority that did, "a peer (either male or female) is the preferred consultant of all respondents." Avraham Leslau and Yisrael Rich, "A Study of 12th Grade Students in State Sponsored Religious Education—1999," *Ten Da`at* XIV (Dec., 2001), pp. 59–60.

21. For an example of such a site see *Haverim Makshivim* at www.kipa.co.il/noar/sot.asp.

each stage is linked and adds to the one before. People usually reach a level of equilibrium at a particular stage until such time that dissonance sets in and they are nudged into creating a new set of structures. "Each stage represents a widening of vision and valuing, correlated with a parallel increase in the certainty and depth of selfhood..." Fowler warns that "transitions from one spiral stage level to another are often protracted, painful, dislocating and/or abortive. Arrests can and do occur at any one of the stages."[22]

One of the implications of this analysis is that not all students are ready for the kinds of questions that teachers may think are "important." Such questions may be too painful, cause too much dissonance, and fall too far beyond the pale of what they are prepared to confront. In short, just because it is an important question does not mean that it is important to the student just yet or that the student is prepared to understand it on a level that will upset the equilibrium.

Similarly, one is frequently struck by the intensity of a student's question at the time that an issue arises and the seeming disinterest that same student sometimes has in the ensuing discussion that a teacher may try to generate or the answers that a teacher may try to offer. Assuming that the teacher is not giving a boring or unintelligible response, how does one account for this gap? Perhaps, again, because the adolescent at this stage takes everything as a unified whole, and the attachment to religious life is non-analytical, this means that questions are not important for the values or truths that they clarify. "Rather, in such discussion he seeks to establish a sense of commonality or relatedness with the other person present."[23] In other words, it may serve more to provide a sense of identification than to give him profound answers to his profound questions. In practical terms, this means that it is important to offer the opportunity to ask questions even if we do not necessarily spend as much time or energy on the responses as we might for those further along in the continuum of religious development. Nor should a teacher be disheartened when the student doesn't seem as interested in the answer as he was in the question. Being able to ask the question and to know that it is taken seriously, knowing that there is an answer available even if he doesn't really understand it or

---

22. James W. Fowler, *Stages of Faith: The Psychology of Human Development and the Quest for Meaning* (San Francisco: HarperCollins, 1995), p. 274. (Originally published in 1981.)
23. *Ibid.*, p. 167

recall the details, may be enough at this stage of religious development.

As much as we may want to use questions and analysis to push our students to reflect upon their beliefs and values so as to create the kind of dissonance that may move them be more reflective, we must understand the perils in pushing too much, too far, too soon. I will never forget the ninth grade student whose faith, he said, was nearly shattered at the beginning of freshman year by the teacher who suggested (the Ramban aside) that Avraham was a human person with frailties and failings. Separate from the theological issues involved, the Jewish educator must always be sensitive to whether his or her approach is appropriate for all students at all ages and stages.[24] The non-analytic nature of belief of some students can be the protective shell which helps maintain their commitment. We should not be so quick to try to consciously break it down, nor should we be oblivious to the inadvertent assaults we sometimes make upon it.

In a similar vein, consider the fact that, according to Fowler, an adolescent at this stage sees symbols as being inseparable from their meaning. Worthy symbols are themselves sacred. They *are* depths of meaning. "Any strategy of demythologization, therefore, threatens the participation of symbol and symbolized and is taken, consequently as an assault on the sacred itself."[25] Much as we may value *lomdus*, much as we may be motivated to teach our students *all kinds of hakirah*s and *halakhic* distinctions, we must also recall that the unexamined nature of belief is such that, for some, it helps maintain *kedushah*. Conversely, breaking down that belief when a student is not yet ready may have the effect of robbing the symbol of its *kedushah* and its uniqueness.

---

24. See, for example, Avishai David, "Perspectives on the *Avot* and *Imahot*," *Ten Da`at*, V:2 (Iyar 5751/Spring 1991), pp. 24–26. Zvi Grumet, "Another Perspective on *Avot* and *Imahot*," *Ten Da`at* VI:1 (Nisan 5752/Spring 1992), pp. 25–27, especially note 15. Joel Wolowelsky, "Moral Education and Patriarchal Critiques: *Kibbud Av* and *Kibbud Avot*," *Tradition* 33:4 (Summer 1999). More recently, see Howard Deitcher, "Between Angels and Mere Mortals: Nechama Leibowtiz's Approach to the Study of Biblical Characters," in *Journal of Jewish Education* 66:1–2 (Spring/Summer 2000), pp. 8–22. Interestingly, such debate often centers upon the controversial comments of Rav Hirsch about the possible mistakes of Rivkah and Yitzhak in the upbringing of their children and the question of whether they took into account the separate and distinct religious development needs of their children.
25. Fowler, *Stages of Faith*, p. 163.

One might tell some students that the *halakhah* does not require one to stand when the *aron kodesh* is open (while the sefer torah remains within), but is it the appropriate thing to say to all students? What is true of symbols may be true of concepts as well: the teacher who tells his students that Judaism is opposed to "spirituality" may have precedent to rely upon, but he may be doing more harm than good by assaulting a key part of a student's religious sensibilities.

The Affective Domain

If religious development were wholly related to cognitive development alone then the process of religious education would be significantly easier. We would simply identify what ideas or knowledge needed to be conveyed, which ones students are capable of understanding at different stages (perhaps accounting for their emotional development), and our work would pretty much be done. In truth, however, religious commitment is related not only to what we know about God but to what we believe as well. One does not need the numerous studies that have been done in other faiths to know that, as one study found, "cognitive knowledge about God did not guarantee conviction, since their exposure to 'rote theology' resulted in their knowing about God but not knowing God."[26] We want our students to know and to love God and to have an ongoing relationship with Him. But how, if at all, do these goals translate into our classrooms and our schools?

What we are speaking about is the affective component of religious education.[27] Yet classrooms, especially those that focus on aca-

---

26. Hyde, *Religion*, p. 72. See the note by Rav Soloveichik *z"l:* "Maimonides' term *leida`* (*Yesodei ha-Torah,* 1:1) transcends the bounds of the *abtract logos* and passes over into the realm of the boundless intimate and impassioned experience where postulate and deduction, discursive knowledge and intuitive thinking, conception and perception, subject and object are one." "The Lonely Man of Faith," *Tradition* 7:1 (Winter 1964–65), pp. 32–33.

27. I have avoided precise definitions of this aspect of religious life for it is beyond my ken and I do not think that it is entirely necessary for our purposes here. One looks forward to the publication of some of the papers presented at a recent Orthodox Forum on the subject of spirituality which may help clarify matters. For the present, I refer to the affective/emotional/spiritual/faith/aspects of Torah life which cannot be understood by cognitive understanding alone.

demic excellence, on acquiring the tools of learning, the skills, the *lehning* of a *blatt*, and the like, do not always make room for affective education. Some do not see a place for it in the curriculum, and I have heard some suggest that either it cannot be taught at all or that it emerges "naturally" from the serious study of text. I contend that it emerges "naturally" only if students see the text as having that potential from the start and, even then, they may need assistance. In any event, this is a subject worthy of exploration in its own right.[28] For the moment, let us assume that it is indeed a value and a goal. What do we need to know about our students that will give us insight into this aspect of their religious training?

Gender Differences

One interesting path of inquiry relates to gender. Research has generated interesting findings about the differences between boys and girls. Many religious educators may intuitively know that, in general (there are always exceptions and large numbers of them), girls tend to be more "serious" than boys about things religious - *davening*, discussions about faith, certain attitudes and the like. This conforms to the "universal finding of the greater religiousness of women."[29] We tend to account for such differences by saying that girls are more "mature" than boys, but I think it would be helpful to try to better articulate how "maturity" may play a role so that we may better understand and help our students.

Adolescents can be somewhat narcissistic or self-centered. They come to identify with those who possess the attributes and ideals that they seek for themselves and this often leads them to peers and/or certain adult role models. This, in turn, can affect the adolescent's conception of God. Girls, for example, "tend to emphasize qualities of loving relationship; God becomes the ideal confidant, who understands everything, and responds to the girl's most intimate wishes and deeds." [30] Boys, on the other hand, tend to look at God as the perfect being, and think of Him in terms of His power and authority. Might

[ED. Cf. Adam Mintz and Lawrence Schiffman: *Jewish Spirituality and Divine Law* (NJ : Ktav, 2005).]

28. This issue often rears its head in discussions about the goals of teaching Talmud and the extent to which it is or should be a subject which lends itself to affective education.

29. Hyde, *Religion*, p. 55.

30. Meissner, *Psychoanalysis*, p. 145.

this distinction not better help us to understand why girls seem to be better *davener*s than boys? Is it not easier and more natural to enter into an intimate dialogue with God as confidant that with God as authority figure, to speak with *Hashem* rather than with *Elokim*? And might this mean that in talking about prayer to different ages and different sexes, we might do well to couch our message in the terms more appropriate to each gender?

At the same time, consider the fact that boys (again at the risk of generalizations) seem to have more difficulty expressing themselves emotionally. Much important work has been done to explain the ways in which boys are raised—by parents, teachers and society—to avoid expressing their emotions or to keep their vulnerabilities a secret.[31] That being the case, how can we expect boys to speak aloud about the affective components of religious life? How can they speak about their feelings about God, about *tefillah*, about crisis or happiness or inspiration, when the vocabulary is foreign to them or causes them such great discomfort? In other words, even if boys at a certain stage may want to enter into the same kind of dialogue with Hashem as girls do, it may be much more difficult for them to do so. Surely we have an obligation to help them overcome these barriers and to create a safe and open environment which gives them permission to express their emotions and their emotional vulnerability. Most important, they need to learn, especially from the adult men in their lives, how to speak this way. Teachers and advisers need to think out loud about their own faith. They need to speak out loud about their own religiosity and spirituality. Both boys and girls are in need of role models who can not only model religious behavior but, to the extent possible, religious feelings as well. Once again, the richness of the English literature curriculum comes to mind here. For in its very use of language, poetry and prose, it not only lends cognitive understanding but also, in the words of Rav Lichtenstein: "Plumbs uncharted existential and experiential depths." In class, in daily announcements, in discussing current events, teachers and administrators need to express their emotions—and they need to talk about what it means to have a relationship with and to feel the presence of *HaKadosh Barukh Hu*.[32]

---

31. See, for example, Dan Kindlon, Michael Thompson, *Raising Cain: Protecting the Emotional Life of Boys* (New York: Ballantine Books, 1999).
32. Rav Lichtenstein, *Torah and General Culture*, p. 244.

Nowhere does the affective component of Jewish education probably rear its head more than in *davening*, for this is one of the few
times where students "do religion" in such an overt way during the
school day. Yet, get most Jewish educators together in a room and they
will eventually admit that *davening* can be one of the most difficult
parts of the day, and what a way to start one's day! If our preceding
analysis is true, then any attempt at making *tefillah* more meaningful must take into account the totality of religious needs of students.
Classes on *be'ur tefillah* will not suffice because *tefillah* is not (only)
an intellectual undertaking but an emotional and experiential one.[33] A
first step, is to begin thinking about the regular *minyan* as a classroom
rather than as a ritual.

The Role of Teachers
    Much of the burden for religious development in schools must
inevitably lie upon the shoulders of teachers, yet few teachers get direction in how to handle students' spiritual needs. As I have tried to
show thus far, there are nuances and complexities to be recognized,
sensitivities and skills that can be acquired and honed. But in how
many schools is a faculty meeting convened in order to discuss just
these issues? Assume a student asks "How do we really know that God
exists?" Are all teachers prepared or capable of answering such questions appropriately? Is there not some science and some art to answering such questions in ways that will give students a number of answers
to choose from? Are there times when we should take a more limited
and limiting approach? Why do we only seem to wrestle with such

33. The challenge of *tefillah* in yeshiva high schools is an incredibly important one that is deserving of attention in its own right. A wonderful first step in
that regard may be found in the recent publication edited by Yoel Finkelman,
Educating Toward Meaningful Tefillah (Jerusalem: Academy for Torah
Initiatives and Directions, 2001). A reflection (at least in print) of the paucity of suggestions for improvement may be found in *Noteworhy Practices
in Jewish Day School Education. Volume II: Tefillah* (Boston: PEJE, 2001).
Approximately 24 pages are dedicated to noteworthy practices in elementary
schools, 11 pages to middle schools and 4 pages to high schools, and the
value of even these for a Modern Orthodox school is not immediately apparent. One notable exception is the selection entitled "The Prayer Experience
as a Joint School-Synagogue Enterprise," by Rabbi Jack Bieler. [Ed. note:
See Moshe Sokolow's chapter on *tefillah* in the Subject Matter section of this
book.]

things in times of crisis, such as when a death occurs, or when a catastrophe strikes, like 9/11? How much discussion do we have about the modeling of our own behavior? As teachers, we would benefit from supervision and collegial collaboration in religious issues as much as academic or psychological ones.

At the same time, we cannot realistically put this all on the teacher's doorstep. We must admit first and foremost that there are teachers who are less capable of handling this role. They give wonderful *shiurim*, they can inspire students to great heights in the intellectual realm, but the human dimension of speaking to students about matters of the heart comes far less easily to them. Alternatively, there are teachers who, because of their enormous teaching loads simply cannot reach out to all students in this way on an individual basis. And there are teachers who are not in the building long enough to connect with students outside the classroom. In this regard, the increasing popularity in some schools of a "religious adviser" or "*yo`eitz*" is a positive step for it recognizes that not all *rebbeim* and teachers necessarily have the time or the wherewithal to deal with students on this level. It also recognizes that there are specific individual needs that can and should be addressed by someone other than the teacher. The adviser is, by definition, someone who is "outside" the normal system and may be viewed by some students as less threatening and more supportive. Indeed, the very creation of such a position is by itself a statement to the student and parent body that religious growth is something that is serious, worthy of discussion and ultimately of great importance to the school.

The Family Component

But precisely because religious development is so complex, it cannot be treated in a vacuum. The teacher, or, in his or her absence, an adviser or administrator, must take into account all of the influences in a child's life and must marshal the assistance of all of the potential players. First and foremost there are the parents. We have parent-teacher conferences and report cards to collaborate with parents about their child's academic development, and we have guidance counselors or advisers who consult with parents about their child; usually when the child is in crisis, but sometimes because the school has developed a healthy sense of cooperation and communication. Yet how many of us really are in touch with parents about their children's religious development? And I refer here not to the phone call we place or the meeting we convene about religious behavior that is treated as a disciplinary issue but, rather, to communication that is about the nurturing or growth of the religious sensitivities of the child. I recall a student who was alternately completely disinterested in *davening* or would constantly talk. He had been disciplined a number of times, didn't really seem like he was oppositional, but couldn't seem to control his behavior either. During parent-teacher conferences, I decided that I was going to talk to the parents about this but I made it perfectly clear that I was not speaking to them as a disciplinarian but rather as someone who was concerned about their child's religious growth.

When I told them about his poor attitude during *davening*, the father finally said to me: "Well, Rabbi, I suppose that's completely understandable, because, unfortunately, I'm not really much of a role model myself during *shul*." I was struck by his candor, so much so that I was speechless. On the one hand, the interchange simply confirmed what we intuitively know about the influence of the home and the possible limitations that there are on our ability to treat the issue of religious development in schools.

On the other hand, in retrospect, this incident was an opportunity lost; an opportunity to enter into collaboration with a family on the subject of religious development. Perhaps it would have been worthwhile to call the family's *shul* rabbi to enlist his insight and his help. Perhaps it would have meant meeting together with the father and child to talk together about the issue. Perhaps it would have provided the prospect to go back to the student to talk about his own perceptions about his father's observance. There are any number of possible avenues and outcomes. The point is that we do ourselves and our students and their parents a disservice by not including parents more in the process. Since that incident, I have spoken to parents numerous times about their children's religious development. I now am struck not by the candor of parents but by their appreciation that someone has taken the trouble to talk to them about an issue, which they themselves are often grappling with at home.

Finally, but most important, let us never take our students for granted. To be sure, there are those who come to us committed and religious, passionate about their *avodat Hashem*. Such students, by virtue of their living in this time and this place, by virtue of their exposure to or embrace of general society or culture, by virtue of their natural development as adolescents, will also have their issues, albeit of a different nature or degree than those less passionate. This does not mean that they do not need our proactive help and guidance in their growth. We need to be sensitive to their developmental needs.

At the other end of the spectrum are those who do not seem to have any passion at all. Dr. Joel Wolowelsky shares an important anecdote about having approached a student who seemed to be out of sorts, having a general gloomy demeanor in school. At the end of the conversation, after the student informed him of numerous family conflicts, Dr. Wolowelsky asked him why he had not come to discuss these issues earlier. Why had he waited for the teacher to approach him first? "What's the matter with you?" the student asked. "I sat in front of you in *minyan* for three weeks staring at a *siddur* held upside down. Don't you notice these sorts of things?"[34]

As for the students who may not seem to yet have the passion we would like, we must recognize that they, too, are a work in progress. I recall speaking to a young woman whom many thought was simply a "talker" in *davening*, who was sent to my office for "disciplining." I asked her what *davening* meant to her and, to my surprise, she burst into tears. She explained that it was such an incredibly important question to her—but nobody had ever really asked her about it before.

In the end, we must not forget that religious growth is an ongoing affair, one that, hopefully, continues beyond adolescence. The present push for students to go to Israel, and the amazing transformation that takes place there, have been noted elsewhere.[35] But it is wrong to suggest that high schools should look upon Israel as a "finishing school" for a job that the high schools themselves were unable to accomplish.[36] To do so ignores the developmental stages that the adolescent goes

---

34. Dr. Joel B. Wolowelsky, "Response," in Y. Finkelman, *Educating Toward Meaningful Tefillah* (Jerusalem: ATID, 2001), p.10.

35. Jay Goldmintz, "The Post-High School Yeshiva Experience: Goals and Benefits," *Ten Da`at* V:2 (Iyar 5751/Spring 1991), pp. 32–34.

36. For a recent reference to this canard and a wonderful response, see Rabbi Yitzchak Blau, "*MeEverLeYam:* Rethinking the Relationship Between Israeli Yeshivot and Diaspora Schools," *Opinions on Jewish Education, Academy for Torah Initiatives and Directions*, January 21, 2002, http://www.atid.org/op-jed.htm. Rabbi Blau makes passing reference to our issue in his statement that Israeli post-high schools for Americans have an advantage over American high schools in that the former "are dealing with eighteen-year-olds that are more mature than the average high school student simply due to the age factor."

through and belittles the importance of late adolescence as a time for reevaluating and restructuring one's beliefs. [37] On the other hand, the accusation has merit to the extent that we did not take advantage of the key stages of development that occurred while the students passed through the classrooms and hallways of our schools.

---

37. "Man does not acquire true religious faith, that is, a really personal faith recognized in its transcendent finality, before the age of thirty years!. Experience has shown that after adolescence the whole religious formation apparently has to undergo revision—not because the child or the adolescent has not hitherto been authentically religious, but because man does not acquire sufficient maturity to make a real personal choice and to recognize reality, before he has become adult." A. Vergote, *The Religious Man* (Dayton, Ohio:Pflaum 1969), p. 300, cited in Meissner p. 146.
Fowler characterizes the late or post-adolescent stage of development as "Individuative-Reflective." "The late adolescent adult must begin to take seriously the burden of responsibility for his or her own commitments, lifestyle, beliefs and attitudes." *Stages of Faith*, p. 182. Reflection is critical for this stage and may only be possible if one can get away from the limiting influence of peers and home.

Instruction

Pictures and Models:
An Exploration in Jewish Educational Thought

Michael Rosenak

Models: A Word of Introduction

In a now classic article, "Philosophical Models of Teaching,"[1] Professor Israel Scheffler distinguishes between activities that may be included in the category of "education" and those, such as indoctrination, or conditioning, that do not qualify. He then notes some questions that characterize the educational venture: "What sort of learning shall I aim to achieve? In what does such learning consist? How shall I strive to achieve it?" He tells us that he will address the questions by way of a consideration of three influential models of teaching which provide, or at any rate suggest, certain relevant answers to the questions above.

In this essay, I hope to do the same with regard to three models that seem to be particularly congenial to Jewish education and that, like Scheffler's models, "do not so much aim to describe teaching as to orient it."

But how, precisely, are we to understand the concept of "models"?

SECTION ONE

The Variety and Educational Uses of Models

Michael Ruse[2] points to certain characterizing features that all models share. For example, models of all types draw analogies between the model and some aspects of reality or of some scientific

---

1. Israel Scheffler: "Philosophical Models of Teaching," in Israel Scheffler: *Philosophy and Education* (Boston: Allyn and Bacon, 1966), 99–114; citation from page 100.
2. Michael Ruse: "Models," in Ted Honderich (ed.): *The Oxford Companion to Philosophy* (Oxford: Oxford University Press, 1995), 582–83.

claim. We may distinguish between physical models, usually small or large scale material constructions, and theoretical models, wherein scientists map limited aspects of reality and introduce simplifying conceptions and assumptions. These models enable us to look at complex realities through prisms that make them manageable. For example: for certain purposes and in certain situations we assume that a map "shows" us an area or a country under consideration, or even lays "the world" before us. We are invited to grasp the world or some aspect of it through particular lenses that focuses our attention on "a way of seeing things" that is particular to the model.

As for educational models specifically, they can be expected to draw pictures relevant to the educational scene and to make educational prescriptions.[3] They describe educational situations metaphorically, and then invite us to see things their way and to accept their guidance in thinking through germane issues. For example, we may have a model that claims to measure achievement by way of letters ('A' to 'F') and then we may plausibly speak of a given learner as "an A student."

Conceptual models that deal with such prescriptive matters as education, then, can be seen as pictures of reality designed for use. They are frameworks within which theoretical work and practical policy discussions are conducted. When these theories are prescriptive and not simply descriptive (as educational issues are, for education is a practical enterprise), they may be expected to suggest normative directions and standards.

Taming and Cultivating

In conceptual models, the pictures drawn frequently come to us in the shape of metaphors. Two well-known examples from within the field of education are, respectively, the "picture-idea" of education as an act of *cultivating* children, on the one hand, and the picture-idea of *taming* them, on the other. The latter picture suggests that children are naturally evil or at least "wild," and that they share with domestic animals the requirement that they be "domesticated" before being given the run of the house or the world. In line with this "picture," moral education constitutes the hoped-for conquest of Mr. Hyde, a loathsome creature, by Dr. Jekyll, the epitome of the educated and

3. On the prescriptive character of educational theory, see T.W. Moore: *Educational Theory, An Introduction* (London: Routledge and Kegan, 1974), 1–26.

virtuous human being. (In Stevenson's classic story, alas, the opposite transpired and Mr. Hyde emerged victorious.)

In the first model-metaphor of "cultivation," the "picture" drawn brings to mind horticulturists who lovingly and carefully tend their young shoots. The metaphor: like tender seedlings, so must children be nurtured and helped to grow. At times they may legitimately be given direction, but they are not to be overpowered or excessively subjected to intervention. Children in this model are like plants: they are endowed with the quality of growth, they are naturally beautiful. Our task as educators is to respect the child's inner development but to appreciate that without gentle intervention the weeds all about may choke our flowers to death. Our vocation, according to the metaphor-model of cultivation, is to care for the plantings, to "help nature along."

Conversely, the "taming" model-metaphor speaks candidly of the need for discipline. In the dire situation of the natural wickedness of humans, discipline is of utmost importance and "tender care" may be a recipe for disaster.[4]

A Way to See the World

Marc Belth places the model in a broad framework where it assumes the dimensions of a paradigm, a total way of seeing the world and exploring it, and sometimes, daring to exchange this way for another.[5] Like Ruse, Belth argues that whatever man studies he is in fact studying some aspect of reality as it is revealed in and through the theoretical model he uses.[6]

This is a comprehensive framework within which we view a given reality, or even our entire world. Once again, the model simplifies so that that the matter under consideration can be clearly grasped and

---

4. On the pedagogical and theological aspects of this "taming" model, see Michael Rosenak: *Tree of Life, Tree of Knowledge* (Colorado: Westview, 2003), 73–90. On the consequences of "taming" for discipline, cf. *Idem.*: "Corporal Punishment in Jewish Education; A Philosophical-Educational Exploration," in Peter Y. Medding (ed.): *Studies in Contemporary Jewry; Jews and Violence* (Oxford, 2003), 168 ff.
5. This conception of paradigms is developed by Thomas S. Kuhn in his groundbreaking *The Structure of Scientific Revolutions* (Chicago: University of Chicago, 1970).
6. Marc Belth: *Education as a Discipline; a Study of the Role of Models in Thinking* (Boston: Allyn and Bacon, 1965), 61.

acted upon. Belth describes what transpires in the world of models, which he also calls "systematic clusters," as follows:

> . . . man is continuously shaping his experience into a whole which can be recalled readily and used in confronting and explaining new events. In this constant shaping, he borrows from everywhere—from his observations, from what he has felt and tasted, from his dreams and illusions, from his desires and dreads. What he sees in the world is what his systematic cluster permits him to see. The meanings which events come to have are derived entirely from this system, [from this] model of reality through which he sees the world.
>
> We sometimes call such models philosophies of life, theologies, developed political systems. . . But a model can also be a word, a design, a plan, a picture. Sometimes models are efforts at copying the events of the world, connected by created concepts: sometimes they are highly abstract symbols that stand for things. But however we may characterize them, they are windows through which we see the world . . . and they make the world meaningful to us in their own terms . . .[7]

How, then, do innovation and change originate? They come about, says Belth, through the work of revolutionaries; people who escaped from conventional thought to envision new models, to draw new pictures.

The task of drawing new pictures is not simple. Consider, for example, George Orwell's superb little novel *Animal Farm* (1946), that pithily describes a failed revolution of "animals," that is, oppressed masses, against human (i.e., capitalist) enslavers. Orwell shows how insidiously old models survive even under new names; as the now regnant pigs in his tale progressively become more "human," i.e., they turn into slave drivers.

But, declares Belth, there are some extraordinary men and women who do step outside their models and thoughtfully examine how these models work. They might argue that these are now inadequate to organize present experience. They create new models and, in some manner and to some degree, persuade others that the world seen through these newly discovered windows is more meaningful, more desirable, more

---

7. *Ibid.*

predictable and more manageable. Not surprisingly Belth points to philosophers as "the most notorious among these model builders."[8]

The Destruction of the Old [the Wise] Is Called Construction[9]

How does this happen? If indeed we always see things through the prism of an already constructed model, how do these talented individuals become builders? We may understand from the rabbinic passage cited in our sub-title above that building first involves the process of undermining and even destroying what was until then sacrosanct. If so, a central task of philosophers, philosophers of education included, is to examine, within their distinct fields, whether certain models still serve to identify "the field" and can still legislate for it with authority; whether existing models still constitute our "world." We must keep in mind that where new models are on the scene, even in nascent form, they tend to cast doubt upon the viability of old ones. But this is a complicated procedure. Determining when to build and when to destroy requires, in addition to great courage, much knowledge and experience. It is best, posits the Tosefta, left to the old, the wise.

One manifestation of this situation of crisis, in which old models seem inadequate or misleading, is that philosophers take on an analytic and descriptive task: they attempt to define and to survey different competing models in a given area of study and experience. Here, the philosopher, in "reviewing" all views, stands implicitly above them all. And sometimes he explicitly criticizes them for playing by the (confining) rules of discourse commonly accepted. S/he may also undermine the authority of existing models by saying that "there is something to be learned from all of them" or by simply describing norm-legislating models dispassionately. Sophisticated descriptions of the models being examined tend to deprive them of their prescriptive or normative status. "Learning something from all of them" is to see them from a new vantage point. Indeed, descriptions of models are often a prelude to discarding them.

---

8. *Ibid.*

9. Tosefta *Avodah Zarah* (I–19). The original context deals with the question of rebuilding the Temple: If the young tell you to build and the old tell you to destroy, listen to the latter, for the building of children is destruction, and the destruction of the old is construction.

Scheffler's Three Models: Locke, Plato and Kant

This point, of studying and describing with a view to possible reshuffling and rebuilding, is implicit in Israel Scheffler's classic description of three models of teaching in the paper already cited: the Impression model, the Insight model and the Rule model.[10] The first "draws the picture" of an initially blank mind, likened to a clean sheet of paper on which teaching and experience inscribe things to be "processed" and made into active knowledge. The agents of learning, i.e., teachers and parents, are charged with filling the paper, i.e., the mind, with materials which the mind can rework, making the connections that form real knowledge.

If this first model derives from a "picture drawn" by John Locke, the second originates in the thought of Plato, and, later, bears the imprint of Augustine.[11] A central focus of this model is that learners grasp, or "envision," only that which they, in some sense, already know. Teachers, then, are engaged in "reminding" the learners of what they know. The model poses the question whether they must also, in some sense, *not* know it, for otherwise, when and how can one be said to have learned something new? The third, the Rule model, which is closely associated with the thought of Immanuel Kant, sees the essence of education in the teaching of principles, of freely accepted yet binding imperatives. Scheffler sees the rule model as complementing the others by adding to the cognitive "discoveries" of the first two models the dimension of actions learned.

The Mansion: A Fourth Model?

As we might expect from our reading of Belth, finding good points in three conflicting models may presage the explication of a fourth one that learns from the alleged shortcomings of the others. This new model incorporates "what is to be learned" from each model but, by so incorporating them, is actually creating another model. In the case before us, we may call it the "mansion model," for it sees education as drawing learners into a house with many rooms and many windows. We enter the mansion armed with principles, insights and rules but, also, with cultural and historical traditions. Our task, says Scheffler,

---

10. Scheffler: *op. cit.*, 100–112.

11. We should note that this model is expounded also in *Midrash Tanhuma Pekudai*. See my discussion of it in *Roads to the Palace; Jewish Texts and Teaching* (Providence: Berghahn, 1995), 91–96.

is to pass on "the multiple live traditions in which [our principles] . . . are embodied and in which a sense of their history, spirit and direction may be discerned."[12]

In this connection, Scheffler cites the English educational philosopher R.S. Peters. The task of the teacher, Peters states, "is to try to get others on the inside of a public form of life that he shares and considers to be worthwhile." This is a model, then, that seeks to make young people "at home" in a many-splendored place where we can freely take in its treasures but according to rules and principles that we have inherited from our historical traditions of science, morality, and culture. Needless to say, this new model may also be scrutinized when needed to determine whether the goods it brings us are "the best that we know" and how they may be improved should the (perceived) need arise. Hence, in teaching, "we do not impose our wills on the student, but introduce him to the many mansions of the heritage in which we ourselves strive to live, and to the improvement of which we are ourselves devoted."[13]

From Scheffler we may learn that theoretical models, including models of teaching, do not so much aim to describe teaching as to orient it. In the act of simplifying, they weave a coherent picture out of epistemological, psychological and normative elements. Models not only enable us to represent and organize the world or some significant part of it by way of a somewhat simplified pictures of reality, but they bear ideological, theological and pedagogical worlds of meaning and obligation.

Ideologies of Instruction

I shall maintain, in line with the thought of the late Israeli educational philosopher Zvi Lamm, that educational models are often used, consciously or unconsciously, to transmit concealed ideologies of instruction.[14] Thus, in studying the ways in which models help us to understand the educational enterprise, we are also examining and evaluating these ideologies and attempting to understand more clearly how they affect our thinking on educational issues and where they are leading us. These ideological questions may be formulated as follows:

---

12. Scheffler: *op. cit.*, 113–114.

13. *Ibid.*

14. Zvi Lamm: *Conflicting Theories of Instruction: Conceptual Dimensions* (Berkeley: McCutchan, 1976), especially 3–35 and his cognitive map, 224.

(a) How do we perceive the current situation in Jewish education, or in whatever field being explored? (b) What is good, but, also, what do we find unacceptable and/or even perverse in the current situation? (c)What would we envision as an improvement or even fundamental change that we can see as a *tikkun*, a repair of this current situation? (d) What must be done to bring about the required *tikkun* or transformation? What is involved in mobilizing "our forces" to achieve the desirable state of affairs?

The Three Educational Models of Zvi Lamm

Lamm lays before us a specifically ideological triad of educational models, two of which he rejects, though they may be said to "survive" as carefully monitored stages within the third model, which is the commended one. There is, first, of all, the ideology of *socialization*, incorporated in an "initiation" model that draws a picture signifying togetherness, say, campers standing around the flagpole in a semi-circle or children sitting in straight rows in the classroom. Here, children are expected to take on the accepted values, funds of knowledge and practices of the educating generation. If they do so, their education can be deemed successful; we may assume that their teachers have utilized appropriate subject matter, created a congenial learning environment, developed the appropriate relationships with pupils and have devised suitable tools of measurement and evaluation (e.g., examinations). The success of teachers becomes evident when their pupils have become good and loyal members of their society. Here, then, is an ideology of loyalty to society, communal togetherness and competence.

A somewhat different model he terms the "molding" one, of *acculturation*. Within this model, children are educated to accept and identify with the principles and ideals of the culture. This differs from the socialization model insofar as learners who have been initiated successfully into the culture are given the freedom to interpret and apply the culture's principles on the basis of their own defensible (!) decisions regarding their application for their generation and in their own situation. To deserve the trust and gratitude of their mentors, they must demonstrate that they wish no ill to the heritage of their culture even, or especially, when they innovate within it. A suitable picture of this model may be students sitting around a table in a graduate seminar in humanities.

Lamm expresses disapproval of both these models which, he declares, lead to inadequate and even pernicious theories of instruction.

The model of socialization, he believes, creates robots. As for the model of acculturation, it denies young people genuine autonomy by feeding them classic "verities" that chain pupils even while claiming to have liberated them.

The only form of instruction that he legitimates as genuine education is grounded in the model of *development*. In this model, instruction does not serve the purposes of socialization or acculturation, but cultivates autonomy in each individual. Education is founded on belief in the fundamental goodness, good sense and intelligence of young people who have not been corrupted by bad "education." Here, children are invited or even required to discover their own principles. They are also to develop the courage to bear the responsibility of applying them freely without having to justify them on the basis of other, often antagonistic, models. A possible picture of this model is Abraham standing "on one side" while all others stood on "the other side." But this picture must incorporate Abraham's covenant with God who, paradoxically, tells him to stand alone.

Imported Models: Freud, Buber and Soloveitchik

Lamm's model is pristinely philosophical-educational. However, many models that are not inherently educational are imported into education from proximate disciplines such as theology, sociology and psychology.

One of the most celebrated models of modern culture that conceptualizes personality is that of Sigmund Freud, who presented us with three characters at loggerheads with one another, jousting within each of us and with the environment. These characters are in constant interaction and, generally, conflict. This picture has invited generations of psychoanalysts to pose varying questions that take off from this fundamental image. How shall we define and manage the neuroses that arise from the deep-seated conflict between these three ogre-like little men and the environment? How may we define mental health in the unfailing presence of these strange characters? What constitutes competence and propriety in the conduct of therapy? As for educational questions: how shall we take the fundamental and gloomy facts of personality and human existence into account so that life may be lived with some contentment and richness, even in the presence of the omnipresent "discontents" of human civilization? In these questions, the prescriptive character of such models is much in evidence.

A theological model that has long been utilized in Jewish and non-Jewish education is based on Martin Buber's distinction between "I-Thou" relationships that bespeak encounter and personhood, and "I-It" situations in which "the other," human or even divine, is no more than an object for use, conceptualization and control. The graphic representation, conveyed by these two (as it were) sets of persons, summons us to build the center of our lives around and within "I-Thou" orientations, rather than "I-It" ones. We are asked to meet the other in a dialogical fashion. The educator, then, is responsible for "arranging encounters" between his or her pupils and for them. At the same time, she must recognize that the learning of skills, also necessary for a fulfilled and responsible life, is legitimately slanted towards the conceptual and objective thinking of "I-It."

Similar is Rabbi Joseph B. Soloveitchik's model of "Adam I" and "Adam II," presented to us in his essay "The Lonely Man of Faith."[15] This has been read as suggesting that education be constructed to generate tension between "majesty" and "covenant" in the life of the educated religious personality yet envisioning ultimate accord between them. Education at its best draws Adam I and his majesty into the circle of authority bestowed by God on the covenantal Adam II.

Developmental Models

Some models, then, are drawn from disciplines such as theology and psychology, co-opted by educators for their own purposes. There are also models that explicitly lead us to think of education as resting on stages in children's cognitive or moral development. In these developmental models, the first stage should lead eventually to the second and then on to the third and further stages; whether it does so adequately is seen to depend largely on the educator.

A consistently developmental model that is anchored in educational rather than psychological theory is that of Kieran Egan,[16] whose four stages of educational development represent the educational ideal and program of leading children towards ever greater understanding of the nature and substance of reality. Here, the key phrase is "stages." The person being appropriately educated is assumed to move steadily

---

15. Joseph B. Soloveitchik: *The Lonely Man of Faith* (New York: Doubleday, 1992).

16. See, for example, Kieran Egan: *Individual Development and the Curriculum* (London: Hutchinson, 1986).

in a specific direction: from the mythic stage to the romantic, then to philosophical and, finally, to ironic thinking. What the model pictures is much like a ladder. The number of rungs to be successfully climbed depends on many factors: physical, mental, and environmental. But development is certainly an educational issue.

It is important to note that all such ideological and prescriptive models leave some researchers and observers skeptical: Why entertain the illusion that such basically differing inclinations—say, that between Adam I and Adam II—can be harmonized, or that there is a dialectic movement toward ultimate concord in human life, say, between "I-It" and "I-Thou"? If there are in fact different types of people who have greatly variegated formative experiences, why should we not expect each person to develop in the direction of her early experience and innate traits? The "I-It" child, or the Adam I child will develop certain traits of controlling behavior, while the one whom William James called the "tender-minded" person will more closely resemble the "I-Thou" or the Adam II profile. These researchers may claim, on the basis of their own sociological, psychological and philosophical models of course, that the Soloveitchik- or Egan-oriented educator tries, by an intellectual sleight of hand, to convert descriptions into prescriptions, as though "facts" of development and cognition could magically be turned into norms, like pumpkins into carriage, simply by drawing interesting pictures.[17]

SECTION TWO

Three Ways of Seeing What Educators Think They Are Doing: A Reiteration

In the preceding pages, we made some preliminary excursions into the landscape of educational models and acquaintance with some pictures, concepts, and characters one may expect to meet on such excursions.

Now, we are ready to briefly examine three possible models for the formation of the educated person with specific reference to the

---

17. See the implicit critique of Charles S. Leibman who brings human "types" into a research pattern that calls into question "harmonizations" of the kind we have considered. Cf. Charles Leibman: "The Sociology of Religion and the Study of American Jews," *Conservative Judaism* XXXIV (May-June 1981), 17–33.

teaching of the Jewish tradition. All three meet the criteria of identifiable models; all make prescriptions for "moving" children towards what their adherents see as the purposes of education and as blueprints for making educated (Jewish) persons. While each is distinct, none needs be seen, in principle, as indifferent to the pictures and metaphors of the others. All draw pictures that help us "store" and organize knowledge and moral insights, all invite us to envision how "it could be different," and all set rules for theory and conduct. All, in an age of valuative crisis, present problems to the normative educational thinker and practitioner, and to all one may pose ideological questions.

The first of my three I shall call the *four-tiered philosophical* model, which is graphic. The second model I shall call the *language-and-literature* model, which is conceptual; and the third, the *traditional-existential* model, which tells stories. What may each separately suggest to us and teach us? Is the statement that "they can all teach us something" in fact a harbinger of a new model? Or, perhaps, they complement one another, for example, by marking progressive stages of development and comprehension?

Finally, what kinds of questions about basic commitment and conviction arise from an analysis of the implications of one or more of them?

Model One:
Principles, Ideals, Aims and Means

What I am calling the four-tiered philosophical-curricular model, was first called to my attention in conversation with my late teacher, Professor Seymour Fox. It is based on four theoretical elements in curricular discussions. In this approach, we begin our conversation with philosophical principles and then move in the direction of theory of practice and, finally, to practice itself.

I am drawing the picture of this model in the form of a four-tiered building. There is a "foundational" ground floor, or tier, of principles, pure and Platonic. These basic principles describe what we hold true with regard to ultimate reality and its significance, or lack thereof. The savants who dwell on the first tier inform us, and then constantly "remind" us, as to what "we" believe about transcendence and what, in the nature of things, we hold to be inherently good and valuable. These answers, and the questions that lie behind them, may be formulated in the shape of a sublime philosophical discourse. But at times, and for many, the philosophy and the principles can be stated more simply: as affirmations of commitment and faith. As such they inform us of our view of things. What we affirm as the body of principle by which we are to live is our picture of the world. Moreover, the ideas we have of the world and ourselves within it are what we educate towards.

On the basis of principles and *ideas* propagated by the savants on the first tier, our second tier people build *ideals* of what the good, the achievable, and the real should look like after they have been brought down to earth and translated into concrete human situations. We may say that here, articles of "faith" and conceptions of the true and the worthy (principles) are re-imagined as practical *visions* for human life.

For example: the principle of (belief in) a revealing God is "brought down" to us in "religion," which constitutes a system of ideals (of practice, commitments, and embodiments of "the good life"). Each principle or belief might be expressed in a number of ideals or religions.

A belief in the ultimate value of freedom can receive principled and concrete expression in diverse ways. We may opine that freedom is an aspect of reality telling us what was "in God's mind" when He created the world, or that it is an imperative of Reason. When we examine the principle of freedom in its various versions and "translate" it into the social, political and historical challenges facing us in this particular time, we are most likely to recognize it in the democratic and liberal ideal of "bringing freedom down to earth." In the discovery of what is ideal and can be justified in the name of principles, we are discovering the fundamental agenda of the education to which we are committed.

Let us summarize by drawing a picture of the first two tiers. With regard to those sitting on the first, the "principled" tier of the four in this model's picture: think of them as elderly, wise and severe. These sage individuals, remember, reside quite abstractly in a rather airless hall, and they are called upon to answer such weighty questions as: What is real, knowable, worth knowing and good?

Those who ask such troubling questions for purposes of translation into their mundane reality are of course sitting on the second tier. They have somewhat more of a view but hesitate to open the windows lest the savants sitting below them catch colds and lose their ability to function. We must keep in mind that in this model the second tier people are assumed capable of acting only after consultation with the first tier sages for they draw their justification from the principles of the first tier's eminences. The task of our second tier characters, it is said, is only and always to bring these embodiments down to earth, articulating them as values, as ideals.

Problems in the Tiers

But this seems overly simplified; in fact, often false. We may entertain the thought that living ideals are not simply translations from abstract ideas, but are also (and, in Judaism, are particularly) decisions made on grounds of revelation and the conversations revelation engenders. Hence, the first tier sages, who represent the world of pure principle, find themselves in the uncomfortable situation of being more revered for their antiquity than respected for ostensible relevance. They may come to feel that while they are lords of educational thought, they are somewhat like members of the contemporary House of Lords; dressed in finery but politely ignored. This situation is variously manifested; I shall mention only two examples.

(1) Even a cursory study of educational ideas and ideals reveals that almost identical ideals can be based on diverse and even opposing principles. For example, a person may be devoted to democracy (an ideal) on the basis of his/her belief in the principle that humans are created in God's image. Yet, conversely, her devotion to democracy may rest on the belief (an idea) that human life is absurd and un-principled. Those who adhere to democracy for the latter reason demonstrate by their commitment their desire to "make something" out of chaos, to redeem themselves from it, to live with others decently, even if absurdly. The "image of God" doesn't enter into it.

Hence, the citizens of Tier One are dismayed to see some men and women of Tier Two insisting that the educator's ideals are in some ways more important or at least prior to her principles in the educational enterprise. Of course, the first tier people may remind their second tier fellows that the Torah, in its two creation stories, "teaches Torah" by beginning with a principled narrative ("In the beginning. . . And God saw that it was good. . . Male and female He created them") and only then moves "down to earth," to a story of the ideal itself, represented by humans, the commandment they were to obey, but didn't, their failed relationship—and their eventual reconciliation. To this, the ideal-oriented educator may respond with the arguments and verses used by Bet Hillel in the classic controversy with Bet Shammai, to show that moving in either direction is equally valid.[18]

---

18. The reference is to the dispute between Bet Shammai and Bet Hillel

(2) We have seen in the case of our two democrats how diverse principles can give rise to common ideals: one theologically-oriented, and the other secular-existentialist in spirit. But it should be clear, also, that people who have the same principles may embrace them in the service of different ideals!

For example: Let me imagine myself running a Jewish school situated next to a Catholic one, the latter headed by a devoted educator and a woman of theological principle. In conversations with her, it becomes clear to me that she and I agree on many principles, first and foremost, the existence of God. We also both affirm that God created the world, that He is good, and that He has communicated with humanity through revelation. We are also at one in believing that He is the redeemer of the human soul.

Yet my colleague understands these tenets of faith in terms of her religion, which is a distinct constellation of ideals and one radically different from my own. Therefore neither of us would ever entertain the idea that our schools be merged. Also, there will be serious doubts as to whether we could ever run a joint activity that specifically testifies to our schools both being "religious" schools.

Why is this so? Speaking from my side, though I share some of the spiritual concerns that animate my colleague's faith, the crucial issue for me is: What are her ideals? For example: Does she observe the mitzvot, that is, does she perform actions, social and individual, that testify to Jewish religious beliefs and acts? Do we share responsibility for a living Jewish people that is a people of revelation? Of course she will have similar but converse concerns. We may respect each other and befriend each other. We may share certain ideals. We have common aspirations for the society in which we both live. We should like to see a more decent one and we are likely to frame this ideal in vaguely religious terms. But we cannot educate towards faith together, under one roof.

All these problems force us to entertain the notion that the first tier can also be the second, and vice versa. This notion raises various questions for Jewish educators who are uneasy with a view of the world which accords pride of place to principles rather than to ideals. But let

---

whether the heavens or the earth were created first, with Shammai offering "principled" reasons for his view and Hillel more down to earth reasons. The Sages declare that the proof texts offered can be combined, as in Genesis 2:1 (*Genesis Rabbah* I:15).

us, at this moment, keep our first two tiers as originally conceived in the model and now visit, even if briefly, the third and fourth tiers.

The Third Tier and the Question of Curriculum

The third tier brings us to the theory of practice. We raise the question of how to formulate goals that can bring the ideals into the real lives of learners. On the basis of recognized ideals (Tier Two), the educator is here asked to state and define his actual aims. What constitutes the curriculum? Why are certain aspects of human experience highlighted and others ignored or played down? What price is paid for each decision? What is the syllabus for each sphere of life and knowledge? How does each syllabus represent our best efforts to make educational ideals come alive; to create competence and genuine feeling in those who live by these ideals? How does the total curriculum address both individuals and society as a whole?

As we might have expected, this tier is a bustling place. There are think tanks galore, guest speakers, inquiry into a range of shapes and forms of education, pilot programs in various realms of knowledge, and experiments into diverse ways of envisioning human abilities and potential. Here, major jumps are to be made—from the heights of the ideal to the animated area of relevance and communicability, achieved or not. What is side-tracked and what is placed at the center of things because it evokes fierce loyalty and concern?

This negotiation, between the ideal and the possible, moves into high gear on Tier Four. Teachers must now decide which means are most useful for achieving the stated goals. If, for example, our ideals are complex and at times paradoxical, the desire to educate toward complexity must always figure in deliberations, and these deliberations must take place in the context of theological and ideological ideals that often present themselves as straightforward prescriptions for specific attitudes required of "good Jews" and loyal citizens. Likewise it must be kept in mind that psychological *descriptions* pertaining to cognitive development may, at a given stage, sabotage certain *prescriptions*, turning normative statements into research data.

The Fourth Tier: A Technical Matter?

Some people come to the fourth tier thinking that finding the right means for the educational enterprise at hand, is a technical matter. Yet, in fact, the availability or non-availability of appropriate means must necessarily affect the goals. Thus, an outstanding curriculum that spells out its goals clearly and reflects lofty ideals can stumble on the training and performance of teachers who have not been taught to understand these goals and whose agreement to its principles has not been secured. In their teaching, members of the teaching staff may conceive of the curriculum, its purpose and processes, differently than did the curriculum writers, or than what their school boards intended. Hence, while the curriculum can be well served by teachers, they may also sabotage it.

The educator, in writing her curriculum, must not forget that means are never neutral or simply techniques, and that realities on the ground may carry more weight in determining what actually happens than statements of aims.

Following Heilman,[19] let us imagine a Modern Orthodox school whose goals are perfectly acceptable to its constituents. Though not all the parents are themselves Modern Orthodox, the school's leadership has devised what it considers to be a reasonable way of dealing with this datum, and has made a sensible policy decision.[20]

But there is a major problem that cannot be solved by setting policies or issuing statements of aims. The problem is that the burgeoning of the Modern Orthodox day school movement requires a far greater number of trained and committed teachers than what is currently available in the community. The educational leadership will then "have no choice" but to turn to secular or ultra-Orthodox teachers. The leadership may institutionalize this situation and ignore or turn down the plea rising up from the third tier, to invest heavily and in a focused manner, in teacher training! As for the teachers employed, they, too, quite legitimately, have a philosophy, and they place on the third and fourth tiers what they learned from *their* mentors!

As my colleague, Seymour Fox, liked to say, one can only hope that the fine cognac of educational philosophy and theory will arrive at the educational table as tasty and healthy grape juice. It could be worse than that.

---

19. Samuel Heilman: "Modern Orthodox Judaism Today: Currents and Trends in America," *Studies in Jewish Education* vol. X (2004), 49–64.

20. For example, traditional Jews who are not themselves fully observant have agreed that, in sending their children to the school, they have expressed their agreement that the school's aim of using the curriculum to promote an Orthodox agenda is acceptable to them, and they commit themselves not to sabotage or undermine it in their parenting.

To sum up: this model looks to present a philosophically-based, hierarchical scheme. On each level, we are to accept the authority of those directly below us. They are to give legitimacy to our ideals, and ultimately to our educational aims and then to means. In this model, the curriculum may seem to be laid out like a "set table." One first clarifies and consults principles, then "translates" them into ideals, which in turn lead us to aims and means. But we must keep in mind that different and even opposing principles may serve as the basis for given ideals. Furthermore, there is a variety of goals that may, under ever changing circumstances, "capture" the ideal and distance it from its original intent.[21] Finally, there is the "give and take" that characterizes the locating of adequate means to carry out the goals; means that are often simply unavailable. It appears, then, that the notion of "a set table" has only limited validity. It is up to the characters on the last two tiers to remind the personages in the first two tiers that education is "not in Heaven." But someone up there has to remind those below that, in this model, education must point to Heaven.

The "Language-Literature" Model

The terms *Language* and *Literature* that are definitive to my second model, I shall explain shortly. But first, let it be noted that we are little concerned here with abstract philosophical questions. Rather, we begin our deliberation with goals. These goals reflect ideals. However, these ideals are not cherished mainly for their reported ability to reflect metaphysical truths, though this, too, is within the circle of their possible significance. Mainly, the goals are perceived in terms of the culture by which we live; *within* which we live. This culture provides our contact with what we consider reality; it is within it that we engage in an ongoing conversation about what is worthy and worth knowing to us.

True, in the consciousness of the educated person, the goals of education are admittedly based on ideals of culture "as it should be." But the normative underpinnings of this model, while reaching out to cultural ideals, have more to do with the identity of the person being

---

21. A pithy example would be the interpretation which is given to the concept of *tsniut* (modesty), which has moved in many school settings to connoting no more than boy-girl relationships and confining these relations as much as possible, whereas the classic understanding of *tsniut* surely takes in the character trait of humility and behavior that is in good taste.

educated than with his or her philosophical acumen. This person is to become a participant in culture; perhaps a builder as well as a son or daughter. This means, also, that she can be expected to know a great deal and to be capable of putting valued artifacts of culture in their proper niches, contexts and perspectives.

Beginning with the goal of initiation, as this model does, means that education, first and foremost, must bring the young person into society and its "Language." What is the picture drawn by the model of *Language*, and its companion concept, *Literature*?

Language Defined

Let me begin by delineating what is meant here by the first of these two metaphors: "Language." "Language," as the term is used here, does not refer mainly to "spoken" languages such as Hebrew, English, or French. Rather, it is indebted to the conception of "civilization" as the British philosopher Michael Oakshott understood it.[22] In my own use of the term, I have referred to Language as the sum total of society's canons: its basic assumptions and procedures; its characteristic modes of behavior and communication; its "inner" truth and self-understood character in the eyes of those who "speak" it. Language, then, is all that is holy to society or perennial within it; all that gives it, and us, a specific and expressed identity. And since our Language is our identity, it is no more to be discarded in times of crisis than is a person wracked by problems to commit suicide. However the history of Language indicates that it constantly undergoes interpretation and that it must remain open to new understandings if its devotees wish to protect it from becoming archaic and unconvincing. "Language," then, could not survive without what we are calling "Literature," to which we shall turn shortly.

A fundamental quality of the Language of Judaism is that it is an historically religious Language that posits a close connection between Language and Revelation as found in its sacred books and traditions. Books that are considered embodiments of Language, or to contain it, or are said to be touched by it, are "holy." They are citadels of Language. This Language is to be impressed upon the hearts of the young by the communities that define themselves as living by it.

---

22. See Michael Oakeshott: "The Study of Politics in a University," in *Rationalism in Politics and Other Essays* (London: Methuen, 1962), for an exposition of his view on "Language" and "Literature."

The status of sacred writings, holy actions, holy times, and even the Hebrew language itself (*leshon hakodesh*) as hallowed (Language, the Word of God), was self-evident until recent generations. Then it was taken for granted that Scripture, studied "day and night," could have no "unacceptable" passages but only "difficult" ones. No wonder that when a holy book fell to the ground, it was kissed. For these tomes conveyed Language—and Language was "from Heaven."

Literature Defined

And when we turn to the concept of *Literature*, we encounter a paradox that is at the heart of this model. Namely, that what was learned in search for contact with the Language was itself largely or mostly Literature. For where people live within a Language, they must "speak" it, and their speech becomes interpretation, commentary; a blend of both tradition and innovation. How so?

Let us state this systematically: The lives of people who live within their Language produce "Literature." Those dedicated to the Language see all worthy Literatures as growing out of it, demonstrating its richness. The Language comes to be cherished as the source of Literatures. Worthwhile Literatures, those that somehow return the learner "to the source" demonstrate what people in the society have done with the Language, how they have expanded and illuminated it by way of new Literatures. No wonder, then, that Literature has been traditionally considered worth "learning" if and where it reflects favorably on the Language, showing the power of the Language to generate new Literature and signifying the devotion of its speakers to the Language.

For those who live by this model, the purpose of education is clear. It is to draw young people into the Language, to get them to "speak it" fluently so that it becomes theirs, and to introduce them to valuable Literatures that have expressed and maintained the Language and, also, built upon it throughout its history. An implicit goal within this model is expressed by the desire of the educator that, hopefully, the person now sitting before him will be capable and worthy of adding Literature, even a footnote, to the common fund of his cultural "world," a footnote that points, once again, to the meaning of the Language itself.

We shall address a major ideological and theological issue inherent in this model in the concluding section. Here, we shall mention the danger that has, in recent generations, given the model some notoriety by way of one of its core images. This image portrays the learning individual, a master of Language and fluent in Literature, sitting in a citadel of the Language, e.g., the Yeshiva, and the "learning" student, who threatens, despite the best intentions, to turn "learning" into an elitist pursuit. Hence, I suggest, an important piece of Literature is the controversy within its corpus as to whether a person's preoccupation with Language will be deemed worthy to the extent that s/he is also capable of self-support (by pursuing a trade), and to the extent that s/he learns to deal with the challenges and dangers posed by the physical environment (for example, by knowing how to swim), in addition to devoting time to Torah (*Kiddushin* 29b).

It is, of course, the latter requirement that returns us to the essence of this model and to its highest aspiration. The duty to "learn Torah for its own sake" may be understood to imply that the learner who lives fully within this model is constantly replenished by living contact with the Language and its classic Literatures. They are his life and the length of his days, and they can create a unique perspective on "literary" pursuits of various kinds. In this context, one may think of the parent of a budding university student who suggests that the young person first spend a year or two "studying Torah."

To "Be Like Moses" Yet Not To Be; A Traditional-Existential Model

Autonomy and Authenticity

We move now to our third model. Here, the picture is a montage of human predicaments, of challenges, dilemmas and discernments. It is a model of storytelling and of shocks of recognition at what is being heard.

But first: What is the reader to understand by this title? What is a "traditional-existential" model? Is it traditional or existential? If existential, how traditional? And where does Moses come into the picture? He was, after all, not traditional but the father of a new entity: the People of Israel. And what is the intellectual casuistry that makes him an existentialist in the light of his life project of creating a kingdom for a commanding monotheism and a home for the thundering voice of prophecy? And, to confound the bewilderment: Is this people a "project" of Moses—or of God? And, a final question, addressed to the present writer: What are you up to?

We are already in the thick of the complexities that characterize this model as it has been presented by modern Jewish thinkers who were themselves heavily invested in education, men such as Martin Buber and Franz Rosenzweig. We must also acknowledge the colossal pedagogic work of Nehama Leibowitz who can largely be credited with making the teaching of Jewish biblical texts a central educational enterprise! And in her wake, we have known many creative teachers who have made us aware of the seeming contradictions, thus, the educational difficulties within the model; difficulties that have been, more often than not, presented as strengths! Clearly this model looks to teachers who are wise and learned and who strive to impart much knowledge to "learners." Yet we also hear an implicit warning by mentors of this model not to confuse education with endless streams of "subject matter." They tell us that education is always of the person rather than of the field, i.e., one teaches material but does not educate it; only people can be both taught and educated.

This model seems close to the educational conception of "vision" but, characteristically, it deals with vision against the backdrop of moral and often religious decisions and dilemmas. But who ever thought of religion as a locus of dilemmas?

A Model of Narratives

The narratives told within this model are its central "pictures." These stories may be divided, like the model itself, into two modes: the religious and the secular, though such categorizations vastly oversimplify the matter. Is the Kafka who authored *The Trial* and *The Castle* secular or religious?[23] In what is called the secular mode, the emphasis is, at first, on stories that depict deliberation towards the solution of problems. They are often inspiring and heroic. They are often biographical. But they are discovered to bear, at the outer limits of experience, a call to the human soul to admit the presence of the incomprehensible, the absurd and tragic in life's path as well as the sublime and significant. This often shocking discovery pulls the person to a search for self, perhaps through classic literature and philosophical

---

23. It is noteworthy that one of this model's significant thinkers, Franz Rosenzweig, upon reading Kafka's novel *The Castle,* expressed the opinion that: "The people who wrote the Bible seem to have thought of God much the way Kafka did," Nahum Glatzer: *Franz Rosenzweig: His Life and Thought* (Philadelphia: JPS, 1953), 160.

anthropology, perhaps via a fascination with poetry or art and film, or perhaps by way of a need to journey to unknown or hidden coves on the face of the earth. All are studied and pondered in search of the complexities with which we must live and in search of guidelines for how to do so. All impress upon the learner that there are problems that must be confronted even if they cannot be solved, problems that will forever remain part and parcel of our situation as human beings.

In the religious manifestations of this educational model, the tension between autonomy and authenticity, often of minor significance for secular-minded thinkers and teachers, is writ large. This tension arises from the decision of the educated religious person and her teachers to acknowledge the presence of Transcendence in the educational situation that is experienced as having been there from the start, in addition to, and alongside of, inquiry-guided-by-intelligence.

As in a life defined as secular, the encounter with this presence teaches that there is perplexity and even mystery and contradiction in the very fabric of life. Thus, autonomy is both illusionary, for "all is in the hand of Heaven", and yet it is at the heart of the matter, for the Fear of Heaven is not in the hands of Heaven. "Heaven" demands responsibility and accords freedom, and, specifically, frees the human being from the sense of tragedy, for not everything is required of the person him/herself. Hence, if we cultivate the sense of tragedy, we may be enticed into evasion and useless introspection into the human soul.

The presence that is there from the beginning is the Torah, and the shape of deliberation it adds to general inquiry, is called "learning." Yet this is not simply traditional learning; as in the secular mode, there is an acknowledgement of dialectics as an avenue of enlightenment. There is conscious decision making and, last but not least, a desire to integrate "everything known" so that faith does not become an escape from reality. *Yir'at Shamayim*, "Fear of Heaven" (and that is what we are talking about within the purview of this model), requires responsibility. And responsibility requires knowledge.

This model, then, whether in its religious or secular modes, is much concerned with both individual responsibility and with the integration of everything we know and experience. This requires a "working out" of what we know and an admission of ignorance. Here, philosophy, and philosophies of various realms (e.g., of law, of education, of science, of history, of religion, etc.), play major roles in helping us to integrate what we know and experience, as well as what we don't. But the model does not exempt the religious person from the quest for "putting it all together", the hallmark of what the educationist, Ernst A. Simon, called "second innocence"—*temimut sheniyah*.[24]

Two Tales

In engaging in abstract discussion as we have done here, we may well be distancing ourselves from understanding the model itself. At this point, therefore, we must take note of our model's discomfort with too many or premature explanations, as though everything can be made clear and simple after all. We move, then, to the broad plains of the model where there are stories and teachings.

Our first tale is unmistakably, yet obliquely, about piety. The story-episode concerns the Hasidic teacher and rabbi Zusya of Hanipol. His disciples, it is told, found him, after many years of illness, on his death-bed, in a state of great trepidation. When they asked him for the cause of his agitation he is said to have replied:

> In the world to come to which I am now being called, I will perhaps be asked why I wasn't like Abraham or Moses. I am not afraid of such questions and I have an answer at hand, namely, that I am neither Moses nor Abraham. The question I dread is, why weren't you Zusya?

We note, first of all, that this, as many stories of its kind, involves a dialogue between the teacher and his disciples. The teacher feels himself called upon to instruct his disciples "this one more time" to teach them Torah. But apparently, it is not to be; the teacher seems powerless, paralyzed by fear. He cannot, so it seems, end his life as he conducted it: as their teacher! The students are shocked.

But the teacher is lifted out of his agitation; he understands his duty to teach after all. The message he conveys is at first disappointing and the pupils may plausibly think that the rabbi is simply "unloading" the reason for his dread in their presence, and that is not an act of genuine teaching. He is warning them that he (and they too?) may be asked, Why weren't you like Moses? Now that I am to be judged, perhaps those above will expect me to be like Moses. A mission impossible, even for persons as righteous as Zusya! At that moment, Zusya probably reflects, after an act of "returning" to himself before God: I

24. See Ernst Akiba Simon: "*Oz Aitam: Al Hatemimut Hasheniyah* (Then I Shall be Innocent: On the Concept of Second Innocence)," *Idem, Ha'im Od Yehudim Anahnu* (Tel Aviv: Sifriat Hapoalim, 1982), 135–69 (Hebrew).

shall have to be brave—even brazen. I shall ask the Heavenly court, Why do you judge me unfairly and harshly? After all, no one can be like Moses!

But then he discovers the source of his fear and the substance of his own teaching: What if the Heavenly court asks me why I was not Zusya, all I should have been? Why wasn't I myself? And to that I have no answer.

A strange confession and a strange teaching. My pupils: I, your teacher, am telling you of my inadequacy. But my telling you this does not deprive me of the right and duty to teach you. And the teaching is: Be, each of you, you yourself. Get close to your own ability to be authentically what you can be, yourselves, as disciples of Moses, our teacher.

The second tale is in the same vein but it is more majestic, and so it expands the discourse about "rabbis on their deathbeds" speaking to their pupils at the hour of ultimate truthfulness (*Berakhot* 28b). It describes the great sage, Rabban Yohanan ben Zakkai, the one who had who received permission from the Roman emperor to found an academy at the coastal town of Yavneh for Torah study, and this, in the last days of Jerusalem and the Commonwealth. Now we are only a few years after the destruction of the Temple by the Romans, and in the hour of Rabban Yohanan's death. Once again, the scene is one of students who have come to visit their rabbi and to receive his final earthly teaching. Here, too, they find their master and teacher weeping. He explains:

> [Even] if I were being taken before a human king, who is here today and tomorrow in the grave, and I can appease him with words and bribe him with money, I would still weep. And now that I am being taken before the King of kings, the Holy One, blessed be He…and if He kills me it is eternal death and I cannot appease Him or bribe Him, and furthermore, when there are two roads before me, one leading to *Gan Eden* [paradise] and one to *Gehinom* [hell] and I don't know by which path I shall be taken, shall I not weep?

Then, after warning them that their fear of God should be no less than their fear of humans, he becomes unexpectedly authoritative and practical, even confident in the appropriateness of his actions:

> At the moment of his departure [from the world], he said to them, Remove the vessels [from the room that they not be-

come ritually impure due to a death in the room], and prepare
a seat for King Hezekiah of Judea who is coming.

As I have suggested elsewhere,[25] R. Yohanan, who weeps at the
prospect of heavenly judgment, having established for himself that he
is indeed a "fearer of God," finds that he is freed from other fears. He
can and does act, making a halakhic ruling about situations of ritual
impurity, as though he were dealing with a theoretical case or one
pertaining to another person. Could an outsider notice, or expect, that
the law's applicability is now occasioned by the teacher's own death?

Rabban Yohanan admits that he anticipates the arrival of King
Hezekiah. Rashi opines that the Judean king of some seven hundred
and fifty years before is coming to accompany R. Yochanan to the
next world. If so, this is a dramatic scene indeed. King Hezekiah, the
embodiment not only of piety but of kingship, is coming to give his
hand to the dying sage who negotiated with Rome for "Yavneh and her
sages" so that study of Torah might outlive the Temple and the commonwealth. Would not the Judean king look upon R. Yochanan, the
man who negotiated with the enemy in wartime, as a traitor?

Rabban Yohanan, who fears Heaven, is not afraid.

A Third Text

Our perplexity grows as we examine a short biblical text and an
even shorter rabbinic commentary on it that seem to say the very opposite of what we might expect from our two previous stories:

And now, O Israel, what does the Lord your God ask of you?
Only this: to fear the Lord your God, to walk in all His ways,
to love Him and to serve the Lord your God with all your heart
and soul, to keep the Lord's commandments and laws which I
command you this day, to your good (Deut. 9:12–13).

To use a concept that this model shares with the previous (Language and Literature) one, these are "difficult" verses. In the presence
of this comprehensive demand, for fear and love and service and obe-
dience, can one really say "Only this (is requested)"? *What more could
God possibly ask?* Here, there is fear of God, and walking in His ways,
and loving Him. What else is there?

---

25. Rosenak: *Roads*, 111–112.

To this question, the Talmud offers a succinct answer (*Berakhot* 33b): The "only this," a great matter for all ordinary mortals, was a trivial matter for the one who spoke to God "face to face:" Moses. The message is clear. Everyone else is to learn from him, to emulate him, to see how this overwhelming and endless task of the spiritual life can come to look like "a small matter." We have for what to aim though we cannot achieve it. Thus, the hero of this model in both his/her religious and secular varieties is constantly afraid; his "fear" is built into his or her existential situation. S/he always, even like Zusya and Rabban Yohanan ben Zakkai, feels inadequate. But it is precisely the realization that one can never rise to the level of Moses that gives strength to the person who must act and who believes that s/he will "only" be judged for not being him/herself. The reward, however conceived, is for the sincere attempt to "*be like* Moses for whom it was a small matter" but without the ability or even the intention to be *him*.

Such are the stories that figure large in the curriculum of the traditional-existential model. We may now briefly discuss two major characteristics of our "Traditional Existential" model of Education.

Freedom and the "Fear of Heaven"

(1) Ideally, the individual being educated should always maintain his or her integrity as an individual, autonomy and responsibility. For the religious teacher and pupil this means that choice and responsibility, however paradoxically, are to play large roles in the curriculum. Elsewhere[26] I have cited Van Cleve Morris, an existential philosopher of education, to the effect that the first time a child who tries to get out of being sent to the grocer dares to tells his mother, "I didn't ask to be born," she should rejoice. What the child is saying is that he is "not guilty" for living and therefore cannot be coerced (he "doesn't have to") buy eggs and milk "for her." Why the joy? Her son now understands that, being relieved of guilt (for having been born), he is now responsible and must decide how to respond. He will judge the request and she will judge his response.

Hopefully, it won't look like that! Hopefully, both mother and son will continue to live in a relationship of ever growing trust. Nevertheless, the rules have changed. The son, we may say, is no longer someone who can be sent to the grocer every five minutes (after all, what

26. Rosenak: *Tree of Life Tree of Knowledge: Conversations with the Torah* (Boulder: Westview, 2001), 258.

about his sister?). In Jewish terms, we may say that he has become a *bar mitzvah*: one who knows himself to be responsible for his decisions and actions. Paradoxically, he is now free to choose and he is responsible for his choice. Now, he is commanded.

Theologically, the most problematic feature of this model—in which responsibility and freedom are equally present—is that while ultimate values are ultimately binding, they become so as a consequence of choice. Once chosen, they make a claim to absolute authority and the religious teacher will do everything that is educationally justified to bring about this choice in her pupils. However she will not consider a child a criminal if he chooses otherwise, no matter how pained she may be.

This acceptance of the individual's choice as legitimate even when painful will be unacceptable in many other traditional models. There it will be argued that absolute values are absolute precisely because they precede us into the world; we do not "have" these values but they "have us;" they are eternally and automatically binding. Yet the fact remains: While moral prescriptions continue to be binding, even if not individually chosen, this is patently not the way the public, even the Modern Orthodox public, perceives religiously non-normative behavior and belief. Indeed, this tolerance of non-normative behavior points precisely to the "modernity" of the model.

Furthermore, since the educated person is always "on the road," the study of Torah is not only an aspect of socialization, nor simply an act of appropriating a Language and significant Literatures. Rather, the person who "sees things" through the prism of this model, studies in an attitude of self-search.

(2) As I have tried to show in a previous work,[27] the teaching of values here evokes a dialectic and deliberative approach. I shall spell this out.

At times, when we think of "teaching values" we envision impressing on the minds and hearts of children that they must distinguish between good and evil, between value and "anti-value." Thus the story of the Golden Calf (Exodus 32–33) impresses on us the iniquitous nature of idolatry. We are bidden to serve God alone. Here, then, we have a clear case of "right and wrong." Similarly we might say, with deceptive simplicity, that loving-kindness is good while hatred is bad. Why deceptive simplicity? Because here the matter is already not

27. Rosenak: *Roads*, 147–185.

quite clear. When is loving-kindness "the value" while hatred is an anti-value? Are there not those (i.e., the incorrigibly wicked) whom we are commanded to hate? Was Aaron the high priest "weak" when he succumbed to the demand of the mob to build the Golden Calf? Or was he demonstrating his character as a "lover of peace"? It transpires that most of the absolute moral values we are to protect and maintain involve us in situations of dilemmas. True the values on the first tier (to borrow a picture from our first model) grant us identity and a clear moral sense, but until we discover the dilemmas in them, we don't know what we should actually do. When do we choose the path of peace and when the path of truth? They are seldom the same!

Take Aaron again. A *midrash* tells us that he loved to make peace between quarrelling people. He did this by telling each of the two, in turn, how the other regretted having offended his friend, whereupon they were reconciled; Aaron had made peace between them. But how about truthfulness? Was Aaron justified in lying to the "enemies" for the sake of peace? When may we tell white lies to reconcile people, and when is this illegitimate? What are possible ways out of the dilemma? We should note that, in this model, we have a deliberation; an instance of (possible) problem solving that revolves around Torah— and "learning" it.

To sum up this point: Teaching values is not mostly about "Do this and be good," but, rather, creating sensitivity to the valuative problem that faces us as we stand before different and even contradictory statements, or recommendations, or norms. How can we reach a resolution? What shall we do if we can't find a resolution? What, in various situations, are the grounds of choice made accessible through the prism of "learning"?

SECTION THREE

Models: Some Illustrative Uses

I have briefly pictured three models for the purpose of clarifying certain central questions in education, and Jewish education in particular. Those models, I have tried to show, are conceptual structures that help us to think about the issues and to locate underpinnings of the positions taken by educators. As noted, the ideological or normative questions that arise in this context can be summarized as follows: what do we consider in the current situation, to be acceptable or unacceptable, what would constitute the repair of the unacceptable and how do we move towards its *tikkun*, mending the world?

Language and Literatures: R. Soloveitchik and Zvi Lamm

How, for example, might Rabbi Soloveitchik utilize the concept of "Language and Literature" that characterizes our second model to explain the current Jewish situation, to argue for its improvement and to envision effective mobilization for change as seen through the prism of the Halakhah? It can be argued that the idea of Language can serve to explicate the Halakhah as the pristine "Language of Judaism," inviting Jews to believe and share in the unique destiny of Israel as normative in form and substance. "Literature," in a Soloveitchikian view, then, would be not only commentary on the Bible and on the words of the Sages but everything that touches on the Language without itself *being* Language. These features of Literature would bring to the fore historical-national dimensions of Jewish existence, and a collective sense of history and obligation. R. Soloveitchik would argue that the inner world of personal religious experience is to be shaped by Language (i.e., by the Halakhah and its inner meaning). Such a conception of Language could "explain" the doctrinal axiom that Jewish halakhic discipline and demands are not to be tampered with. At the same time, the Halakhah should be explained and its "difficulties" addressed in the framework of a living and Language-driven Literature.

Clearly, one could enter the discussion of Language and Literature in contemporary Jewish life and education at a radically different point. Let us imagine, for example, Zvi Lamm's response to the very notion of Language which, to him, is part and parcel of the problem of reactionary and enslaving indoctrination. He is likely to posit that modern thought and experience have exposed such conceptions as "Language" to be mere wishful thinking, grounded in an ultra-conservative ideology. In his model, those who have recourse to this term construct a static future in the light of a feverishly imagined past.

The argument about what we are calling Language brings into view a paradox within the Language-Literature model. In relatively serene epochs, Language had the status of the self-understood and it delineated "the world." It was, in a sense, the model itself. Thus there would be little occasion to define this sentiment and give it a name except in the presence of non-Jews who "didn't understand" or heretics who refused to. That which is self-understood needs no explication!

So what happens to Language in the contemporary situation of doubt and suspicion? Does it not become an indicator of ideological conviction "of some people" rather than an encompassing social reality of everyone? It would appear that that is indeed the case. To illustrate: we have seen see that Lamm's development model rejects Language and thus maintains that everything is Literature. The "world" constitutes an arena of cultural activity without walls. Here, then, is an example of how various understanding of Language and Literature helps us to categorize and give form to differing ideologies of education. Those who look forward to an education of total openness and self-development without imposed norms posit that our problem, that prevents repair, is the very concept of "Language." They will find the "Literature only" conception congenial. On the other hand, there are those who say that all is Language, and think of education as being, ideally, an uncompromising transmission of the sacred or the pristinely classical.

And what about those who wish to be modern (living within plural and ever-changing Literatures), yet traditional (dedicated to enduring forms of Language and to classic "Literatures")? What are their options? Shall they endeavor to teach by the traditional model, somewhat modified for pragmatic reasons (in ways that the tradition allegedly finds acceptable), or shall they praise the "old" (i.e., wise) philosophers who construct a new model that incorporates not only new Literature, but even, however hesitatingly, new Language?

Tradition and Modernity: A New Model

We shall illustrate. Israel's long-time Minister of the Interior, the late Yosef Burg, a very sophisticated person, was once asked which word in such hyphenated terms as *Torah-V'Avodah* (Torah and productive work), *Dati-Leumi* (National-Religious), or *Modern-Orthodoxy* was the really important one: the more obviously traditional-Jewish Language oriented one or the more modern one? His answer was that the hyphen between each set of pairs was the most important of the three signs.

Burg was making a philosophical model-making statement. Even in the presence of the old model, he felt that a new one was being constructed that reflected a specific ideology, hence a specific model of change. In this model, *Avodah*, i.e., the word picture in which we see people working with their hands, engaged in worldly affairs and combining Zionist and religious activity, needs no apologies. Torah is not a frill and *Avodah* is not a compromise with the mundane in this new model, which has learned from many others. Modern Orthodoxy is not an accommodation that makes room for both tradition and innovation, nor is it, as Haredi thinkers would say, a pernicious form of modernity that converts Judaism into a type of pale Literature, leaving the wide plains of experience and identity devoid of "Yiddishkeit." Nor is it a form of tradition that gingerly makes overtures to modernity for the sake of its own (traditional) survival. Rather, so says the hyphen of Dr. Burg, it is a new model, with some destruction (such as the demystification of the ghetto experience) for the sake of construction (of Eretz Yisrael) before the heavenly redemption.

Separately and Together: Two Questions

I shall briefly pinpoint questions raised by each model separately and then raise a question about their possible inter-actions.

The first of our models begins its curricular explorations by turning to philosophers for adequate understandings of basic principle. As a result, its adherents will say that they alone implement principled education, in which difficult questions receive forthright answers. Yet, despite the orderliness that seems to characterize this model and its ability to cover the field of educational activity and to address all aspects of it, there is a crucial question to be addressed to it, namely, whether the metaphysical-principle model is meaningful and appropriate?

In examining whether this model is both of the above, we may ask: do teachers, even those who speak unequivocally of "a Torah of truth," primarily mean by this that education—as such—and Jewish education—in particular—rests on doctrinal explorations and pronouncements? Perhaps the narratives of the forefathers and mothers, of the giving of the Torah, of wanderings in the desert and the conquest, figure more prominently in our teaching? Do we not find our ideals often preceding our principles?

We have seen the issue arise in the controversy between Bet Hillel and Bet Shammai as to whether the heavens or the earth preceded in the Creation. What distinguishes one view and perspective from the other is obviously not simply "the facts of the case" or the doctrinally correct way of seeing things. Indeed, the Sages resolve the problem by saying to each party to the dispute: Why shall we not agree that you are both right? The argument need not be useful in arriving at some objective truth though all would agree that there is much Torah to be learned from it. What we seem to have here is a conversation about what *meanings* can be found in the narrative of creation!

In moving once again to the Language-Literature model, we note that closely knit communities, in which Language really connotes an overwhelming reality, yet which are in some contact with modern rhetoric, are particularly well served by this model. Only publics that live faithfully by them, that are both drawn to modernity yet are profoundly suspicious of it for it scorns the truth of their model, can make good use of it. A primary example would be the Haredi public. For example, they can use it to discover—and rediscover—that "everything serious is Language." In a different fashion, Modern Orthodox communities find it useful for making diverse Literatures available, without sacrifice, so it is said, of (Jewish) Language. If, for example, someone maintains that "everything in Jewish Language is Halakhah" then vast expanses are left free for "universal" Literature!

Peters' Paradox

The question I shall address with regard to the third model is a distinctly educational one. It was raised many years ago by the aforementioned British philosopher of education, Richard L. Peters, in his well-known essay, "Habit and Reason: The Paradox of Moral Education."[28]

What is the paradox of which he speaks? It is that we wish to educate to "Reason" (or to whatever overriding value and virtue stands at the pinnacle of our ideology) while the facts of gradual human development and maturation make it obvious that children, at an early stage, cannot really comprehend the ideal of the curriculum or what is "normative" about it. Thus, they must learn "Habit" before they are ready for "Reason." The problem and paradox is that the Habits learned may undermine Reason. Habits are hard to break! How can one educate the whole personality to Reason (or, for traditional Jews who are "inside" the model of *Yir'at Shamayim*, to love and fear of God), when the deep or "real" motivations for pursuing this ideal are not yet comprehensible to the child?

We may suggest that the paradox may be addressed in Judaism as a matter of stages. We teach the performance of mitzvot before we talk

---

28. Richard L. Peters: "Reason and Habit: the Paradox of Moral Education," in Peters: *Moral Development and Moral Education* (London: George Allan and Unwin, 1981), 45–60.

about values. We stress the teaching of what I have called "explicit religion" (norms of behavior, socialization, initiation, and imitation) before we deal directly with "implicit religiosity," that which wells from the heart, conveys significance, and emphasizes personality.[29] This does not mean that elements of implicit religiosity should not be part and parcel of the curriculum from the first, or that children cannot philosophize, but that explicit teaching conveys the identity of the child, makes him or her part of the community and prepares the child for a life of mitzvot.

The devotee of the third model may fail to see the problem. She will point out that there are stories and commentaries for young children as well as for the mature. And also, that there is poetry and song in the life of commandment and community as well as in the inner life of spiritual search.

If this blending of spirit and law is to be cultivated, reaching towards some common Language in all three of our models, we may be able to learn from all of them and with all of them. That venture of learning together may indeed undermine all existing and self-sufficient models. But the Torah did not descend from Sinai as a paradigm. Jewish faith must qualify the claim that there is one model, all-encompassing and exclusive; we are not bidden to serve conceptual models, but to serve God. If we confuse the one with the other, we may find ourselves worshipping idols. Indeed, if there is a striving for a common Language, the plentitude of models from which we can learn may be fortuitous.

---

29. For my recent discussion of this issue, see Michael Rosenak: "Zelophehad's Daughters, Religion and Jewish Religious Education," *Journal of Jewish Education* 71:1 (2005), 3–21.

The Ethics of Exclusion:
Pedagogical, Curricular, Leadership, and Moral Imperatives for Inclusive Practice in Jewish Schools

Jeffrey Glanz

Introduction

"The best of leaders recognize . . . [the] dilemmas [they face] as opportunities for doing what is right, not necessarily what is expedient. As school leaders, we have an obligation to set ethical and moral examples for the organization we serve."
(Sorenson & Goldsmith, 2006, p. 169)

"To teach B'tzelem Elokim will require that all of us engaged in the education of our children lose no opportunity to affirm the inestimable worth of every life . . ."
(Shapiro, 2006, p. 174)

"Vision . . . is an invitation to pupils, educators, families, and communities to create, through reflection, a desired and meaningful tomorrow. . . . The contemporary challenge to Jewish education is clear and severe. What is required is fresh and energetic thinking about the Jewish future and its rationale, in view of the desperate circumstances we face."
(Fox, Scheffler, & Marom, 2006, p. 8)

"Hopelessness is a form of silence, of denying the world and fleeing from it. The dehumanization resulting from an unjust order is not a cause for despair but for hope, leading to the incessant pursuit of the humanity denied by injustice."
(Freire, 2004, p.15)

"And you shall do that which is right and good . . . ."
(Devarim, 6:18)

Inclusive practice in education and schooling, public or private, is cutting-edge, not commonly in use. Yet, this essay posits that such practice is a moral necessity and an ethical imperative incumbent on Jewish educators to articulate, philosophically, and to actualize, in practice. An ideological, social, political, and intellectual commitment to justice, equity, and excellence for *all* students must be continuously affirmed and reaffirmed. This essay will posit that such ideals are lacking in many schools, public and private. Too many Jewish schools, in particular, exclude the "non-traditional" student possessing different learning needs and requiring special educational services. Many Jewish day schools and yeshivot are not philosophically committed to inclusive pedagogy, nor have they been able to commit sufficient resources, financial and otherwise, to support such initiatives organizationally. Teachers too, for the most part, are not prepared (pre-service and in-service) to teach in diverse, inclusive learning environments that include students with learning and other disabilities.

Exclusionary educational practices do not only refer, however, to students with disabilities taught outside the mainstream of the general education classroom (see, e.g., Ferri & Connor, 2006). Students may also be excluded culturally. Sephardic students' rich cultural heritage, for instance, may be given short shrift as evidenced in curricular exclusion whereby Sephardic traditions and practices are not actively taught in Ashkenazi schools, even where Sephardic students attend. Anecdotal evidence exists for the reverse situation as well, although the numbers of Ashkenazi students attending Sephardic schools are much lower by comparison. Parenthetically, Sephardic exclusion from *Haredi* Yeshivot in Israel is an even more acute problem. Educators should commit to constructing inclusive curricula and policies that acknowledge and appreciate cultural diversity.

This chapter, then, moves beyond usual parameters of inclusionism to also consider aspects unique to *limmudei kodesh* related to Sephardic and Ashkenazi traditions. Although other examples of exclusionism related to, for instance, new immigrants from Eastern Europe and their assimilation and acceptance in schools and in society as a whole can be discussed (see, e.g., Schnall, 2006), or the *Haredi* and Modern Orthodox Judaism divide, our discussion here, will focus on the examples stated above related to students with disabilities, and Sephardim and Ashkenazim. The role and responsibility of Jewish schools to address exclusionary educational and cultural practices and behaviors form the main focus of this monograph. Although inclusive practice is also important for programs of informal education, summer camps, youth organizations, etc., the focus here will remain on Jewish schools. Other educational contexts deserve more complete attention in another monograph or essay.

Educational and cultural exclusionary attitudes and practices have significant pedagogical, curricular, leadership, and moral implications for the work of progressive and idealistic educators as well as concerned community members. The theoretical frame supporting the viewpoints taken in this monograph is based on concepts and issues of social justice, cultural diversity, constructivism, differentiated instruction, and an ethic of caring. Inclusive practice, however, will serve as the moral frame and research perspective of the monograph. The author is cognizant of the possible controversial nature of some of the ideas expressed. Transformational (Northouse, 2003) and moral leadership (Sergiovanni, 1992), however, compel a serious and forthright discussion of these issues so that concerned, committed educators and others might continue their Herculean efforts to ensure high quality instruction for *all* students in an environment of educational opportunity and cultural sensitivity.

What is inclusion? Inclusion is a belief system (Stainback & Stainback, 2000). It is a process of facilitating an educational environment that provides access to high quality education for all students (Lambert et al., 2003). Related to the disabilities issue, inclusion is premised on the notion that "all" children learning together in the same school and the same classroom, with services and supports necessary so that they can succeed, is critical. Advocates say that students with disabilities should be educated with students without disabilities (see, e.g., Karagiannis, Stainback, & Stainback, 2000b). Special classes or removal of children from the general education environment (note that the term "general" is preferred over "regular" because "regular" implies that students not in the "regular" classroom are "irregular") should occur only when the nature or severity of the disability is such that education in the general classroom cannot be achieved satisfactorily with the use of supplementary support services (Individuals with Disabilities Education Act, 33, U.S.C., 1400, 1997; Kochhar, West, & Taymans, 2000;

Viachou, 2004; Young, 2000). Inclusion, however, must also address cultural exclusion. In this case, the school curriculum must adequately address the histories, customs, and *halakhot* of both Sephardic and Ashkenazic students.

Next, a theoretical frame supporting inclusive practice is presented, followed by some practical suggestions for moving schools closer to an inclusion model. The chapter ends with a discussion of the moral imperatives and ethical implications of inclusion.

Theoretical Background
Overview
Table 1 charts the approach taken in this essay that questions the moral and ethical foundations of exclusionism in two distinct areas that have serious implications for educational practices in Jewish day · schools and yeshivot. After describing the "problem" by presenting sample scenarios drawn from actual school incidents, the research base and practice of inclusion will be highlighted. Then, the following theories or conceptual approaches will be reviewed in brief fashion: social justice, the ethics of caring, differentiated instruction, constructivism, and cultural diversity. The research base for inclusion is then highlighted. While this essay introduces theoretical, conceptual and some practical approaches to fostering inclusion, it is not meant as a manual or guide to establish an inclusive classroom or school.

Table 1: Theoretical Frame

Classification	Students with Disabilities	Sephardim/Ashkenazim
Problem	Segregated from mainstream	Curricularly excluded
Theory	Social justice (Brown, 2004); ethics of caring (Held, 1995); differentiated instruction (Tomlinson, 2004); constructivism (Twomey Fosnot, 2005)	Social justice; ethics of caring; cultural diversity (Banks, 2005)
Recommendation	Inclusion through differentiation (Reid, 2005)	Inclusion through curriculum integration (Beane, 1997)

Methodology	Teacher training (Darling-Hammond & Bransford, 2007); professional development (Gordon, 2003); prejudice reduction (Ponterotto, Utsey, & Pedersen, 2006)	Teacher training; professional development; prejudice reduction

The Ethical Problem and its Parameters

Scenarios presented below are fictionalized for purposes of reporting, although they are based on actual incidents. They are meant as caricatures, not representative of all situations, but they do have a basis in reality. Exclusionism has not infrequently been reported in the literature, nor is it unique to schools as evidenced by an examination of class organization sheets, courses of study and other curricular approaches, and commonplace pedagogical strategies employed in many classrooms. As a consequence of this essay, the author is in the process of beginning a formal study to survey educators, current and former students, and parents to document attitudes, experiences, and views of exclusionism as manifested in Jewish day schools and yeshivot. The author hopes to write a follow-up article reporting results of this descriptive study.

Some of the scenarios that follow are rather straightforward while others, like the first one, deal with complex ethical issues. They are of an ethical nature because they deal with issues of individual rights and justice (see, e.g., Mahoney, 2006, 2008). They are issues that reasonable people may differ about because of personal experiences, misinformation, or ideology. Profound differences in points of view are rarely gratuitous. For one person, inclusion may be the road to justice and equity for all students; yet for another, the road to intrusion and miseducation. However, considering its normative, social, educational, and even political dimensions, the issue of inclusion touches the very heart or foundation of what we think about the function of our schools, the way children learn, the best way to teach our children, and our expectations for their academic, social, emotional, and spiritual growth as individuals.

Scenario 1a:
Students with Disabilities—*"I don't want that 'kind' of child in the same class with my child."*

Judith Lazarus served as president of the P.T.A. for several years at the Winston Jewish Elementary School (fictitious) in a mid-west metropolitan city. Despite her busy personal and professional schedule, she remained committed to community service and especially to the Jewish School. A Harvard graduate and child neurologist as well as mother of two precocious children attending the school, Dr. Lazarus was an active spokesperson in the community on a range of social, medical, and educational issues. Respected by many parents and colleagues, she ran unopposed for two consecutive terms as P.T.A. president. She was a strong supporter of the newly appointed elementary school principal who had a reputation as a caring, intelligent, and creative administrator. Shortly after his inauguration as principal, he announced at a P.T.A. meeting his plans to initiate an inclusion philosophy and even inclusion classes at the school. He didn't believe that students with special needs should be, in his words, "segregated" from the rest of the student population, but rather "students could be offered high instructional programming in the same classroom." "We can educate our children equally well," he stated, "in the same classroom with teachers well prepared to address individual learning needs of all the students." "Our school," he continued, "should and will provide the proper resources to ensure that this inclusion project benefits all children." After reviewing research findings on the benefits of inclusion for both students with and without disabilities, he asked for parent volunteers to join a steering committee of teachers and others to help implement the inclusion program. Dr. Lazarus, not one to shy from conversation or debate, stood up at the meeting and respectfully but assertively said, "There are without doubt some students with special needs whose needs cannot be adequately addressed by any sort of 'inclusion'. These students often thrive when provided with the correct special-ed setting. An example is the sort of student with a constellation of emotional and learning problems—and I have many of these in the BOCES setting in which I work—

*that simply cannot be handled in any mainstream setting."
She continued, "We have an intensive support program, na-
tionally recognized, that brings together child psychiatrists, a
child neurologist (me), child psychologists, psychiatric social
workers, and special-ed teachers, in special schools, to help
care for these kids and their families (who often need a lot of
support, and guidance). The fact remains is that some kids
have serious attentional, emotional, or brain-based problems
(severe dyslexia comes to mind)—and to subject mainstream
students, mainstream teachers, etc, to all the adaptations
these children would require will in my experience not work
as well as having these kids treated in separate classes." Silence filled the auditorium after her comments. All eyes turned
to the principal. "I don't think we totally disagree," retorted
the principal. "Certainly, inclusion will not work for some
kids with very, very severe disabilities; I feel the same way.
The students you speak about are a very, very small minority. What I am advocating, however, is an elimination of the
historic way we've excluded so many 'normal' children from
the mainstream because they simply learn differently and because we have developed, quote unquote, 'sophisticated' testing procedures to identify presumed intellectual deficiencies.
Schools have been reluctant to accommodate them. I want
our school to join other cutting-edge schools by saying 'we
will not exclude, whenever possible, any child from the mainstream.' Dr. Lazarus, I am discussing the 'basic' student with
a different learning style, maybe she has retention issues, mild
learning disabilities, etc., . . . we need to 'push in' these children, not 'pull them out'." He continued, "But I also believe
we can include students with significant disabilities if we are
committed to really helping all, or most children who deserve
better treatment." "Even Down-Syndrome children?" que-
ried the P.T.A. president. "Yes, in some cases they can succeed in the classroom (Wurzburg, 1992, 2001). Dr. Lazarus
looked incredulous; she hesitated. Suddenly, one parent stood
up near the rear of the auditorium and shouted, "I don't want
that 'kind' of child in the same class with my child." Another
parent after hearing someone else speak out chimed in by saying, "My child is normal. These other kids have problems.*

*They'll slow down the learning of my child." Still another
parent said, "These special children, uh, I mean, the handicapped you know, . . . they ought to be educated alone . . . I
mean given services they need to help them. What's wrong
with that? That way everybody will be happy."*

Inclusion remains an ill-conceived idea for many educators and
parents. Unaware or unwilling to accept its benefits for both special
and general education students, detractors adhere to traditional conceptions of teaching and learning.

Paradigm paralysis (see, e.g., McBeath, 1994) is all too common
in education. Our assumptions are fixed and we utilize a single paradigm or lens through which to perceive our work and world. Whether it is our conception of organizing schools, formulating curricula,
teaching, supervising instruction, or views of how students learn best,
paradigm paralysis has thwarted alternate ways of conceiving education and schooling. This paradigm effect, as it is called, is natural but
becomes problematic when we rigidly follow the prescribed path even
when it is no longer functional or when we are confronted by other
more efficacious possibilities. Exclusionism has become our paradigm
effect. We are paralyzed to the idea of inclusion. It just doesn't fit with
our conventional ways of structuring work in classrooms.

In terms of our conceptions of the notion of "disability," we operate, according to Hahn (1989) from two perspectives. The one adhered
to traditionally and still accepted by many people today is known as
the "functional limitations" perspective. In this paradigm, the problem
resides with the student of special needs. The role of the school is to
remediate, if it can, the disability, or at least, ensure that the student
does not interfere with the majority of students without a disability.
These students, under this paradigm, are given services but in separate
educational environments (e.g., resource rooms or special schools).
Under the "functional limitations" perspective, schools do not change
or adapt at all to the needs of these special needs students.

An alternate way of meeting the needs of special learners is known
as the "minority group" perspective. Within this paradigm, schools
indeed adopt and accommodate to the needs, interests, and abilities
of all students. According to Karagiannis, Stainback, and Stainback
(2000b), "Segregation and practices such as identification and labeling, which usually absorb a large amount of resources, are seen as

social discrimination and a denial of the provision of skills for participatory citizenship" (p. 10).

Resistance to inclusive practice in schools has been formidable (see, e.g., Fuchs & Fuchs, 1994). According to Karagiannis, Stainback, and Stainback (2000a), several states have made their teacher certification for special education more rigid and "some organizations and states have proposed the reinstitution of segregated schools for students with disabilities" (p. 22). These authors bring further evidence of exclusionism by pointing out that since 1970 there has been a marked increase in the identification of students with disabilities, yet the numbers placed in inclusive classrooms are "minimal" (p. 22). They cite further statistical evidence that students with learning disabilities, who constitute the largest category of students with disabilities, have not received adequate remedial assistance "in general education classrooms and resources rooms" (p. 23). Some states, though, they say, have made much progress towards inclusion such as "Idaho, North Dakota, Oregon, and Vermont" (p. 23). They claim that a reason why these states have progressed on a more rapid pace towards inclusion rests on the wide dissemination of "innovative, successful organizational and instructional arrangements for achieving inclusion" (p. 23). The momentum for inclusion is growing according to these authors. Support from local, state, national, and international professional organizations has fueled interest and advocacy for inclusion. Court cases, too, have challenged schools from continuing their segregation of students with disabilities. Lay groups, parent advocates, and educators too have begun a groundswell to "push" for inclusion on a human rights basis (see, e.g., International League of Societies for Persons with Mental Handicap, 1994, June). Reviewing the literature on inclusion, Fisher (2006) reports much progress over the past ten years. He explains, "As a profession, we are now asking *how* more often than *why* in regard to inclusive schooling" (p. 206).

As Scenario 1a above indicates, exclusionism manifests itself sometimes in rationalized arguments that, on the surface, seem reasonable. What is unreasonable about placing severely disabled children in separate facilities? Why place strains on the teacher and other general education students by placing a child with autism in a fifth grade classroom? It wasn't too long ago that similar questions were posed about African-American youngsters attending integrated schools. It also wasn't too long ago that the notion of integrating students with physical challenges (e.g., in wheelchairs) was criticized with the major reason, at least the articulated one, being that school facilities cannot provide for wheelchair accessibility. We are simply used to one paradigm for educating children and treating differences, and are unable to remain open enough to accept alternate ways of structuring classrooms and schools.

One colleague, upon hearing this thesis of inclusion, stated, "My wife knows more about this than I do, and she actually teaches courses in special ed, etc, and feels even more strongly about it than I do; both of us are clinicians, so we also deal with these issues every day professionally. We both know that there are many children for whom inclusion is much worse than 'special' classes. There is a lot of money at stake in that if governments, etc. can convince parents to go with inclusion, it's much cheaper. I'm not saying every kid needs a special ed class, I'm saying that every special needs kid cannot be accommodated in a mainstream inclusion class, and that it often harms the kid, making him feel even more inferior. Obviously, for kids with relatively minor problems, this is not the case."

My response was as follows: "I think the distinction centers on what we mean by the term 'inclusion'. When schools cannot provide adequate resources, when teachers are not properly prepared, when services of specialists are not readily available, inclusion will indeed not work. It is not really inclusion. Inclusion by definition means availability of adequate resources, evidence of teacher training, ideological commitment, etc. You can't knock something that is not working effectively because 'other' factors are inhibiting it. Furthermore, regarding the financial side of the matter, if real inclusion is operable it wouldn't necessarily be cheaper since the same personnel and material resources would be needed *in* the school building. Moreover, according to Karagiannis, Stainback, and Stainback (2000b), "Inclusion is not, nor should it become, a convenient way to justify budgetary cuts that may jeopardize the provision of essential services. Genuine inclusion," they continue, "does not mean dumping students with disabilities into general education classes without support for teachers or students." In other words, the authors conclude, "the primary goal of inclusive schooling is not to save money: It is to adequately serve all students" (p. 11). Certainly, students with special needs require additional services and may need specialized instructional technologies and equipment to help them. The idea is to make these services and instructional capacities available for all students as part of the standard operational procedures of running a school. They should not be viewed as supplementary or peripheral, but rather as central, endemic, and natural. This is certainly a new paradigm from which to operate.

Additional discussion of inclusive schooling, pros and cons, will appear in the section on inclusion research and practice later in the chapter.

Scenario 1b:
Students with Disabilities—*"It's unfortunate, but we simply can't accommodate your child's 'peculiar' learning style."*
> Sara spoke at a relatively young age. Born to professional educators, Sara was continually exposed to a rich and varied literate environment. Despite her seemingly precocious development, Sara experienced difficulty in her early grades, one through three, keeping up with her classmates. In grade 5, she had problems with retention of information and could not learn as many psukim as other students. Rashi was out of the question. Sara came home each evening with much homework. The work was frustrating her and she would inevitably cry. As the school year progressed, the workload also increased as did her frustration levels. Sara asked her parents to send her to another school. "I hate my school; the kids tease me and they call me 'dummy'." Despite extra help at home with a special tutor, Sara's educational and social woes continued. At a parent-teacher conference, her parents were told that Sara "tries hard but just can't keep up." A meeting with the principal proved memorable. After praising Sara's sweet demeanor and fine midot, the principal suggested that perhaps finding another school would be in Sara's best interests. "It's unfortunate, but we simply can't accommodate your child's 'peculiar' learning style." Shocked by the principal's naivety, if not ignorance of current pedagogic and learning theories, the parents reluctantly registered their precious Sara into the local public school that provided resource room assistance as well as inclusion class options.

Many schools neither recognize nor appreciate that all children learn differently, or if they do they take little or no action to match pedagogical strategies to varied learning styles. The one-size-fits-all approach to pedagogy and curriculum is ingrained in the minds and actions of many educators. Teachers, until recently, have not been prepared to teach a diverse group of students with varied learning styles. Research consistently demonstrates that most classrooms, especially at the middle and high school levels "use traditional instructional methods such as lecture, assigned readings, drill, and independent practice" (Lauria, 2005, p. 68). Although many students do thrive in traditional classroom settings, many more do not (see, e.g., Dunn, Gianitti, et al., 1990). Extensive research has been conducted that demonstrates that poor academic achievement is often a consequence of a teacher's inability to match instructional strategies to a child's preferred learning style (Dunn & DeBello, 1999). Students whose learning styles do not match the teacher's instructional approaches are often excluded from classroom discourse.

Some people might claim that in today's Jewish schools, girls like Sara do have options. Programs like P'Tach are available. Aside from exorbitant costs and stigmas associated with such programs, these programs do provide opportunities for some children to succeed. When well-run, such programs can elevate a child's self-esteem and engender long term academic and social accomplishment. When such programs do not work well, they are a detriment emotionally and otherwise. One program this author is familiar with, not P'Tach, ran their classes in trailers with few options for mainstreaming. In fact, research indicates that once placed in a special education setting, few students are ever fully mainstreamed (see, e.g., Madden & Slavin, 1983; Terman, Larner, Stevenson, & Behrman, 1996). P'Tach, while noble and probably still necessary in the Jewish community, is a stopgap measure needed momentarily.

Scenario 2a:
Sephardim and Ashkenazim- *"Why don't they just do it the 'normal' way?"*

> *Yossi was invited to hear Sion's son's lehning at the local Sephardic school the week prior to the bar mitzvah. It was Yossi's first time in a 'real' Sephardic minyan, and for that matter the first time in a Sephardic school. Yossi thought to himself, "it feels like I'm in another universe." "What's this 'sing song-ing' of pesukei dezimra all about?" "Wow, look at that Torah in that strange looking box?" "Now see how hagbah is being done, wow." And just listen to the bar mitzvah's grandmother*

yodeling . . . or something?!" Yossi's wife, who was sitting obviously in the women's section, was equally bewildered. She whispers to Yossi afterwards, "Why don't they just do it the 'normal' way?"

Such attitudes are common when a person is ignorant of others' cultural traditions. Normalcy is often perceived from one's perspective. Otherness is perceived as different, alien, or uncommon (Allport, 1987). I am certain if we would interview Yossi and his wife, they would say, "Sure, we heard mention in *halakhah shuirim* in school or elsewhere that Sephardic customs are different, but we never really experienced anything like this." They might even say, "It's kind of nice, but . . . ." What is our responsibility as educators to dispel misconceptions, to include more active and concrete learning experiences of other Jewish cultural traditions, and to encourage heightened cultural sensitivity and diversity? Many Jewish schools do not expose their students to different Jewish cultural traditions. The school curriculum that excludes, by omission, the cultural traditions of others does a disservice to the student, if not the entire Jewish educational community.

Ashkenazim and Sephardim, developing under different circumstances and conditions, gradually established differing customs, traditions, and norms of behavior (Zohar, 2005; Sperber & Elman, 1999). Despite these differences in *minhagim*, reflected too in *halakhah*, they shared a common historical bond. In most countries in which they resided they were excluded or marginalized, at the very least, socially, politically, religiously, and culturally (Stillman, 1995).

Rivalries and discord between both cultural groups were not uncommon as well (see, e.g., Davies, 2004; Gilad, 1990). Where Sephardim were minorities among Ashkenazi communities, social and educational disparities were common. Disparities, for example, in academic achievement were evident (Shavit, 1984; Shmueli, 1977; Willms & Chen, 1989). As differences increased, prejudices too were more common (Schwartz, Link, et al., 1991). Nuances among Sephardi customs became blurred in the eyes of non-Sephardim. The tendency to cluster non-Ashkenazi traditions under the rubric of Sephardi was commonplace (Zohar, 2005). Sephardim have felt the pangs of exclusionism (Matza, 1998). [In a study I am currently conducting, Sephardic students, within an Ashkenazic school system, relate some

emotional experiences they have felt including, among others, embarrassed by their cultural traditions, e.g., not wanting their Ashkenazi
friends to meet their parents or visit their homes especially on holidays, or wishing they too were Ashkenazi. Another Sephardic adult
recalled experiences in grade school when he was "made to study the
Kitzur Shulhan Arukh." Still another adult lamented that when a Sephardi marries an Ashkenazi, it is seen as "intermarriage in the eyes
of Ashkenazim."] Expressions of dissatisfaction (Rafael & Sharot,
1991) were expressed in a collection of stories, poems, and plays by
American Jews of Sephardic descent. This collection, according to the
authors, gives voice to a culture previously unheard in a literary canon
with a predominantly Eastern European and Ashkenazic tradition.

Despite exclusion of Sephardic customs in the curriculum of
many Ashkenazi day schools and yeshivot, Sephardic holiday customs
and traditions reflect a rich and deeply spiritual Jewish culture that
flourished for many centuries on the Iberian Peninsula in Spain and
Portugal (Paretzky, 1996). Such customs are not unitary, nor uniform.
Sephardic Passover customs and traditions, for instance, can vary
from region to region, country to country, and even family to family.
"Many Sephardic customs and traditions involved assimilating Passover rituals with the culinary, musical, and linguistic traditions of the
surrounding peoples in the areas where Sephardim lived" (Sephardic
Passover Customs and Traditions, http://www.angelfire.com/pa2/pass-
over/ Sephardicpassovercustoms.html). Students in school should be
actively taught about Sephardic Passover dietary rulings that permit
kitniyot, as well as special foods that Ashkenazim never saw let alone
tasted (including the *Huevos Haminados* dish). The actual conduct of
the *seder,* too, is educationally instructive (e.g., the "different" order
in which the Four Questions might be posed).

Complicating the nature of the issue, we must take into account
the diversity and variety of experience that generally gets lumped
under the title "Sephardi." "Sephardi" correctly refers to the descendants of the Jews who were exiled from Spain in 1492. Many of them
went to Muslim countries where there were already indigenous Jewish
populations with no connection to Spain. This includes North Afri-
cans, Yemenites, some Syrians (usually Damascus, rather than Aleppo
which was largely Sephardi), Iraqis, Iranians, Bukharians, etc. These
Jews are more correctly referred to as Mizrahim (Orientals) and do
not prefer to be "lumped together" with the Sephardim, for a variety
of reasons (see, e.g., Patai, 1971)

The responsibility of the educator, as curricularist, is to create or design an educational environment that facilitates and provides opportunities for students of all Jewish cultural traditions to explore and learn about each other's customs. No time or place in the curriculum? The matter depends, I think, on the kind of outcomes, social and intellectual, we want for our students. Do we want our children to respect and remain culturally attuned to other Jewish traditions and cultures? Do we want to create an inclusive curriculum that is appreciative of other Jewish cultures? Do we want to encourage intercultural understanding and opportunities for learning? Do we want our own children to feel included and appreciated based on who they are and what they believe? These are some of the fundamental questions schools need to pose in addressing this form of exclusionism.

Scenario 2b:
Sephardim and Ashkenazim- *"Their classrooms are just not 'warm' places for learning."*

Etzion Madmoni and her husband Yosef were initially pleased with the local Ashkenazi day school for their 5-year old. Living in a largely Ashkenazi community, the parents felt that sending their child to an Ashkenazi school would assist their child's assimilation; i.e., the making of new friends. Within a short time, however, the parents were unhappy. Their child came home, according to the parents, "forlorn, frustrated, and unhappy." The Madmonis felt they had no other option but to send their child to another school. This time they'd select a Sephardi school, even though it was much farther from where they now lived. "Their (Ashkenazi) classrooms are just not 'warm' places for learning" explained Etzion to her neighbor.

Etzion and Yosef Madmoni's own personal experiences with Ashkenazi traditions were minimal and episodic. What they perceived as "just not warm enough" may have been affected by their own expectations and prejudices towards Ashkenazi schools. Unless exposed to an inclusive curriculum that encourages intercultural understanding such feelings will fester. Certainly parents have the right to send their child to any school they wish, but they should base their decision on reality and not on erroneous or misinterpreted expectations. Sephardim not exposed to inclusive curricula, are as likely to hold provincial and prejudicial views as are Ashkenazim. It should be noted, however, that Sephardim, since they are minorities in many communities in the United States, for instance, have learned quite well, out of necessity, to accommodate to and learn about many Ashkenazi customs. The reverse is not always true.

* * *

Segregation of special education populations from general education and curricular exclusion among both Ashkenazi and Sephardi schools is problematic, and certainly antithetical to inclusive educational theory and practice. The problem, as framed in this essay, centers on exclusionary practices and the responsibility of schools and their educators to encourage an educational milieu conducive to academic excellence for all students regardless of learning ability and cultural preference or tradition. In the sections that follow, several critical theoretical frames are discussed that provide support for inclusive practice in schools. Although secular sources, studies, and authorities are cited to lend support for these theories, Jewish tradition and culture has much to say about them as well, as will be cited. Understanding these concepts and ideas is essential to form a solid foundation for inclusionism in education, while minimizing or eradicating exclusionary practices and attitudes.

The Concept of Social Justice in Jewish Schools

"*. . . , principle-centered leaders operate in alignment with 'self-evident, self-validating natural laws'. These include such basic principles as fairness, equity, justice, honesty, trust, integrity, and service. These principles point the way for leaders.*"
(Kaser, Mundry, Stiles, & Loucks-Horsley, 2006, p. 26)

"*You shall relentlessly pursue justice and righteousness.*"
(Devorim, 16:20)

Jewish tradition is rich in its advocacy for justice. In *Sefer Tehillim* (99:4), it says "Mighty is the King, Who loves justice. You founded fairness." Also, "He has told you; O Man, What is Good, and What does God require of you- but to act justly, to love *hesed* and to walk humbly with your God" (*Micha*, 6:8 from opening quotation of *Sefer Ahavat Hesed*, Hafetz Hayyim). Such views are expressed even more fundamentally in the *Torah*. In *Devarim* (16:20), "Justice, justice," we are commanded, "you shall pursue." *Vayikra* (19:15) teaches "You shall judge your fellowman justly"—*b'tzedek tishpot amitekha*.

One of the fundamental principles of Judaism is the attempt to emulate the Creator derived from the mitzvah of *ve-halakhta bi-de-rakhav* (*imitatio Dei;* Devarim, 28:9). Although its application is intricate (see, e.g., Blau, 2000; Korn, 1997), Blau (2000) citing the Rav says that this is "not just another mitzvah" but is the "foundation of Jewish ethics" (p. 21). As such we are enjoined to emulate God's character traits (see Blau, 2000 for pivotal discussion about advocacy of *imitatio Dei* of "action" and "attributes"). In *Sefer Tehillim* (9:9–10) it says, "And He will judge the world with righteousness, judging the nations in fairness. Hashem will be a fortress of strength for the oppressed, a fortress of strength in times of distress." Likewise, says the *Rambam* and other commentaries, we are commanded to attend to the oppressed and downtrodden. Seeking social justice, then, is intrinsic to Judaism and, hence, an obligation for Jews. Jewish educators, too, are not exempt from such responsibility.

The concept of social justice has received wide attention in secular literature (see, e.g., Bogotch, 2000; Bowers, 2001; Brown, 2004; Connell, 1993; Furman & Shields, 2005; and Rapp, 2002). The subject of promoting social justice in schools is so vast that our attention to it in this section will remain limited. Calls for social justice abound because many critics over the years have pointed to significant social, political, economic, and educational inequities in schools (see, e.g., Apple, 1986; Giroux, 1991; Ogbu, 1978; Spring, 1994). Schooling, for these critics, perpetuates and reinforces social, racial, and gender stratifications. Inequities in allocations of school finances (Kozol, 1991), socially stratified arrangements through which subject matter is delivered known as tracking practices in schools (Oakes, 1985), biased content of the curriculum (Anyon, 1981), patriarchal relations through authority patterns and staffing (Strober & Tyack, 1980), differential distribution of knowledge by gender within classrooms (Sadker & Sadker, 1994), and the influence of teacher expectations (Rosenthal & Jacobson, 1968) are examples of inequities decried by these critics. An example related to teacher expectations makes a point in this context.

Teacher Expectations

What are teacher expectations, how might they function to stifle individual autonomy and perpetuate stereotypical relationships, and what impact might they have on students are important questions (Good & Brophy, 2007)? Coined by Robert Merton and first researched by Rosenthal and Jacobson (cited by Tauber, 1997), the self-fulfilling prophecy is a phenomenon that has relevance in education. Aware of the limitations of this concept, researchers have documented its effects in and outside the classroom (see, e.g., Ogbu, 2003; Seyfried, 1998). Expectations are sometimes communicated directly, more often indirectly or unconsciously. Assumptions are sometimes made based on a student's family background, religious or cultural environment, or past academic performance. A teacher who tells Chaim he might as well not study for the *behinah* since he's failed prior exams, may affect the student in marked emotional and academic ways. Social justice advocates point out that educators should remain vigilant and aware of the force of expectations so that students are not treated differentially due to some unfounded or grossly misinterpreted characteristic. Educators who seek to promote social justice in the classroom might posit the following question: "How might I, as the classroom teacher, promote the ideals of equality, justice, and opportunity in my classroom by communicating positive expectations to students?" (see Yonezawa & Jones, 2006, wherein they report findings of a study in which students, who oppose tracking, call for teachers to teach for equity and to have positive attitudes towards all students). Tauber (1997) proffering advice to teachers about remaining conscious of the power of their expectations, asks:

> Do you assign tasks on some gender basis? Does it just seem natural to assign heavier and dirtier tasks (i.e., carry this, move that) to the "stronger sex" and the more domestic activities (i.e., wash this, clean that, serve this) to the "weaker sex"? When leaders are selected, whether for a classroom or a playground activity, are males more often chosen than females? When creative activities (i.e., decorating for an upcoming holiday) are undertaken, are females more likely than males to be called upon?
>
> When you conduct demonstrations, are males more often asked to assist you and females more often asked to be "recording secretaries"? Do you let female students get away with inappropriate behavior that you would discipline male

students for? If you are female, do you catch yourself identifying more with the female students than with the male students? And the list goes on and on. (pp. 47–48)

Although Tauber discusses gender issues, which may or may not relate to a day school or yeshiva setting, the inferences are nonetheless pertinent, if not obvious. If a teacher lowers expectations for a student simply because of an academic or intellectual label placed on her (see, e.g., Rist, 1970), or because of some cultural consideration, then social justice activists would point to this as an injustice.

In *halakhah,* mindful attention is certainly given to the relationship of pre-conceived notions (i.e., expectations) to outcomes. Stringent *halakhot,* for instance, governing the frame of mind that *dayyanim* must possess when confronting some case involving someone's wealth, appearance, age, background, even religiosity have been codified. A judge must remain impartial (see selected excerpts from the *Rambam* below) not only to serve as a judge but because he is a teacher. When listing the characteristics of *dayyanim* in *Shemot* (18:21), the Torah also makes it clear that a judge is required to be a model citizen so that he is always teaching by example. Professional educators, too, are placed in situations of judging students and situations, and are obligated to assume an even-handed disposition. The commandment in *parashat Ve-zot Ha-berakhah* (33:10) for the *kohanim: yoru mishpatekha le-ya`akov vetoratekha le-yisrael* (to be teachers), seems to be very intrinsically related to the charge of *Yoreh Yoreh Veyadin Yadin* that our Rabbis/*Dayyanim* are given when they head out into the world.

מנין המצוות לרמב"ם

רעד: שלא ליקח שוחד שנ' ושוחד לא תקח.

רעה: שלא לכבד גדול בדין שנ' ולא תהדר פני גדול.

רעו: שלא יירא הדיין בדין מאדם רע שנ' לא תגורו מפני איש.

רעז: שלא לרחם על עני בדין שנ' ודל לא תהדר בריבו.

רעח: שלא להטות משפט אדם חוטא שנ' לא תטה משפט אביונך, למדו מפי השמועה שזה אביון במצוות.

רפ: שלא להטות משפט גרים ויתומים שנ' לא תטה משפט גר יתום.

What is our moral commitment to avoiding negative or low expectations so that we ensure justice in our schools for all students? Research is needed to explore a host of questions related to expectations.

The call for social justice talks to the heart of concepts of respect, equality, and equity. John Dewey (1916) articulated a commitment to these ideals in his monumental *Democracy and Education*. In the ensuing years other progressive and neo-progressive educators made similar pleas. Recently, attention has been drawn to the ethical and moral responsibilities of school leaders to pursue and uphold such concepts (Theoharis, 2007a, 2007b).

John Rawls (1971), moral philosopher and academician, in his groundbreaking work in political philosophy, *Theory of Justice*, provides the conceptual grounding for educational leaders and others committed to respect, equality, and equity. He posits a Kantian interpretation that conceives of justice idealistically as fundamentally grounded in human respect. On a more pragmatic level, he sees justice as an accommodation between competing political and philosophical positions in which individuals with differing opinions learn to cooperate without coercion. For Rawls, moral persons are ones who are willing and able to appreciate both the idealistic and pragmatic views of justice. Rawls believes that development of a sense of justice is a high order human characteristic or personality state that includes developing multiple relationships with diverse groups of people and learning to respect and treat each justly. For Rawls, such action is moral affirmation. Education, in general, and schools in particular, play a critical role in fostering such respect and cooperation (Strike, 1991).

The social justice literature differentiates between issues of equality and equity. Individuals concerned with fostering social justice ensure that each individual or group receives what is needed (Strike & Soltis, 1992). An ethic of justice is affirmed when equality and equity are employed. The authors cite Aristotle who held "that justice consists of treating equals equally and unequals unequally." Using this premise, "if high-school grades are the basis of admission into a university, then two people with the same grades should receive the same treatment, either both should be admitted or both should be rejected" (p. 46); thus justice is affirmed on the basis of equality. Equity on the other hand, in the Aristotelian sense means if a student is need of an accommodation to assist learning, I treat him fairly by providing that instructional prompt, for instance; in other words, he gets what he needs. No one else would complain of unfairness for not receiving that particular prompt. So, when people differ in relation to some characteristic or condition, they receive different treatment based on their particular needs. Thus, in the ethics of justice, both are affirmed.

More fundamentally, Rawls (1971) bases his theory of justice on a notion of fairness as well. In a school setting, one fourth grader might need remedial assistance in reading, for instance, while another enrichment. Equity, not equality (i.e., getting the same thing), is achieved given the fact both students' needs are accurately and unbiasedly assessed. Both individuals are treated even-handedly in pursuit of a good life, liberty, and happiness. On an individual level, social justice advocates ensure that all individuals are treated equally; i.e., given what each needs without preferential treatment or differences in resources expenditures. Expectations here are held in check and dispensed fairly without bias. Equality doesn't really address group differences though. Let's say student one is African-American, and student two Caucasian. If African-American students are placed uniformly in remedial classes without attention to their academic ability and needs, and Caucasian students automatically placed in upper tracks, inequity and thus injustice prevail. An inequitable situation is one in which a group has not historically been treated fairly, justly, or given equal treatment. Members of the group are often viewed as inferior, or at the very least considered less, and consequently oppressed or disadvantaged. Equity goes beyond racial, ethnic and gender inequalities to also include social class, disability, and exceptionalities (Shapiro & Stefkovich, 2005).

Parenthetically, in regards to the Aristotelian idea of treating equals equally and unequals unequally, and equality versus equity, the *gemara* and halakhic works make it clear that *tzedakah* is not just about giving people the same amount. Charity does not necessarily ensure that all people receive an equal amount. Based on a *pasuk* in *Parashat Re'eh*, (see *Rashi* to *Devarim* 15:7–8) the *hakhamim* define the obligation to provide for a person according to his needs as providing the basic requirements of existence such as food and clothing, and they interpret the extra phrase, "that which he lacks" as referring to a person who was previously wealthy but has now become impoverished. The *Midrash Tannaim*, (on *Devarim* 15) as well as the *gemara* in *Ketubot* (66b) has the story of Hillel Ha-Zakken, that he bought a horse to ride on and a slave to run before a certain poor man who was from a wealthy family and was used to living luxuriously. When, on one occasion, he could not find a slave to run before the man, he himself ran before him. See also the *Shulhan Arukh* (*Yoreh De`ah* 250:1) for codification of charitable equity.

In regards to Rawls seeing justice as an accommodation between competing political and philosophical positions in which individuals with differing opinions learn to cooperate without coercion, the *Tosefta* tells us that the highest form of justice in this world is not in fact strict *din* (*Sanhedrin* 1:9) Rather, it is *pesharah*, loosely translated as compromise but encompassing much more. *Pesharah* involves the idea that sometimes the right answer must, in fact, involve multiple practical realities and considerations, instead of taking an ivory-tower, strictly academic approach. Lest we think that this form of justice is "diluted" in some way, the *Tosefta* goes out of its way to point out that it is, indeed, the purest form. One might suggest that *pesharah* is so because it actually allows the system of justice to affect people in a very real and meaningful way.

תוספתא סנהדרין פרק א הלכה ט

רבן שמעון בן גמליאל אומר: כשם שהדין בשלשה, כך פשרה בשלשה.

יפה כח פשרה מכח הדין.

כיזה צד? שנים שדנו יכולין לחזור בהם, ושנים שפישרו אין יכולין לחזור בהם.

Finally, the connection between the call for social justice and inclusion is critical. ". . . [I]nclusive education is needed as a means to achieve social justice for students with disabilities" (Artiles, Harris-Murri, & Rostenberg, 2006, p. 261). Citing Dyson's (1999) work, Artiles, Harris-Murri, and Rostenberg (2006) discuss two discourses of inclusion relevant to social justice. This monograph has relied on both discourses. The first is the "justification" discourse that offers reasons for and advantages of inclusive practice. The second is the "implementation" discourse that addresses the ethical perspective and the "efficacy" position, both of which are amplified throughout the monograph.

Building an Ethic of Caring

"An abundance of caring is a signal quality found in most educators. This propensity to step outside of oneself, to see, hear, and appreciate another human being, increases insight, aids communication, and promotes excellence in instruction. Learners served by caring educators feel more important, demonstrate higher motivation, learn faster and better, and reveal greater confidence about their future. That is education as its best." (Draayer, 2003, p. 139)

*"He who joins in the distress of the community, will be worthy
of witnessing the consolation of the community."*
(Ta'anit 11a)

Dealing with others justly, with care (compassion) is, very much
a priority in Judaism. An educator underscoring the importance of
care might, for instance, cite Vayikra (19:18), *ve-ahavta le-re'akha
ka-mokha*—"You shall love your fellow as yourself." How would we
want our child, who might need special education services, treated in
a school/classroom? Studies, as will be indicated later, indicate the
negative emotional impact of segregation or labeling. Exclusionary
educational or cultural behaviors are antagonistic to dealing with others justly or with compassion. Interestingly, the terms *rahamim* and
rahmanut ("mercy" and "compassion") are derived from the word *re-
hem* ("womb"), thus indicating that our feelings and acts of kindness
to others, i.e., treating them justly and with compassion, is endemic to
our existence from birth; we are to relate to our fellow human being as
if he or she were a member of our own flesh and blood family (Borowitz & Weinman Schwartz, 1999). Many other sources within Judaism
support an ethic of caring for the "other."

Within the secular community, the moral commitment to inclusion is informed by the work of Nel Noddings (1984, 1986, 1992) on
the ethic of caring. An "ethic of caring" affirms a belief that educators
and children alike are to be caring, moral, and productive members of
society (Jordan Irvine, 2001). As Noddings (1992) posits, "The traditional organization of schooling is intellectually and morally inadequate for contemporary society" (p. 173). Although appropriate at
some point in educational history, the traditional model of bureaucratic school organization in which organizational needs supersede
individual interests is no longer appropriate. Dewey (see Mayhew &
Edwards, 1965) knew this well when he said, the problem of education
was the "harmonizing of individual traits with social ends and values"
(p. 465). Nurturing an "ethic of caring," principals and teachers alike,
realize their ultimate motive is to inspire a sense of caring, sensitivity, appreciation, and respect for human dignity of all people despite
travails that pervade our society and world. Organizations are not au-
tonomous independent entities but are rather made to conform to and
meet the needs of people. Noddings (1992) makes the point related to

the purpose of education, "We should educate all our children not only for competence but also for caring. Our aim should be to encourage the growth of competent, caring, loving, and lovable people" (p. xiv).

Feminist organizational theory (Blackmore, 1993; Regan, 1990) informs this "ethic of caring" by avoiding traditional conceptions of teaching and leading. Feminist theory questions legitimacy of the hierarchical, patriarchical, bureaucratic school organization. Challenging traditional leadership models, feminist theory encourages community-building, interpersonal relationships, nurturing, and collaboration as of primary interest (Ferguson, 1984). Supportive of this feminist view of school organization, Henry (1996) explains how feminist theory opposes bureaucracy:

> The feminist approach that I have developed in this study places people before mechanical rules or bureaucratic responses. Feminism stems from a concern not just with humankind, but with all living things and their interdependence in the universe, with a view to redefining male-female and other relations away from a notion of dominance and subordination and toward the ideal of equality and interconnectedness. . . . All human beings are seen as enriched by a feminist way of seeing and relating to the world. Instead of autonomy, separation, distance, and a mechanical view of the world, feminism values nurturing, empathy, and a caring perspective. (pp. 19, 20)

Noddings (1992) has led a feminist critique challenging traditional conceptions of education by advocating an ethic of caring "to enable schools to become caring communities that nurture all children, regardless of their race, class, or gender" (Marshall, Patterson, Rogers, & Steele, 1996, p. 276), and ability or culture. Unlike traditional humanistic models of administration, "caring" is inclusionary, non-manipulative, and empowering. Whereas the main objective of bureaucracy is standardization, caring inspires individual responsibility. Caring "is a situation- and person-specific way of performing in the world that requires being fully and sensitively attuned to the needs of the cared for by the person caring. Caring cannot be transformed into policies mandated from above, but caring can give form and coherence to our schools" (Marshall, et al., 1996, pp. 278–279).

Starratt (1991) also provides support for an ethic of caring in educational administration. According to Starratt, an administrator committed to an ethic of caring will "be grounded in the belief that the integrity of human relationships should be held sacred and that the school as an organization should hold the good of human beings within it as sacred" (p. 195). Thus, school leaders affirmed by an ethic of caring will ensure notions of social justice in their schools and remain vigilant to safeguard the best interests of all learners.

Although defining "caring" has been difficult (Beck, 1994), scholars who have explored this topic in depth note that caring always involves, to some degree, three activities. They are: (1) receiving the other's perspective; (2) responding appropriately to the awareness that comes from this reception; and (3) remaining committed to others and to the relationship.

What do caring educators do? According to Marshall et al., (1996), they "frequently develop relationships that are the grounds for motivating, cajoling, and inspiring others to excellence. Generally thoughtful and sensitive, they see nuances in people's efforts at good performance and acknowledge them; they recognize the diverse and individual qualities in people and devise individual standards of expectation, incentives, and rewards" (p. 282). With students, teachers would remain sensitive to their social, emotional, and academic needs.

Caring educators would make certain that students respect each other, and that the values and traditions of each individual, regardless of religious affiliation or cultural background, are affirmed. Caring educators would remain sensitive to the feelings of students with disabilities. They would avoid exclusionism and would support a policy of inclusion as is most feasible under the circumstances (see, e.g., Villa & Thousand, 2000).

The relationship between an ethic of justice and an ethic of caring is instructive (see Katz, Noddings, & Strike, 1999). An educational commitment to seeking justice in terms of promoting equality, equity, and respect in the classroom for all students is fundamentally premised on an ethic of caring. Caring about the worth and needs of the individual student, not necessarily the needs of the school as an organization, is of utmost concern to educators who work from an ethic of caring and justice. Parenthetically, one difference between the two ethics should be pointed out as well. Justice generally strives for a sense of impartiality; i.e., right is right, wrong is wrong. An ethic of care, in contrast, avoids impartiality. Moral reasoning is passionate and involved. Gilligan (1993) and Noddings (2003) argue that moral detachment is not feasible. Caring places philosophical laurels on compassion in which equity is placed at the core, not equality.

A Rationale for Differentiating Instruction

". . . Classes should include students of diverse needs, achievement levels, interests, and learning styles, and instruction should be differentiated to take advantage of the diversity, not to ignore it."
(Jackson & Davis, 2000, p. 23)

"On that day they removed the doorkeeper and permission was given to any student to enter (the beit midrash) for Rabban Gamliel announced that no student whose character does not correspond to his exterior may enter the house of study. That day many benches were added. Rav Yohanan said: Abba Yosef ben Dostai argued this point with the sages. One claims that four hundred benches were added and one claims that seven hundred benches were added ... On that day, Tractate Eduyot was written ... and there was not a single law in the study hall that had been left unresolved."
(Berakhot 27b–28a)

Fundamental to differentiation of instruction is a belief that a heterogeneous class is a most viable method for grouping students. The debate between ability and heterogeneous grouping can be traced back directly to Talmudic times. The Talmud in *Berakhot* 27b, quoted in part above, tells the story of a dispute that took place between Rabban Gamliel, who at the time was the head of the academy in Yavneh, and Rav Yehoshua. As a result of this dispute, Rabban Gamliel was relieved of his duties as the Nasi, and was replaced by Rav Elazar ben Azarya. The Talmud dictates that a heterogeneous educational environment affected the quality of learning that took place in the yeshiva. An argument can therefore be made based on this *gemara* that *Hazal* did, in fact, favor a more heterogeneous academic setting. Presumably, the success in learning cited in this *gemara* was attributable not merely to an increase in students in the yeshiva, but rather to the teaching methodology that enabled a more diverse body of *talmidim* to succeed. Jewish tradition stresses the importance of addressing each student's needs. In the *Midrash Tanhuma*, cited below, commenting on the inherent diversity of human beings (i.e., just as they look differently, so too they think, and presumably learn, differently), Moshe prays for *Hashem* to provide a leader (read: teacher) who will be able to deal with each one of them according to his needs while still being able to tend to the whole flock (a differentiated approach).

מדרש תנחומא (בובר) פרשת פינחס סימן א

אבל אם ראה אוכלוסין של בני אדם, אומר ברוך חכם הרזים. כשם שאין פרצופותיהן שוין זה לזה, כך אין דעתן שוה, אלא כל אחד ואחד יש לו דעה בפני עצמו. וכן הוא אומר לעשות לרוח משקל (איוב כח כה), משקל של כל אחד ואחד. תדע לך שהוא כן, שכן משה מבקש מן הקב"ה בשעת מיתה, ואומר לפניו רבונו של עולם גלוי לפניך דעתו של כל אחד ואחד מהם, ואין דעתו של זה דומה לדעתו של זה, ובשעה שאני מסתלק מהם בבקשה ממך אם ביקשת למנות עליהם מנהיג, מנה עליהם אדם שיהא סובל כל אחד ואחד לפי דעתו. מנין ממה שקראו בענין יפקוד [ה'] אלהי הרוחות לכל בשר וגו' (במדבר כז טז).

Calls for differentiating instruction have gained strength in secular education literature over the past decade. Conceptually and theoretically grounded in the work of progressive education (Dewey, 1900), child development (Erikson, 1995), social and intellectual development (Vygotsky, 1934/1986; Piaget, 1936), learning styles (Dunn, 1995), and multicultural education (Banks, 2004), differentiated instruction has been most recently articulated and promulgated through the work of Carol Tomlinson (2001; 2003). Teaching for a diverse student population is certainly challenging. Then again, teaching well is itself a challenging enterprise requiring knowledge expertise, talents in communication, pedagogical savvy, appreciation of varied student learning styles, etc. (Parkay & Stanford, 2006). The problem of reaching all students academically, however, has become more critical as schools have become more ethnically and linguistically diverse. Teaching, historically, has been plagued by a one-size-fits-all mentality. As Tomlinson (2005) simply yet accurately posits, "[W]e teach as we were taught" (p. 183). Classrooms have always been heterogeneous. Yet when students appear to teachers to be alike ethnically, linguistically, or culturally, educators have made the erroneous assumption that all students learn the same way, hence teaching becomes unifaceted.

Oakes (1985) has uncovered the fallacies inherent in homogeneous grouping and convincingly debunked explanations for maintaining its use. Certainly, teachers may claim it is "easier" to teach a homogenous class. Such arguments may in fact underlie an inability or unwillingness to address learning needs of all students in a class. For these teachers, teaching becomes teacher-directed wherein a whole-class instructional model is often used.

Recently, George (2005) has articulated a rationale for differentiating instruction. He argues that a heterogeneous classroom is critically important for several reasons that have relevance for Jewish educators. Since students in the future will likely live and work in diverse environments, classrooms should model such diversity. He explains, "[T]he heterogeneous classroom can provide a real-life laboratory for the development of important interpersonal and social knowledge, skills, and attitudes essential to success in adult life, while simultaneously providing opportunity for varied types and degrees of academic achievement" (p. 186). Besides goal consistency, George asserts that heterogeneous grouping will aid in accurate placement of students without erroneous labeling. "When students learn together in diverse classrooms, without the need to classify students according to their ability, there is also much less risk of labeling or stigmatizing high or low achievers" (p. 187). Furthermore, George states that such grouping accentuates the awareness of individual differences. If a teacher perceives his class as uniform, she is more likely to teach in a uniform manner. Teachers, he continues, are more sensitive to individual learning needs of students in mixed ability classrooms. "In an effective heterogeneous classroom (one where curriculum and instruction are properly differentiated), students and teachers, I think, are more likely to view their differences as assets that strengthen the whole school" (p. 187). Moreover, he argues that effort and persistence are enhanced in a differentiated classroom. The classroom is also more equitable in that "there is a much greater chance for equitable distribution of teaching talent and other school resources" (pp. 187–188). "Heterogeneous classrooms help ensure that all students are exposed to a complex, enriched curriculum, and to spirited instruction" (p. 188). The benefits of heterogeneous classrooms extend to both able and disabled learners. Among the benefits to able learners are enhanced self-esteem and personal growth (Also see ben-Ari, R., http://www.lookstein.org/heterogeneous/ hetero_edu_ complex.htm).

Differentiation of instruction has recently gained greater attention in Jewish education literature (see, e.g., Focus on: Differentiated instruction, 2006, in the *Jewish Educational Leadership*, entire theme).

Constructivism as Pedagogy

"An empowered teacher is a reflective decision maker who finds joy in learning and in investigating the teaching/learning process—one who views learning as construction and teaching as a facilitating process to enhance and enrich development."
(Twomey Fosnot, 1989, p. xi)

". . . Form groups upon groups and engage in Torah study, for the Torah is not acquired except [through studying] with companions. This is in accordance with [the words of] R' Yose the son of R' Hanina. For R' Yose the son of R' Hanina said: [Regarding] that which is written: 'There will be a sword against those who are alone, ve-no`alu.' [Its meaning is as follows]: There will be a sword against the enemies of [those] Torah scholars who sit each one alone and engage in Torah study. And not only that, but they [i.e., those who study alone] become foolish [as well, i.e., they err in their rulings]. [For] here [i.e., in the verse regarding the Torah scholars] it is written: ve-no`alu—and there [in a verse regarding Aaron and Miriam's sin against Moses] it is written: asher no`alnu, [which means: that which we have acted foolishly.] And not only that, but they sin [as well], as it is stated [in the verse] that which we have acted foolishly: - and that which we have sinned."
(Berakhot 63b)

How do people learn best? John Dewey (1899) said that people learn best "by doing." Hands-on instructional tasks encourage students to become actively involved in learning. Active learning increases students' interest in the material, makes the material covered more meaningful, allows students to refine their understanding of the material, and provides opportunities to relate the material to broad contexts. Constructivism also supports the social dimensions of learning; i.e., people learn best when actively working with others as partners, as in cooperative learning (see e.g., Johnson, Johnson, & Johnson-Holubec, 1994). Thus, constructivist pedagogy is aligned with the moral commitment to provide all students with developmentally appropriate instruction in an inclusive environment (Nalder, 2007; Udvari-Solner

& Kluth, 2007). Although constructivist practices are viable in non-inclusive settings since good pedagogy is good pedagogy, its incorporation in inclusion classes is more vital given the diverse student learning styles and needs in such placements.

Constructivism is aligned with progressive thinking. Constructivism is not a theory about teaching and learning per se; rather, it is a theory about the nature of knowledge itself. Knowledge is seen as temporary, developmental, socially constructed, culturally mediated, and non-objective. Learning, then, becomes a self-regulated process wherein the individual resolves cognitive conflicts while engaged in concrete experiences, intellectual discourse, and critical reflection (Foote, Vermette, & Battaglia, 2001; Rodgers, 2002). The principles of constructivist paradigms support the view of educators as informed decision-makers. Accordingly, learning is a socially mediated process in which learners construct knowledge in developmentally appropriate ways and that real learning requires that learners use new knowledge and apply what they have learned (Vygotski, 1934/1986; Bransford, Brown, & Cocking, 1999). These beliefs emphasize "minds-on" learning. This endorses the belief that all learners must be intellectually engaged in the learning process by building on their previous knowledge and experiences, and applying their new learning in meaningful contexts. To become a constructivist (mediator of learning), the teacher preparation candidate must be guided by the development of the child, motivation, and learning. Thus, central to expert instruction is a deep understanding of child development and a broad knowledge of the principles of pedagogy that serve as the blueprint for design of instruction that leads to student learning.

More specifically, students who are encouraged to "gather, assemble, observe, construct, compose, manipulate, draw, perform, examine, interview, and collect" are likely to be engaged in meaningful learning opportunities (Davis, 1998, p. 119). Students may, for example, gather facts about Sephardic history by exploring primary and secondary sources, even exploring the Internet, and then compose essays about key Sephardic figures. Students, Ashkenazic and Sephardic, may become involved in cooperative group activities aimed at learning more about each other's traditions and customs. Students may record their observations about reading selections and react to video segments in personal reaction journals. Students may construct posters demonstrating Sephardic artifacts, while teams of students may interview Sephardic rabbis.

Many of us would applaud such efforts because students are actively involved in meaningful and relevant learning activities. However, as O. L. Davis, Jr. (1998) has reminded us, hands-on "activities that do not explicitly require that pupils *think* about their experience" can simply mean "minds-off" (p. 120). Davis explains further:

Raw experiences comprise the grist for thinking. They are necessary, but not sufficient, instructional foci. For the most part, hands-on activities must include *minds-on* aspects. That is, pupils must think about their experience. They must, as Dewey noted, reflect about what they have done. Consciously, they must construct personal meanings from their active experience. . . . Indeed, for hands-on activities to qualify as educationally appropriate tasks, teachers must work with pupils before, during, and after these engagements so that pupils maintain a minds-on awareness of their unfolding experiences. (p. 120)

Constructivist pedagogy's strongest anchor in its alignment with inclusive practice comes from the social constructivism of Lev Vygotsky (1934/1986). He argued that since knowledge is constructed in a sociocultural context, social interaction, cultural tools, and activity shape individual development and learning. Knowledge construction is enhanced in a diverse learning environment wherein multiple perspectives on a particular issue or subject are available. Explaining Vygotsky's approach, Woolfolk and Hoy (2003) posit that "By participating in a broad range of activities with others, learners appropriate (take for themselves) the outcomes produced by working together" (p. 91). Vygotsky's best known concept, the zone of proximal development (ZPD), demonstrates the import of inclusive learning. On one hand, the ZPD demonstrates how the learner mediates and negotiates knowing; the learner stretches just enough to construct new knowledge slightly above the current level of knowledge. On the other hand, it is with the support of another that the problem is solved.

Working from a constructivist pedagogic frame is challenging (Windschitl, 2002). Teaching in an inclusive setting is challenging as well. Constructivism can certainly apply in general education classrooms. However, given the nature of an inclusive classroom environment with the more natural diversity of learners, constructivist pedagogy is a more natural fit. Research affirms constructivist pedagogy as instrumental in an inclusive classroom (Beck & Kosnik, 2006; George, 2005; Palincsar, Magnusson, Cutter, & Vincent, 2002; Reid, 2005). A strong argument can be made that early Jewish education systems clearly saw the value in inclusionary practice and constructivism. The *gemara* quoted at the outset of this sub-section (*Berakhot* 63b), explains that we learn *be-havruta* because of the different styles of the two participants (note that they are, ideally, actively engaging in learning, as opposed to listening to a lecture; see Brown & Malkus, 2007 for a recent study on this point). The *gemara* goes so far as to call one who learns alone (or, perhaps, it could be argued, in a homogenous environment) both a fool and a sinner; a fool because he will never gain new perspectives in his *own* learning, and a sinner because through his lack of well-roundedness in understanding he will end up propagating false rulings in Israel.

Promoting Cultural Diversity

"Multicultural education is a concept that incorporates cultural differences and provides equality in schools. For it to become a reality in the formal school situation, the total environment must reflect a commitment to multicultural education. The diverse cultural backgrounds and microcultural memberships of students and families are as important in developing effective instructional strategies as are their physical and mental capabilities. Further, educators must understand the influence of racism, sexism, classism on the lives of their students and ensure that these are not perpetuated in the classroom [and in the school]."
(Gollnick & Chinn, 1997, p. 12)
"Ve-ha`amidu talmidim harbeh"
Pirkei Avot (1:1)

According to Avot D'Rabbi Natan (2:3) in regard to Pirkei Avot (1:1) *Ve-ha`amidu talmidim harbeh*, Beit Shammai says, "One should teach only one who is smart, meek, of good ancestry and rich." In contrast, Beit Hillel says, "One should teach every man, for there were many transgressors in Israel who were brought close to Torah, and from them descended righteous, pious, and worthy folk." So *harbeh* could mean, teach a diverse group of students thus providing educational opportunities to all. Jewish tradition clearly values diversity.

The arena of cultural diversity and multicultural education is vast. In order to provide theoretical grounding for the positions taken in this essay, I have decided to focus on one aspect of the topic; i.e., the relevance of culturally relevant teaching. Multicultural education, though, serves as the moral underpinning for this discussion. According to Boyer and Baptiste (1996), multicultural education transforms "education so that its reality for students includes equity for all, a true spirit of democracy, freedom from prejudice and stereotypes of discrimination, and appreciation for cultural diversity" (p. 2). Multicultural education consists of five dimensions (Banks, 1997): Content integration (the degree to which, for example, teachers use examples from a variety of cultures), equity pedagogy (teaching, for example, that facilitates achievement for all students), empowering school culture and structure (practices, for example, that avoid labeling), prejudice reduction (activities, for example, that promote positive interactions with those different from oneself), and knowledge construction (examining, for example, who determines what gets taught).

Appreciating and capitalizing upon cultural diversity to enhance learning is very much an extension of the work of those educators committed to multicultural education. Support for deep learning based on sound psychological learning theory was reported by Lambert and McCombs (2000) in a comprehensive review of the latest research on learning theory amplified by a fundamental psychological principle relating to the learning process and the learner. They explain that social and cultural diversity are important factors in enhancing the learning experience. Learning, they explain is "facilitated by social interactions and communication with others in a flexible, diverse (in age, culture, family background, etc.) and adaptive instructional setting" (p. 509). Learning is enhanced by interacting with diverse abilities, cultures, values, and interests. Learning environments should allow for the appreciation of and interaction with diverse learning styles. The principle states that "Learning settings that allow for and respect diversity encourage flexible thinking as well as social competence and, moral development" (p. 509). Multicultural communities, according to Strike (2007) are characterized "by a sense that we are all in this together while also respecting differences and individual rights" (p. 146).

Educators who teach from a culturally relevant frame understand that all students can learn, albeit at different paces and in different ways. Although not the first to articulate a culturally relevant stance in regards to teaching, Ladson-Billings (1994) compares culturally relevant teaching with what she terms assimilationist teaching. An assimilationist believes that ethnic groups should conform to the norms, values, expectations, and behaviors of the dominant social and cultural group. Culturally relevant teachers, by contrast, believe that all students can learn, albeit differently. Assimilationist teachers believe that failure is inevitable for some students.

Culturally responsive teachers (Jordan Irvine & Armento, 2003) are responsive to their students by incorporating elements of the students' culture in their teaching. They make special efforts to get to know their students well. They might ask their students to share stories about their family and cultural heritage. Students are encouraged to express themselves openly about their culture. Students obtain a tremendous sense of pride and a feeling of being appreciated. A teacher, for instance, might assign her students a homework assignment to write a story about their family. Culturally responsive pedagogy is integrated into the curriculum and lessons on almost a daily basis, not just around holidays or special commemorations.

According to Lindsey, Roberts, and Campbell Jones (2005), culturally relevant educators affirm justice and opportunity for all students in their school and work to create an inclusive learning environment that supports and encourages all students to succeed, academically and socially.

Inclusion Research and Practice

"I would prefer my children to be in a school in which differences are looked for, attended to, and celebrated as good news, as opportunities for learning. The question with which so many school people re preoccupied is, 'What are the limits of diversity beyond which behavior is unacceptable?' . . . But the question I would like to see asked more often is, 'How can we make conscious deliberate use of differences in social class, gender, age, ability, race and interest as resources for learning?' . . . Differences hold great opportunities for learning. Differences offer a free, abundant, and renewable resource. I would like to see our compulsion for eliminating differences replaced by an equally compelling focus on making use of these differences to improve schools. What is im-

*portant about people—and about schools—is what is differ-
ent, not what is the same."*
(Barth, 1990, pp. 514–515)

Inclusion, as stated at the outset of this chapter, is cutting-edge
practice (Alton-Lee, Rietveld, Klenner, Dalton, Diggins, & Town,
2000). What is inclusion? What are some of its antecedents? What
does research inform us about such practice? Later in the chapter, we
will present some suggestions for implementing inclusion.

"An inclusive school is one that educates all students in the mainstream," according to Stainback and Stainback (2000). They continue,
"Educating students in the mainstream means that every student is in
general education and general classes." Moreover, they explain, "It
also means that all students are provided with appropriate educational
opportunities within the mainstream that are challenging yet geared
to their capabilities and needs; they are likewise provided with any
support and assistance they or the teachers may need to be successful in the mainstream." Fisher (2006) amplifies with more specificity:
"Related services, such as speech or physical therapy, are provided
within the context of the general education class, rather than being offered in the more traditional pull-out model" (p. 205). Yet, inclusion is
more than this according to leading researchers in inclusion (Clough,
& Corbet, 2000). "An inclusive school is place where everyone be-
longs, is accepted, supports, and is supported by his or her peers and
other members of the school community in the course of having his or
her educational needs met" (p. xi).

The history of inclusion begins with exclusion. Historically, the
"deformed," "feebleminded," "insane," "socially maladjusted," "stu-
pid," "incapable," "unteachable," and "handicapped" have been la-
beled as uneducable and isolated from the mainstream educational
system (Winzer, 1993). From time immemorial, many societies practiced infanticide for children considered physically deformed or mentally incapable. Greek civilization, for instance, lauded for its inspiring literature, culture, and seminal philosophers and artisans, practiced
infanticide on a regular basis. Parenthetically and curiously, the Jews
living under Greek rule, in contrast, were far more advanced in their
treatment of these children. Jewish communities took these children
in and, although they were often shunned from communal view, their
physical needs were cared for. Margaret Winzer's noteworthy history

of special education, titled *The History of Special Education: From Isolation to Integration*, documents the horrendous treatment of these children prior to the 18th century. In the 19th century, she explains, exclusion was commonplace, although the beginnings of "charity" towards them, if not education, emerged. She cites the pioneering work of people like Denis Diderot for the blind, G. M. A. Ferrus for the mentally retarded, and William Tuke for the deaf, among prominent others, whose worked formed the basis for caring and educating what was termed "handicapped" students. Her history ends with the emergence of special education classes in schools.

Winzer's (1993) observations about a society's awareness of its obligations to treat and educate its disabled is historically revealing but also instructive in terms of the obligations of educators today in dealing with "difference." She observes:

> A society's treatment of those who are weak and dependent is one critical indicator of its social progress. Social attitudes concerning the education and care of exceptional individuals reflect general cultural attitudes concerning the obligations of a society to its individual citizens. Every society recognizes certain extreme forms of human difference as abnormality. Along the range of human behavior from normal to abnormal there is some point at which a social judgment is made and an individual comes to be regarded as exceptional, disabled, different, or deviant. To what extent a society can accept such differences and how to deal with them are perennial problems. (p. 3)

We will again underscore this essential observation in the section on moral implications.

For the past several decades increased attention has been given to the educational and social needs of students with disabilities. Language about special education students too has evolved. The term "handicapped students" is no longer in vogue because of negative connotations. We avoid labeling a human being in a unitary way as "handicapped" because that designation certainly does not define the person wholly. Rather, they are whole, normal people who have certain physical, emotional, or learning needs. Hence the term "students with disabilities" has become more popular. The phrase "students with exceptionalities" or "exceptional students" is also in vogue. Some educators, including this author, however, have issues with these latter designations as well. The term "disabilities" is not sufficiently descriptive and it offers a condescending or at least negative image. Calling these students "students with possibilities" not "disabilities" affirms our collective commitment and belief that all students are capable to some degree and our obligation as educators is to address each student's "possibilities." Some might argue that we can go only so far with language before we find it difficult to define or label anything. Remaining sensitive about another's personhood and educational future is not a light matter. Much of the literature on inclusion reinforces such understandings of the power and use of language to address the needs of these and all students.

Legal rulings in significant court decisions have reinforced awareness of students with disabilities. In 1975, Congress passed Public Law 94–142 (Education of All Handicapped Children Act). Wiebe Berry (2006) reviews the more recent legal mandate to provide equitable educational opportunities to students with disabilities (No Child Left Behind, 2001, Individuals with Disabilities Education Act (IDEA), 1997, 2004). "In order to receive federal funds, states must develop and implement policies that assure a free appropriate public education (FAPE) to all children with disabilities. The state plans must be consistent with the federal statute, Title 20 United States Code Section 1400 et.seq. (20 USC 1400)" (http://www.scn.org/~bk269/94-142.html). Since the passing of IDEA, inclusion has been discussed much more than in the past. Although not on the forefront of educational practice, inclusive schooling and practices have been advocated in the literature and established in schools (Ainscow, 1997). In many New York City schools, for example, Collaborative Team Teaching (CTT) classes have been established with two teachers (one special education certified and one general education certified) teaching a heterogeneous class. According to Artiles, Kozleski, Dorn, and Christensen (2006), "From a historical perspective, special education was created as a parallel system for serving students with specific identifiable needs and disabilities." They continue, "This created ongoing dilemmas related to allocation of resources, divisions or professional labor, professional identity issues in personnel preparation, and barriers for the education of disabled populations to access mainstream practices and contexts. The educational project of inclusion aims to change this historical separation" (p. 66).

Parents, educators, and other concerned citizens have highlighted the historic inequitable treatment of students with disabilities and have advocated for inclusive practices as a means to ameliorate past injustices (Reid & Valle, 2004). Evidence demonstrates that services to students with disabilities have been inferior in segregated situations (Blackorby, Wagner, Cameto, Davies, Levine, Newman, et al., 2005). Educators today "now recognize that instructional practices effective for most learners are also effective for students with disabilities if they are delivered in an explicit and systematic manner" (Wiebe Berry, 2006, pp 489–490). Although teachers need to be prepared to teach in inclusive heterogeneous settings (Cook, 2002), research indicates that inclusion, when properly in place, provides all students increased access, encourages acceptance of all students, maximizes student participation, and increases academic achievement of both the abled and disabled (Artiles, Kozleski, Dorn, & Christensen, 2006).

What does additional research have to say about inclusion? In a review of the literature, Salend and Garrick (1999) found "increases in academic achievement, increased peer acceptance and richer friendship networks, higher self-esteem, avoidance of stigma attached to pull-out programs, and possible lifetime benefits (e.g., higher salaries, independent living) after leaving school" (as cited in Wiebe Berry, 2006, p. 490). Vaughn, Elbaum, Schumm, and Hughes (1998) have cited positive social outcomes for students with and without disabilities (also, see Hunt & Goetz, 1997; Staub & Peck, 1994–1995). Studies indicate that inclusive classrooms do not contribute to academic decline of non-disabled students (Peltier, 1997; Power-deFur & Orelove, 2003; Sharpe & York, 1994). Research also indicates that acceptance of inclusive practices is based on the amount of administrative support, resources, and training teachers receive (Ainscow, Howes, Farrell, & Frankham, 2003; Bishop & Jones, 2002). Effective inclusion also "depends on classroom climate factors as well as effective instructional strategies" (Erwin & Guintini, 2000; Myklebust, 2006; Wiebe Berry, 2006, p, 520).

Limits of or cautions about inclusion have also been noted in the literature (see, e.g., Zigmond, 2003). Some studies indicate that parents in favor of inclusion tended to be more satisfied compared to parents of mainstreamed children. Feiler and Gibson (1999) explain that advocacy of inclusion does not minimize or ignore a number of important issues that must be addressed about the inclusion movement. The authors point to four concerns that need more attention.

One, inclusion may mean one thing in one school, yet quite another thing in another. Precise definitions are necessary, and a consensus about practice has not yet been achieved. Such consensus does not exist. A second concern is a call for additional research on inclusion in terms of its long-term social and academic benefits or dangers (Armstrong, 2004). Third, just having an inclusive classroom doesn't by itself mean no exclusion is occurring. Wiebe Berry (2006) makes the point that "inclusive" settings can themselves "exclude." Good pedagogy is good pedagogy regardless of the educational setting. If teachers are not philosophically committed to inclusion and if their espoused theories for inclusion do not match their theories-in-action (Osterman & Kottkamp, 2004), then inclusion will not work. Parenthetically, I witnessed such exclusion in one CTT class I observed a few years ago. After the end of a mathematics lesson, one teacher announced to the class, "Okay, now let's get ready for language arts. Those in special ed move to the back of the room." A fourth caution proffered by Feiler and Gibson is that best practice inclusion may exist in one or several classrooms, but not appreciated or reinforced by the larger school culture (also see, Lindsay, 2003; Wedell, 2005).

Most recently, Volonino and Zigmond (2007) call into question co-teaching practices where general and special educators work together to teach a diverse group of students. Relaying the pros and cons of inclusion early in their review of the literature, they conclude that co-taught classrooms, a common occurrence in full inclusion placements, "is complicated by the theory-practice divide." "Although, theoretically, co-teaching could enhance instruction . . . , in practice, co-teaching is not often implemented as proposed." They continue, "co-teaching may hold future educational promise for some students, in some classrooms, at present, the research base does not provide sufficient support . . . ." (p. 298).

In conclusion, notwithstanding the views expressed in the preceding paragraph, sufficient research, overall, indicates that inclusive practice is warranted, at least as an alternative model. Research also indicated that problems have occurred in its proper implementation. Further research, including carefully designed experimental and additional qualitative studies, is to be encouraged. But as Wolfe and Hall (2003) suggest, "Let's end the debate about whether to include students with severe disabilities in the general education classroom. Let's focus on *how* and *when* and *where*" (p. 56; italics in original).

Recommendations

Thus far, we have alluded to several areas in which inclusive practice is needed in Jewish education and schooling. We have laid a theoretical framework for inclusive practice. In this section, based on Table 1 excerpted in part below, two groups of practical recommendations are offered, each relating to one of the two areas of classification identified as problematic:

Classification	Students with Disabilities	Sephardim/Ashkenazim
Recommendation	Inclusion through differentiation (Reid, 2005)	Inclusion through curriculum integration (Beane, 1997)

A separate monograph can be written for each area of recommendation. Suggestions are brief and, in many cases, presented in outline or bullet form along with some recommended readings. Please note, again, that this essay is not intended to discuss creating an inclusive classroom or school.

Differentiating Instruction for Students with Disabilities in Inclusive Classrooms

One of the common arguments by teachers, themselves, against working in an inclusive classroom is the perceived inability to "handle so many students with different learning needs." Teachers prepared to teach in inclusive classrooms, however, have essential knowledge, skills, and dispositions to deal with students' learning differences. The literature on differentiated instruction, which provides practical teaching tools and methodologies to teach an inclusive class, is extant and growing.

Some Guidelines for Differentiated Instruction include:
- Differentiated instruction can occur when teachers are aware and able to consider and deal with different learning needs and abilities of their students.
- Differentiated instruction is possible when teachers find opportunities for every student to succeed.
- Differentiated instruction occurs when teachers can multi-task.

- Differentiated instruction occurs when teachers can manage a classroom well enough to allow for "structured chaos" but know how to minimize excessive noise and disruptions.
- Differentiated instruction occurs when a range of activities is provided: whole-class instruction, small-group activities (pairs, triads, quads), individualized activities (e.g., learning centers, independent study), and student-teacher conferences (e.g., working on contracts for learning).
- Differentiated instruction occurs when teachers allow students to express themselves in diverse ways (e.g., artistically, musically, technologically, scientifically, athletically, etc.).
- Differentiated instruction allows students to express themselves in different ways (e.g., traditional compositions/essays, speeches, drama, music, building models, etc.).
- Differentiated instruction occurs when students discuss ideas freely and openly, giving all students a chance to participate in the discussion.
- Differentiated instruction occurs when the whole class listens to each other as individuals or as small groups about how they plan to learn or study a particular topic.
- Differentiated instruction occurs when the teacher works with selected students while providing meaningful activities for others.
- Differentiated instruction occurs when teachers allow students to take responsibility for their own learning.
- Differentiated instruction occurs when teachers use peer tutoring (i.e., advanced learners on particular topics work with students not as advanced).
- Differentiated instruction occurs when teachers realize students will complete work at different paces and that the teacher must plan for and provide learning activities for students who complete work before others.
- Differentiated instruction occurs when students can form their own interest groups to explore a topic of interest.
- Differentiated instruction incorporates cooperative learning, multiple intelligences and learning styles.

Teachers attuned to differentiation keep in mind these affirmations:

_____ 1. I call on students equitably.
_____ 2. I care for all students.

_____ 3. All students, regardless of ability, can learn from one another.

_____ 4. I am attuned to the different learning needs and abilities of my students.

_____ 5. I display the work of all students, regardless of ability or achievement

_____ 6. I help students appreciate, tolerate, and accommodate their similarities and differences in learning, culture, and interest.

_____ 7. I celebrate the successes of all students.

_____ 8. I consciously incorporate multiple intelligences whenever feasible.

_____ 9. I consciously incorporate learning styles whenever feasible.

_____ 10. I pre-assess students' knowledge prior to instruction so that I can develop appropriate lessons.

_____ 11. I use a variety of assessment strategies throughout the unit of instruction.

_____ 12. I am flexible in allowing students to demonstrate different ways that they have learned the material (in other words, I give students choices about how to express their learning).

_____ 13. I offer different homework options.

_____ 14. I give different kinds of tests.

_____ 15. I grade holistically, not relying on one sole test or measure.

_____ 16. In questioning all students, I prompt and probe equitably.

_____ 17. I give the same wait time to slow learners as I do to advanced learners.

_____ 18. I use a variety of grouping procedures, including whole-class instruction and small grouping.

_____ 19. I use peer tutoring as necessary.

_____ 20. I find ways for all students to excel.

_____ 21. I use a variety of teaching strategies.

_____ 22. I take into consideration students' interests and needs in planning instruction.

_____ 23. I give students texts that are at varied levels and readability.

_____ 24. I incorporate technology into instruction wherever feasible and useful.

_____ 25. I differentiate instruction when appropriate.

Recommended resources and readings include Bowe (2005), Carolan and Guinn (2007), Choate (2004), Dodge (2006), Drapeau (2004), National Professional Resources, Inc. (2003), Sapon-Shevin (2007), Tomlinson (2001, 2004), and Villa and Thousand (1995).

Also, consult www.corwinpress.com for an extensive list of excellent resources on the subject.

Curriculum Integration in the Inclusive Classroom

Efforts to integrate curriculum in secular education abound (see, e.g., Beane, 1997; Etim, 2005; Glatthorn, 2000). Integrating curriculum is important because it addresses the learning needs of all students. In Jewish education, calls for integrating curriculum have been made. For instance, Blau (2003) makes the point for greater attention to *aggadah* in the teaching of *gemara* because it provides opportunities for students who are not inclined to the kind of analytical thinking required in halakhic sections. Also, Rothstein (2003) emphasizes the need to devise a curriculum that "meets the needs of all its constituents" (p. 325). He states that it is certainly challenging but imperative nonetheless.

Considering discussion in the theoretical framework that emphasized the importance of cultural diversity as well as issues of justice and caring, an inclusive, integrated curriculum is warranted. An inclusive classroom and school will ensure that attention is given to the historic, religious, social, and halakhic traditions of different Jewish cultural groups. The extent and nature of curriculum attention will vary from school to school depending on demographic and other considerations. Still, each school should examine its curriculum to ensure proper attention is given to this subject.

Guidelines for Integrating Curriculum:
- Structure the curriculum to allow for greater depth and less superficial coverage. Discussion of any cultural tradition should be undertaken seriously.
- Meet with school curriculum leaders to design appropriate curricula and learning experiences/activities designed to meet pre-specified goals.
- Structure and deliver the curriculum so that it addresses the rich and deep cultural heritage of the group under study.
- Structure the curriculum so that it is closely coordinated. Coordinating content within lessons and among units over the course of the school year is imperative so that curriculum is sequential and well organized (Glatthorn, 2000).
- Emphasize both the halakhic theory or law and the practical. Relating content to the lived experiences of students is important to

increase student learning. Hands-on activities, when feasible, are very much warranted (Glatthorn, 2000).

- Organize curriculum discussion groups at faculty and grade conferences with teachers, and assess the impact of the new curriculum on students from all cultural groups.
- Review all instructional materials and resources to ensure inclusivity and coverage.
- Make recommendations to revise the curriculum based on some evidence.
- Solicit input from others in the curriculum process (e.g., curriculum specialists, rabbis, parents, and students).
- Examine the relationship between teaching and curriculum.
- Explore the impact of the hidden curriculum on the formal curriculum (e.g., What is happening outside the classroom as a result of discussing Sephardic and/or Ashkenazic traditions?).

Other curricular suggestions may include, in brief:
- Opportunities to include comparisons between Sephardic and Ashkenazic traditions and customs in *parashat ha-shavu`a, humash*, and *halakhah*.
- Opportunities to incorporate model lessons from Dobrinsky's (1988) *Teacher's Guide* that highlights teaching suggestions with practical and detailed information derived from Sephardic laws and customs (Dobrinsky, 2001).
- Opportunities for schools and educators to collaborate to develop standards in *limmudei kodesh* including benchmarks (see, e.g., Sokolow, 2007). For instance, a standard could include "Knowledge of Early Sephardic History." A benchmark at the high school level might state "Students will be able to cite Jewish Sephardic connections with the Iberian Peninsula." Students, instructionally, might engage in reading excerpts from the books of *Yesha`yahu, Yirmiyahu, Melakhim Alef,* and *Yonah*. They might examine archeological artifacts of the era, family histories, and a biography of the Abrabanel. Again, much curricular work—not in the purview of this essay—is needed.

Conclusion

This chapter has focused on a controversial topic. Pointing out exclusionary educational practices may put some people on the defensive. Yet, it has been stressed that educators committed to social justice and an ethic of caring, so integral in Jewish tradition, are morally obligated to point out ways of improving Jewish education.

Exclusion, as described in this essay, is morally unconscionable. Although attending to the needs of all students can occur in various ways, this chapter has described inclusion as one model worthy of consideration. Parenthetically, many public schools are not wholly inclusive. Many are traditional schools that have several inclusive classrooms. The movement towards inclusion can be made gradually and carefully. Not all teachers are properly trained to teach differentially, nor are they all committed to an inclusive philosophy. Teacher training in schools of education and professional development in schools are required to prepare teachers to work in inclusive settings. The fact that inclusion also takes additional resources, financial and otherwise, is another reason to proceed with caution. Although roadblocks towards inclusion exist, educators and others morally committed to such educational practices can do much to ensure the best education for all students.

Besides attention to the inclusion of students with disabilities, this chapter has also emphasized cultural curricular exclusion. Cultural exclusion can occur when a given group's customs and traditions are ignored or marginalized in the school curriculum. Schools, it has been argued, can play a critical role in terms of addressing these forms of exclusion by creating a more just, caring, and inclusive curriculum.

An inclusion model has been explicated with some recommendations to include students with disabilities via differentiated instruction and to create a more integrated or inclusive curriculum (Nind, Rix, Sheey, & Simmons, 2005). We conclude with a word about the ethics and morality of inclusion.

Moral Imperatives: The Ethics of Inclusion

This essay has presented a non-consequentialist ethical approach towards inclusive practice, in contrast to consequentialist theories that espouse the principle of benefit maximization in which the best choice is one that results in the most good for the greatest number. As Strike, Haller, and Soltis (2005) explain, this principle "judges the morality of our actions by their consequences. It says that the best action is the one with the best overall results" (p. 17). What is considered a "benefit," or a "good result" is often left to conjecture, at worst, or to further analysis, at best. In contrast, the principle of equal respect, as a non-consequentialist ethical stance, according to the aforementioned authorities, "requires that we act in ways that respect the equal worth of moral agents." It requires "that we regard human beings as having intrinsic worth and treat them accordingly" (p. 17). Thus, according to this line of thought, the rightness or wrongness of an action or position is based on the intrinsic needs of people often marginalized by their community, not on its consequences. As has been demonstrated, a review of the literature on inclusion indicates the efficacy of inclusive practice in many areas for all children, although admittedly additional research is needed, particularly in regards to Jewish school settings. My read of extant research in the field reveals that inclusive practice is often not adopted, not solely on the basis of research findings on its effectiveness or lack thereof for children's academic, emotional, and social development, but on such factors, among others, as adherence to educational tradition, lack of professional preparation, misguided leadership initiatives, and not least of which is an insensitivity to or ignorance of the ethical moral dimensions of work in schools.

On this latter point, the position taken here is that educators who do not consider the benefits of inclusion or its implementation are not necessarily acting immorally or unethically. Educators might, in fact, fall into one of four categories regarding these issues. The first group, and probably the least in number, are those educators and others concerned with supporting education in schools who do act immorally in the sense that their actions are concerned more with personal self-interest or politicalization of the educational enterprise, and not establishing policies and practices in the best interests of promoting student learning. The second, more numerous, category includes those people who simply have not considered the moral and ethical implications of their work or actions. These include educators of good-will, but they do not possess the requisite "ethical knowledge" (Campbell, 2003) to fully assess and appreciate the moral consequences of their behaviors in the classroom or school. Teacher training programs, for instance, often focus on the technical aspects of teaching (e.g., lesson planning, curriculum development, and classroom management) without sufficient attention to moral and ethical principles embedded in the act of teaching or leading. A third group includes educators and others who share the views and positions espoused here and wish to continue research in the area, which is very much needed, and who might be willing to form an inclusive network of some sort to further discussion of inclusive practice. A final group is comprised of those individuals who after considering the existing research and experiences of practice legitimately take a different position on what is best for students. They are not morally absent or corrupt. They struggle with difficult and challenging ethical dilemmas and come up with alternative strategies or approaches to educational practice.

Ethics, fundamentally, deals with actions that are commonly seen as right or wrong. Showing favoritism to a colleague who is Ashkenazic, for instance, over someone who is not in terms of hiring as a Jewish day school principal, in a case in which one's cultural background is irrelevant to job performance, is prejudicial and discriminatory. An ethical educator strives to do the right things as well as do things right. Morality deals with a system of values that undergirds ethical behavior. A moral leader might value social justice and equity for all people. If one's behavior is consistent then one will act "morally" when called to do so. Because a leader values social justice, she or he will consciously remain on guard for possible prejudicial behavior in selecting a new hire (Glanz, 2006).

Exclusionary educational practice, we have argued, is unethical. Jewish educators committed to justice, caring, cultural sensitivity, constructivist practice, differentiation within an inclusive learning environment are aware of the pedagogical and curricular implications of their work. They, thus, try to create an ethical school and classroom environment (Starratt, 1994; Zubay & Soltis, 2005). This final section of the essay will further deepen our understanding of the moral imperatives necessary for inclusive schooling.

Inclusive practice, to its fullest extent, cannot occur without moral commitment. Some Jewish educators have written and shared their beliefs and values that favor inclusive practice. Zweiter's (2006) incisive critique raises serious questions for Jewish educators about fundamental assumptions of Jewish education itself. Challenging Jewish educators to critically examine their own practices on many levels, Zweiter questions the practice of grouping students homogeneously. Zweiter evidently questions the efficacy of non-inclusive educational settings. He says of homogeneous grouping, ". . . while it may be easier for the teacher to teach students who are at a similar ability level, it is far from clear that bright children learn less when they are with a mixed group of students than when they are with other bright children" (p. 15). As for pedagogy and student involvement he is even more precise, "Active student involvement, independence, critical thinking and questioning need to replace passive learning" (p. 16). Most of our classrooms are homogeneously grouped because, according to Oakes (1985), traditional conceptions of learning remain with us even though they no longer make sense. Although not discussing inclusion, Zweiter refers to such educational traditions:

> *So much of what we do is the product of inertia, it's the way we've always done it or the way it has always been done. Even worse is when those unquestioned practices become dogma— we must do it this way because that's the way it has always been done. That dogma stifles and inhibits any possibility for change and growth, and we are left with practices whose rationale has long been forgotten. Remember Rav Hanokh of Alexander's comment that the real slavery of Israel in Egypt was that they learned to endure it. (p. 25)*

Advocacy of inclusion is also grounded in the critique of classroom life (Jackson, Boostrom, & Hansen, 1993). Alfie Kohn (1999) says our schools and classrooms are joyless. Mel Levine (2004) charges that "instructional practices and curricular choices fail to provide educational opportunities for diverse learners" (p. 8). He asks, why do "children like Michael, with his impressive mechanical aptitude" have to "be sentenced to wait until adulthood to experience success"? (p. 10). According to Svi Shapiro (2006), "students learn in the competitive, test-driven, and grade-obsessed school environment that what counts has little to do with the pleasure of learning, or the intrinsic value of greater understanding" (p. 9). Shapiro says "It is a process that starts from the moment one steps into a typical classroom and kids are placed in differential groups for reading, or treated by teachers with quite different amounts of respect and value depending on how they look, speak, or perform on assigned tasks" (p. 40). "School," he continues, is a place that "conveys, and endlessly reinforces, the idea that people are necessarily and inevitably to be ranked in ability and worth, and that those who are deemed of most worth are recognized and celebrated. . . ." (p. 40).

Continuing this line of thinking, Eliott Eisner (2004) observes, "Part of our press toward standardization has to do with what is inherent in our age-graded school system. Age-graded systems work on the assumption that children remain more alike than different over time and that we should be teaching within the general expectations for any particular grade." Eisner debunks such an assumption of uniformity in student aptitude and achievement. He continues, "yet, if you examine reading performance, for example, the average range of reading ability in an ordinary classroom approximates the grade level. Thus at the second grade, there is a two-year spread; at the third grade, a three-year range; at the fourth, a four-year range. Consider how various the picture would be if performance in four or five different fields of study were examined. Children become more different as they get older, and we ought to be promoting those differences and at the same time working to escalate the mean" (p. 304). He concludes, "We need a fresh and humane vision of what schools might become because what our schools become has everything to do with what our children and culture will become" (p. 305).

The vision Eisner is debunking is morally corrupt. Dwayne Huebner (1996), one of my doctoral mentors, astutely commented that education and teaching is "moral activity." "It is never amoral," he says. "It can be, and sometimes is, immoral" (p, 267). Schools and classrooms that do not "enable" and consequently "ennoble" all students (an idea generated by Yeshiva University President Richard Joel, albeit said in another context) are morally bankrupt. A moral vision is one founded on a deep commitment to inclusion by remaining steadfast in the belief that all children can learn at some developmentally appropriate level and that Ashkenazic and Sephardic customs and laws are of equal value.

Inclusion has been a historic goal in Jewish education, although not always actualized. As Seymour Fox, Israel Scheffler, and Daniel Marom (2006) in their volume titled *Visions of Jewish Education* state: "Jews in the Western world have aspired to civic and social equality." Jews, they continue, "have argued and worked for full political rights, for admission to universities, for access to the professions, and for the right to participate in all branches of commerce" (p. 5). In other words, they have called for and demanded inclusion, socially, politically, economically, and intellectually. Such societal and constitutional inclusion has been achieved by Jews as they have "become full and active participants in the civic and political life of their communities" (p. 5). Jewish schools should aspire to no less. We need a vision.

The moral vision needed goes beyond the ordinary, mundane, or established ways of conceiving teaching and learning (Brown & Duguid, 1991). From a Deweyian (1916) perspective, this vision "entails a constant expansion of horizons and a consequent formulation of new purposes and new responses" (p. 206). We need new responses to deal with a plethora of challenges we face in Jewish education, many not articulated in this essay. This new vision cannot be framed in isolation from a community of concerned individuals seeking to improve education and curriculum, more specifically, in Jewish schools. Discussions of vision have begun (see, e.g., Fox, Scheffler, & Marom, 2006). Educators and others must meet to discuss the kind of vision needed to address inclusive practices as highlighted here.

Finally, such a vision is only possible with moral and transformational leadership (Riehl, 2000). Transformational leadership has received much attention in the educational leadership literature (see, e.g., Leithwood & Jantzi, 2005). Although transformational leadership has been examined by other theorists (e.g., Bass, 1997), Kenneth Leithwood and Doris Jantzi have most recently addressed implications of transformational leadership for schools. Their ideas find relevance for our work in fostering inclusive practice. According to Leithwood and Jantzi (2005), "three broad categories of leadership practices" can be identified: setting directions, developing people, and redesigning the organization. The authors explain that setting directions is a "critical aspect of transformational leadership . . . [by] . . . helping staff to develop shared understandings about the school and its activities as well as the goals that undergird a sense of purpose or vision" (pp. 38–39). They explain that people are more likely to participate when they have had a say in developing ideas and practices. Transformational leaders realize that anyone can set a direction for an organization, but it is the effective leader who considers and solicits the participation of other key school personnel to share in the development and actualization of the institutional vision and purpose.

Summarizing how transformational leadership works, Northouse (2003) explains: "Transformational leaders set out to empower followers and nurture them in change. They attempt to raise the consciousness in individuals and to get them to transcend their own self-interests for the sake of others" (p. 142). Northouse highlights the following characteristics of transformational leaders: serve as strong role models, have a highly developed sense of moral values; a self-determined sense of identity; visionary, confident, articulate; willingness to listen to followers; engender trust in followers, and act as change agents within and for the organization. Both Fullan (2003) and Starratt (1995) concur that change, without addressing a change in core beliefs and values, is doomed to remain temporary and superficial. "Transformational leadership," says Starratt (1995), "is concerned with large, collective values . . . " (p. 110). Leadership is predicated on the foundation of changing core beliefs and values. Fullan (1991, cited by Fullan 2003) has identified "five crucial mind and action sets that leaders in the 21st century must cultivate: a deep sense of moral purpose, knowledge of the change process, capacity to develop relationships across diverse individuals and groups, skills in fostering knowledge creation and sharing, and the ability to engage with others in coherence making amidst multiple innovations" (p. 35).

What is our moral commitment to such ideals in regards to inclusive practice? Ryan (1996) makes a strong case for the role of leaders to promote inclusive practice. He states: "Leadership practices need to be organized to promote inclusion because we live in a world that increasingly embraces values, views, and practices that are not consistent with inclusion" (p. 105). The moral imperative of inclusion involves much work as we strive to enhance an ethic of caring, justice, and constructivist work within an inclusive differentiated instructional environment. To accomplish this imperative requires moral commitment to an "ethics of inclusion."

Questions for Reflection
1. From your experience, in what ways have schools/classrooms excluded students?
2. In what ways have schools/classrooms successfully included students?
3. Can you provide personal examples of how you or someone you know has been excluded or included in a school?
4. What specific examples can you provide to demonstrate that students with disabilities have been included or excluded?
5. What specific examples can you provide to demonstrate that Sephardic customs and traditions have/have not received curricular or pedagogical attention?
6. Can you describe situations in which Sephardic customs and traditions have received curricular and pedagogical attention?
7. To what extent have Ashkenazim experienced exclusion?
8. How might the school curriculum address the Ashkenazic/Sephardic issue discussed in this chapter?

9. How might you remain more culturally sensitive as an educator?
10. What would you do to encourage or ensure that a child's culture is appreciated and respected school-wide?
11. How might you counter someone who would say that classroom management issues would be too cumbersome in an inclusive class?
12. How would you address a parent's concern that she doesn't want her "normal" child in the same classroom as a "learning disabled one" or "a physically disabled one?"
13. What strategies may educational leaders employ to ease apprehensions of parents who make similar complaints as in the previous question?
14. Do you think placing students who are working well above their capacities in the same classes as students with mild learning disabilities may impede the educational progress of students with disabilities? Explain.
15. Given the premise of the previous question, would the progress of these above average students be impeded in any way? Explain.
16. How might someone who favors inclusion using the examples in the previous two questions respond to a claim that progress of each group would indeed be impeded?
17. Isn't inclusion, diversity, and multiculturalism a leftist, socialist agenda that tries to treat everyone the same? Explain why or why not.
18. Do you see inclusionary practice as blurring differences in ability among students? Explain.
19. To what extent do you see inclusion an issue in Jewish schools?
20. What factor or factors would inhibit implementation of inclusion in your school?
21. What strategies might you utilize to overcome the roadblocks alluded to in the previous question?
22. What kind of additional professional development would teachers need to work in an inclusive class?
23. What can a principal or any other school building leader do to support inclusionary work?
24. Can you think of an instance wherein some educator espouses a philosophy that calls for "achievement for all students" but does not advocate inclusion? Explain.
25. What other inclusionary/exclusionary issues need further analysis?

26. What else would you like or need to know about inclusion?
27. Have you experienced an inclusive classroom? Explain.

If you are interested in further discussion of issues of inclusion, please contact the author at: glanz@yu.edu.

The author would also like to thank Yamin Benarroch, Moshe Goldfeder and Leon Zacharowitz for their assistance in the preparation of this chapter.

References

Ainscow, M. (1997). Towards inclusive schooling. *British Journal of Education, 24*(1), 3–6.

Ainscow, M., Howes, A., Farrell, P., & Frankham, J. (2003). Making sense of the development of inclusive practice. *European Journal of Special Needs Education, 18*(2), 227–242.

Allport, G. (1987). *The nature of prejudice.* Reading, MA: Addison-Wesley.

Alton-Lee, A., Rietveld, C., Klenner, L., Dalton, N., Diggins, C., & Town, S. (2000). Inclusive practice within the lived cultures of school communities: Research case studies in teaching, learning and inclusion. *International Journal of Inclusive Education, 4*(3), 179–210.

Anyon, J. (1981). Social class and the hidden curriculum of work. In H. A. Giroux, A. N. Penn, & W. F. Pinar (Eds.), *Curriculum and instruction: Alternatives in education.* Berkeley. CA: McCutchan Publishers.

Apple, M. (1986). *Teachers and text: A political economy of class and gender.* London: Routledge.

Armstrong, F. (2004). *Action research for inclusive education: Changing places, changing practices, changing minds.* London: RoutledgeFalmer.

Artiles, A. J., Harris-Murri, N., & Rostenberg, D. (2006). Inclusion as social justice: Critical notes on discourses, assumptions, and the road ahead. *Theory into Practice, 45*(3), 260–268.

Artiles, A. J., Kozleski, E..B., Dorn, S., & Christenssen, C. (2006). Learning in inclusive education research. *Review of Research in Education, 30*(1), 65–108.

Banks, J. (1997). *Educating citizens a multicultural society.* New York: Teachers College Press.

Banks, J.A. (2004). *Multicultural education: Theory and practice* (3rd ed.). Boston: Allyn and Bacon.

Banks, J. A. (2005). *Cultural diversity and education: Foundations, curriculum, and teaching* (5th ed.). Boston: Allyn and Bacon.

Barth, R. (1990). A personal vision of a good school. *Phi Delta Kappan, 71,* 512–571.

Bass, B. M. (1997). Does the transactional/transforamtional leadership transcend organizational and national boundaries? *American Psycholgist, 52,* 130–139.

Beane, J. A. (1997). *Curriculum integration: Designing the core of democratic education.* New York: Teachers College Press.

Beck, C., & Kosnik, C. (2006). *Innovations in teacher education: A social constructivist approach.* New York: State University of New York Press.

Beck, L. G. (1994). *Reclaiming educational administration as a caring profession.* New York: Teachers College Press.

ben-Ari, R. http://www.lookstein.org/heterogeneous/hetero_edu_complex.htm, Retrieved September 9, 2007.

Bishop, A., & Jones, P. (2002). Promoting inclusive practice in primary initial teacher training: Influencing hearts as well as minds. *Support for Learning, 17*(2), 58–63.

Blackmore, J. (1993). In the shadow of man: The historical construction of educational administration as a "masculinist" enterprise. In J. Blackmore & J. Kenway (Eds.), *Gender matters in educational administration and policy* (pp. 27–48). London: The Falmer Press.

Blackorby, J., Wagner, M., Cameto, R., Davies, E. Levine, P. Newman, L., et al. (2005). *Engagement, academics, social adjustment, and independence.* Palo Alto, CA: SRI.

Blau, Y. (2003). Redeeming the Aggadah in yeshiva education. In J. Saks & S. Handelman, (Eds.). *Wisdom from all my teachers: Challenges and initiatives in contemporary Torah education* (pp. 305–322). Jerusalem: Urim Publications.

Blau, Y. (2000). The implications of a Jewish virtue ethic. *The Torah U-Madda Journal, 9,* 19–41.

Bogotch, I.E. (2000). *Educational leadership and social justice: Theory into practice.* Revised version of paper presented at the annual conference of the University Council for Educational Administration, Albuquerque, NM. ERIC document no. ED 452 585.

Borowitz, E. B., & Weinman Schwartz, F. (1999). *The Jewish moral values.* Philadelphia: The Jewish Publication Society.

Bowe, F. (2005). *Making inclusion work.* Upper Saddle River, NJ: Pearson.

Bowers, C.A. (2001). *Educating for eco-justice and community.* Athens: University of Georgia Press.

Boyer, J. B., & Baptiste, Jr., H. P. (1996). *Transforming the curriculum for multicultural understandings: A practitioner's handbook.* San Francisco, CA: Caddo Gap Press.

Bransford, J.D., Brown, A.L., & Cocking, R.R. (Eds.). (1999). *How people learn: Brain, mind, experience, and school.* Washington, DC: National Academy Press.

Brown, K. (2004). Leadership for social justice and equity: Weaving a transformative framework and pedagogy. *Educational Administration Quarterly,40*(1), 79–110.

Brown, J. S., & Duguid, P. (1991). Organizational learning and communities of practice: Toward a unified view of working, learning, and innovation. *Organization Science, 2,* 40–57.

Brown, S., M., & Malkus, M. (2007). *Hevruta* as a form of cooperative learning. *Journal of Jewish Education, 73,* 209–226.

Campbell, E. (2003). *The ethical teacher.* Philadelphia: Open University Press.

Carolan, J., & Guinn, A. (2007). Differentiation: Lessons from master teachers. *Educational Leadership, 64*(5), 44–47.

Choate, J. S. (Ed.). (2004). *Successful inclusive teaching* (4th ed.). Boston: Pearson.

Clough, P., & Corbet, J. (2000). *Theories of inclusive education.* Thousand Oaks, CA: Sage.

Connell, R.W. (1993). *Schools and social justice.* Philadelphia, PA: Temple University Press.

Cook, B. G. (2002). Inclusive attitudes, strengths, and weaknesses of pre-service general educators enrolled in a curriculum infusion teacher preparation program. *Teacher Education and Special Education, 25,* 262–277.

Darling-Hammond, L., & Bransford, J. (2007). *Preparing teachers for a changing world: What teachers should learn and be able to do.* San Francisco: Jossey-Bass.

Davies, C. (2004). Taking root: Narratives of Jewish women in Latin America. *Progress in Development Studies,4,* 75–76.

Davis, Jr., O. L. (1998). Beyond beginnings: From "hands-on" to "minds-on." *Journal of Curriculum and Supervision, 13,* 119–122.

Dewey, J. (1899). *The school and society*. Chicago, IL: The University of Chicago Press.

Dewey, J. (1900). *School and society*. Chicago: University of Chicago Press.

Dewey, J. (1916). *Democracy and education*. New York: Macmillan.

Dobrinsky, H.C. (2001). *A treasury of Sephardic laws and customs: The ritual practices of Syrian, Moroccan, Judeo-Spanish and Spanish and Portuguese Jews of North America*. New York: Yeshiva University Press.

Dobrinsky, H. C. (1988). *Teacher's guide for a treasury of Sephardic laws and customs*. New York: Yeshiva University Press.

Dodge, J. (2006). *Differentiation in action: A complete resource with research-supported strategies to help you plan and organize differentiated instruction and achieve . . . Learners*. New York: Scholastic.

Draayer, D. R. (2003). *Retirement straight talk: Stories and wisdom from educators*. Lanham, MD: ScarecrowEducation.

Drapeau, P. (2004). *Differentiated instruction: Making it work: A practical guide to planning, managing, and implementing differentiated instruction to meet the needs of all learners*. New York: Scholastic.

Dunn, R. (1995). A meta-analytic validation of the Dunn and Dunn Model of Learning-Styles Preferences. *Journal of Educational Research, 88*(6), 353–362.

Dunn, R., & DeBello, T. C. (Eds.). (1999). *Improved test scores, attitudes, and behaviors on America's schools: Supervisors' success stories*. Westport, CT: Bergin & Garvey.

Dunn, R., Giannitti, M. C., Murray, J. B., Rossi, I., Geisert, G., & Quinn, P. (1990). Grouping students for instruction: Effects of learning style on achievement and attitudes. *Journal of Social Psychology, 130,* 485–494.

Dyson, A. (1999). Inclusion and inclusions: Theories and discourses in inclusive education. In H. Daniels & P. Garner (Eds.), *World yearbook of education 1999: Inclusive education* (pp. 36–53). London: Kogan Page.

Eisner, E. W. (2004). What does it mean to say a school is doing well? In D. J. Flinders & S. J. Thornton, (Eds.), *The curriculum studies reader* (2nd ed.) (pp. 296–305). London: Routledge.

Erikson, E. (1995). *Childhood and society* (Rev. Ed.). New York: Vintage.

Erwin, E. J., & Guintini, M. (2000). Inclusion and classroom membership in early childhood. *International Journal of Disability, Development and Education, 47,* 237–257.

Etim, J. S. (2005). *Curriculum integration K–12: Theory and practice.* Lanham: MD University Press of America.

Feiler, A., & Gibson, H. (1999). Threats to the inclusive movement. *British Journal of Special Education, 26*(3), 147–152.

Ferguson, K. E. (1984). *The feminist case against bureaucracy.* Philadelphia: Temple University Press.

Ferri, B. A., & Connor, D. J. (2006). *Reading resistance: Discourses of exclusion in desegregation and inclusion debates.* New York: Peter Lang.

Fisher, D. (2006). This issue. *Theory into Practice, 45*(3), 205–206.

Focus on: Differentiated instruction. (2006). *Jewish Educational Leadership, 5*(1), entire issue.

Foote, C.S., Vermette, P.J., & Battaglia, C.F. (2001). *Constructivist strategies: Meeting standards and engaging adolescent minds.* Larchmont, NY: Eye on Education.

Fox, S., Scheffler, I, & Marom, D. (Eds.). (2006). *Visions of Jewish education.* New York: Cambridge University Press.

Freire, P. (2004). Pedagogy of the oppressed. In. D. J. Flinders & S. J. Thornton, (Eds.), *The curriculum studies reader* (2nd ed.) (pp. 125–133.). London: Routledge.

Fuchs, D., & Fuchs, L. (1994). Inclusive schools movement and the radicalization of special education reform. *Exceptional Children, 60,* 773–796.

Fullan, M. (2003). *Leading in a culture of change.* San Francisco: Jossey-Bass.

Furman, G. C., & Shields, C. M. (2005). How can educational leaders promote and support social justice and democratic community in schools? In W. A. Firestone & C. Riehl (Eds.), *A new agenda fort research in educational leadership* (pp. 119–137). New York: Teachers College Press.

George, P. S. (2005). A rationale for differentiating instruction in the regular classroom. *Theory Into Practice, 44*(3), 185–193.

Gilad, G. (1990). *Discord in Zion: Conflict between Ashkenazi and Sephardi Jews in Israel.* Scorpion Publishing.

Gilligan, C. (1993). *In a different voice: Psychological theory and women's development.* Cambridge, MA: Harvard University Press.

Giroux, H. A. (Ed.). (1991). *Postmodernism, feminism, and cultural politics.* Albany, NY: SUNY Press.

Glanz, J. (2006). *Ethical and spiritual leadership.* Thousand Oaks, CA: Corwin.

Glatthorn, A. A. (2000). *Developing a quality curriculum.* Alexandria, VA: Association for Supervision and Curriculum Development.

Gollnick, D., & Chinn, P. C. (1997). *Multicultural education in a pluralistic society.* NJ: Prentice Hall. Good, T. L., & Brophy, J. E. (2007). *Looking in classrooms* (10th ed.). Boston: Allyn & Bacon.

Gordon, S. P. (2003). *Professional development for school improvement: Empowering learning communities.* Boston: Allyn and Bacon.

Hahn, H. (1989). The politics of special education. In D. K. Lipsky & A. Gartner (Eds.), *Beyond separate education: Quality education for all* (pp. 225–242). Baltimore: Paul H. Brookes.

Held, V. (1995). *Justice and care: Essential readings in feminist ethics.* New York: Westview Press.

Henry, M. (1996). *Parent-school collaboration: Feminist organizational structures and school leadership.* New York: State University of New York Press.

Huebner, D. (1996). Teaching as moral activity. *Journal of Curriculum and Supervision, 13*(3), 267–275.

Hunt, P., & Goetz, L. (1997). Research in severe disabilities. *Journal of Special Education, 31,* 3–29.

Individuals with disabilities Education Act, 33, U.S.C., $ 1400 (1997).

Individuals with disabilities Education Act, 20, U.S.C., $ 1400 (2004).

International League of Societies for Persons with Mental Handicap. (1994, June). The Inclusion Charter. UNESCO World Conference on Special Educational Needs: Access and Quality. Salamanca, Spain.

Jackson, P. W., Boostrom, R. E., & Hansen, D. T. (1993). *The moral life of schools.* San Francisco: Jossey-Bass.

Johnson, D. W., Johnson, R. T., & Johnson-Holubec, E. (1994). *Cooperative learning in the classroom.* Alexandria, VA: Association for Supervision and Curriculum Development.

Jordan Irvine, J. J. (2001). *Caring, competent teachers in complex classrooms.* Washington, DC: American Association of Colleges for Teacher Education.

Jordan Irvine, J. J., & Armento, B. J. (2003). *Culturally responsive teaching.* Boston: McGraw Hill.

Karagiannis, A., Stainback, S.., & Stainback, W. (2000a). Historical overview of inclusion. In S. Stainback & W. Stainback (Eds.). *Inclusion: A guide for educators* (pp. 17–28). Baltimore: Paul H. Brookes.

Karagiannis, A., Stainback, W., & Stainback, S. (2000b). Rationale for inclusive schooling. In S. Stainback & W. Stainback (Eds.). *Inclusion: A guide for educators* (pp. 3–15). Baltimore: Paul H. Brookes.

Kaser, J., Mundry, S., Stiles, K. E., & Loucks-Horsle, S. (2006). *Leading every day: 124 actions for effective leadership.* Thousand Oaks, CA: Sage.

Katz, M. S., Noddings, N., & Strike, K. A. (Eds.). (1999). *Justice and caring: The search for common ground in education.* New York: Teachers College Press.

Kochhar, C.A., West, L.L., & Taymans, J.M. (2000). *Successful inclusion: Practical strategies for a shared responsibility.* Upper Saddle River, NJ: Merrill.

Kohn. A. (1999). *The schools our children deserve.* Boston, MA: Houghton Mifflin.

Korn, E. (1997). *Tselem Elokim* and the dialectic of Jewish morality. *Tradition: A Journal of Orthodox Thought, 31*(2), 5–30.

Kozol, J. (1991). *Savage inequalities.* New York: Crown Publishers.

Ladson-Billings, G. (1994). *The dreamkeepers.* San Francisco: Jossey-Bass.

Lambert, N. M., & McCombs, B. L. (Eds.). (2000). *How students learn: Reforming schools through learner-centered education.* Washington, DC: American Psychological Association.

Lambert, L., Walker, D., Zimmerman, D. P., Cooper, J. E., Lambert, M. D., Gardner, M. E., & Szabo, M. (2003). *The constructivist leader* (2nd ed.). New York: Teachers College Press.

Lauria, J. (2005). Effects of learning-style-based homework prescriptions on the achievement and attitudes of middle school students. *NASSP Bulletin, 89*(642), 67–89.

Leithwood, K., & Jantzi, D. (2005). Transformational leadership. In B. Davies, (Ed.), *The essentials of school leadership* (pp. 31–43). Thousand Oaks, CA: Corwin Press.

Levine, M. (2004). Helping those in need: Celebrating diverse minds. *Educational Leadership, 61,*8–12

Lindsay, G. (2003). Inclusive education: A critical perspective. British Journal of Special Education, 30(1), 3–12.

Lindsey, R. B., Roberts, L. M., & CampbellJones, F. (2005). *The culturally proficient school: An implementation guide for school leaders.* Thousand Oaks, CA: Corwin.

Madden, N. A., & Slavin, R. E. (1983). Mainstreaming students with mild handicaps: Academic and social outcomes. *Review of Educational Research, 53*(4), 519–569.

Mahoney, D. (2006). *Ethics and the school administrator: Balancing today's complex issues.* Lanham, MD: Rowman & Littlefield.

Mahoney, D. (2008). *Ethics in the classroom.* Lanham, MD: Rowman & Littlefield.

Marshall, C., Patterson, J. A., Rogers, D. L., & Steele, J. R. (1996). Caring as career: An alternative perspective for educational administration. *Educational Administration Quarterly, 32,* 271–294.

Matza, D. (Ed.). (1998). *Sephardic-American voices: Two hundred years of a literary legacy.* Danvers, MA: University Pres of New England.

Mayhew, K. C., & Edwards, A. C. (1965). *The Dewey School: The laboratory school of the University of Chicago, 1896–1903.* New York: Atherton Press.

McBeath, R. J. (1994). The impact of paradigm shifts in education. *Educational Media International, 31*(3), 165–170.

Myklebust, J. O. (2006). Class placement and competence attainment among students with special educational needs. *British Journal of Special Education, 33*(2), 76–81.

Nalder, N. L. (2007). *Cooperative learning in an inclusive classroom: The impact on students with special needs.* Dissertation Abstracts. Retrievable at http://www.amazon.com/Cooperative-learning-inclusive-classroom-Dissertation/dp/B000GKHR8M/ref=sr_1_2/103-1694125-4367017?ie=UTF8&s=books&qid=118 8996703&sr=8-2

National Professional Resources, Inc. (2003). *Differentiated instruction: A focus on inclusion.* VHS Video Training Tape.

Nind, M., Rix, J., Sheey, K., & Simmons, K. (Eds.). (2005). *Curriculum and pedagogy in inclusive education: Values into practice.* London: RoutledgeFalmer.

Noddings, N. (1984). *Caring: A feminist approach to ethics and moral education.* Berkeley, CA: University of California Press.

Noddings, N. (1986). Fidelity in teaching, teacher education, and research for teaching. *Harvard Educational Review, 56,* 496–510.

Noddings, N. (1992). *The challenge to care in schools: An alternative approach to education.* New York: Teachers College Press.

Noddings, N. (2003). *Caring: A feminine approach to ethics and moral education* (2nd ed.). Berkeley: University of California Press.

Northouse, P. G. (2003). *Leadership: Theory and practice.* Thousand Oaks, CA: Sage.

Oakes, J. (1985). *Keeping track: How schools structure inequality.* New Haven, CT: Yale University Press.

Ogbu, J. U. (1978). *Minority education and the caste: The American system in cross cultural perspective.* San Diego, CA: Academic Press.

Ogbu, J. U. (2003). *Black American students in an affluent suburb: A study of academic disengagement.* Mahwah, NJ: Erlbaum.

Osterman, K. E., & Kottkamp, R. B. (2004). *Reflective practice for educators: Improving schooling through professional development* (2nd ed.). Thousand Oaks, CA: Corwin.

Paretzky, Z. T. (1996). *Reservoirs of faith: The yeshiva through the ages.* Jerusalem: Feldheim.

Parkay, F. W., & Stanford, B. H. (2006). *Becoming a teacher* (7th ed.). Boston: Allyn and Bacon.

Palincsar, A. S., Magnusson, S. J., Cutter, J., & Vincent, M. (2002). Supporting guided-inquiry instruction. *Teaching Exceptional Children, 34*(3), 88–91.

Patai, R. (1971). *Tents of Jacob.* Englewood Cliffs, NJ: Prentice-Hall.

Peltier, G. L. (1997). The effects of inclusion on nondisabled students: A review of the research. *Contemporary Education, 68,* 234–240.

Piaget, J. (1936). *Origins of intelligence in the child.* London: Routledge & Kegan Paul.

Ponterotto, J. G., Utsey, S. O., & Pedersen, P. B. (2006). *Preventing prejudice: A guide for counselors, educators, and parents.* Thousand Oaks, CA: Sage.

Power-deFur, & Orelove, D. (Eds.). (1997). *Inclusive education: Practical implementation of the least restrictive environment.* Gaithersburg, MD: Aspen Publishers.

Rafael, E. b., & Sharot, S. (1991). *Ethnicity, religion, and class in Israeli society.* Cambridge University Press.

Rapp, D. (2002). Social justice and the importance of rebellious, oppositional imaginations. *Journal of School Leadership, 12*(3), 226–245.

Rawls, J (1971). *A theory of justice.* Cambridge, MA: Harvard University Press.

Regan, H. B. (1990). Not for women only: School administration as a feminist activity. *Teachers College Record, 91,* 565–577.

Reid, G. (2005). *Learning styles and inclusion.* London: Paul Chapman.

Reid, D. K., & Valle, J. W. (2004). The discursive practice of learning disability: Implications for instruction and parent-school relations. *Journal of Learning Disabilities, 37,* 466–481.

Riehl, C. J. (2000). The principal's role in creating inclusive schools for diverse students. *Review of Educational Research,* 70(1), 55–81.

Rist, R. (1970). Student social class and teacher expectations: The self-fulfilling prophecy in ghetto education. *Harvard Educational Review 40*, 3, 411–451.

Rodgers, C. (2002). Seeing student learning: Teacher change and the role of reflection. *Harvard Educational Review 72*(2), 230–253.

Rosenthal, R., & Jacobson, L. (1968). *Pygmalion in the classroom: Teacher expectation and pupils' intellectual development.* New York: Holt, Rinehart & Winston.

Rothstein, G. (2003). Walking before running: Towards a more practical Judaic studies curriculum. In J. Saks & S. Handelman, (Eds.). *Wisdom from all my teachers: Challenges and initiatives in contemporary Torah education* (pp. 323–340). Jerusalem: Urim Publications.

Ryan, J. (2006). *Inclusive leadership.* San Francisco: Jossey-Bass.

Sadker, M., & Sadker, D. (1994). *Failing at fairness: How our schools cheat girls.* New York: Simon and Schuster Publishers.

Salend, S. J., & Garrick, L. M. (1999). The impact of inclusion on students with and without disabilities and their educators. *Remedial and Special Education, 20,* 114–126.

Sapon-Shevin, M. (2007). *Widening the circle: The power of inclusive classrooms.* Boston: Beacon Press.

Schnall, D.J. (2006) Perspectives for the future of Jewish education. In Z. Grumet (Ed.). *Jewish education in transition: Proceedings of the first international conference on Jewish education* (pp. 75–82). Teaneck, NJ: BenYehuda Press.

Schwartz, S., Link, B. G., Dohrenwend, B. P., Naveh, G., Levav, I., & Shrout, P. (1991). Separating class and ethnic prejudice: A study of north African and European Jews in Israel. *Social Psychology Quarterly, 54*(4), 287–298.

Sephardic Passover customs and traditions, http://www.angelfire.com/pa2/passover/ Sephardicpassovercustoms.html). Retrieved September 3, 2007.

Sergiovanni, T. J. (1992). *Moral leadership: Getting to the heart of school improvement.* San Francisco: Jossey-Bass.

Seyfried, S. (1998). Academic achievement of African-American preadolescents: The influence of teacher perceptions. *American Journal of Community Psychology, 26,* 381–402.

Shapiro, H.S. (2006). *Losing heart: The moral and spiritual miseducation of America's children.* Mahwah, NJ: Lawrence Erlbaum.

Shapiro, J. P., & Stefkovich, J. A. (2005). *Ethical leadership and decision making in education: Applying theoretical perspectives to complex dilemmas* (2nd ed.). Mahwah, NJ: Erlbaum Associates.

Sharpe, M. N., & York, J. L. (1994). Effects of inclusion on the academic performance of classmates without disabilities. *Remedial and Special Education, 15,* 34–44.

Shavit, Y. (1984). Tracking and ethnicity in Israeli secondary education. *American Sociological Review, 49*(2), 210–220.

Shmueli, E. (1977). Problems in educating Oriental Jewish children in Israel. *Equity & Excellence in Education, 15*(3), 3–5.

Sokolow, M. (2007). *Va-Yasem 'Oto 'Al Nes*: Standards in *limmudei kodesh* for Modern Orthodox day schools. *Ten Da'At, 19,* 4–17.

Sorenson, R. D., & Goldsmith, L. M. (2006). *The principal's guide to school budgeting.* Thousand Oaks, CA: Corwin.

Sperber, D., & Elman, Y. (1999). *Why Jews do what they do: The history of Jewish custom throughout the cycle of the Jewish year.* New York: Ktav Publishing.

Spring, J. (1994). *The American school, 1642–1993* (3rd ed.). New York: McGraw-Hill Publishers.

Stainback, S., & Stainback, W. (Eds.). (2000). *Inclusion: A guide for educators.* Baltimore: Paul H. Brookes.

Starratt, R. J. (1991). Building an ethical school: A theory for practice in educational leadership. *Educational Administration Quarterly, 27*(2), 185–202.

Starratt, R.J. (1994). *Building an ethical school: A practical response to the moral crisis in schools.* London: The Falmer Press.

Starratt, R.J. (1995). *Leaders with vision: The quest for school renewal.* Thousand Oaks, CA: Corwin.

Staub, D., & Peck, C. A. (1994/1995). What are the outcomes for non-disabled students. *Educational Leadership, 52,* 36–40.

Stillman, N. A. (1995). *Sephardi religious responses to modernity.* Luxembourg: Harwood Academic Publishers.

Strike, K. A. (1991). The moral role of schooling in a liberal democratic society. In G. Grant (Ed.). *Review of research in education.* Washington, DC: American Educational Research Association.

Strike, K. A. (2007). *Ethical leadership in schools: Creating community in an environment of accountability.* Thousand Oaks, CA: Corwin.

Strike, K. A., & Soltis, J. F. (1992). *The ethics of teaching* (2nd ed.). New York: Teachers College Press.

Strike, K. A., Haller, E. J., & Soltis, J. F. (2005). *The ethics of school administration* (3rd ed.). New York: Teachers College Press.

Strober, M. M., & Tyack, D. B. (1980). Why do women teach and men manage? *Signs,* n.a.

Tauber, R. T. (1997). *Self-fulfilling prophecy: A practical guide to its use in education.* Westport, CT: Praeger.

Terman, D. L., Larner, M. B., Stevenson, C. S., & Behrman, R. E. (1996). Special education for students with disabilities. *The Future of Children, 6*(1), 4–24.

Theoharis, G. (2007a). Navigating rough waters: A synthesis of the countervailing pressures against leading for social justice. *Journal of School Leadership, 17*(1), 4–27.

Theoharis, G. (2007b). Social justice educational leaders and resistance: Toward a theory of social justice educational leadership. *Educational Administration Quarterly, 43*(2), 221–258.

Tomlinson, C. (2001). Differentiated instruction in the regular classroom: What does it mean? How does it look? *Understanding Our Gifted, 14*(1), 3–6.

Tomlinson, C. (2003). *Fulfilling the promise of the differentiated classroom.* Alexandria, VA: Supervision and Curriculum Development.

Tomlinson, C. (2004). *How to differentiate instruction in mixed ability classrooms?* (2nd ed.). Alexandria, VA: Association for Supervision and Curriculum Development.

Tomlinson, C. (2005). This issue. *Theory Into Practice, 44*(3), 183–184.

Twomey Fosnot, C. (1989). *Enquiring teachers, enquiring learners: A constructivist approach to teaching.* New York: Teachers College Press.

Twomey Fosnot, C. (2005). *Constructivism: Theory, perspectives and practice.* New York: Teachers College Press.

Udvari-Solner, A., & Kluth, P. (2007). *Joyful learning: Active and collaborative learning in inclusive classrooms.* Thousand Oaks, CA: Corwin.

Vaughn, S., Elbaum, B. E., Schumm, J. S., & Hughes, M. T., (1998). Social outcomes for students with and without learning disabilities in inclusive classrooms. *Journal of Learning Disabilities, 31,* 428–436.

Viachou, A. (2004). Education and inclusive policy-making: Implications for research and practice. *International Journal of Inclusive Education, 8*(1), 3–21.

Villa, R.A., & Thousand, J.S. (Eds.). (1995). *Creating an inclusive school.* Alexandria, VA: Association for Supervision and Curriculum Development.

Villa, R.A., & Thousand, J.S. (2000). *Restoring for caring and effective education: Piecing the puzzle together.* Baltimore: Paul Brookes Publishing.

Volonino, V., & Zigmond, N. (2007). Promoting research-based practices through inclusion? *Theory into Practice, 46*(4), 291–300.

Vygotsky, L. (1934/1986). *Thought and language.* Cambridge, MA: The MIT Press.

Wedell, K. (2005). Dilemmas in the quest for inclusion. *British Journal of Special Education, 32*(1), 3–11.

Wiebe Berry, R. A. (2006). Inclusion, power, and community: Teachers and students interpret the language of community in an inclusion classroom. *American Educational Research Journal, 43*(3), 489–529.

Willms, J. D., & Chen, M. (1989). The effects of ability grouping on the ethnic achievement gap in Israeli elementary schools. *American Journal of Education, 97*(3), 237–257.

Windschitl, M. (2002). Framing constructivism, in practice as the negotiation of dilemmas: An analysis of the conceptual, pedagogical, cultural, and political challenges facing teachers. *Review of Educational Research, 72,* 131–175.

Winzer, M. A. (1993). *The history of special education: From isolation to integration.* Washington, DC: Gallaudet University Press.

Wolfe, P. S., & Hall, T. E. (2003). Making inclusion a reality for students with severe disabilities. *Teaching Exceptional Children, 14,* 56–61.

Woolfolk, A., & Hoy, W. K. (2003). *Instructional leadership: A learning-centered guide.* Boston: Allyn and Bacon.

Wurzburg, G. (Dir.). (1992). *Educating Peter.* Film.

Wurzburg, G. (Dir.). (2001). *Graduating Peter.* Film.

Yonezawa, S., & Jones, M. (2006). Students' perspectives on tracking and detracking. *Theory into Practice, 45*(1), 15–23.

Young, I. M. (2000). *Inclusion and democracy.* Oxford: Oxford University Press.

Zigmond, N. (2003). Where should students with disabilities receive special education services? Is one place better than another? *Journal of Special Education, 37,* 193–199.

Zohar, Z. (Ed.). (2005). *Sephardic and Mizrahi Jewry: From the golden years of Spain to modern times.* New York: New York University Press.

Zubay, B., & Soltis, J. (2005). *Creating the ethical school: A book of case studies.* New York: Teachers College Press.

Zweiter, S. (2006). From the inside looking in: Some musings on day school education. In Z. Grumet (Ed.). *Jewish education in transition: Proceedings of the first international conference on Jewish education* (pp. 11–27). Teaneck, NJ: BenYehuda Press.

SUBJECT MATTER

Making the Bible Come to Life:
Biblical Archaeology and the Teaching
of *Tanakh* in Jewish Schools

Lawrence H. Schiffman

Introduction

The archaeology of the Bible, as we know it, began to flourish in the late eighteenth century and, as a result of numerous factors, grew into great prominence in the nineteenth and twentieth centuries. To be sure, chance archaeological finds had taken placed beforehand, and this was the case in the Jewish community as well.[1] The tremendous rise of and interest in classical archaeology during the Renaissance had less of an effect on the Jewish community than among non-Jews, although some Jews were stimulated to explore the material culture of the land of Israel or to seek material evidence for Jewish history.[2] Further, Jewish scholars had also become involved in the identification of ancient biblical sites in the Land of Israel.[3] As the European powers gradually gobbled up control of much of the Near East, eventually including the Land of Israel, archaeology expanded in the lands of the Bible.[4] By the nineteenth and twentieth centuries, Christian scholars,

---

1. J. Tigay, "'Archaeology' of the Bible and Judaism in Late Antiquity and the Middle Ages," *The Archaeology of Jordan and Beyond. Essays in Honor of James A. Sauer*, ed. L.E. Stager, J.A. Greene, and M.D. Coogan (Harvard Semitic Museum Publications, Studies in the Archaeology and History of the Levant 1; Winona Lake, IN: Eisenbrauns, 2000), 490–97.
2. C. Roth, *The Jews in the Renaissance* (New York: Harper and Row, 1965), 30–33.
3. Yehoseph Schwartz, *Tevu'ot ha-Aretz* (Jerusalem, 1855), trans. I. Leeser, *A Descriptive Geography and Brief Historical Sketch of Palestine* (Philadelphia, 1850); Estori ha-Farhi, *Kaftor va-Ferah* (Jerusalem, 1899).
4. N. A. Silberman, *Digging for God and Country, Exploration, Archaeology and the Secret Struggle for the the Holy Land, 1799–1917* (New York: Knopf, 1982).

and, later, Jewish scholars as well, unearthed numerous sites mentioned in the Bible and archaeologists continue to rediscover the life of ancient Israel and its ancient Near Eastern neighbors. Numerous texts, including ancient Hebrew inscriptions,[5] literary and religious texts,[6] and early biblical and Jewish manuscripts,[7] have been unearthed in more than two centuries of systematic scientific exploration. Despite the widespread popularity of archaeology today—even among members of the Orthodox community, most of whom have extensively visited the important archaeological sites and museums in Israel—[8] these discoveries have had little or no impact on Jewish education on the elementary and high school levels in the American Orthodox context.

It is possible that in a different Orthodox intellectual climate we would not be discussing this question, as the introduction of biblical archaeology into the educational curriculum would be self-evident. However, the discussion of the Bible in the contemporary American Orthodox community is dominated by commentaries and homiletical discussions that do not seek to interpret the *Tanakh*, as did the medieval commentators. Rather they seek to use the Bible to convey messages generated centuries after the close of the Bible.[9] Such com-

5. Hebrew material is conveniently collected in G.I. Davies, *Ancient Hebrew Inscriptions, Corpus and Concordance* (Cambridge: Cambridge University Press, 1991). Unfortunately this book uses transliteration, making it necessary to re-transliterate into Hebrew characters for use in Jewish educational contexts.

6. Ancient Near Eastern texts are collected in J.B. Pritchard, ed., *Ancient Near Eastern Texts Relating to the Old Testament* (3rd ed. with supplement; Princeton: Princeton University, 1969) and W. Hallo and K.L. Younger, eds. *The Context of Scripture* (3 vols. Leiden: Brill, 1997–2002).

7. For an introduction to the Dead Sea Scrolls, see L.H. Schiffman, *Reclaiming the Dead Sea Scrolls* (Philadelphia: Jewish Publication Society, 1994).

8. See M. Broshi, "Archaeological Museums in Israel: Reflections on Problems of National Identity, *Bread Wine, Walls and Scrolls* (Journal for the Study of the Pseudepigrapha Supplement Series 36; London and New York: Sheffield Academic Press, 2001), 52–59.

9. B.B. Levy, "The State and Directions of Orthodox Bible Study," *Modern Scholarship in the Study of Torah, Contributions and Limitations*, ed. S. Carmy (Orthodox Forum Series; Northvale and London: Jason Aronson, 1996), 39–80; idem., "Our Torah, Your Torah, and Their Torah: An Evaluation of the ArtScroll Phenomenon," *Truth and Compassion: Essays on Judaism and Religion in Memory of Rabbi Dr. Solomon Frank*, ed. H. Joseph, J. N. Lightstone and M. D. Oppenheim (Waterloo, Ont.: Wilfred Laurier University Press, 1983), 157–89.

mentaries dominate the market so exclusively that the focus of Bible study has been redirected away from the text and its ancient context. While this approach has the advantage of maintaining the eternal validity of the Bible's message, it greatly reduces interest in such areas as language and style, history, archaeology, and geography. In this atmosphere, at least in the American Orthodox community, interest in the great archaeological discoveries pertaining to the Bible has not found much of a place. This is despite the large number of Orthodox lay people who have become archaeology buffs and subscribe to such periodicals as *Biblical Archaeology Review*.

This is even more the case in the school curriculum. Fears of wandering into possible heterodoxy add to the de-emphasis of this fascinating and significant material. While a full-scale Orthodox commentary on the Bible aimed at the modern American Orthodox community would go a long way to helping this situation, in the manner that the *Da`at Miqra'* series functions in Israel,[10] we write here in the hope that even while such a desideratum is not available, progress is still possible and highly desirable in the educational sphere.

This study seeks to deal first with the underlying ideological, religious, and intellectual issues connected with the use of archaeological material as well as to propose concrete avenues for making use of such data to enrich the teaching of *Tanakh* in our day schools and Jewish high schools.

Theoretical Considerations

In many ways, the fundamental issue regarding the use of archaeological material to illuminate the Bible in Orthodox education is the classic *Torah u-Madda* issue. When secular learning, much of which has been developed beyond the confines of our community, can contribute to our understanding of Torah, to what extent and how should this information be used? Even assuming that archaeological data totally supported the factuality of the biblical narrative, the use of external material might very well be understood by some as an implicit challenge to the exclusive demands of our Jewish faith which ought not to need scientific or academic support.[11] Such a position is

---

10. The English translation of *Da`at Miqra'* to Psalms has just appeared in 3 vols. It is the first of a projected full series.

11. Cf. N. Lamm, *Torah Umadda, the Encounter of Religious Learning and Worldly Knowledge in the Jewish Tradition* (Northvale and London: Jason Aronson, 1990) 39–75.

untenable on a practical level in view of the large-scale contact that our children have with a large variety of external influences, many a formal part of our secular studies curriculum, which either challenge or support their religious faith. Put simply, in today's Orthodox world, faith will be tested and evaluated—in any case—in light of numerous secular disciplines. The issue is more serious in regard to biblical archaeology, for the very same discoveries in the hands of different interpreters can be used to bolster or challenge—even to prove or disprove—the biblical narrative. We submit that it is exactly this situation that calls upon us to assimilate this material into our study of Torah so that our students will come to understand our perspective as Orthodox Jews before coming in contact, often at the university level, with radically different approaches.[12]

It may be objected that the teaching of such material necessarily gives credence to research of non-Jewish or non-observant Jewish biblical scholars. Early generations of biblical archaeologists, who were Christian to the last man, sought to prove the truth of the Bible through their research.[13] Recent developments in this field have led to the entry of large numbers of Israelis and other Jews into this area but, at the same time, to growing academic independence from the desire to prove the historicity of the Bible. In fact, there are some groups of archaeological scholars who have taken it to be their life's work to debunk the Bible and the biblical historical tradition.[14] In some cases, the motivation has been post-Zionist or even anti-Semitic or anti-Israel. Again, it is precisely these facts that call upon us to integrate archaeological discoveries into our teaching so that our community will come to understand this material within the context of the ongoing traditions of Jewish biblical interpretation. It is precisely this consideration that led to the inclusion of this material in the *Da`at Mikra* series of biblical commentaries.[15] In fact, archaeological evidence has already

---

12. M.J. Bernstein, "The Orthodox Jewish Scholar and Jewish Scholarship: Duties and Dilemmas," *The Torah U-Madda Journal* 3 (1991–1992) 8–36.

13. Broshi, "Religion, Ideology and Politics and Their Impact on Palestinian Archaeology," *Bread, Wine, Walls and Scrolls*, 14–38.

14. On the nexus of politics and archaeology, see N.A. Silberman, *Between Past and Present* (New York: Doubleday, 1990), especially 87–136.

15. Cf. the fascinating letter of the Lubavitcher Rebbe, of blessed memory, from 5721 (1960/1) in M.M. Schneersohn, *Sha`are `Emunah* (Jerusalem: Hekhal Menahem, 1991) 174–77. Here, while discussing a new Bible commentary which he had initially been asked to edit, he suggests inclusion of

been integrated to some extent into the teaching of the Bible in Israeli modern Orthodox circles, as can be seen by examining textbooks and publications of teachers' seminaries.

The most significant argument for the inclusion of this material is that otherwise we may continue to teach false information where correct information is readily available. The simplest place to observe this is in locating biblical sites where modern archaeology and historical geography have produced biblical atlases allowing us to fully understand the details of a biblical narrative that would otherwise be confusing. Nevertheless, unwillingness to accept information from non-Jewish or non-Orthodox sources on geographical matters is observable in many contemporary Orthodox publications, clearly a rejection of the *Torah u-Madda* perspective. Such information is especially meaningful in a generation in which we can all visit these sites and often see the archaeological remains from the biblical period.

We realize fully that our concern with providing maximum information and preparing our students for the future challenges of higher education and adult life may not be shared by all readers. Yet we hope that the illustrations which will follow in this article will convince parents and educators of the value of biblical archaeology as a means of enhancing traditional Torah study.[16]

The Yeshivah High School Curriculum

Certainly, the most important age level for serious discussion of the issues raised by biblical archaeology is that of high school. It is here that students, especially those going off to universities, need to be prepared to meet challenges to the Jewish tradition which they will encounter. Some of these challenges may even be involved with serious political issues, such as those concerning the historical relationship of the Jewish people to the land of Israel and the Temple Mount.

Two options for including this field of study in the yeshivah high school curriculum present themselves. These issues could be the subject of a special twelfth grade class, or part of some series of mini-courses or units. A separate mini-course would allow concentrated reading and discussion of these issues with a teacher having particular

---

archaeological material, even where cautioning that the commentary should reflect nothing new, only the traditional commentaries in a new form.

16. Cf. Lamm, 199–210, who, however, does not discuss archaeology or, for that matter, academic Jewish studies in any of its aspects.

expertise. On the other hand, it would be limited to certain particular issues and not integrated with the study of the biblical text and traditional commentaries. Alternatively, biblical archaeology could be part of the ongoing study of *Tanakh* in high school. The advantage of integration with the regular curriculum is that it allows the archaeological data to be presented in context and by a teacher regarded as an authority by the students. Further, the integrated approach gives a more representative picture of biblical archaeology, rather than creating a false emphasis on particular issues or challenges. Finally, integration into the curriculum as a whole would allow discussion of archaeological material and texts from the ancient Near East in religious terms, not simply as a historical appendage separate from traditional study.

The availability and training of personnel are likely to be the major factors in such decisions in schools that seek to include this field. In the absence of appropriate text material for student and teacher, the decision is likely to be affected by whether the *Tanakh* teacher or someone else—often a Jewish history teacher with wider training—is available to teach this subject.[17] So we have to assume that both methods will be followed, and that different schools will adapt differing approaches.

Let us now turn to fundamental areas of discussion that need to be dealt with in high schools. It seems best to include in the curriculum several issues which students will face, especially at general universities. We will briefly discuss each of the following: ancient Near Eastern literature and the Bible, the exodus and conquest, the period of the kings, and Jerusalem and the Temple.

The Bible and Ancient Near Eastern Literature

Ancient Near Eastern literature has been a rapidly expanding corpus since archaeologists began digging up clay tablets in Mesopotamia and Syria, hieroglyphic documents in Egypt, and inscriptions on stone in Canaan/Israel. These documents testify to the advanced cultures in which Israel developed and also to the simultaneously close and contrasting relationships between Israelite religion—emerging

---

17. Related issues may come up in the study of Talmud where archaeological material, especially in the area of realia, can make many passages clearer. Here the only possible option is inclusion in the ongoing regular text curriculum.

Judaism—and the religions of its neighbors.[18] In fact, these texts show the specifics of the unique contribution of the Bible to human civilization, something that should be a matter of pride to students. At the same time, in the hands of some, these texts can be misrepresented as detracting from the greatness of biblical tradition.

Let me give a few examples. From the Atrahasis epic, we learn of one particular version of the Mesopotamian creation and flood epic.[19] If we look at this text we see immediately the contrast between the Atrahasis account and the biblical story. In this creation story, we see humanity created to serve the gods, not as the pinnacle of creation. Further, the god does not breathe his spirit into man, but expectorates into the dirt to create him. Again, here we see that humanity has no great aspirations; humans are not "a little lower than the angels" (Ps. 8:6), created in the image of God, but earthy creatures. The flood takes place in this Mesopotamian epic not because of the sinfulness of humanity, a moral issue, but because some of the gods think that humans made too much noise. Here, again, the moral stance of the Bible is absent, and all that matters is the capricious desire of the gods—similar to the Greek pantheon. The well-known flood epic of Gilgamesh, read by many in college humanities courses, also provides numerous biblical parallels, and can be discussed from the moral and ethical point of view as well.[20] In spite of the very different way in which these stories are told, the widespread account of a great flood leads us to assume that there must have been some historical event that was recorded by all these ancient civilizations.

When we look at the great law codes of Mesopotamia, we find a similar differentiation between Mesopotamian codes and the Bible. In the Prologue to the eighteenth century B.C.E. Code of Hammurabi, there is a call for true justice in the name of the gods. However, even free people are treated unequally, the *lex talionis* (an eye for an eye) is actually understood and presumably applied literally, and justice is ultimately determined through trial by ordeal. In all these Mesopotamian cases, one can truly understand the innovation represented by biblical morals and standards of justice.[21]

18. Cf. B. Eichler, "Study of Bible in Light of Our Knowledge of the Ancient Near East," *Modern Scholarship in the Study of Torah*, 81–100.

19. W.G. Lambert and A.R. Millard, *Atrahasis: The Babylonian Story of the Flood* (Oxford: Clarendon Press, 1969) 43–105.

20. Trans. by B. R. Foster in Hallo, *Context of Scripture* 1.458–60.

21. [Ed.: Cf. Moshe Sokolow: "Discovering the Biblical Value of Human

Let us take another example: the biblical laws against superstition and idolatry. The texts from Ugarit (Ras Shamra in northern Syria), dating from c. 1400 B.C.E., allow a deeper understanding of the Canaanite cults against which our prophets fought so strongly. The battle against Canaanite religion exemplifies the issue of loyalty to the God of Israel and His Torah in an open society, an issue of great importance to our students today. [22] The mythology of these texts makes clear the background of this biblical struggle. Maimonides stated that certain Jewish religious practices stemmed from a divine desire to separate Israel from the idolatrous practices of their neighbors.[23] This is readily observable in Canaanite, Egyptian, and Mesopotamian texts. Marital practices of the Pharaonic dynasties and Egyptian religious literature amply illustrate the point as well. In ancient Egypt, the Pharaohs regularly entered into incestuous marriages. Further, biblical opposition to the cult of the dead can be understood readily in light of the excessive burial practices of the Egyptian aristocracy, predicated on the divine nature of the dead king and the need to supply the mummified body with material goods (and even companions, duly killed for the purpose) for the afterlife.

The Controversial Evidence of Archaeology: The Exodus and Conquest

The physical remnants of these civilizations also attest to their idolatrous practices and allow us to understand the various biblical passages dealing with ancient Near Eastern religion. Archaeologists have unearthed numerous physical representations of gods and god-

---

Life; A High-School Tanakh Lesson Utilizing Active Learning," *Ten Da`at* vol. 10 (1997), 41–57.]

22. A later example of the same issue is the Maccabean Revolt against extreme Hellenism and syncretism.

23. Guide for the Perplexed 3.29–30. He derived his information on ancient idolatry from South Arabian practices reported in a tenth century Arabic text. Maimonides portrays Abraham as throwing off the yoke of this pagan cult, the religion of the Sabeans. Note that Maimonides was perfectly willing to read contemporary works about the ancient Near East and to use them to reconstruct the background of biblical literature. The historical inaccuracy of these accounts in no way detracts from the hermeneutical approach followed by Maimonides. Cf. S. Pines, "Translator's Introduction," in M. Maimonides, *The Guide for the Perplexed* (Chicago: University of Chicago Press), cxxiii–cxxiv.

desses, fertility figurines, gods in the shape of animals, and parapher-
nalia used for polytheistic worship.

In these cases, ancient Near Eastern material allows us to gain a
sense of perspective on the environment in which the Bible came into
being and functioned in its original setting. We are able to understand
the revolution in religion and morals that the Bible created, and still
creates, and we can see here, in Maimonides' adaptation of the view
of Rabbi Ishmael, that "the Torah speaks in the language of humans."

More difficult is the set of questions relating to the historicity of
the exodus from Egypt and the conquest of Canaan. Students will have
to confront this debate among archaeologists which is complex, and
often tied to the contemporary Arab-Israeli conflict and to attempts of
the Palestinians and their supporters to deny the archaeological data
attesting to the long history of the people of Israel in the Land of Israel.

Earlier biblical archaeologists placed the conquest in the thirteenth century B.C.E. and identified evidence of a destruction layer in
Canaan which they attributed to the Israelite army. From this conclusion, it was one step to the assumption that the sojourn in Egypt and
the exodus were historical events, even if not all the details were to be
taken literally.[24] This essentially pro-traditional point of view was recently challenged by scholars of varying motivations. These scholars
argue that there is no evidence for either the exodus or the conquest,
and that this paucity of evidence proves that the events did not happen.[25] We reject these claims, since there is evidence for both events,
and since we see the motivation of some of the main European pro-
tagonists as anti-Israel, pro-Palestinian sentiments.

Here, we need to teach students what can reasonably be expected of historical and archaeological evidence for this period. We need
to show them the Merneptah Stele from Egypt[26] that testifies to the

---

24. W. F. Albright and his students have been identified with what is incor-
rectly known as the maximalist position that accepts the basic historicity of
the biblical narrative. See W.F. Albright, *Archaeology and the Religion of
Israel* (Garden City, N.Y.: Doubleday, 1969), *From Stone Age to Christianity*
(2nd ed.; Garden City, N.Y.: Doubleday, 1957), and *The Archaeology of
Palestine* (Baltimore: Penguin, 1961).
25. The results of this approach, known as minimalism, are summed up in
I. Finkelstein, N.A. Silberman, *The Bible Unearthed: Archaeology's New
Vision of Ancient Israel and the Origin of its Sacred Texts* (New York: Free
Press, 2001).
26. Trans. J. K. Hoffmeier, in Hallo, *Context of Scripture* 2.40–41. The text

conquest; the evidence for a complete cultural change in thirteenth-twelfth century B.C.E. Canaan, as described in the book of Judges more than in Joshua, the book actually detailing the conquest; and the Egyptian historical accounts as preserved by the fourth century B.C.E. Egyptian historian Manetho, preserved, in turn, by Josephus in the first century C.E.[27] All of this, plus Egyptian material that helps in understanding the environment and historical background, must be taught and explained. Here, where we truly do lack direct proof, we need to carefully explain to students that the role of archaeology remains merely to be an aid to understanding the Bible and an ancillary support for our beliefs.[28]

Further, we need to explain to students that the approach to biblical history assumes that absence of evidence proves that something did not happen. This is counter both to logic and to the progress of archaeology and the constant new discoveries that frequently supply evidence not available before.

The Monarchy and Jerusalem

Once we reach the period of the monarchy, the clear relevance of the evidence and ease of incorporating it into the curriculum make our task easier. The Tel Dan Stele, mentioning the House of David,[29] demonstrates that David and his descendants existed, and confirms

describes the situation in Canaan in the thirteenth century B.C.E. with Israel alone pictured as a people without a geographical designation. This clearly refers to the period between the invasion and the actual settlement of the various Israelite tribes.

27. M. Stern, *Greek and Latin Authors on Jews and Judaism* (Jerusalem: Israel Academy of Sciences and Humanities, 1976), 1. 62–86. Cf. J. Assman, *Moses the Egyptian, the Memory of Egypt in Western Monotheism* (Cambridge: Harvard University Press, 1997), 29–44, who mistakenly sees Akhenaten, the monolotrous Egyptian ruler, as figuring in Manetho's exodus traditions. Manetho's two different exodus accounts cannot derive from the Bible as it was unavailable to him (the Septuagint is a century later), and so must reflect the ancient Egyptian "narrative" of Israel's departure from slavery in Egypt.

28. Cf. J. K. Hoffmeir, *Israel in Egypt, The Evidence for the Authenticity of the Exodus Tradition* (New York: Oxford University Press, 1977). Hoffmeir does require an earlier date than most modern scholars accept, but one more in agreement with the traditional Jewish dating. See also E. S. Frerichs, L. H. Lesko, eds., *The Exodus, The Egyptian Evidence* (Winona Lake, IN: Eisenbrauns, 1997).

29. Trans. A. Millard, in Hallo, *Context of Scripture* 2.161–2.

the basic lines of the history of Northern Israel's relations with Aram. Students can be shown other texts and inscriptions that illustrate the history of Judah and Israel in the ancient Near East and can be taken on virtual visits to many of the great sites of the events described in the Bible, like Meggido or Hazor where the district capitals have been recovered. The Siloam Tunnel Inscription,[30] for example, truly brings to life not only the biblical account but also the rabbinic evaluation of it.[31] Various ancient Near Eastern texts from Mesopotamia provide both background data and specific mention of certain rulers in Judah and Israel. These materials also testify to the immense size of the cities and armies of the time, confirming that Judah and Israel were large kingdoms. Here, ample material about daily life can also be brought to bear on the teaching of all kinds of verses. Why not let students see houses, pots and pans, burial sites, jewelry—all the appurtenances of daily life that somehow bridge the gap between our ancient ancestors and ourselves?[32]

Finally, we see Jerusalem and the Temple as an important subject, to a great extent because it is also so closely linked to the modern political debate. Our students need to have a sense of the geography and archaeology of ancient Jerusalem and of the Temple area, despite the fact that the twice-built Second Temple has obscured the remains of the First. Nevertheless, evidence for First Temple period Jerusalem does stand, and its presence in ancient Near Eastern texts can help our students in facing some of the false claims they may hear today, let alone in understanding the Bible itself. Students, for example, can follow the tragedy of the destruction of Judah and Jerusalem in the contemporary Lakhish Letters.[33]

Archaeology as Concretization

In what follows, we will attempt to call attention to very particular aspects of the archaeological record that can help to illustrate material taught to elementary school children in Humash class. Here, the point is not to engage young children in issues, but rather to illustrate and give a sense of reality and veracity to what they are studying. At this

---

30. Tans. K. L. Younger, in Hallo, *Context of Scripture* 2.146–6.

31. M. Pesahim 4:9; Avot de-Rabbi Nathan Version A, chap. 2.

32. An excellent resource is P.J. King and L.E. Stager, *Life in Biblical Israel* (Louisville: John Knox Press, 2001).

33. D. Parde, in Hallo, *Context of Scripture* 3.78–81.

age level, videos are available that can provide a sense of reality to the world of our biblical ancestors. Ample material may be gathered to illustrate the nature of the Mesopotamian society which the Patriarchs left. This will give children a sense of the sacrifice made by Abraham, Isaac, and Jacob when moving to Canaan, a land then much less advanced. For both places, houses, cities, and temples may be shown. Ancient Mesopotamia has yielded numerous buildings and objects of daily and religious life that can lead children in this direction. For example, in Genesis 4, the early professions are set out—husbandry, farming, music, metal working. Objects from ancient Mesopotamia illustrate the performance of these tasks and the result of this labor. Numerous available photographs illustrate the great architectural classics of ancient Mesopotamia and allow a sense of the culture and civilization Abraham and his family left. The cities and villages that Abraham would find in Canaan can also be illustrated.

Later on, when the Israelites were in Egypt, Egyptian art and architecture can illustrate that environment. Here the letters from Deir el-Medina can be employed to illustrate the lives of people in the service of Pharaoh, very much like the early period of Israelite slavery. Children can be taught to appreciate the conditions that the Israelites must have suffered from a sense of conditions in Egypt in general. For elementary school children with less rigorously controlled requirements, some time can be devoted in the secular curriculum to units on ancient Egypt and Mesopotamia that will provide increased background for study of Tanakh.

Once we reach the period of the conquest and children begin to study the books of *Nakh*, especially *Nevi'im Rishonim*, the great wealth of archaeological material from virtually every important place mentioned in the Bible, makes it easy to show students the reality of the stories they are studying. Here, the wealth of information on the Israelite four-room house, and on daily life in general, can be used to concretize the biblical stories. Since these books are primarily taught in junior high school, it is also possible to introduce students to the geographic side, especially in the Land of Israel where mapping biblical events and learning where they happened can be undertaken together with looking at the archaeological evidence for these places in antiquity.[34] At this level, the combination of archaeology and geog-

---

34. Conveniently collected in E. Stern, ed., *The New Encyclopedia of Archaeological Excavations in the Holy Land* (4 vols.; Jerusalem: Carta, 1993).

raphy can greatly help to instill a historic connection to the Land of Israel at the same time as it helps to bring about greater understanding of the biblical narrative.

A final area that can be included at all levels, and which has special significance in showing our children the age-old continuity of our religious practice, may loosely be described as archaeological evidence for ritual objects. Large numbers of *mikva'ot* found throughout the Land of Israel—and even in the Diaspora—testify to age-old adherence to the laws of purity, initially in all areas, and, after the destruction of the Temple, particularly in marital life. Evidence for *tzitzit* from Mishnaic times, including vegetable-dyed (that is, false) *tekhelet*, tied as *tzitzit*,[35] can be shown and discussed in relation to the modern quest for *tekhelet*. Excavated *tefillin* from Qumran[36] and the Bar Kokhba Caves illustrate this mitzvah as well.

Showing children the oldest scrolls of biblical books found among the Dead Sea Scrolls allows them to see the continuity of scribal techniques and to feel the reality of the antiquity of the Bible, even if we have to admit, as do the rabbis, that some scrolls differ from the Massoretic Text. While Talmudic studies are beyond the scope of our discussion, we should note that coins, and other representatives of the material culture of ancient times, often illustrate rabbinic teachings. To cite just one example, we note the two-part lamp inscribed "Shabbat" that was excavated. In accord with Mishnah Shabbat 2:4, a secondary oil supply had been attached to the lamp to allow it to burn longer on Shabbat. The Bar Kokhba documents provide contracts, *ketubot* and *gittin* similar to those required by Mishnaic and Talmudic law.[37] A tremendous amount of material is available pertaining to ancient synagogues, which have been discovered in large numbers in the Land of Israel and the Diaspora.[38] All these objects, at various age levels,

---

35. Y. Yadin, *Bar Kokhba, The Rediscovery of the Legendary Hero of the Second Jewish Revolt Against Rome* (New York: Random House, 1971), 81–85. These falsely dyed fringes have played a role as color samples in attempts to prepare halakhically valid *tekhelet* in modern times.

36. Y. Yadin, *Tefillin from Qumran* (Jerusalem: Israel Exploration Society and Shrine of the Book, 1969).

37. Yadin, *Bar-Kokhba*, 222–53.

38. See, for example, S. Fine, ed., *Sacred Realm, The Emergence of the Synagogue in the Ancient World* (New York: Oxford University Press, 1996). This volume is the catalogue of an exhibit that was organized by the Yeshiva University Museum.

can help to illustrate the reality of our law and tradition as practiced by our forefathers.

Teaching Materials

A final aspect of our proposal to include the results of archaeology in our curricula, whether in the format of a separate course or in the regular teaching of *Tanakh*, is the need for teaching materials that will make this possible. To be sure, as long as textbooks and other teaching materials, such as teachers' manuals, software, and audio-visual aids for presenting biblical archaeology for the day school market, do not exist, we are not likely to see much progress. Here, also, in the area of Bible and archaeology, we are not helped by the lack of a modern American Orthodox Bible commentary that would integrate this material, at least on the adult level. This leaves teachers and curriculum planners with the difficult job of using sources designed for the secular academic community or the Christian community, or Israeli materials—usually intended for the secular schools. It is clear that without an organized effort, the fate of biblical archaeology in our schools will remain minimal, and at best episodic.

Because we are proposing including this material in the day school curriculum in a variety of ways, two approaches seem to make the most sense for the training of teachers and for disseminating the relevant material. First, we would suggest teacher workshops with scholars from America and Israel able to discuss not only the archaeological discoveries but also the religious and political issues surrounding them.[39] Such workshops should be full day events with reading materials and sample lessons.

It is not simply a matter of providing material derived from biblical archaeology for teacher use and letting instructors know what exists. Extensive preparation is needed so that the teachers can truly integrate this material into traditional study. Even at the elementary level, the ability to illustrate and supplement in order to strengthen the main themes of biblical study has to be developed.

Second, a list of relevant archaeological material in the order of biblical passages needs to be assembled, and it needs to be made easily

---

39. Such workshops with scholars could be helpful for many areas of study that are part of our day school curricula, and would greatly enhance teaching at all levels.

accessible on a website. Such a website[40] could also include articles on the wider issues involved, but the key value is in providing the actual material: texts, archaeological finds, and analysis. Such a website should provide ancient Near Eastern texts in translation and relevant pictures and captions so that they can be regularly downloaded and distributed to children. Teacher guides need to be prepared and provided for each item. Maps designed especially for the day school student should be made available as well. Sets of images for projection should be prepared and made available on CD. Without such a sustained, organized effort, and in the absence of textbooks, little will be accomplished.

Conclusion

The introduction of biblical archaeology into our study of *Tanakh* in elementary and high school classes, like any curricular innovation, requires effort, training and suitable materials. But given the value of archaeological evidence and the excitement it generates in students and in the wider community, it should be introduced into our schools. Further, as an example of *Torah u-Madda*, it represents an opportunity to inculcate fundamental concepts about our Jewish faith and its connection to the wider world of learning. Finally, it will help to prepare young people for their eventual exposure to other approaches to the Bible and enable them to justify their own beliefs to themselves and others. It is a challenge that we ought to undertake and in which we will succeed.

---

40. [Ed.: A site that lists prominent archaeological finds according to the sequence of the Biblical text is http://prophetess.lstc.edu/~rklein/ (retrieved 1/4/2010; under: Old Testament/History tables). This site also provides (under: Ancient Near East/archaeology) 70 links to "general archaeological resources" and well over 200 links to "specific archaeological sites."]

תפילת רב: *Educating for Prayer,*
Utilizing the Writings of Rabbi Joseph B. Soloveitchik
(the Rav): **Curricular and Instructional Guidelines**

Moshe Sokolow

Introduction

There are three parts to this essay. In the first part, we offer a
sampling of alternative approaches to overall curriculum design and
indicate how each would respond to the pedagogical challenges of
prayer and spirituality. In the second, we describe the fundamental,
"essential" questions raised by the study and teaching of prayer, and
present selections from the writings of the Rav in response. In the third
and largest part, we have matched the Rav's insights on prayer to six
specific lessons in Torah according to a didactic format that can be followed by day school—primarily secondary school—teachers.

This essay has its genesis in an invitation from the Van Leer Insti-
tute in Jerusalem to participate in a conference on the influence of
Rabbi Joseph B. Soloveitchik, ז״ל, the Rav. I am grateful to Dr. Naftali
Rothenberg for issuing the invitation and to Dean David Schnall of the
Azrieli Graduate School for supporting my participation and offering
to publish the essay as part of the Azrieli Papers.

Prologue
The Problem with Prayer: The Rav as Solution

It is commonplace that a problem *stated* is well on its way to
solution, for statement of the nature of a problem signifies that
the underlying quality is being transformed into determinate
distinctions of terms and relations or has become an object of
articulate thought.

John Dewey[1]

---

1. "Qualitative Thought" by John Dewey, in *Philosophy and Civilization*
(New York, 1931), 198.

There is scarcely a subject that so frustrates modern Orthodox religious education as prayer. Day in and day out—at least once and as often as three times—day schools confront the pedagogical expectation (not to mention the halakhic obligation) of engaging their students in prayer. Abundant anecdotal evidence and a plethora of publications on the subject[2] testify to the exasperation experienced by many religious educators in their ineffectual attempts to get their students to *daven* (pray) properly. Their most frequent complaint (misbehavior notwithstanding) relates to their perception that their students lack adequate or appropriate *kavvanah* (attitude), a symptom they attribute to a nonchalant attitude towards religion, in general, and towards prayer in particular.

Some day schools tackle the problem head on with formal courses of instruction on prayer. Primary grades concentrate on oral recitation, reading comprehension and the "geography" of the *siddur* (prayerbook); middle-schools focus on laws and customs of the synagogue service; secondary schools deal with the complications introduced by special circumstances such as *Shabbat*, festivals, and the Days of Awe.[3] True to form, these curricular measures tend overwhelmingly to the "cognitive"—academic or intellectual—dimension of education, with comparatively less consideration for the "affective"—emotional or value appreciation—dimension.

---

2. On-line forums such as LookJed and ATID provide the anecdotes and also address the problem formally. Cf. http://atid.org/news/25-10-01.asp, and http://www.google.com/u/lookstein?q=prayer&sa.x=11&sa.y=2.

3. Cf. The *Tefillah* Curriculum of the Fuchs-Mizrachi Lower School of Cleveland:*http://www.fuchsmizrachi.org/2004-2005%20parent%20guide. pdf* (p. 61) and the RAMAZ Middle School: *http://ramaz.org/school_middle/ curriculum_tefillah.cfm*.

Precious little formal curricular attention is devoted to prayer in modern Orthodox secondary schools—at least insofar as published curricula indicate. This situation contrasts with that which prevails in most community day schools. There, the major emphasis is on prayer as introspection and contemplation, with recitation and comprehension of the formal service—let alone *halakhah* and *minhag*—getting comparatively short shrift. E.g., "Students should be encouraged to debate the nature of tefilah and its value." Cf. *http:// www.akibaweb.org/plural.htm#recommendations* (Akiba Community Day School of Philadelphia).

We have diagnosed this malaise as a devotional deficit disorder (from which educators themselves are hardly immune!) and have written a detailed prescription of the curricular and instructional steps that day schools may take to enhance the spiritual education of their students.[4] In the present essay, we shall address the challenge of educating for proper prayer within the larger framework of educating the soul. We shall attempt this by presenting the writings of Rabbi Joseph B. Soloveitchik (the Rav), ז"ל, as a palliative to the pervasive inattentiveness and apathy that educators bemoan.

The subject of prayer is woven throughout the warp and woof of the Rav's halakhic and hashkafic writings.[5] Beset by the anxiety of existential loneliness, the Rav welcomed the fellowship provided by what he called "the community of prayer" (*Community*, 19), in which "every individual experiences not only his pain, but also that of countless others" (*op. cit.*, 22). Describing prayer as "the quintessence of Judaism" (*Worship*, 4) and defining it as "the hierarchy of needs, clearly defined and evaluated" (*Redemption*, 67), the Rav offers a prescription for the spiritual malaise affecting prayer that day school education should be able to fill.

Synopsis:

The Rav had an abiding concern for day school education; applying his teachings to the problems of prayer is a "natural." Prayer is a subject about which he lectured and published copiously.[6] His views

---

4. Moshe Sokolow: "Teaching Spirituality in Day Schools and Yeshiva High Schools," in Adam Mintz, Lawrence Schifman (ed.): *Spirituality, The Quest for Religious Meaning* (NY, 2004), 235–268.

5. Here is a list of the bibliographical abbreviations we use in the essay:
- Community: "The Community," *Tradition* 17:2 (Spring, 1978)
- Worship: *Worship of the Heart; Essays on Jewish Prayer* (NJ, 2003)
- Redemption: "Prayer, Redemption, Talmud Torah," *Tradition* (*op. cit.*)
- Lonely Man: "The Lonely Man of Faith," *Tradition* 7:2 (Summer, 1965)
- PRC: David Hartman: "Prayer and Religious Consciousness; an Analysis of Jewish Prayer in the Works of Joseph B. Soloveitchik, Yeshayahu Leibowitz, and Abraham Joshua Heschel," *Modern Judaism* 23,2 (2003)
- Dialogue: "Prayer as Dialogue," *Reflections of the Rav* (ed. Abraham Besdin; Jerusalem, 1966)
- Family: *The Family Redeemed* (NY, 2000)
- Teaching: "Teaching with Clarity and Empathy," *Reflections of the Rav* (ed. Abraham Besdin; Jerusalem, 1966)

6. In addition to the bibliography cited just above, there are several hun-

on the gamut of existential concerns are deemed authoritative by most modern Orthodox day school educators. Day school students are likely to be attracted to his formulations of the issue in contemporary terms, and, finally, they are likely to be entranced by the lyrical beauty of the terms in which he couches his proffered solutions.

We have selected a half-dozen units in Torah study, apropos of what we regard as the ordinary pedagogical and methodological instruction of the text and its commentaries, into which we have interpolated passages from the writings of the Rav that address essential and enduring educational concerns about prayer. It is our expectation that by exposing our students to the Rav's thoughts on prayer throughout the traditional *limmudei kodesh* curriculum, they will be encouraged to match the Rav's questions to problems of their own, and judge the answers he proposes by the yardstick of their own intelligence guided by their own experience.

Indeed, the singular relationship between pedagogy and prayer is captured by the following Midrash:

> God said to Moses after the incident of the golden calf, "Let go of me, and my anger will rest on them and I will get rid of them." Is Moses holding back God's hand, so that God must say "Let go of me"? What is this like? A king became angry at his son, placed him in a small room, and was about to hit him. At the same time the king cried out from the room for someone to stop him. The prince's teacher was standing outside, and said to himself, "The king and his son are in the room. Why does the king say 'stop me'? It must be that the king wants me to go into the room and effect a reconciliation between him and his son. That's why the king is crying, 'Stop me'." In a similar way, God said to Moses, "Let go of me." Moses said, "Because God wants me to defend Israel, He says 'Let go of me'." And Moses immediately interceded on their behalf.
>
> (*Shemot Rabbah* 42:10)[7]

---

dred pages of handwritten notes in circulation, which were taken during a course on prayer that the Rav taught at Yeshiva University's Bernard Revel Graduate School of Higher Jewish Studies, during the 1956–57 academic year. Additional secondary sources include Rabbi Aharon Lichtenstein: "Prayer in the Teachings of Rav Soloveitchik, zt"l," [*http://www.vbm-torah. org/archive/ralpray1.htm*].

7. Translation by Yohanan Muffs: "Who will stand in the breach? A study of prophetic intercession," *Love and Joy* (NY, 1992), 34.

PART ONE

Curriculum Development: Method and Meaning

Preface to an Eclectic:

In the expectation that this essay will be read by people who are unfamiliar with curriculum development, we shall try to provide a précis of the practice. A number of theories compete for preeminence in the field of curriculum development; rather than describe them all—however briefly—we will attempt to present an eclectic process that draws upon their several common denominators.[8]

Our preferred definition of curriculum is:

"All the learning which is planned and guided by the school, whether it is carried on in groups or individually, inside or outside the school."[9]

From this definition, several operative pedagogical and didactic consequences ensue:

(1) The emphasis on "learning" rather than "teaching" acknowledges the need of the students to take an active role in their own education. Using professional jargon, it testifies to the replacement of the "transmission of knowledge" model—in which knowledge "flows" from the teacher to the student—with something more akin to the "experiential" model, in which students seek to "construct" knowledge from the many sources and stimuli to which they are exposed.[10]

(2) The qualification "planned and guided" indicates that we have to specify in advance what we are seeking to achieve, how we are to go about its implementation, and how we will determine how much of it has been achieved and how well.

(3) The limitation of curriculum to "the school" is a constant reminder that we are obliged to operate within the real confines of a school, both spatial and temporal. The "school year," "school day," and "school building" are no less defining and delineating than subject matter, instructional material, and tools of assessment.

---

8. For the comprehensive exposition, see the article cited in n. 4, above.

9. John Kerr quoted in Kelly, A. V.: *The Curriculum. Theory and Practice* (4e, London, 1983; 1999), 10.

10. See Roland Barth: *Learning by Heart* (San Francisco, 2001), 32 ff., 48 ff.

This definition is accompanied by a preferred definition of school-work:

> "In sum, the business of schools is to produce work that en-gages students, that is so compelling that students persist when they experience difficulties, and that is so challenging that students have a sense of accomplishment, of satisfac-tion—indeed, of delight—when they successfully accomplish the tasks assigned."[11]

The following are the common denominators of curriculum develop-ment, on which we shall elaborate in the continuation:

1. designating the "larger" purpose of education through a statement of mission or vision;
2. determining who are the "stakeholders" in the educational enter-prise, whose views and values it must reflect;
3. choosing and articulating the various "objectives" of the educa-tional process, usually distributed among three "domains:" the cognitive (what the students will know), the affective (what they will value), and the behavioral (what they will be able to do);
4. selecting suitable and (age-)appropriate "subject matter" and stip-ulating the preferred instructional modalities ("learning experi-ences");
5. conducting an "assessment" of the learning that has taken place and a determination of the extent and intensity of its effectiveness.

Mission and Vision

Procedurally, curriculum development has generally begun with a declaration of educational purpose embodied in a school's statement of its mission or vision. The formulation of this statement enables the educating parties (see the section on "Commonplaces" that follows) to clarify and articulate their shared assumptions about, and expectations of the educational enterprise. Reference to the statement throughout the development process insures that the curriculum remains "on task."

We have chosen the mission statement of the Maimonides School of Brookline, MA, as a paradigm[12] both out of deference to the Rav, its

---

11. Phillip Schlechty: *Inventing Better Schools* (San Francisco, 2001), 58.
12. A "generic" mission statement would resemble the mission statement of the Association of Modern Orthodox Day School (AMODS), which reads:

founder, and because it captures the essential purpose to which most modern Orthodox day school education is devoted. It reads:

"To produce religiously observant, educated Jews who will remain faithful to their religious beliefs, values, and practices as they take their place as contributing members of the general society. Maimonides provides its students with both an outstanding religious education and an excellent college preparatory secular education in an atmosphere that reinforces their commitment to Torah and observance of Mitzvot."[13]

Pursuant to such a mission, we would expect a school to provide the type of instruction in the subject of prayer that would produce the kind of educated, religious observance to which a student would remain faithful throughout a life that is expected, in large part, to be conducted within the perimeters of a largely secular American society.

Schwab: The Commonplaces

Joseph Schwab, professor of education at the University of Chicago, proposed a model of curriculum development based upon the recognition of "commonplaces"—fixtures that control and mediate the formal educational enterprise. They are: the learner; the teacher; the subject matter; and the milieu.[14] The curricular specialist, who ne-

---

We are a group of modern Orthodox day schools and yeshiva high schools that recognize:
- the importance of excellence in both Torah and general studies;
- the preeminence of moral virtue and ethical integrity in personal, business and professional life;
- the equal educational needs of boys and girls, young men and women;
- the centrality of the State of Israel to the religious and national existence of the Jewish people;
- the inherent value of all segments of the Jewish community and the need to work with them to address mutual concerns.

Retrieved from: http://www.msdcs.org/AMODS.cfm?section=For%20Educators, on April 20, 2005.

13. Maimonides School, Brookline MA (*www.maimonides.org/mission.htm*). On the role of the Rav in the establishment of Maimonides, see Seth Farber: *An American Orthodox Dreamer; Rabbi Joseph B. Soloveitchik and Boston's Maimonides School* (Hanover, 2004).

14. Joseph Schwab: *Science, Curriculum and Liberal Education* (Chicago 1978), 365.

gotiates the needs and desires of each constituency and prevents any single commonplace from monopolizing the discussion and the development, conducts the deliberations.

In day school terms, a deliberation over a curriculum for prayer would involve:

- An educational psychologist (a.k.a. learning specialist), representing the student, to comment on modalities of learning;
- A master teacher, to advise on available instructional methodologies;
- A member of the school's board of education, to advocate for parental and communal interests;
- A scholar, philosopher, or rabbi, to provide enlightenment and direction on the textual and thematic substance of prayer.

Bloom: Educational Objectives

Educational goals are traditionally formulated according to "Bloom's taxonomy."[15] We shall endeavor, here, to formulate several objectives each in the *affective* (values) and *behavioral* (skills) domains as well as one objective in each of the six levels of the *cognitive* (knowledge) domain. Our subject matter will be the *Amidah*.

Affective:
1. The student will appreciate the need for prayer as a fundamental religious obligation.
2. The student will appreciate the relationship between prayer and the sacrificial [Temple] order.
3. The student will value the *Amidah* as the core of daily prayer.
4. The student will commit to required prayer—daily and on special occasions—as prescribed by Halakhah.

Behavioral:
1. The student will locate the three daily *Amidah* services in the *siddur*.
2. The student will locate the passages in the *Amidah* that are either altered or replaced on prescribed occasions.

---

15. Benjamin S. Bloom: *Taxonomy of Educational Objectives; the Classification of Educational Goals* (NY, 1956). There are currently several revisions of the taxonomy, some by Bloom's co-authors and others by his students. The objectives we will formulate (below) follow the classic paradigm.

3. The student will demonstrate proper behavior and physical comportment during the recitation of the *Amidah*.

Cognitive:

1. **Knowledge** (remembering information): the student will list the *berakhot* of the *Amidah*.
2. **Comprehension** (explaining the meaning of information): the student will translate the titles of the *berakhot* into English.
3. **Application** (using abstractions in concrete situations): the student will divide the *berakhot* into the categories of *shevah*, *bakkashah* and *hodayah*.
4. **Analysis** (breaking down a whole into components): the student will divide the *bakkashot* into individual and collective petitions.
5. **Synthesis** (forming a new, integrated whole): the student will account for the sequence of all the *berakhot* of the *Amidah*, individually and categorically.
6. **Evaluation** (judging ideas on their merits): the student will elaborate on whether the formulation and arrangement of the *Amidah* is ideal, adequate or unsatisfactory.

Tyler: The Four Questions

While Schwab's construct informs the essence of curriculum deliberation and Bloom's model informs its cognitive psychological considerations, Ralph Tyler guides its practical operation. Tyler[16] would have us chart, sequentially, our aims or objectives, our means of implementation and, finally, the process of assessment by which we can evaluate our success. Procedurally, Tyler would have us pose four questions, whose answers would dictate the form and content of the curriculum. They are:

1. What are the purposes of the school?
2. What educational experiences are related to those purposes?
3. What are the organizational methods which will be used in relation to those purposes?
4. How will those purposes be evaluated?

Translated into the "idiom" of prayer, these questions would be reformulated as:

---

16. Ralph W. Tyler: *Basic Principles of Curriculum and Instruction* (Chicago, 1949; pb ed. 1969).

1. How is prayer relevant to the common, current purpose of the school?
2. How do we provide students with the learning opportunities (including course content, instructional methods, and experiential dimension) required to accomplish those purposes?
3. How do we organize those learning experiences and distribute them over the students' tenure in the school to achieve the greatest possible effect with regard to prayer?
4. How will we know whether we have taught the content and processes of prayer effectively, and whether the students have learned them?

An idiosyncratic Orthodox problem with Tyler's model, however, is the penchant to define curricular objectives in textual terms, rather than the standard "cognitive" and "affective" goals of Bloom's "Taxonomy." Ask a 4th grade day school teacher for her curriculum and she invariably answers: The Book of Exodus and The Book of Joshua. An alternative schema that allows us to begin with our textual objectives follows.

Adler: The Paideia Proposal

The *Paideia* group, headed by Mortimer Adler, editor-in-chief of the *Encyclopaedia Britannica* and initiator of the "great books" concept, advanced an alternative model of curriculum development. Advocating a revamping of public education, the group devised its own curricular structure—one intrinsically more compatible with traditional day school education. According to the *Paideia* model, one stipulates the "organized knowledge" to be acquired, the "intellectual skills" of acquisition and analysis, and the "enlarged understanding of ideas and values" to be derived from the application of those skills to that body of knowledge.[17]

Applying the *Paideia* corollary to Schwab, a curriculum deliberation on education for prayer within day schools would encourage the commonplaces (as delineated above) to direct their remarks to:
• Which subject matter—already part of the traditional curriculum—offers the greatest potential for spiritual development, in general, and prayer, in particular?

17. Mortimer Adler: *The Paideia Proposal: An Educational Manifesto* (NY, 1982).

- Which learning skills have to be cultivated and refined to make prayer accessible and meaningful?
- What are the spiritual values that the students should discover, deliberate and internalize in the course of their encounter with the texts and themes related to prayer?

The actual deliberations—led by the experienced curriculum designer—and the ongoing follow-up—led by the head of school and master teachers—will provide the optimal situation in which the desirable values of spirituality can be infused into the curriculum for prayer.

Understanding by Design

The most recent entry in the curriculum theory sweepstakes is entitled "Understanding by Design" (abbreviated: *UbD*). While not actually introducing any new components, its value reposes in its restructuring of the entire deliberation featuring a three-part process of development called "backward design:"

1. Identify desired results—consisting of enduring understandings, essential questions, knowledge and basic skills.
2. Determine acceptable evidence—via informal checks, observation and dialogue, quizzes and tests, academic prompts, performance tasks and projects.
3. Plan learning experiences and instruction.[18]

Translating *UbD* into the idiom of prayer, the three steps would be:

1. What are the essential questions we expect our students to pose to the subject of prayer, and what are the enduring understandings we would like them to obtain?
2. How will the students persuade us that they know what we expect them to know about prayer, that they value what we hold dear about it, and that they possess the skills particular to its practice?
3. How do we plan to inculcate those values, practice those skills and obtain that knowledge? In other words, how do we insure that posing those essential questions will obtain those enduring understandings in response?

---

18. Grant Wiggins, Jay McTighe: *Understanding by Design* (Alexandria Va., 1998). Cf. *www.ascd.org/readingroom/books/wiggins98book.html*

"Enduring understandings" go beyond discrete facts or skills to focus on larger concepts, principles, or processes, while "essential questions" go to the heart of a discipline, recur naturally in the history of a field and throughout one's learning, and raise other important questions.[19] The success of a curriculum is proportional to the degree to which the "essential" questions it raises find their answers in those particular understandings that meet the definition of "enduring." As an introduction to the series of instructional units that follow in Part Three, we provide here a selected list of such questions pertaining to prayer—drawn from actual pedagogical experience—and a corresponding list of understandings, which are drawn from the voluminous writings of the Rav.

---

19. *Op. cit.*

Essential Questions:	Enduring Understandings:
What is prayer and why must I pray at all? Is everyone capable of prayer? Is anyone? Why must I pray at fixed intervals and not when the mood/need strikes me?	Prayer is the quintessence of Judaism (*Worship*, 4). Prayer is the doctrine of human needs (*Redemption*, 63). To pray means to discriminate, to evaluate, to understand; in other words, to ask intelligently (*Redemption*, 67); it is not a function of mood.
How can prayer be personalized if I can only use someone else's words? Why should the presence of a *minyan* make a difference to my personal prayers—isn't it unlikely that we're all praying for the same thing/reason?	You cannot arrange all your prayers in thought alone without speech (*Kuzari*, cited in *Worship*, 6). Membership in the covenantal community sanctions prayer. Prayer is restricted to the traditional forms and language of the covenantal community (Hartman, *PRC* 109).
What is the relationship between the standardized action (מעשה המצוה) and the inner, experiential, spiritual activity (קיום המצוה)? What is the relationship between fixed prayer (קבע) and "spontaneous" prayer (תחנונים)?	The very essence of prayer is the covenantal experience of being together with and talking to God and that the concrete performance, such as the recitation of texts, represents the technique of implementation of prayer and not prayer itself (*Lonely Man*, 35).
What is כוונה in prayer? What value is there in prayer if its כוונה has been compromised?	[The] intention to discharge one's duty in accordance with God's will… The physical performance divorced from the inner experience is worthless … a meaningless, stereotyped ceremonial (*Worship*, 20–21).

PART TWO

The Rav on Prayer

Intersections

In order to give greater gravity to the Rav's ideas on prayer, to insure that students have more occasions to encounter them and opportunities to internalize them, and in light of the fact that many day schools do not teach prayer formally beyond primary school, we have designed a series of "intersections" between the Rav and the study of *Humash*. They are:

1. Adam and the Prayer for Rain (Genesis 1–2)
2. Abraham and Sedom (Genesis 18)
3. Prayers were Established by the Forefathers (Genesis, *passim.*)
4. From Slavery to Freedom (Exodus 1–2)
5. The Proximity of Redemption to Prayer (Exodus, *passim.*)
6. God and Moshe: Prayer as Dialogue

In several of these units, we have attempted to focus the instruction and learning on a "didactic dichotomy," i.e., to direct the students' attention to a textual, logical or ideological contradiction, and to accomplish the educational objectives of the lesson via its resolution.

Before we do so, however, we will present a unit that will introduce the Rav's thoughts on prayer in general, thereby setting the stage for the specific, text-bound, units that follow.

In this introductory lesson, we shall attempt to answer some *essential questions* regarding prayer by reading excerpts from several essays by the Rav. While the Rav does not answer these questions in a systematic fashion, his essays are profoundly illuminating and stimulate considerable thought. The sources cited here are open to various interpretations and some thoughts and ideas expressed here—as well as the pedagogic suggestions—are my own.

The questions are [cf. the end of Part One for additional questions]:

1. Why must I pray at all?
2. Is it not presumptuous to assume that God is going to listen to *me*? How do I know if/when He is listening?
3. Why should I continue to pray to Him if I don't get what I pray for?

4. Why must I pray at fixed intervals and not when the mood/need strikes me?
5. How can prayer be personalized if I can only use someone else's words?
6. Why should the presence of a *minyan* make a difference to my personal prayers—isn't it unlikely that we're all praying for the same thing/reason?

Terminology: "Prayer" is a Misnomer

Let us begin with a quick analysis of the technical terms we employ for what we, colloquially, call *davening*.[20] We customarily use the English word "prayer" as though it were entirely synonymous with *Tefillah*. A closer look at the etymologies of the two words, however, shows that they are definitely not identical. The verb "to pray" actually means to entreat, or to beseech, and the noun "prayer" means a request or petition. In Hebrew, the corresponding verb is בק״ש, and the noun form *bakkashah*, while properly designating one aspect of *Tefillah*, is hardly synonymous with the entire enterprise.

Tefillah, on the other hand, derives from the verbal root פל״ל, which has the connotation of intervention or arbitration. The noun פלילים (Exodus 21:22), for example, means a court, and the reflexive verbal form להתפלל means to intercede on behalf of, or, possibly, to judge oneself or another.[21] A far better English definition of *Tefillah* than "prayer" would be "introspection." While standing in self-judgment, a person might be inclined to "pray," that is, to petition God to meet a perceived need. That same person, however, might judge that all his needs have been met, and will incline, instead, to offer God praise rather than petition. If his recent experience includes deliverance from jeopardy, he might "pray" to God with thanksgiving.

We "pray," then (for the sake of comprehension, we will continue to use the colloquialism), for a variety of purposes, including petition, praise, and thanksgiving. Of these three categories, the one we have selected to treat here, on account of its prominence, is petition. If we take the *Amidah*, for example, we find that although the first three *berakhot* comprise praise and the last three—thanksgiving, the core (the middle 13 *berakhot*) of this most repeated Jewish prayer consists

20. The etymology of *daven* is highly speculative, and ranges from Aramaic (*de-avinan* = of our [fore]fathers) through Old French (cognate with "divine") to Turkish.
21. See *Rashi* on Genesis 30:8, s.v. נפתולי אלהים נפתלתי.

of petitions. Indeed, the Rav notes: "Petition is the main form of human prayer" (*Worship*, 10–11, 28 ff), and: "Even two of the last three benedictions (רצה and שים-שלום) are of a petitionary nature" (*Redemption*, 65).

> [**DIDACTIC NOTE:** Among the essential questions we posed at the outset were: Why must I pray at all? How do I know if/when God is listening? Why should I continue to pray to Him if I don't get what I pray for? Challenge students to answer these questions based upon the following selections from the Rav.]

Dialogue and the Covenantal Experience

The very essence of prayer is the covenantal experience of being together with, and talking to, God, and that the concrete performance—such as the recitation of texts—represents the technique of implementation of prayer, and not prayer itself (*Lonely Man*, 35).

Prayer, according to the Rav, is a dialogue between man and God. Here are some of his poignant observations on the nature of that dialogue:

In prayer ... we have a dialogue which is reciprocal and bilateral. Man climbs the mountain toward God while He descends, figuratively, from the mountain top. Two hands embrace, as in a handshake. "And the Lord came down upon Mt. Sinai, on the top of the mountain; and the Lord called Moses to the top of the mountain and Moses went up" (Exodus 19:20)... In prayer both God and man move...

Prayer, we said, is a dialogue, not a monologue. A dialogue exists when one person addresses another, even if the other is temporarily silent. In prophecy, God speaks and man is silent; in prayer, there is the reverse situation. We have the assurance that He is a *shome'a Tefillah* [He hears our prayers], even if He does not accede to our wishes. He is not necessarily a *mekabbel Tefillah* [responsive to our specific requests]...

In prayer we do not seek a response to a particular request as much as we desire fellowship with God. Prayer is not a means for wheedling some benefit from God. Despite our prayer: *utekabbel berahamim uberatzon et tefillatenu* [accept our prayer with compassion and pleasure], it is our persistent hope that this may be fulfilled, but it is not our primary motivation.

Our sages felt that the acceptance of our prayers is beyond our understanding and is governed by unknowable considerations. We do not really understand why some prayers are accepted and others rejected. Nevertheless, prayer in the sense of petition does play a central role in our *Shemoneh Esreh*... Dialogue means communication, engagement, and interaction. When we pray, God emerges out of His transcendence and forms a companionship with us; the Infinite and the finite meet and the vast chasm is bridged (*Dialogue*, 77–78).[22]

Tefillah and "Mood": Rambam and Ramban

[**DIDACTIC NOTE**: Another of the essential questions we posed at the outset was: Why must I pray at fixed intervals and not when the mood/need strikes me? Challenge students to provide an answer by means of the distinction the Rav draws between the positions of *Rambam* and *Ramban* on the origin of the mitzvah of *Tefillah*.]

Rambam (Maimonides) and *Ramban* (Nahmanides) disagree whether the mitzvah of *Tefillah* is *de-oraita* (of Torah origin) or *de-rabbanan* (of rabbinic origin). *Rambam* regards it as a Torah require-

---

22. The notion of utilizing prayer to bridge the "finite" and the "Infinite" is quintessentially Hassidic. Indeed, numerous aspects of the Rav's writings on prayer display a greater affinity to R. Shneur Zalman of Liady (founder of Lubavitch Hassidism) than to R. Hayyim of Volozhin (disciple of the Gaon of Vilna and "father" of the intellectual-scholarly school with which the Soloveitchik family was identified over several generations). The Rav himself acknowledges his debt to Lubavitch *hassidut*, which accumulated over the time he spent as a child with a Lubavitch *melammed*. [Cf. Aaron Rakeffet: *The Rav* (New Jersey, 1999) II, 178: "The Future of Jewish Education in America."].

The contrasts between the Hassidic and Mitnagdic views on prayer in specific reference to the Rav, have been noted by Norman Lamm: "Study and Prayer; Their Relative Value in Hassidism and Mitnagdism," *Samuel K. Mirsky Memorial Volume* (NY, 1970), 37 ff., and Bezalel Naor: "Two Types of Prayer," *Tradition* 25/3 (1991), 26 ff.

This felicitous combination of the intellectual and the emotional/experiential is likely to enhance the appeal the Rav's approach to prayer has for adolescent students.

ment, listing it in his *Sefer haMitzvot* as the fifth of the 613 command-ments. *Ramban*, however, considers prayer, in general, to be rabbinic; only prayer in distress (עת צרה) is a Torah imperative.

According to the Rav:

The views of Maimonides and Nahmanides can be reconciled. Both regarded prayer as meaningful only if it is derived from a sense of *tzarah* [distress]. They differ in their understanding of the word (*Dialogue*, 80).

The Rav proceeds to draw a distinction between external dis-tress—caused by poverty, illness, or oppression—and an internal, "ex-istential," malaise which derives from feelings of insecurity and lone-liness (prominent themes in the Rav's writings). This intellectual and emotional distress, the Rav claims, provoked the Psalmist to exclaim: "מן המיצר קראתי י'ה," from the straits I call out to God (Psalms 118:5), and they produce the urge to pray.

Out of this sense of discomfiture prayer emerges. Offered in comfort and security, prayer is a paradox, modern methods of suburban worship and plush synagogues notwithstand-ing. The desire for proximity of wife and children at services comes from a need for security and comfort. Real prayer is derived from loneliness, helplessness, and a sense of depen-dence (*op. cit.*, 81).

The public distress (the Rav calls it: "surface crisis"), which *Ram-ban* envisions as a cause for prayer, is the kind which comes sud-denly, openly, and strikes everyone. The personal crisis (the Rav calls it "depth crisis"), which *Rambam* views as sufficient cause for prayer, however, can grow gradually, clandestinely, affecting some individu-als and not others. Even the most insensitive people will realize when they are in public, common, danger, but only the reflective and intro-spective will appreciate the onset of a personal crisis.

The Torah bids man actively to combat and possibly eliminate superficial, external crises. The ills of poverty, disease, and war are debilitating and impair our spiritual freedom. The To-rah, however, encourages man to embrace the experience of the "depth crisis." Thereby does man fully grasp the reality of his condition and become stirred to great heights of the spirit (*ibid.*).

The challenge of a "surface crisis" is met with solutions; a "depth crisis," on the other hand, can only be met by prayer.

Prayer as Petition: The Biblical Evidence

[**DIDACTIC NOTE**: Thus far we have established that petition is: (a) one of the three principal ways in which we can relate to God from a posture of introspection or self-judgment; (b) the most prominent and most significant of the three. Before continuing with the Rav's analysis, however, have students turn directly to the *Tanakh* and explore several examples of Biblical petition.][23]

1. Moshe (Numbers 12:13)
The most concise petition in *Tanakh* is the one which Moshe recited on behalf of his sister, Miriam. It consists of 5 words: א-ל נא רפא נא לה, which can be divided as follows:
   (a) an address: God
   (b) a petition: cure her

2. Shimshon (Judges 16:28)
A slightly longer and more complex prayer was recited by Shimshon as he stood chained to the pillars in the temple of Dagon:
ה'...זכרני נא, וחזקני נא אך הפעם הזה...ואנקמה נקם אחת משתי עיני מפלשתים
It may be divided as follows:
   (a) an address: God
   (b) a petition: take note of me and strengthen me this once
   (c) his motivation: that I may avenge myself on the Philistines for the loss of my sight

3. Hannah (I Samuel 1:11 ff.)
Hannah's prayer for a son includes all of the elements we have seen in the previous petitions (address, petition, and motivation), plus a fourth element: self-deprecation:
ה'...אם-ראה תראה בעני אמתך, ונתת לאמתך זרע אנשים, ונתתיו לה' כל ימי חייו...
   (a) the address: Lord of hosts
   (b) self-deprecation: Your oppressed maidservant
   (c) the actual petition: grant Your maidservant male children

---

23. We are indebted to the systematic and enlightened presentation of these elements in Moshe Greenberg: *Biblical Prose Prayer* (Berkeley, 1983).

(d) motivation for the petition: that I may devote him to a lifetime of God's service

[In *Berakhot* (31 a-b), Hannah's petition serves as the paradigm for all Jewish prayer.]

4. Ya`akov (Genesis 32:10–13)

The most sophisticated prayer of petition in the *Tanakh*, however, is the one which Ya'akov offered on the eve of his reunion with Esav:

ה' האמר אלי שוב לארצך ולמולדתך...קטנתי מכל החסדים ומכל האמת...ועתה הייתי לשני מחנות...הצילני נא מיד אחי...פן-יבא והכני...ואתה אמרת היטב איטיב עמך...

Here we have no fewer than seven separate elements (including those we have already observed in the prayers of others):

(a) an address: God of my fathers

(b) a description of the addressee: Who commanded me to return home

(c) a statement of self-deprecation: I am unworthy of even Your grace

(d) detail of self-deprecation: from the staff with which I crossed the Jordan (on my way to Mesopotamia) I have grown to encompass two camps

(e) the actual petition: rescue me from Esav

(f) description of distress: lest he smite me, my wives and children

(g) his motivation: that You may fulfill Your promise: "I shall surely do well to you"

[**NOTE**: Additional examples (cited by Greenberg, *op. cit.*) include King Hezekiah (2 Kings 19:15–19) and the sailors in Jonah (1:14). Note that in each and every case we have cited from the *Tanakh*, the "address," with its overtones of praise or thanksgiving, precedes the "actual petition."]

Tehinah vs. *Bakkashah*: How Do We Approach God in Prayer?

[**DIDACTIC NOTE**: Part of our very first essential question was: "Is it not presumptuous to assume that God is going to listen to me?" In other words, is not prayer an act of "*hubris*" (unforgivable arrogance)? In this section we will see that the Rav's definition of *tehinah* provides us with an important insight into the way we approach God to petition Him.

Ask the students: Why do we take three steps forward before reciting the *Amidah*? In dealing with this question, refer to Rabbi Saul
Berman's introduction to the R.C.A. edition of the ArtScroll *Siddur*,
p. xii, entitled: "An Overview—The 'Approach' in Prayer."]

In an earlier section, we provided an analysis of the word *Tefillah*.
Here we must pause to analyze another pair of technical terms: *tehinah* and *bakkashah* The Rav notes that *bakkashah* designates a claim
or a demand, something to which we feel entitled, while he defines
tehinah (based upon the commentary of *Rashi* on Deuteronomy 3:23)
as something we have no reasonable expectation of receiving:

> The word *tehinah* suggests an unearned grace, something not
> due to us... We prefer *tehinah* to *bakashah*, because the lat-
> ter suggests a claim, a demand. The principal topic of Jew-
> ish prayer is *tehinah*; praise and thanksgiving are merely
> prologues and epilogues... We petition without offering any
> apologies; it is most legitimate, but the request is always for
> *mattenat hinam*, a gift which we do not deserve (*Prayer as
> Dialogue*, 84).

This notion of entreating God for a favor can be tied into the halakhic prescription of how God should be approached in prayer. The
Shulhan Arukh mandates that three forward steps should be taken pri-
or to the recitation of the *Amidah* (which we have already identified as
being, quintessentially, a prayer of *tehinah*). The reason for these three
steps is not stipulated. The author of *Sefer Rokeach* (1165–1230),
however, suggests that the three forward paces are patterned after the
three times the word *va-yiggash* (approach) is utilized in *Tanakh*: once
each for Avraham, Yehudah, and Eliyahu.

When Avraham approached God on behalf of Sedom (Genesis
18:23),[24] he had no reasonable expectation of having his petition
granted. God had declared Sedom an evil city whose wickedness had
prompted Him to destroy it. He was already extending a courtesy to
Avraham by sparing his nephew, Lot; by what right did Avraham seek
to have the entire city spared? Surely not because it was deserving of
it!

When Yosef threatened to imprison Binyamin, Yehudah stepped
forward to plead for his release (Genesis 44:18). He was so certain that

---

24. See Part Three, Unit Two "Avraham and Sedom."

his appeal would be denied that he had already volunteered to be enslaved in his stead. The language he employed ("please, sir," "you are just like Pharaoh") reflects his subservience to Yosef and his recognition that he was asking for something to which the second to Pharaoh would not think him entitled.

Finally, when Eliyahu confronts the priests of Ba`al atop Mt. Carmel, he, too, prays to God for success (1 Kings 18:36). Eliyahu doesn't merely petition God, however; he tries, as it were, to "coerce" God into granting his request. He sets up a challenge to the priests of Baal and then demands that God back him up. Where does he come up with such audacity?

Rabbi Saul Berman distinguishes between these three plaintiffs based upon three considerations:

(1) By what right did they pray to God?
(2) On whose behalf did they pray?
(3) To which quality of God did they appeal?

The following schematic demonstrates the results of Rabbi Berman's investigation:

	by what right	for whom	quality of God
Avraham	as *ben-brit*, a party to a covenant	mankind	justice
Yehudah	as a servant	the Jewish people	mercy
Eliyahu	as a prophet, a party to an intimate relationship with God	God Himself (God's presence)	revelation

These three examples provide us with an answer to the question of how to approach God with the presumption that our prayers will be answered. We see, now, that there are indeed several grounds on which to base that assumption: God is likely to respond to a party to His covenant, to His faithful servants, and to those with whom He enjoys a special relationship. As Psalms records (99:6): משה ואהרן בכהניו ושמואל בקראי שמו, קראים אל ה' והוא יענם. "like Moshe and Aharon amongst His priests and like Shemuel amongst those who proclaimed His name; all call out to God, Who answers them."

MINYAN: The Company of Others and the Words of Others

[DIDACTIC NOTE: Two other essential questions we posed at the outset deal with the private vs. public nature of prayer: What advantage does *tefillah be-tzibbur* have over private prayer, and why are the words of the *siddur* superior to our own? In this final section we will guide students to answer these questions by means of the distinction the Rav draws between *tefillah* and *tze'akah*, in an essay entitled: "Redemption, Prayer, Talmud Torah," *Tradition* 17/2 (1978).]

We may now draw a final distinction—between *tefillah* and *tze'akah*, two terms for prayer that appear to be used, in *Tanakh*, synonymously. The Rav distinguishes between *tze'akah*, a cry of pain and suffering, and *tefillah*, which is the articulation of need.

Using the slavery in Egypt as the paradigm of suffering and the exodus as the model of redemption, the Rav draws a lesson in prayer from the story of Moshe.[25]

What is the connection, he asks, between the episodes in which Moshe protects a Jewish slave and intercedes to stop a quarrel (Exodus 2:11 ff.), and the statement which follows (vs. 23): "And it came to pass in the course of many days... that the Children of Israel sighed on account of their bondage and they cried out..."? The *Zohar*'s explanation, expanded by the Rav, is that in the state of slavery the Jews were mute, incapable of sound, let alone articulate speech. They knew pain—in the physical sense—but not suffering, which is not a physical sensation, but a spiritual experience; they thought their condition was normative. Only after Moshe demonstrated to them that they were the victims of injustice did their sensitivity return, and, with it, their ability to cry out.

The ability to cry out to God is the prelude to prayer, but not yet prayer itself. Crying out is an awareness of need, as the need of the sufferer for relief, but it does not yet recognize what the Rav calls "a hierarchy of needs." To cry out to God is to release pent up emotions almost arbitrarily; to pray to God is to have reflected, analytically, on a variety of needs and to prioritize one's requests intelligently.

Judaism... wants man to cry out aloud against any kind of pain, to react indignantly to all kinds of injustice or unfair-

---

25. See Part Three, Unit Four: "From Slavery to Freedom," and Unit Five: "The Proximity of Redemption to Prayer."

ness... Whoever permits his legitimate needs to go unsatisfied will never be sympathetic to the crying needs of others... For Judaism, need-awareness constitutes part of the definition of human existence...

Prayer is the doctrine of human needs. Prayer tells the individual, as well as the community, what his, or its, genuine needs are, what he should, or should not, petition God about... In short, through prayer man finds himself. Of course, the very instant he finds himself, he becomes a redeemed being (*Redemption*, 65–66).

Just as man cannot pray for others until he has prayed for himself, so he cannot pray for himself without including others in his prayers. Once he recognizes his responsibility to pray for others, according to the Rav, he has created "a community of prayer."

What does this mean? It means a community of common pain, of common suffering. The Halacha has taught the individual to include his fellow man in his prayer. The individual must not limit himself to his own needs, no matter how pressing those needs are and how distinguished he is. Halacha has formulated prayer in the plural... Even private prayers, such as those offered on the occasion of sickness, death, or other crises, are recited in the plural...

Knesset Yisrael is a prayerful community, in which every individual experiences not only his own pain, but also that of countless others. I still remember the distress we young boys experienced when we heard of a pogrom in some Jewish town thousands of miles away. Our anguish was not due to fear, but to sympathy and compassion. We felt the pain of the nation as a whole (*Community*, 19–22).

Halakhah prescribes *tefillah be-tzibbur* as an antidote to man's existential loneliness, but loneliness is but one of the two sides of man's slavish existence; the other is his ignorance.

When I say that man is ignorant, I do not refer to his scientific achievements; in this area modern man is clever and ingenious. What man fails to comprehend is not the world around him, but the world within him, particularly his destiny, and the needs of which he is supposed to have a clear awareness...

Because of this misidentification, man adopts the wrong table
of needs which he feels he must gratify. Man responds quickly
to the pressure of certain needs, not knowing *whose* needs he
is out to gratify.

At this juncture, sin is born. What is the cause of sin if
not the diabolical habit of man to be mistaken about his own
self? ...Does the young man understand his basic needs? If
he did, we would have no problem of crime, drugs and per-
missiveness in general... Modern man is, indeed, existentially
a slave, because he is ignorant and fails to identify his own
needs (*Redemption*, 61–63).[26]

Just as the presence of other worshippers alleviates the loneliness
of man's existence, the use of liturgical formulas relieves him of the
burden of identifying and classifying his needs before making proper
petition to have them met. Instead of leaving man to blunder in the
maze of real or presumed needs, the Halakhah canonizes them and
requires him only to recite them.

In Review and Conclusion

Here, again, are the questions with which we began. Granting our
premises that: (a) *Tefillah*, conceptually, is a form of arbitration and
self-judgment, and (b) normative, operative, prayer is petition; here
are the answers which the Rav offers:

1. Why must I pray at all?

Since petitionary prayer stems from the recognition of need, an intelligent, introspective person imposes upon himself the obligation to pray.
The ability to pray, i.e., to engage in spontaneous "needs-awareness,"
is one of the distinguishing characteristics of a free, sentient, being.

2. Is it not presumptuous to assume that God is going to listen to *me*?

By virtue of either: (a) the covenantal relationship (*ben-berit*, modeled
by Avraham); (b) the master-servant relationship (Yehudah); or (c) the
intimate, *ben-bayit*, relationship (Eliyahu), we have the right and confidence with which to approach God at all times, even for what amount
to a *matenat hinam*, a favor we have no right to expect.

---

26. Note the Rav's recurring reference to "needs."

3. Why should I continue to pray to Him if I don't get what I pray for?
If we are committed to prayer as dialogue, we should continue to speak to God even in the face of His apparent silence. He offers us no guarantee that He will accept our prayers/petitions (מקבל תפילה), only that He will listen (שומע תפילה).[27]

4. Why must I pray at fixed intervals and not when the mood/need strikes me?
The dispute between *Rambam* and *Ramban* offers an insight into the establishment of fixed intervals for prayer. (קבע) Taking *Rambam's* understanding of prayer as personal need rather than public danger, coupled with the understanding that greater sensitivity is required for *tefillah* than for *tze`akah*, if there were no fixed prayers we would be at risk of praying infrequently or failing to pray at all! Under such conditions, we would be unable to maintain a proper relationship with God.

5. How can prayer be personalized if I can only use someone else's words?
The Rav invites us to understand that it is man's essential ignorance that leads to his misidentification of his own needs, and, ultimately, to sin. Were man left entirely to his own petitionary designs, he might never make the proper requests of God. The formulaic pattern of the *Amidah*, for instance, insures that man's real needs are addressed regularly.

6. Why should the presence of a *minyan* make a difference to my personal prayers? Isn't it unlikely that we're all praying for the same thing/reason?
The Rav cites man's essential loneliness as one of the principal problems of human existence. The presence of a quorum in prayer is an invitation to man to overcome his loneliness, even temporarily. By joining with others in prayer—even by praying alone in the grammatical plural—man creates "community."

---

27. When the kidnapped Israeli soldier Nahshon Wachsman, ה"יד, was murdered by Palestinian terrorists, his father, Yehudah Wachsman, was asked whether his belief in God had been shaken by God's denial of his, and so many other people's prayers to spare his son. His answer was: מותר לאבא גם לומר לא; a father is also entitled to say: No!

PART THREE: THE INSTRUCTIONAL UNITS

With these descriptions and illustrations of curricular theory and process in mind, we can now proceed to the final part of our essay. Here, we shall construct several curricular units that are intended to integrate the Rav's ideas about prayer into the traditional study of *Humash/Tanakh*.

UNIT 1
Adam and the Rain: The First "Needs Assessment"

In this lesson, we shall examine the case of a petition that demonstrates an indispensable principle of the prayer relationship between Man and God, although the prayer's very existence is only inferred from the Torah text.

Enduring Values[28]

The Rav's quintessential definition of prayer is "to ask intelligently" (*Redemption*, 67), i.e., to conduct an accurate "needs assessment." The Rav also addresses the singular importance of "petitionary" prayer: "Petition is the main form of human prayer" (*Worship*, 10–11, 28 ff); "Even two of the last three benedictions [of the *Amidah*] are of a petitional nature" (*Redemption*, 65).

In explaining the fundamental dispute between *Rambam* and *Ramban* on the origin of the mitzvah of prayer, the Rav introduces a distinction between "ordinary" prayer (*tefillah*) and "extraordinary" crying-out to God (*tze'akah*), as on the occasion of a public catastrophe. The latter, even according to *Ramban*, originates in Torah law.

Educational Objectives[29]
Cognitive: The student will…
- Provide the details of each day's creation.
- Compare the descriptions of the creation of man and woman in chapters 1 and 2 and relate them to the rule of: כל כלל שאחריו מעשה אינו אלא פרטו של ראשון that RASHI cites in his commentary to Genesis 2:8.

---

28. Formulated according to "Understanding by Design," as described in Part One and illustrated in Part Two.
29. Formulated according to Bloom's "Taxonomy," as described in Part One.

- Distinguish (cf. *Lonely Man*) between "Adam I" and "Adam II."
- Explain the nature of their "crime" and their "punishment."
  - Distinguish (cf. *Rambam: Guide* I:2) between מפורסמות and מושכלות

Affective: The student will...

- Appreciate Man's singular role in creation, as its climax and apex.
- Appreciate that God "needs" man's assistance to bring His creation to completion and perfection.
  - Recognize prayer as a form of assistance
- Sympathize with other people who are in need and pray on their behalf.
- Recognize the prayer for rain as, arguably, the most basic of all human needs.

Behavioral (Skills): The student will...

- Read the text aloud, with proper pronunciation and punctuation—as indicated by the טעמי המקרא.
- Arrange the differences between the two narratives of creation in a table, to facilitate their comparison and contrast.
- Use a concordance to locate the importance of rain elsewhere in the Bible.

THE LESSON

Part One: Resolving a Contradiction

1. In Genesis 1:12, the Torah states: ותוצא הארץ דשא, עשב מזריע זרע למינהו..., indicating that grass had begun to grow on day three of creation.

2. In 2:5, however, it states:
וכל שיח השדה טרם יהיה בארץ, וכל-עשב השדה טרם יצמח; כי לא המטיר ה' אלקים על-הארץ, ואדם אין לעבד את-האדמה, which implies that there was no vegetation—because there was no precipitation!—prior to the creation of man on day six.

3. The Talmud (*Hullin* 60b) provides a resolution:
מלמד שיצאו דשאים ועמדו על פתח קרקע,
עד שבא אדם הראשון ובקש עליהם רחמים, וירדו גשמים וצמחו;
ללמדך: שהקב"ה מתאוה לתפלתן של צדיקים.

R. Assi resolves this contradiction by positing that the vegetation was kept poised just below the surface of the earth from day three until day six, when Adam came and recited a prayer for rain. From this resolution, he then infers a momentous theological postulate: שהקב"ה מתאוה לתפלתן של צדיקים; God craves the prayers of the righteous.[30]

Part Two: Extracting the Significance

Reducing this theological proposition to more existential terms, it places man—rather than the earth—at the focus of creation and indicates that God's principal purpose in creation was not the earth itself but the earth-dweller: Man. Man, for his part, was not intended to emerge upon the background of a completed and perfect world, but to be co-opted into partnering with God in its completion and perfection. God, therefore, did not provide man with merely the opportunity or even just the incentive to pray for the rain that would complete creation; He positively craved man's prayer without which God's own plan and intent would have been frustrated.

The consequences of this realization are exceedingly far-reaching. As much as we are dependent upon Him and His grace, so do His actions depend upon our participation in His worldly enterprise. That would appear to give us considerable leverage to wield in our dealings with Him.[31]

Part Three: Some Thoughts about the *"Complementarity"* of Prayer[32]

In regard to the "regular offerings" (קרבן תמיד ; Numbers 28:2), God puts us in charge of what He calls: "MY near-offerings (קרבני), MY food (לחמי), MY fire-offerings (לאשי), MY soothing savor (ריח ניחחי)."[33]

This permits—or, perhaps, even mandates—the following syllogism:

1. Sacrifices are God's "food," and He is dependent on us for His satisfaction.

---

30. This interpretation undoubtedly rests on the Talmudic identification of the root שי"ח with prayer: "אין שיחה אלא תפילה". Cf. *Talmud Yerushalmi Berakhot* (4:7:1), *Bereishit Rabba* (68:9), *et al.*
31. See our elaboration on this point in Unit 2: "Avraham and Sedom."
32. The state or quality of being complementary, defined as: "mutually supplying each other's lack" (Webster).
33. Translations follow Everett Fox: *The Five Books of Moses* (NY, 1995).

2. Prayer is the substitute for sacrifice ("ונשלמה פרים שפתינו", Hoshea 14:3).

3. God depends upon our regular prayer just as He previously depended upon our regular sacrifice.

Our prayer then, is decidedly NOT a one-sided affair, in which we beseech God for unmerited divine assistance, favor or grace. On the contrary, it is part of a pact, a covenant if you will, between parties who, however unequal in capacity, are nonetheless mutually dependent.[34]

Part Four: Some Halakhic Consequences

Ordinarily, the nature of petition restricts its recitation to weekdays; hence, the elimination of the intermediate *berakhot* from the *Amidah* of *Shabbat* and *Yom Tov*. The same principle appears to govern the similar restriction against the recitation of *Avinu Malkeinu* on *Shabbat*:

ונוהגין לומר ''אבינו מלכנו'' על הסדר, ואם הוא שבת—אין אומרים אותו (רמ''א, תקפ''ד:א).

הטעם—שאין שואלין צרכים בשבת (משנה ברורה, שם, ס''ק ד).

It is customary to recite *Avinu Malkenu* in its proper place.

If it is *Shabbat*, however, it is not recited.

The reason is that we do not recite petitionary prayers on *Shabbat*.

A fine distinction, however—one that is in tune with the Rav's distinction between prayer and crying-out—is drawn by R. Shlomo Zalman Auerbach with regard to other forms of existential "needs assessments:"

שאלה: אם כן, מדוע מותר לשאול את צרכיו בראש השנה, הרי גם בראש השנה אסור להצטער, ככתוב: ''חדות ה' היא מעוזכם''?

תשובה: ''מתריעים בשבת'' (תענית ג:ז). רואים שעל צרות גדולות מותר להתפלל גם בשבת. ובראש בשנה, שהוא יום הדין ואנחנו בצרה גדולה, מותר גם לשאול את צרכיו.

Q: Why, then, is it permissible to recite petitions on *Rosh ha-Shanah* when it is equally inappropriate to experience distress...?

A: It is permissible to "sound the alarm" on *Shabbat*. It is permissible to pray on account of great (public?) distress even on *Shabbat*. On

---

34. Further on "complementarity," cf. Unit 6: "Prayer as Dialogue."

Rosh ha-Shanah, the Day of Judgment, on which we are all in great distress, it is thus permissible to petition.[35]
And in a similar vein:

כתבו האחרונים דמותר לומר בשבת אלהי עד שלא נוצרתי, יהי רצון וכו', דאינו
אסור שאלת צרכיו אלא כשמבקש על חולי, או פרנסה, ודומה לו—שיש צער לפניו.
אבל חרטת עוונות טוב לומר בכל יום כיון שאינו בלשון וידוי (משנה ברורה, סי'
רפ"ח, ס"ק כב).

Others have written that it is permissible on *Shabbat* to recite *Elohai ad shelo notzarti*, or *yehi ratzon*, because the only petition that is prohibited is on account of illness or livelihood, where there is evident distress. It is appropriate, however, to express remorse daily, since it is not, strictly speaking, a "confession."

UNIT 2
Avraham and Sedom: Prayer, Intercession, and "Divine Intimacy"

Enduring Values
* Avraham, the first of the *Avot*, is cited in the Torah several times as "calling out in God's name" (e.g., Genesis 12:8), apparently an early designation for prayer. So accomplished did Avraham become at prayer, that he became a paradigm of intercessory prayer in his own lifetime. After chastising the Philistines on account of Sarah, God advises Avimelekh to "return the man's wife; indeed, he is a prophet and can intercede on your behalf and you will live" (20:7).[36]
* Recognition of the *Avot* as paradigms of prayer may also account for the Halakhic ruling (by *Rambam*, via R. Hayyim) that *kavvanah* is only required of *birkhat avot,* the first blessing of the *Amidah.*
* In time of need, we would do well to turn to a righteous person to assist us through prayer.

---

35. *ועלהו לא יבול* (ירושלים, תשנ"ט), כרך א, עמ' 351.
36. By "intercessory" prayer, we mean prayer offered on another's behalf. Our use of this concept is informed by Yohanan Muffs: "Who will stand in the breach? A study in prophetic intercession," *Love and Joy* (NY, 1992).

Educational Objectives

Cognitive: The student will...

- Describe the situations in which Avraham (and other *Avot*) interceded with God, via prayer, on behalf of themselves or on behalf of others.
  - Cite God's reaction to their intercession and characterize it.
- Describe the strengths of character or leadership that the *Avot* (Avraham in particular) brought to their task.
  - Contrast the qualities that characterized Avraham with those of Yitzhak and Yaakov, particularly as regards their contributions to prayer.
- Describe Avraham's confrontation with God over Sedom and its consequences.
- Compare Avraham's willingness to confront God over the fate of Sedom with Noah's resignation over the fate of the world.
- List the principle characteristics of petitionary/intercessory prayer in the Bible and cite several paradigms of same.

Affective: The student will...

- Recognize the "intimacy" that the *Avot* (and other, singular, Biblical characters) enjoyed with God.
- Appreciate how incredible it was for Avraham to confront God over Sedom.
- Appreciate that God essentially invited his opposition, as He essentially invites intercession at all times.
- Value the qualities of the *Avot* and seek to emulate them.
- Recognize prayer as instrumental in interceding with God.
- Sympathize with other people who are in jeopardy and recognize the need to intercede on their behalf.

Behavioral (Skills): The student will...

- Read the text aloud, with proper pronunciation and punctuation—as indicated by the *ta`amei ha-mikra*.
- Identify the verbs that designate forms of intercession (e.g., גישה,עמידה, שיחה, פגיעה) and translate them into English, utilizing an appropriate dictionary, if necessary.

- Use a concordance to locate appearances of such verbs elsewhere in the Bible.
- Correctly identify other contexts in which these verbs signify intercession.

THE LESSON

Part One: Why tell?

In Genesis 18, God is about to destroy the cities of Sedom and Amorah on account of their great iniquity and the cry that has ascended to Him. At what appears to be the last moment, He recalls that He is not supposed to launch such a catastrophe as this without providing prior notice to His servant: "Am I going to hide from Avraham what I am about to do?" (18:17). Given the information, Avraham proceeds to remonstrate with God, praying and pleading for Sedom. The question, of course, is: Did God expect Avraham to respond otherwise? If it was His intention to destroy the cities, why open the door to negotiation?

In fact, the same question can be asked of any of a number of instances reported in Tanakh in which God informs people of their own, or others', fate, only to have them argue with Him over His decision and attempt to intercede with Him on behalf of the intended victims. (Moshe, Shemuel, Yesha'ayahu and Yonah come quickly to mind.) It is as though God does not really want to carry out His verdict and He is looking to be talked out of it; He invites prayer.[37]

Part Two: The Paradox of Prophecy

In the specific case of the prophet, however, this partnership (in the previous lesson, we entitled it "complementarity") has a paradoxical outcome: The prophet, who is—at first—the medium for the transmission of the divine threat of punishment for transgression, becomes—in the continuation—an advocate for the defendant before the Chief Justice, interceding in order to have his sentence mitigated.

The fulfillment of this function is what inspired prophetic intercessory prayer:

Prophetic prayer is the most characteristic indication of the prophet's total intellectual independence and freedom of

---

37. See the point made in Unit One, Part One: "God craves the prayers of the righteous."

conscience. The divine strong hand does not lobotomize the prophet's moral and emotional personality. Prophecy does not tolerate prophets who lack heart, who are emotionally anaesthetized. Quite the contrary, one could even argue that, historically speaking, the role of intercessor is older than the messenger aspect of prophecy. After all, Abraham is not a prophetic messenger, yet he is considered a prophet nonetheless. His prophetic nature manifests itself only in his prayer... (Gen. 20:7). There is no better example of prayer and petition than that of Abraham in the case of Sodom, which distinguishes itself in its unbridled audacity against heaven: "Shall the Judge of the world not do justice?" (Gen. 18:25).[38]

Part Three: Precedent

This curious, counterintuitive situation has a precedent. In Unit One: "Adam and the Rain," we stipulated that Man is God's partner in creation. Before man would pray for rain, there was no apparent vegetation; without man's active and consensual participation, creation is incomplete.

Man's responsibility to assist God to realize the full potential of creation didn't end with his expulsion from the Garden of Eden; it continues, undiminished, throughout history and is still ongoing today.

Part Four: The Right Approach

Avraham's intercession at Sedom is a paradigm of yet another feature associated with *Tefillah*: the right way to approach God. When the impending fate of Sedom is first revealed to him, the Torah describes his approach to God using the word *va-yiggash*, literally—to approach. R. Eliezer ben Yehudah Roke'ah (c. 1165–c. 1230) observes that the same word is used to describe the approaches made by two other Biblical figures, Yehudah (Genesis 44:18) and Eliyahu (1 Kings 18:36), prior to their own acts of intercession. He concludes that the three steps forward we customarily take before the *Amidah* match the strides taken by these three figures.

[**NOTE**: A detailed examination of all three cases was presented in Part Two, in which we posed three questions to each of the three cases: By what right was the approach made? On whose behalf? Appealing to which qualities of God?]

---

38. Muffs, *op. cit.*, 11.

Part Five: Petition and Regular Prayer

The example of Avraham at Sedom illustrates yet another principle of prayer—the integration of petition (*bakkashah*) into the fixed liturgical order (*tefillah kevu`ah*). The Rav has written:

> It [prayer] consists of both experiencing the complete helplessness of man, his absolute dependence upon God, and the performance of the ritual of prayer, of reciting fixed texts (*Family*, 40).

> Does *avodah she-ba-lev* exhaust itself in standardized action, in the recital of a fixed text thrice daily, or in an inner experiential reality, in spiritual activity?... The physical deed of reciting a fixed text serves only as a medium through which the experience finds its objectification and concretion. It is not to be identified with the genuine act of praying, which is to be found in an entirely different dimension, namely, in the great, wondrous God-experience (*Worship*, 19–20).

As the three messengers leave Avraham and turn towards Sedom, the Torah (18:22) describes Avraham as: "Still standing before God" (עודנו עומד לפני ה'). *Targum Onkelos* renders the word עומד as: משמש בצלו, engaged in prayer.

- In what kind of prayer was he already engaged prior to God's revelation to him of the fate of Sedom?
- What is the relationship between this preexisting prayer and the petition on behalf of Sedom that follows?

The *Netziv* replies: "This was his regular everyday prayer (תפילה קבועה)." Only in the following verse (23; ויגש אברהם) does he begin to pray specifically for Sedom. He elaborates:

> The Torah informs us about all these details to teach us that one should pray for something only as part of his regular prayer, since that is the most propitious time (עת רצון). As the Talmud records (*Avodah Zarah* 7b): "When does the verse apply: 'A prayer of a lowly man when he is faint? When 'He pours forth his plea (שיחו) before God'" (Psalms 102:1). That is to say, during regular prayer, which is called a plea (שיח)... For this reason, Avraham did not have to preface his prayer [for Sedom] with praise [of God] as the law requires, since he

was already engaged in regular prayer, which contains praise
(הרחב דבר, *ad. loc.*).

[NOTE: The *Netziv* contrasts Avraham's petition on behalf of Sedom with Yaakov's petition on his own behalf (32:10 ff.), noting
that since Yaakov was not otherwise engaged in prayer, his petition
had to commence with praise of God. See Unit Three: "Tefillot Avot
Tikkenum" (Part Three), where we deal with Yaakov's petition in
detail.]

Part Six: Petition within Prayer; A Halakhic Dimension

In an essay entitled: *Semikhat Ge'ulah li-Tefillah*,[39] which deals,
inter. alia., with the relationship of petition (*bakkashah/tehinah*) to
prayer (*tefillah*), the Rav asks, rhetorically:

> How can man—short-lived and anxiety-ridden—approach the
> King in petition and supplication? The entire matter of prayer
> is a gift of a gracious God to mortal man... [Therefore,] it is
> forbidden to cry out to God without utilizing the form and
> framework of prayer (42).

Citing the statement of R. Simlai: "One should always arrange his
praise of God [first] and afterwards he may pray" (*Avodah Zarah* 7b),
he stipulates two points about *Tefillah*:

(A) There is an obligation to pray; one is obliged to pray and gratify his creator, and place his petition before Him.

(B) One may not petition for his needs outside of the framework
of [fixed] prayer.

By inserting his petition for Sedom into the context of his regular
[fixed] prayer, Avraham serves as a paradigm of this principle.

UNIT 3

תפילות—אבות תקנום
Personifying our Prayers

Enduring Values

- תפילות—אבות תקנום (*Berakhot* 26b). The prayers of the *Avot* are the
  "historical precedent" on which the אנשי כנסת הגדולה based our

---

39. שיעורים לזכר אבא מרי, ז"ל (Jerusalem, 1985; vol. 2), 35–57. See Unit Five:
"The Proximity of Redemption to Prayer."

Tefillah. "We find that our forefathers, Moses and the prophets prostrated themselves before God in prayer, spoke with Him conversationally, revealed to Him their innermost secrets and forced Him as it were, to meet their needs; they both argued and demanded" (*Ra`ayonot*, 245).

*   "The fact that we commence the recital of the "eighteen benedictions" by addressing ourselves to the God of Abraham, Isaac and Jacob, is indicative of the covenantal relationship which, in the opinion of our sages, lies at the very root of prayer" (*Lonely Man*, 35).

*   Recognition of the *Avot* as paradigms of prayer may account for the Halakhic ruling (by *Rambam*, via R. Hayyim) that *kavvanah* is required only of the first blessing of the *Amidah*, known as אבות.

Educational Objectives

Cognitive: The student will…

*   Describe the situations in which Avraham and other *Avot* interceded with God, via prayer, on their own behalf or on behalf of others.
    *   Cite God's reaction to their intercession and characterize it.
*   Describe the strengths of character or leadership that the *Avot* (Avraham in particular) brought to their task.
    *   Contrast the qualities that characterized Avraham with those of Yitzhak and Yaakov, particularly as regards their contributions to prayer.
*   Cite the three classic "approaches" to authority that were made by the *Avot* and translate them into the requirements we follow prior and subsequent to prayer.
*   List the principal characteristics of petitionary/intercessory prayer in the Bible and cite several paradigms of same.

Affective: The student will…

*   Recognize the "intimacy" that the *Avot* (and other, singular, Biblical characters) enjoyed with God.
*   Appreciate that God essentially invites intercession at all times.
*   Value the qualities of the *Avot* and seek to emulate them.
*   Recognize prayer as instrumental in interceding with God.
*   Sympathize with other people who are in jeopardy and be prepared to intercede on their behalf.

- "The very essence of prayer is the covenantal experience of being together with and talking to God and that the concrete performance, such as the recitation of texts, represents the technique of implementation of prayer and not prayer itself" (*Lonely Man*, 35).

Behavioral (Skills): The student will…
- Read the text aloud, with proper pronunciation and punctuation—as indicated by the טעמי המקרא.
- Identify the verbs that designate forms of intercession and approach (e.g., גישה,עמידה, שיחה, פגיעה) and translate them into English, utilizing an appropriate dictionary, if necessary.
- Use a concordance to locate appearances of such verbs elsewhere in the Bible.
- Demonstrate the proper approach to, and recessional from the *Amidah*.

THE LESSON

Part One: Conformity and Individuality

While we have a tendency to speak of the *Avot*, collectively, as though they were interchangeable, the truth is that with all the similarities in their actions and reactions each of them possessed distinctive traits of character and personality. Each of those traits, in turn, can be identified with the Jewish people, as an entity, giving palpable proof to what *Ramban* designated: מעשה אבות—סימן לבנים.

The two statements that follow capture the essence of their similarities and differences in a manner particularly well-suited for the understanding of *Tefillah*.

A. *Berakhot* 26b	B. *Pesahim* 88a
Avraham established *shaharit*…	Avraham appears on a mountain…
Yitzhak established *minhah*…	Yitzhak appears in a field…
Yaakov established *ma'ariv*…	Yaakov appears in a house…

We shall now proceed to clarify what the Sages intended to convey via these associations.

Part Two: The Characterizations[40]

Avraham was called עברי because he had the capacity to confront
his idolatrous environment with his belief in one God.[41] The light he
shed on true faith and belief is represented by the *shaharit* prayer,
which is recited after dawn, and the standard he set for others to follow
is represented by a mountain, which is visible even at a distance. Avraham's conduct both in his emigration to God's Promised Land, as well
as his itinerary after his arrival, are models of devotion to the cause of
monotheism and its dissemination.

> Avraham expresses the historical chapter in which the people
> of Israel bears God's name throughout the world and the gen-
> tile nations relate to them as a 'divine prince' in their midst.

Yitzhak represents continuity. He strengthened the structure that
Avraham erected, thereby insuring that it would not be just a passing phase. Even the wells that he dug received the same names that
had been conferred on them by Avraham. Since his lot was not one
of innovation, Yitzhak often appears passive—as in the case of the
akeidah, and in the arrangement of his marriage to Rivkah. This pas-
sivity/continuity is represented by the *minhah* prayer, which is recited
at twilight—a time that is neither entirely day nor night, and by the
field, which represents something at once both stable and unyielding.

> Yitzhak expresses the humdrum chapters in national life; the
> periods in which the nation resided in its land, living accord-
> ing to the heritage of its fathers.

Yaakov's life, from birth and on, is characterized by struggle;
hence, the attribution to him of *ma'ariv*, the prayer that is recited only
by night—in darkness. He succeeds, however, by drawing clear lines
of demarcation that keep his restless family intact, and inside. Whereas Avraham and Yitzhak are represented by a mountain and a field—
symbols of expansiveness—Yaakov's symbol is the house; enclosed
and, perhaps, even forbidding.

> Yaakov's life spans the dark periods of national exile. The
> gathering within the house is the necessary result of the ongo-
> ing emergency that characterizes Yaakov's life.

---

40. We base these remarks upon the insights provided by the staff of Herzog
Teachers' College (Har Etzion) in their teachers' guide to *Bereishit-Shemot*
(5758), p. 27.

41. (*Bereishit Rabba* 42:8) כל העולם כולו מעבר אחד והוא מעבר אחד.

Part Three: Models of Petition

As Yaakov is about to be reunited with Esav, he addresses God with an urgent plea for deliverance from what he describes as impending doom and destruction. This prayer (Genesis 32:10–13), which serves as a model of what Moshe Greenberg has called "Biblical Prose Prayer,"[42] is the only such model to contain all seven elements we have come to expect of petition: address, description (of addressee), self-deprecation, detail (thereof), petition, distress, and motivation.

Address:	אלקי אבי אברהם ואלקי אבי יצחק
Description	האמר אלי, שוב לארצך ולמולדתך
Self-deprecation	קטנתי מכל החסדים ומכל האמת
Detail	כי במקלי עברתי את הירדן הזה
Petition	הצילני נא מיד אחי, מיד עשו
Distress	כי ירא אנכי אתו פן יבא והכני
Motivation	ואתה אמרת היטב איטיב עמך

[NOTE: The other models presented by Greenberg, consist of Moshe (Numbers 12:13), Samson (Judges 16:28), Hannah (1 Samuel 1:11 ff.), and the sailors aboard Jonah's ship (1:14).][43]

In Unit Two: "Avraham and Sedom" (Part Five), we presented the explanation of the *Netziv* that Avraham didn't need to begin his petition with praise of God because he was already engaged in regular (fixed) prayer. Yaakov, on the other hand, had to begin his petition by praising God because he was not otherwise engaged in prayer. Why were their situations different? Since Avraham entertained his guests at noon (18:1) and they arrived at Sedom in the evening (19:1), his plea to God—which followed his separation from his guests—had to have been in the afternoon, at which time he would have been reciting *minhah*.

Yaakov, on the other hand, had spent the day making frantic preparations for his encounter with Esav and subsequently he goes to sleep (32:14). It would appear that he had already recited *minhah* and felt he could not delay his petition until the next regular prayer time arrived.

---

42. Cf. n. 23, *supra*.

43. We have dealt with these examples at greater length in Part Two: "Prayer as Petition; the Biblical Evidence."

Part Four: Another Comparison

There are similarities and differences among the *Avot* other than those we contrasted in Part Two. Avraham's stance before God is referred to as עמידה (rising up; 19:27), Yitzhak's is called שיחה (conversation, discussion; 24:63), and Yaakov's is פגיעה (encounter; 28:11).

These three verbs, as expounded by Rabbi Avi Weiss, signify three distinct actions that ought to characterize our *Tefillah*.

> As one rises up, it is important to remove all the clutter, all the disturbances that could impede one's ability to communicate with God…In conversation, one must obviously comprehend the contents of his/her words… [and] it is important to feel God's presence.[44]

The last two elements: comprehending the prayers and feeling God's presence, are the twin pillars of the Rav's definition of *kavvanah*. Based upon a distinction first drawn by R. Hayyim Brisker, *kavvanah* is said to comprise the understanding of the liturgy coupled with the awareness that one is standing in the presence of divinity.

חידושי ר' חיים הלוי על הרמב"ם

(הלכות תפילה פרק ד, הלכה א)

תרי גווני כוונות יש בתפילה.

האחת: כוונה של פירוש הדברים, ויסודה הוא דין כוונה.

ושנית: שיכוון שהוא עומד בתפילה לפני ה'.

UNIT 4

Slavery and Redemption: Knowing how to Pray

Enduring Values

• In explaining the fundamental disagreement between *Rambam* and *Ramban* on the origin of the mitzvah of prayer,[45] the Rav introduces a distinction between "ordinary" prayer (*tefillah*) and "extraordinary" crying-out to God (*tze'akah*), as on the occasion of a public catastrophe. The latter, even according to *Ramban*, originates in Torah law.

---

44. *A Taste of Torah*, Va-yetze, 5759. *http://www.hir.org/torah/rabbi/5759/vayetze59.htm*, downloaded on May 17, 2005.

45. We have dealt with this question at greater length in Part Two.

- According to the Rav, slavery is characterized by silence (*Redemption*, 59). Since slaves have only biological needs (as opposed to "human" ones), they may cry out, but they do not pray. Yet, only when they find their voice in prayer can they be redeemed.
  [**NOTE:** The Rav makes the same point about the experience of Holocaust survivors (*Redemption*, 57) and a similar lesson could be constructed for a Jewish history class.]
- Indeed, the Rav identifies the oft-repeated mitzvah of סיפור יציאת מצרים as a paradigm of the equation: redemption=speech (*op. cit.*, 56). This characterization serves several purposes for the Rav, among them the distinction between *tefillah* and *tze'akah*, a distinction that plays a significant role in his support for *Rambam*'s position on the Torah origin of prayer.
- "The very essence of prayer is the covenantal experience of being together with and talking to God and that the concrete performance, such as the recitation of texts, represents the technique of implementation of prayer and not prayer itself" (*Lonely Man*, 35).

Educational Objectives
Cognitive: The student will…
- Compare and contrast the role of slaves in at least two of the following regions.
  - Ancient Egypt
  - Roman Empire
  - Pre-Colombian Mesoamerica
  - Plantations in the U.S.A.[46]
- Describe the conditions of slavery imposed on the Jews in Egypt, and how the Jews responded to them.
  - List the verbs in Shemot 1–2 that describe forms of articulation, assess their significance, and note their appearance in the context of prayer elsewhere in the Bible.
  - Cite God's reaction to their response (Exodus 3:23–25) and characterize it.
- Describe the strengths of character or leadership that Moshe and Aharon brought to their task.
  - Contrast the relationship between Moshe and Aharon de-

---

46. See Kenneth Chelst: *Exodus and emancipation: Biblical and African-American slavery* (Jerusalem: URIM, 2009).

scribed in 4:16 with that described in 7:1 and draw a conclusion from their equation.
- Compare Moshe's demurral at the burning bush (3:11; 4:2, 10, 14) with his demurral subsequent to the initial confrontation (6:12, 30).
- Describe the initial confrontation with Pharaoh and its consequences.
- Contrast prayer and crying-out in light of the Rav's explanation of the disagreement between *Rambam* and *Ramban* on the origin of the mitzvah of prayer.

Affective: The student will…
- Appreciate the enormity of the oppression and slavery in Egypt, and of our redemption.
- See the hand of God in both the slavery and redemption.
- Value the qualities of leadership in Moshe and seek to emulate them.
- Recognize prayer as instrumental in the process of redemption.
- Recognize the exodus from Egypt as a universal symbol of deliverance from suffering and oppression.[47]
- Sympathize with other people who experience slavery [or other forms of oppression and injustice] and pray for their redemption.
- Appreciate that "modern man is, indeed, existentially a slave, because he is ignorant and fails to identify his own needs" (*Redemption*, 63).

Behavioral (Skills): The student will…
- Read the text aloud, with proper pronunciation and punctuation—as indicated by the *ta`amei ha-mikra*.
- Identify the verbs that designate forms of articulate speech (e.g., זעק, צעק, קרא) and translate them into English, utilizing an appropriate dictionary, if necessary.
- Use a concordance to locate appearances of such verbs elsewhere in the Bible.
- Correctly identify other contexts in which these verbs signify forms of prayer.

---

47. E.g., Michael Walzer: *Exodus and Revolution* (NY, 1985), which examines the "political meanings" of the exodus narrative and the uses to which it has been put in modern times.

THE LESSON

Part One: A Discussion of Slavery

The Jews in Egypt were rendered mute by their oppression and the process of their redemption was consequently delayed. At this point, students will be asked to recite observations of slavery from history and literature (e.g., *Uncle Tom's Cabin, The Gulag Archipelago*) and characterize the common denominators of the experience of slaves. These observations will be compared and contrasted with those of the *peshat* of Exodus 1:13–14 and with *Midreshei Aggadah* on the subject [e.g., Louis Ginsberg: *Legends of the Jews*]. Particular attention will be paid to the several interpretations of עבודת פרך and to the reappearance of פרך in the laws of Israelite servitude (Leviticus 25: 43, 46, 53).

Part Two: Crying Out vs. Praying

We shall next look through the early portions of Exodus for the appearance of verbs that denote the articulation of sound. We will distinguish between verbs that only indicate calling or crying-out, and verbs that are synonymous with prayer. This will enable us to conclude—with the Rav, and his source in the *Zohar*—that the appearance of Moshe and the hope that he symbolized enabled the Hebrew slaves to find their voice, pray to God, and secure their promised redemption.

The verbs we will identify include: אנ״ח, זע״ק, שו״ע, נא״ק, צע״ק.

Part Three: Redemption in Stages

The *Zohar* divides the redemption into three stages: (1) slavery=total silence; (2) redemption begins with sound, but no words; (3) total redemption=sound+words.

The textual focus here will be on Exodus 2:23, which indicates that prior to the arrival of Moshe on the scene, the Jews had not called out to God because they lacked the "need awareness" for freedom. The protest that Moshe lodged with Pharaoh over their treatment, while initially unsuccessful, heightened their sensitivity to their own needs. In this context, we will also examine the reasons Moshe gave for declining his mission, paying particular attention to their relationship to the capacity for speech.

Part Four: To "Know" is to Empathize"

A special focus of this lesson will be Exodus 2:25: וירא אלקים את בני ישראל, וידע אלקים; "God saw the Israelites and God knew." What did

He see, and what did He know? There is a broad range of commentary on this question that is relevant to the Rav's definition and qualification of prayer.

(1) *Onkelos*. וגלי קדם יי' שעבודא דבני ישראל, ואמר במימריה למפרקהון 'יי; The enslavement of the Israelites was exposed before God, and He decided to extricate them.

(2) *Sa`adiah*. ונט'ר אללה אלי בני אסראיל, ורחמהם; God observed the Israelites and had compassion on them.

(3) *Rashi*. נתן עליהם לב, ולא העלים עיניו מהם; He paid attention to them and didn't overlook them.

(4) *Ibn Ezra* (long version). וירא, שהיו המצרים עושים בגלוי; וידע, העשוי בסתר; He saw that the Egyptians were [oppressing them] openly, and He knew what was being done secretly.

(5) *Ibn Ezra* (short version). Philosophers have stated that there are two categories of knowledge: knowledge of things that exist (דעת היש), and knowledge of things that will be (דעת העתיד).

(6) *Ramban*. Rashi's interpretation is true to the *peshat*. Initially, God hid His countenance from them and left them vulnerable. Now, He heard their cry and noticed them—i.e., He no longer hid Himself from them; He knew of their affliction and what they required. The text tells of several causes of their redemption: "God heard their cry," "God recalled His covenant," "For I have known his affliction" (3:7), because they were not yet worthy of redemption—although the time had come—as Ezekiel prophesied (20:6–10). It was only on account of their anguished cry that He compassionately accepted their prayers.

(7) *Sa`adiah Gaon*, in his commentary on Psalms 1: 6, enumerates no fewer than 12 (!) uses of the verb י"דע.[48]

Out of all these nuanced definitions, we may suggest the following interpretation—one particularly well-suited for the purposes of education:

"To know" is a multifaceted enterprise. In the *cognitive* domain, it includes awareness and comprehension (and other items in Bloom's taxonomy[49]); in the *affective* domain, it embraces intimacy and commitment. In the metaphysical domain indicated by our verse, however, it signifies empathy. God was already "aware" of their predicament,

---

48. Curiously, his translation here: "to show compassion," is not one of them.
49. See our description of the taxonomy in Part One.

and "committed" to their redemption; with the latest chapter in their travail, He became one with their suffering: עמו אנכי בצרה.

Part Five: To "Teach" is to "Empathize"

Apropos of empathy, it is worthwhile noting that the Rav regarded empathy as a prerequisite for successful pedagogy.

In an essay entitled: "Teaching with Clarity and Empathy" (*Reflections*, 150–159), he distinguishes between the role that Moshe played after the sin of the golden calf and the one he later played after the sin of those who craved meat (קברות התאוה). To the former, Moshe reacted as a teacher, by making forceful pronouncements and taking forthright and powerful action. This, the Rav explains, was a suitable response to an incident involving idolatry.

The latter incident, however, was characterized by paganism and hedonism, and the "intellectual" approach of argument and persuasion that Moshe took towards the golden calf would have been ineffectual. To counter this threat, Moshe had to become an אומן, a nursing father.

Besides teaching, he would have to reach out emotionally to the people, nurture them through their national infancy, with patient, sympathetic understanding and empathy... Our age is demonstrably pagan... It consists of uninhibited *peritzut* (indulgence). The teaching role may have been sufficient in the past to counter the allurements of other religions, philosophies, and the pseudo-ideologies which still abound nowadays... We must have, in addition to teaching: dedication, personal commitment, for otherwise the burden is unbearable; *selflessness*, a readiness to subordinate personal career and egotistical ambitions; and *empathy*, an ability to teach with feeling, not only with clarity (*Reflections*, 157–158). [50]

Part Six: What else Can we "Know"?

According to *Rambam*, we have an obligation to "know" God. Indeed, the very first laws of the *Mishneh Torah*, הל' יסודי התורה, begin with the stipulation that "the most fundamental principle and the pillar of all knowledge is to know (לידע) that there is a first cause..." What

---

50. Cf.: "Engaging the Heart and Teaching the Mind," *Reflections* 160–168. Regarding the Rav's combination of the intellectual and the emotional/experiential, see our note 22, *supra*.

sort of knowledge does that obligation entail? Are we to "know" Him the way He "knows" us?

The answer of philosophy has generally been that one knows God through the ability to provide rational proofs of His existence. The Rav, however, is critical of such proofs because they lack the experiential dimension he believes is indispensable to the true religious experience. He asks:

> Does the loving bride in the embrace of her beloved ask for proof that he is alive and real? Must the prayerful soul clinging in passionate love and ecstasy to her Beloved demonstrate that He exists? ...
>
> Maimonides' term לידע transcends the bounds of the abstract *logos* and passes over into the realm of the boundless intimate and impassioned experience where postulate and deduction, discursive knowledge and intuitive thinking, conception and perception, subject and object, are one (*Lonely Man*, 32–33, note).

[The Rav also notes that *Rambam* begins by describing God in ("aboriginal") experiential terms and only in the fifth halakhah of יסודי התורה does he introduce a philosophical (Aristotelian) proof for His existence.]

Unit 5

סמיכת גאולה לתפילה
The Proximity of Redemption to Prayer

To illustrate the variety of methodological presentations of which the Rav's writings on prayer avail themselves, we shall alter the format of this unit to meet the requirements of a lesson whose focus is on *Halakhah* and *Hashkafah*, rather than on *Humash*.

* * *

אמר ר' יוחנן: איזהו בן עולם הבא? זה הסומך גאולה לתפילה של ערבית (ברכות ד ע"ב)

> R. Yohanan said: Who merits the world to come?
> Whoever brings nigh redemption to prayer in the *Arvit* service (*Berakhot* 4b).

Preface

The *Netziv*'s observation that Avraham was already engaged in תפילה קבועה, fixed prayer, prior to presenting his petition on behalf of Sedom,[51] provides us with an opportunity to discuss two additional dimensions of prayer—one hashkafic and one halakhic—that we will consign under the rubric of סמיכת גאולה לתפילה. The hashkafic dimension pertains to the juxtaposition of praise and petition within the *Amidah*, while the halakhic dimension pertains to the proximity of praise to petition within the juxtaposition of the *Amidah* and קריאת שמע וברכותיה.

The commentaries of *Rashi* and the *Tosafot* to the statement of R. Yohanan with which we began this section, will prove enlightening.

Rashi (s.v. Whoever brings nigh redemption… [in the *ma'ariv* service]):

- How much more so if he does it in *Shaharit*, because the essence of the redemption from Egypt occurred during *Shaharit*, to wit: "On the morrow of the *Pesah* the Jews left" (Numbers 33:3).
- David, in Psalms, alluded to bringing nigh redemption to prayer, by saying "God is my rock and redeemer" (Psalms 19:15), to which he brought nigh "God will answer you on a day of distress" (20:2).
- The *Talmud Yerushalmi* in *Berakhot* states: To whom can we compare one who does not bring redemption nigh unto prayer? To a courtier who knocks on the king's door and leaves before the king opens the door. Here, too, he has left.
- Rather, one should bring God nigh to himself and appease Him with praise and encomium on account of the exodus. God will come nigh unto man, and as a result of that proximity man can place his petitions before Him.
  - "Man was commanded to redeem himself in order to attain full being. This can be achieved only through prayer. ונצעק אל 'ה, 'and we cried unto God'. The redemption from Egypt was initiated through prayer" (*Redemption*, 64–65).[52]

Tosafot (s.v. R. Yohanan says)
- If bringing nigh redemption unto prayer in *Shaharit* precludes any interruption between them, how does *Arvit* accommodate two—and possibly even three—interruptions?

51. See Unit Three: "Avraham and Sedom" (Part Five).
52. See Unit Four: "Slavery and Exodus"

- What about our own practice to recite יראו עינינו and other verses after השכיבנו? (Is that not an intrusion on the proximity?) It would appear that since they are a rabbinic enactment they constitute an "extended redemption" (גאולה אריכתא) [implemented in order to enable all the congregants to return home together after the service].

- In addition, those verses contain 18 references to God [אזכרות]—complementing the 18 blessings of the *Amidah*—apropos of which they also enacted the closing of יראו עינינו.

- The Halakhah follows R. Yohanan, whose position is supported by a ברייתא, and the *Halakhot Gedolot* also rules in his favor.

- Therefore, it is prohibited to talk between the גאולה blessing of *Arvit* and the *Amidah*.

- The *Siddur* of R. *Amram Gaon*, however, stipulates that the recitation of *Kaddish* between redemption and prayer of *Arvit* signifies that we do not require them to be brought nigh at that time, because the *Arvit* service is optional.

- This is problematic. R. Yohanan's position here indicates that he regards *Arvit* as mandatory, and in a disagreement between R. Yohanan and Rav [who rules it is optional] we would be bound to follow R. Yohanan, so it is best to adopt a stringent position and beware of talking in between.

- Alternatively, if there is a contradiction in Halakhah—we generally rule that *Arvit* is optional while here we appear to follow R. Yohanan who maintains it is mandatory—we would have to say that even if R. Yohanan agreed with Rav that *Arvit* is optional, he still requires that [redemption and prayer] be brought nigh, in which case we would do well to do so, too.

The Hashkafic Dimension:[53]

The proximity to redemption transforms prayer from a manner of expressing oneself in words into a veritable spiritual activity; a commitment to God and an acceptance of His moral authority. Redemption is the goal of the covenant, and *Shema`* is its epitome. Man has no right to come before God in quest of redemption without owning up to his covenantal commitments. As the Rav writes:

> Through prayer, they [Abraham, Isaac, Jacob, Moses, David and Solomon] achieved the covenant with God, and through

---

53. Cf. *Lonely Man*, 41, note.

prayer, we expect eventually to realize that covenant (*Redemption*, 55).

To promote this realization, Halakhah imposed the requirement that redemption and prayer be seamless, and yet the intention required of the recitation of *Shema`* is not identical to that which is required of the *Amidah*. Whereas *Shema`* confers upon man the "ontological (existential) legitimacy" of a moral being engaged in a moral task, the *Amidah* actually negates the value of human existence by forcing man to appear before God as a humble, even enslaved, supplicant. The condition that the Talmud (*Berakhot* 14b–15a), designates קבלת עול מלכות שמים, accepting the yoke of heavenly majesty, combines these two contradictory elements "into one comprehensive awareness of man who is at the same time the free messenger of God and His captive as well."

The Halakhic Dimension:[54]

We will enter the halakhic dimension via a "didactic dichotomy" based upon the question introduced by *Tosafot* (above):

If bringing nigh redemption unto prayer in *Shaharit* precludes any interruption between them, how does *Arvit* accommodate two—and possibly even three—interruptions?

Tosafot resolve the question by recourse to the concept of "an extended [blessing of] redemption;" we shall deal with it by stipulating that the blessing of redemption—in both *Shaharit* and *Arvit*—is a prerequisite (מתיר) for the recitation of the *Amidah*.[55] In the following passage, the Rav explains how the relationship between the obligation to pray and its performance is different from that of other mitzvot and their performance.

...*Tefillah* differs from all other mitzvot in which a person is obligated. With respect to other mitzvot, first the obligation of its performance falls upon the person. That obligation then transforms his [subsequent] action into the performance of a mitzvah, and awards it a special status.

For example, a person assumes an obligation [to recite] a blessing following his nourishment and this obligation begets the [mitzvah] object of the grace after meals. So it is with re-

---

54. "בענין סמיכת גאולה לתפילה," שיעורים לזכר אבא מרי ז"ל (ירושלים,תשמ"ה), לה וכו'.

55. This parallels the point made earlier in the Hashkafic Dimension.

gard to praise and thanksgiving; personal obligation is made
manifest in the [subsequent] articulation of a blessing...

Tefillah, however, being a feature of [seeking divine]
compassion and not a permanent [mitzvah performance] fix-
ture, reverses the sequence. The blessings of prayer do not
achieve the status of blessing—with all its signification and
prerequisites—by means of an individual's obligation but on
their own accord. There exists an object of *Tefillah* in its fixed
liturgy that is totally independent of personal obligation, [an
object] whose prerequisite derives from its independent status
as [seeking divine] compassion. Even if a person has already
fulfilled his obligation [towards formal prayer], the signification of prayer as [seeking divine] compassion has not been
removed... the obligation derives from the fact that it exists
as an object of prayer in reality (*Shi`urim*, 40).

It is on account of this distinction that the Rav maintains that
women share with men the personal obligation to pray, despite prayer
belonging to the category of time mandated mitzvot from which wom-
en are generally exempt.[56]

UNIT 6

Prayer as Dialogue: Talking with God

Enduring Values

In *The Lonely Man of Faith*, the Rav stipulates that "Adam II"
requires a community to promote his redemption. The relationship between man and God in this community, which the Rav labels
"covenantal,"[57] is characterized by their proximity and even equality.
As he writes there:

We meet God in the covenantal community as a comrade and
fellow member. Of course, even within the framework of this
community, God appears as the leader, teacher, and shepherd.

56. It is our intention to develop this particular point in a unit devoted to
Hannah's prayer in 1 Samuel chapter 2. In this context, we also plan to examine the Rav's recorded and reported views on women's prayer groups and
their educational implications.
57. See Unit One: "Adam and the Rain" (Part Three).

Yet the leader is an integral part of the community, the teacher is inseparable from his pupils, and the shepherd never leaves his flock...The covenant draws God into the society of men of faith (30).

In this lesson, we shall see that the historical dialogue between God and Moshe, as well as the ongoing dialogue between God and ourselves, epitomizes a form of what we have called "complementarity,"[58] an idea that constitutes an indispensable principle of the prayer relationship between Man and God.

Educational Objectives

Cognitive: The student will....

* Compare the descriptions of the creation of man and woman in chapters 1 and 2 and relate them to the rule of ,כל כלל שאחריו מעשה אינו אלא פרטו של ראשון.[59]
    * Distinguish (a la Soloveitchik) between "Adam I" and "Adam II."
    * Discriminate between an "I-Thou" and an "I-Thou-He" relationship.
    * Describe the qualities and characteristics of the community that the Rav calls covenantal, existential or faith.
* Locate the *kapporet* in the *mishkan* and describe its function.
* Locate and discuss the passages in Torah that direct Moshe how to communicate with God.
* Suggest what the words כופר, כפורת and כיפורים have in common.

Affective: The student will...

* Appreciate Man's singular role in creation, as its climax and apex.
* Appreciate that God and Man meet on intimate and complementary terms in a covenantal/prayer community.
* Appreciate the opportunities of יום הכיפורים to enter into a dialogue with God based on the principle of complementarity

Behavioral (Skills): The student will...

* Read the text aloud, with proper pronunciation and punctuation—as indicated by the *ta`amei ha-mikra*.

58. *Op. cit.*
59. Cf. *Rashi,* Genesis 2:8.

- Arrange the differences between the two narratives of creation in a table, to facilitate their comparison and contrast.
- Locate verbs and nouns in Tanakh that derive from the root כפ"ר and determine their semantic relationship.

THE LESSON

Part One: Complementarity and Kavvanah

The concept that our prayer and God's satisfaction are mutual[60] appears to be the basis for a Talmudic prescription for the proper "direction of the heart" (כוונת הלב) to which prayer should be addressed:

תלמוד בבלי מסכת ברכות דף ל עמוד א

היה עומד בחוץ לארץ - יכוין את ליבו כנגד ארץ ישראל שנאמר:
(מלכים א' ח') והתפללו אליך דרך ארצם.
היה עומד בארץ ישראל - יכוין את לבו כנגד ירושלים, שנאמר:
(מלכים א' ח') והתפללו אל ה' דרך העיר אשר בחרת;
היה עומד בירושלים - יכוין את לבו כנגד בית המקדש, שנאמר:
(דברי הימים ב' ו') והתפללו אל הבית הזה;
היה עומד בבית המקדש - יכוין את לבו כנגד בית קדשי הקדשים, שנאמר:
(מלכים א' ח') והתפללו אל המקום הזה;
היה עומד בבית קדשי הקדשים - יכוין את לבו כנגד בית הכפורת;
היה עומד אחורי בית הכפורת- יראה עצמו כאילו לפני הכפורת;
נמצא: עומד במזרח - מחזיר פניו למערב, במערב - מחזיר פניו למזרח,
בדרום- מחזיר פניו לצפון, בצפון - מחזיר פניו לדרום;
נמצאו כל ישראל מכוונין את לבם למקום אחד.

One standing in the Diaspora should direct his heart towards the Land of Israel... in the Land of Israel—towards Jerusalem... in Jerusalem—towards the Temple... in the Temple—towards the Holy of Holies... in the Holy of Holies—towards the *kapporet* ...One standing behind the *kapporet* should pretend he is before it.
The result is that one standing in the east—faces west; west—faces east; south—faces north; and north—faces south.
The result is that all Israel direct their hearts towards one place.

---

60. Cf. Unit One: "Adam and the Rain" (Part Three).

Q. Why did the *kapporet* become the narrowest focus of the prayers of all Israel?

(שמות פרק כה: כב) ונועדתי לך שם ודברתי אתך מעל הכפרת מבין שני הכרבים
אשר על ארן העדת את כל אשר אצוה אותך אל בני ישראל:

I shall meet with you there, and I shall speak with you from above the *kapporet*, from between the two *keruvim*, which are atop the Ark of the Covenant...

(במדבר פרק ז:פט) ובבא משה אל אהל מועד לדבר אתו וישמע את הקול מדבר אליו
מעל הכפרת אשר על ארן העדת מבין שני הכרבים וידבר אליו:

When Moshe entered the tent of meeting to speak with Him, he heard the voice discoursing with him from above the *kapporet* atop the Ark of the Covenant, from between the two *keruvim*...

A. Because it was from the *kapporet* that the voice of God emanated in addressing Moshe, it is to that selfsame *kapporet* that Israel addresses its voice in prayer.

Part Two: Kofer, Kapporet, Kapparah, and Yom ha-Kippurim

The root כפ"ר is a homonymous one in the Bible. The aspect with which we will deal, here, is the one signifying the noun "pitch" (כופר), and the verb "to coat" [with pitch; see Gen. 6:14: וכפרת אותה מבית ומחוץ בכופר "coat it, inside and out, with pitch"]. By metaphorical extension, this verb also designates "to cover over, pacify, or propitiate" (see Gen. 32:21: אכפרה פניו "I shall pacify/ propitiate him"), whence we derive the noun "ransom, or price of life" (כופר לנפש; Exodus 21:30: אם כופר יושת עליו...‏ "Should ransom be designated, he shall pay the price of his life").

Coming closer to our purpose—both textually and contextually— is Exodus 32:30: ...אולי אכפרה בעד חטאתכם; "You have erred/sinned grievously...perhaps I can cover over your error/sin." *Rashi, ad. loc.*, appreciating both the literal and metaphorical usage of כפ"ר, comments: אשים כופר וקינוח וסתימה לנגד חטאתכם, להבדיל ביניכם ובין החטא; "I shall place a coating, or filling, at the site of the 'sin' to keep you disengaged from it." כופר, in these terms, is the stuff with which we fill in the chinks in our spiritual armor that חטא causes to develop.

When do we apply this כופר? On the "Day of Atonement," a word that has a decidedly delicious derivation from the Middle English "at one," meaning: "agreed." *Yom ha-Kippurim* is—literally as well as homiletically—a "Day of At-one-ment," or, recasting *Rashi*'s metaphor, a "Day of Bonding." By closing the apertures of the soul and sealing them against erosion due to the friction of error and sin, man becomes one with God and that is his ultimate כפרה.

The כפורת was a slab of pure gold that reposed atop the Ark of the Covenant in the Tabernacle (Exodus 25:17 ff.), fitted to its outer dimensions. Its relationship to the usages of כפ"ר that we have already demonstrated is illustrated by its translation, in older English versions (based upon the Septuagint and the Vulgate), as: "mercy seat," deriving its name from the notion of propitiation. In order to secure כפרה for the Jewish people on יום הכיפורים, Aaron is instructed to sprinkle the blood of the sin-offering (חטאת) "on and before the כפורת" (Leviticus 16:15–16).

Part Three: Conclusion

Just as Moshe, at Sinai, stood in the cleft of the rock clutching the tablets of the Law, as God, in a cloud, first revealed His attributes of compassion and grace, so was Aharon instructed to seek atonement for the Jewish people by replicating the circumstances of Moshe's revelation. The *kapporet* replaced the "cleft of the rock" (נקרת הצור) in which Moshe stood, and the "cloud of incense" (ענן הקטורת) replicated the "thickness of the cloud" (עב הענן) from within which God spoke.

We, who have neither the cleft of the rock nor the "mercy seat," and who can produce neither genuine clouds nor those of incense, must rely upon the סדר התפילה, the order of prayer, invoking the thirteen attributes of grace and compassion, and the סליחות, the liturgical order of *Yom ha-Kippurim*, invoking God's juridical capacity to pardon and atone.

As the Talmud reports (*Rosh ha-Shanah* 17b):

אמר רבי יוחנן: אלמלא מקרא כתוב אי אפשר לאומרו, מלמד שנתעטף הקדוש ברוך
הוא כשליח צבור, והראה לו למשה סדר תפלה. אמר לו: כל זמן שישראל חוטאין -
יעשו לפני כסדר הזה, ואני מוחל להם.

R. Yohanan said: Were it not an explicit verse, we would be unable to express it... God wrapped Himself as an emissary of the congregation and showed Moshe the order of service, saying: Whenever the Jews sin, let them perform this service before me and I shall forgive them.

Finally, it was only after Adam sinned and was banished from Eden that he was assigned the task "to work the earth whence he was taken" (Genesis 3:23). Assumedly, this is the juncture at which he prayed.

Additional significance, then, attaches to the fact that immediately thereafter God sets up two *keruvim* "to guard the way to the tree of life" (3:24). These are, arguably, the same two *keruvim* that crowned the *kapporet*, from between whose outstretched wings God spoke. The hermeneutic circle is, again, complete. In the words of the *Netziv* (3:23):

> The purpose of Creation—that the glory of God should fill the earth—was hereby completed insofar as everything was now dependent upon Man's deeds, by way of reward and punishment.[61]

---

61. As I write these concluding lines, the city of New Orleans struggles to cope with the aftermath of Hurricane Katrina and people have begun to ask the same question that was asked after the lethal tsunami struck Indonesia last year: "How could a compassionate God allow this to happen?" I believe that some of the insights we have obtained from the Rav and from his sources of information and inspiration can provide a response to this question.
The Talmud (*Ta`anit* 22b) records:

תנו רבנן: על כל צרה שלא תבוא על הצבור מתריעין עליה, חוץ מרוב גשמים. מאי טעמא? -
אמר רבי יוחנן: לפי שאין מתפללין על רוב הטובה.

> The Rabbis taught: On the occasion of every distress that befalls the public, we sound the alarm [i.e., we call for prayer and fasting]—with the exception of excessive rain. Why? R. Yohanan says, because we do not offer prayers over an abundance of good.

According to the explanation we provided in Unit One: "Adam and the Rain," God created a world with the potential for natural growth, but did not enable this potential to be realized until man appreciated it and made provision for it through prayer. As recorded by the Talmud (*Hullin* 60b):

מלמד שיצאו דשאים ועמדו על פתח קרקע,
עד שבא אדם הראשון ובקש עליהם רחמים, וירדו גשמים וצמחו

> Vegetation was poised to emerge from below the earth's surface until Adam came and sought compassion on their behalf [through prayer], the rain fell, and they grew.

The result, as we elaborated in this last unit, was the establishment of a relationship of mutuality (we called it "complementarity") between man and God that makes us partners in creation *provided* we fulfill our proprietary responsibilities, paramount among which is the obligation of לעבדה ולשמרה; to cultivate the earth and to guard it. Prayer, as the Rav maintains, is the means of intelligent "needs analysis" and, as such, it is the handiest instrument of ongoing communication within our relationship with God. And from God's perspective, prayer is the means by which He obtains our "input" into the creative process and by which He charts and grades our spiritual progress. In the words of R. Assi: "God craves the prayers of the righteous" (שהקב״ה מתאוה לתפלתן של צדיקים).

And as the *Netziv* wrote:

> The purpose of Creation—that the glory of God should fill the earth—was hereby completed insofar as everything was now dependent upon Man's deeds, by way of reward and punishment.

New Orleans is not the first city that man has built on a particularly precarious site. It is neither the first time that he has taken measures to protect such a city against the "elements," nor the first time that his mistaken priorities have led to the thwarting of his intent and the destruction of his endangered city.

The city of Babylon, according to the Torah's record, was situated in "a valley in the Land of Shin`ar" (שנער; Genesis 11:2), which was so called, our Sages tell us, because שם ננערו מתי המבול; there the victims of the flood had collected (*Bereishit Rabba* 37:4). Man persisted in its construction, despite the obvious disadvantages, on account of his confidence in its construction with ראשו בשמים; its head in the clouds, which, according to our Sages, implied man's determination to "beat the odds" by outsmarting God.

אמרו אחת לאלף ושש מאות חמשים ושש שנים הרקיע מתמוטט כשם שעשה בימי המבול, בואו ונעשה לו סמוכות:

> They said: The sky falls in once every 1656 years, as evidenced by the flood. Let us build something to prop it up (*Rashi, ad. loc.*).

Man's hubris, his awful arrogance in the face of God's intent, led to the confounding of his plans and the cessation of the construction: ויחדלו לבנות העיר (v. 8). But man is nothing if not persistent and in London, Amsterdam and New Orleans, he has thrown caution to the winds and challenged God by constructing cities against the dictates of "nature." If he is prudent, he invests wisely in building and maintaining the proper infrastructure and escapes "nature's" direst consequences. From time to time, that prudence is supplemented by serendipity and a timely finger in the dike prevents catastrophe. If he acts imprudently and impudently, however, squandering precious time and resources on other and more selfish projects, then he is—proverbially and poignantly—hoist with his own petard.

Rain, as the Talmud carefully considers, is a blessing at *all* times and prayers for rain remain unaffected by the consequences that may ensue. God, in His cosmic beneficence, let it rain. Man, in his individual and institutional arrogance, built a city on a site that was singularly susceptible to flooding and then allowed the levees to deteriorate.

Contributors

David Schnall is Dean of the Azrieli Graduate School of Jewish Education and Administration and Herbert Schiff Professor of Management and Administration at Yeshiva University. He is the author of several books, including: *The Jewish agenda: Essays in contemporary Jewish life,* and: *By the sweat of your brow: Reflections on work and the workplace in classic Jewish thought.*

Daniel Pollack is a Professor at the Wurzweiler School of Social Work of Yeshiva University. He is the author of *Contrasts in American and Jewish Law,* and his other research interests include prison conditions, foster care and child abuse, and social work issues pertaining to natural disasters.

Howard Deitcher is on the faculty of the Melton Center for Jewish Education at the Hebrew University of Jerusalem and has also has served as its director. His research interests include the child's understanding of the Biblical story, philosophy for children, and models of educational leadership. He is co-author, with Alex Pomson, of *Jewish day schools, Jewish communities.*

Alex Pomson is a senior lecturer at the Melton Center for Jewish Education at the Hebrew University of Jerusalem. He has also served as the chair of the Network for Research in Jewish Education. He is co-editor, with Randal Schnoor, of *Back to school; Jewish day school in the lives of adult Jews.*

David Pelcovitz is Gwendolyn & Joseph Straus Chair in Jewish Education at the Azrieli Graduate School of Jewish Education and Administration of Yeshiva University. He is the author of *The parenting path* and co-author of *Balanced parenting: a father and son—a rabbi and a psychologist—examine love and limits in raising children.*

Rona Novick is Associate Professor and the director of the Fanya Gottesfeld Heller Division of Doctoral Studies at the Azrieli Graduate School of Jewish Education and Administration of Yeshiva University. She is the founder of BRAVE, a highly regarded anti-bullying program that serves both public and private schools.

Jay Goldmintz is Headmaster of the Rabbi Joseph H. Lookstein Upper School of Ramaz. He recently received his EdD from the Azrieli Graduate School of Jewish Education and Administration of Yeshiva University, and is involved in research into adolescent spiritual development.

Michael Rosenak is Emeritus Professor of the Philosophy of Jewish Education at the Hebrew University of Jerusalem. He is the author of numerous books and articles, including *Commandments and concerns: Jewish religious education in secular society* and *Tree of life, tree of knowledge: Conversations with the Torah.*

Jeffrey Glanz is Raine and Stanley Silverstein Chair in Professional Ethics and Values at the Azrieli Graduate School of Jewish Education and Administration of Yeshiva University. He is the author or co-author of twenty books in the field of education, including: *Supervision that improves teaching and learning* and *Finding your leadership style: A guide for educators.*

Lawrence Schiffman is Ethel and Irvin A. Edelman Professor of Hebrew and Judaic Studies, and Chairman of the Skirball Department of Hebrew and Judaic Studies at New York University. He is the author, co-author or editor of nearly thirty books and numerous articles in Judaic studies, including *From text to tradition: A history of Second Temple and Rabbinic Judaism, Texts and traditions: A source reader for the study of Second Temple and rabbinic Judaism,* and *Jewish spirituality and divine law.*

Moshe Sokolow is Associate Dean and Fanya Gottesfeld Heller Chair in Jewish Education at the Azrieli Graduate School of Jewish Education and Administration of Yeshiva University. He is the author of *Studies in the weekly parashah based on the lessons of Nehama Leibowitz,* and is the editor of *Ten Da`at: A journal of Jewish education.*